HACIENDA AND

MARKET IN

EIGHTEENTH-CENTURY

MEXICO

Hacienda and Market in

Eighteenth-Century Mexico

The Rural Economy of the

Guadalajara Region, 1675-1820

Eric Van Young

University of California Press   Berkeley, Los Angeles, London

For Loli and Oscar, and for Maggie,
but mostly for Marin

University of California Press
Berkeley and Los Angeles, California

University of California Press, Ltd.
London, England

Printed in the United States of America

1 2 3 4 5 6 7 8 9

Library of Congress Cataloging in Publication Data

Van Young, Eric.
  Hacienda and market in eighteenth-century Mexico.

  Bibliography: p. 363
  Includes index.
  1. Agriculture—Economic aspects—Mexico—Guadalajara
region—History. 2. Haciendas—Mexico—Guadalajara
region—History. 3. Produce trade—Mexico—Guadalajara
region—History. I. Title.
HD1795.G78V36   330.972′35   80-39888
ISBN 0-520-04161-5

CONTENTS

MAPS, FIGURES, AND TABLES

Tables

ACKNOWLEDGMENTS

In the preparation of this study I have incurred a great many debts—financial, intellectual, and emotional—which it is a pleasure to acknowledge here in some small way. The research and much of the writing were supported by a Foreign Area Fellowship from the Social Science Research Council and the American Council of Learned Societies, and a Bancroft Library Fellowship from the University of California at Berkeley. The Center for Latin American Studies at the University of California, Berkeley, provided a supplementary travel grant as well as generous financial assistance in preparing the original manuscript.

My intellectual debts are harder to define. Woodrow Borah, teacher and friend, has shaped my basic interests, provided many kinds of support over the years, and set a challenging example of intellectual integrity. David Brading shared with me his interest in the social and economic history of colonial Mexico and has consistently encouraged and supported my efforts in historical research. Arnold Bauer has also encouraged my work, and gave this study a close reading at an early stage. For their reading of various parts of the manuscript and for helpful comments I want also to thank James Parsons, Tom Flory, Murdo J. MacLeod, and Ed Ehmke.

In Guadalajara the directors and staffs of the archives in which I worked were unfailingly courteous and occasionally allowed me exceptionally broad access to documentary materials. I am especially indebted to the late Lic. Alejandro Hernández Alvirde, director of the Archivo de Instrumentos Públicos de Guadalajara, and Professor José Luis Razo Zaragoza, paleographer of the Archivo and official city historian; Sr. Salvador Gómez García, director of the Archivo Histórico Municipal de Guadalajara, and his particularly gracious staff; the late Professor José Cornejo Franco, director of the Biblioteca Pública del Estado, who allowed me to examine and partially catalog two hitherto little-used collections of documents; and Father Eucario López of the Archivo del Arzobispado de Guadalajara and related collections in the Catedral de Guadalajara. Other friends in Guadalajara, deeply interested in local history in their own right, aided me in many ways; I would like particularly to single out Professor Salvador Reynoso and Sr. Jesús Toscano Moreno. I owe a special debt of gratitude to Enrique Florescano for his encouragement in a field to which he himself has made distinguished contributions, and for first setting my feet on the road toward Nueva Galicia.

The friends who have helped and encouraged me along the way are too numerous to mention here, but they will know who they are. I particularly want to thank Sayre Van Young, Delia Nicholls, Richard Lindley, and Bob Callaway. Special thanks go to my daughter Marin for not scribbling on my notes and for sacrificing so many Saturday mornings with comparatively good grace, and to my wife, Marjorie Milstein, for her impatience and for her patience.

CONVENTIONS AND ABBREVIATIONS

Conventions

Documentary citations from the Archivo General de la Nación (AGN) are limited to transcriptions of documents from the Ramo de Jesuítas, lent to me by Sr. Salvado Reynoso of the Universidad Autónoma de Guadalajara. The citations are not complete, but what information there is follows the standard notation of section, legajo, and expediente.

Citations from the Archivo Histórico Municipal de Guadalajara (AHMG) are of the *actas de cabildo*, the minutes of the city council meetings, with annexed documents. The boxes (*cajas*), numbering about fifty, are arranged roughly in chronological order, but the contents are in disarray. The boxes are numbered according to two different systems; I have consistently used the old system, beginning with the first box (the oldest materials) as no. one. In general, the citations give the number of the box and the year, or just the box number if the year is mentioned in the text; occasionally they include legajo and expediente numbers, where these are available.

In the Archivo de Instrumentos Públicos de Guadalajara (AIPG), the Libros de Gobierno (LG) are cited by volume and page number, and sometimes by year if the year is not given in the text. The Protocolos— notary records—are cited with the abbreviation "prot." followed by the last name of the notary, the volume number, and in most cases, the page numbers. Again, dates are given where they do not appear in the text. Documents from the Ramo de Tierras y Aguas (Tierras) are cited with the legajo and expediente number only, not the page numbers (these documents are most often unpaginated), and the year, where necessary.

In the Biblioteca Pública del Estado de Jalisco (BPE), documents from the Archivo Judicial de la Audiencia (AJA) are cited by the box number, the document number within the box, and the serial number of the document, in that order. Thus, for example, "BPE-AJA, 136:5:1320" would indicate box no. 136, document no. 5 within that box, and document serial no. 1320. Documents from the Archivo Fiscal de la Audiencia (AFA) are cited by volume and year, and those from the section Bienes de Difuntos (BD) by legajo and expediente. Documents from the section Manuscritos Catalogados (MC) are cited according to the form legajo, volume, and expediente, though the designation of this material in the BPE is not always consistent.

For collections in the Catedral de Guadalajara (CG), citations of the Archivo del Arzobispado de Guadalajara (AAG) are given by year only, since that is the only information available on the documents. Citations of materials from the Archivo de la Secretaría del Cabildo (Eclesiástico) (ASC) are given by legajo number and year.

Spanish words and phrases are italicized the first time they appear in the text, but not thereafter. Footnote citations of published and manuscript sources are given in shortened form; for fuller information, the reader is directed to the bibliography.

Abbreviations

AGN   Archivo General de la Nación

AHMG Archivo Histórico Municipal de Guadalajara

AIPG   Archivo de Instrumentos Públicos de Guadalajara
        LG—Libros de Gobierno de la Audiencia de Nueva Galicia
        prot.—Protocolos de notarios públicos
        Tierras—Ramo de Tierras y Aguas

BPE   Biblioteca Pública del Estado (de Jalisco)
        AFA—Archivo Fiscal de la Audiencia de Nueva Galicia
        AJA—Archivo Judicial de la Audiencia de Nueva Galicia
        BD—Archivo del Juzgado General de Bienes de Difuntos
        MC—Manuscritos Catalogados

CG   Catedral de Guadalajara
        AAG—Archivo del Arzobispado de Guadalajara
        ASC—Archivo de la Secretaría del Cabildo (Eclesiástico)

INTRODUCTION

During the eighteenth century the area around Guadalajara, the principal city of western Mexico, was progressively integrated into a regional economic system which relied upon the city as a market for agricultural products and a source of credit and capital. The growth of the urban population spurred the commercialization of agriculture in the city's hinterland and drew all groups of rural society into an expanding network of relations mediated by a cash economy. The main components of this system were already present and well established in the seventeenth century, but in the eighteenth century the traditional equilibrium shifted dramatically in favor of the great rural estates at the expense of the peasant sector, particularly the village Indian population.

The dominance of rural economic and social life by the *hacienda* has been a continuing theme in the work of those historians concerned with the history of pre-Revolutionary Mexico, especially economic and agrarian history. Concern with a number of important historical problems—the structure of colonial society and economy, the nature of the Porfiriato, and the post-Revolutionary development of Mexico—has nourished a long tradition of interest in the economic and social life of the countryside.[1] As research advances, it is becoming increasingly clear that the

1. Andrés Molina Enríquez, *Los grandes problemas nacionales* (1909); Helen Phipps, *Some Aspects of the Agrarian Question in Mexico* (1925); George M. McBride, *The Land Systems of Mexico* (1923); Frank Tannenbaum, *The Mexican Agrarian Revolution* (1930); Nathan M. Whetten, *Rural Mexico* (1948); Silvio Zavala, "Orígenes coloniales del peonaje en México," *Trimestre Económico* 10 (1944); François Chevalier, *La formation des grandes domaines au Mexique* (1952); Woodrow Borah, *New Spain's Century of Depression* (1951); Lesley Byrd Simpson, *Exploitation of Land in Central Mexico in the Sixteenth Century* (1952); Charles Gibson, *The Aztecs Under Spanish Rule* (1964); Ward Barrett, *The Sugar Hacienda of the Marqueses del Valle* (1970); William B. Taylor, *Landlord and Peasant in Colonial Oaxaca* (1972); and Enrique Florescano, *Precios del maíz y crisis agrícolas en México* (1969), and *Estructuras y problemas agrarios de México* (1971). For a survey of literature on the agrarian history of Latin America in general, see Magnus Mörner, "The Spanish American Hacienda," *Hispanic American Historical Review* 53 (1973); and below, Chapter 6 and notes.

traditional, monolithic model of the hacienda is falling apart as a viable analytical category. In very general terms, that model pictured the hacienda as an exceedingly large, undercapitalized, self-subsistent seigneurial estate supporting the social aspirations of an elite absentee landlord through reliance upon an impoverished, serf-like labor force and the production of small agricultural surpluses which earned a minor income in an almost natural economy. Certainly there were estates which approached this model, but the exceptions outnumbered those which conformed to it. Furthermore, the development of the hacienda, particularly during the colonial period, was seen as taking place in a historical vacuum, in a moon-like landscape without cities, provincial towns, Indian population concentrations, mining areas, external markets, or other points of economic crystallization.[2]

The rural economy and society in Mexico, as in other parts of Latin America, consisted of a number of complex symbiotic relationships, not only between landlords and laborers, but also between producers and urban markets and between and among Indian villagers, haciendas, and non-Indian peasants. Production and social control in the countryside involved all kinds of commercial linkages as well, extending through hacienda stores to provincial towns and regional metropolises, and even across the Atlantic to Spain. The notion of the personal greed and social aspirations of colonial landowning elites as the prime motivating forces behind the consolidation of the hacienda system has been replaced by more complex explanations hinging on long-term demographic and economic factors. In general, the amazing range of observed variation among types of rural production units has focused attention upon a group of economic and social variables—land, labor, capital, markets, and technology—whose relationships have changed over time, rather than upon static models.[3]

Within the burgeoning tradition of scholarship on Latin American agrarian history, there seem to be three basic approaches. The first of these may be called *entrepreneurial* history, or the close study of one enterprise, in most cases some kind of large agricultural estate with surviving serial records.[4] The second approach can be called *sectoral*, in that it isolates one

2. The work of Chevalier, *La formation des grandes domaines*, while it played a pivotal role in the conceptual development of this model, was in fact very precise in discussing the particular historical and regional context of the north Mexican hacienda.

3. See in particular the article by Eric R. Wolf and Sidney W. Mintz, "Haciendas and Plantations in Middle America and the Antilles," *Social and Economic Studies* 6 (1957); and below, Chapter 6.

4. A relatively early example of such entrepreneurial history is Richard Pares' study of the Pinney family's sugar plantation on Nevis, *A West-India Fortune* (1950). More recent studies are those of Barrett, *The Sugar Hacienda of the Marqueses del Valle*, and Charles H. Harris III, *A Mexican Family Empire* (1975).

strand of relationships in a given agrarian economy, such as labor, land tenure, technology, or credit, or one kind of activity, such as livestock-raising, and examines it closely in terms of its own history and its relationship to other strands or activities.[5] The third approach, more properly called *regional* history, focuses on an analysis of the agrarian structure within a given region, simultaneously dealing with a number of variables.[6] The lines of division among these approaches are certainly not rigid, and many historical studies will partake of more than one. Yet the emphasis in each type, the analytical focus, is clear enough, and presents somewhat different problems of method, evidence, and interpretation. This study falls into the third group, that of regional agrarian history.

Many of the new views on Mexican agrarian history have come out of investigations of regional social and economic structure. Yet much of the best current work in regional agrarian history, on Mexico as on other parts of Latin America, demonstrates a real lack of precision in using the idea of "region" as the basic theater of its analysis—though some of it is very good on other grounds. The notion of the region, a concept of spatial relationship borrowed from the geographers, has become something of a buzz-word in studies of agrarian history, like "capitalism" or "crisis." This is not to suggest that a rigid, technical definition of the term is desirable in such research, or even that it is possible, but only that we should think a bit more seriously about what we mean when we discuss geohistorical regions.

What exactly is a region? The most important components of a working definition would probably be a geographical space of some kind and a

5. An example of this approach is Ramón María Serrera Contreras, *Guadalajara ganadera* (1977), a recent work on the region under study here. Also falling into this category would be institutional studies which bear on agrarian structures, such as Lesley Byrd Simpson's *The Encomienda in New Spain* (1966) and *The Repartimiento System* (1938), and much of the work of Silvio Zavala.

6. Mexico has proved to be a particularly rich field of inquiry for regional studies. The modern development of regional history on Mexico really does not extend much further back than the early 1940s at most, say to Woodrow Borah's work on colonial Oaxaca, *Silk Raising in Colonial Mexico* (1943), and Robert C. West's on Parral, *The Mining Community of Northern New Spain* (1949); it got a major push with Gibson's *The Aztecs Under Spanish Rule* (1964). More recent works include William Taylor's *Landlord and Peasant in Colonial Oaxaca* (1972); Ida Altman and James Lockhart, eds., *Provinces of Early Mexico* (1976), and David A. Brading, *Haciendas and Ranchos in the Mexican Bajío* (1978). Elsewhere the development of modern regional history, as opposed to the often valuable but less sophisticated type of local history, was also relatively late. One thinks of Jean Borde and Mario Góngora's work on Chile, *La propiedad rural en el Valle del Puangue* (1956), for example, or Stanley J. Stein's on Brazil, *Vassouras* (1957). A major recent contribution is that of Arnold J. Bauer, *Chilean Rural Society* (1975), which deals mainly with central Chile. It is possible to detect in all this the influence of the French school of regional history, with its emphasis on structural analysis, long-term trends, and quantitative data. See the provocative piece by David J. Robinson, "Introduction to Themes and Scales," in Robinson, ed., *Social Fabric and Spatial Structure* (1979), esp. pp. 5, 9-10, and 16-18.

boundary or boundaries to set it off. In this context, an agricultural or an economic region may not necessarily be coterminous with the more familiar and easily identifiable political or administrative divisions, or even with topographical features. Here we might add a third element to the definition—that of a geographical space with boundaries determined by the effective reach of some kind of system whose parts interact more with each other than with outside systems. It should be acknowledged, of course, that it is often necessary to limit the field of inquiry to some sort of representative subset or sample of regional reality, but the definitional point still holds. The main thing is that we need to be more sensitive and more precise, and that perhaps some a priori definitions or models would be helpful in our using the regional concept more effectively.

The region, though never a completely self-contained entity, nonetheless provides geohistorical or physiographic boundaries which minimize the unique or eccentric, while still allowing meaningful generalizations. When we look at agrarian structure on the regional level, the importance of resource endowment, geography, and population distribution emerges clearly. Similarly, the economic division of labor among production units of various types becomes susceptible of analysis over time. Examining such factors as distance from a market or markets, for example, helps the historian to spotlight economic factors which give certain types of producers a competitive advantage over others. The relationship of the countryside to a regional capital or major city, so full of reciprocal movements and pressures, is best examined at this level as well. For many reasons, then, the regional study of historical agrarian structures has much explanatory power, combining the depth of the microhistorical approach with the breadth of a structural analysis over time.

The notion of regional history is related to that of urban history, and in fact the two are conceptually interdependent.[7] Colonial as well as modern cities had hinterlands or spheres of influence. Most important colonial cities sat like spiders at the center of administrative, political, and commercial networks with identifiable regional boundaries. Cities were not only supplied by their regions with food, primary products, and immigrants, but sent out lines of commerce, credit, and capital, not to mention political and cultural control. From the perspective of urban history, then, regional studies are important in allowing us to see how cities grew, how their areas of influence expanded or contracted over time, and whether they consti-

7. See, for example, the collection of essays edited by Jorge E. Hardoy and Richard P. Schaedel, *Las ciudades de América Latina y sus áreas de influencia a través de la historia* (1975); Richard M. Morse, ed., *Las ciudades latinoamericanas*, vol. 2, *Desarrollo histórico* (1973); and Rolando Mellafe, *The Latifundio and the City in Latin American History* (1971).

tuted poles of growth and economic crystallization or were merely atrophied appendages of a feudal countryside.

This study deals with both rural and urban history, and in that sense is regional in emphasis. It examines a historical region with a major city at its center, but it is not *about* that city. By the same token, the economic and social changes which occurred in the countryside around colonial Guadalajara cannot be viewed in isolation from the development of the city and outward expansion of its influence—political, economic, social, and cultural. What we will examine in the following chapters is the process by which the Guadalajara region became internally integrated during the eighteenth century. The motive force of that integration was the growth of an urban market, and its mechanism was the expansion of commercialized agriculture to supply that market. The exploration of these relationships constitutes a case study in regional economic change.

The second major emphasis of this work, linked to the concrete instance of regional economic development but theoretically distinct, is the relationship of population growth per se to changes in agrarian structure. Specifically, the idea presented most forcefully in recent years by Ester Boserup —that population increase is an independent variable, and changes in agricultural productivity and agrarian structures dependent variables—is addressed in detail in the body of this study, and somewhat more generally in the Conclusion.[8] This emphasis on the primacy of population growth is a reversal of the more traditionally held view that change in the availability of food supply controls the course of population movement. That this statement of the two models is oversimplified need not be labored here. But while the population-primacy model does seem to fit the facts of the Guadalajara region in the late colonial period, it is subject to important modifications.

In the first place, change in the agricultural system stimulated by regional population increase does not seem to have brought about any particular innovation in farming technology, but may actually have been responsible for an involution in agriculture, a turning of resources to less productive but more profitable types of farming. In the second place, the major problem underlying the restructuring of traditional agriculture was not technical, but distributional. That is to say, a large, dependent rural labor force and a growing urban center had to be carved out of a predominantly peasant population which, at the beginning of the period, was only imperfectly integrated into the regional economy. The weight of the evidence presented here indicates that population increase itself, channeled by certain economic and institutional factors, was the major force behind change in the

8. Ester Boserup, *The Conditions of Agricultural Growth* (1965).

rural economy, but hardly in any simple manner and certainly not through technological improvement. Examination of the shifting equilibrium between peasant and commercial agriculture, then, constitutes a second case study, that of change in a peasant society.

Rural economy and society in the late colonial period were more complex in their structure than is portrayed here. In emphasizing only the dynamic factors within the market economy, I have left out of my description much of the texture of life in the countryside. Particularly, small agriculturists and stockmen—the *rancheros* from whom the famous regional "charro" culture is said to have derived its basic characteristics—have been given short shrift in these pages. Similarly, the limited but important group of rural middlemen and brokers of all sorts—hacienda administrators, *corregidores* and *subdelegados*, provincial merchants—who mediated economic and social life and helped to link the rural districts to the city have not been treated on their own, but only mentioned in passing. Finally, the independent economic life of Indian villages—the small-scale, interstitial farming, gathering, and craft activities upon which much of the provincial and urban consuming public came to depend—has been largely ignored. In the thesis presented in the following chapters, the "maximizing peasant," around whom so much debate has centered in the last decade or so, finds little place.

The decision to pass over these groups and their activities results partly from the nature of the documentation on them, which is plentiful but fragmentary. There is a strong documentary bias in favor of entities with definite institutional bounds and corporate identities, such as large estates, Indian villages as corporate landowners, and the agencies of municipal government. This means that descriptions of the ranchero or small-merchant groups, for example, often have a certain static quality which accords ill with the emphasis on change in the present work, especially from the structural perspective I have chosen here. Ultimately more important, however, is that a detailed description of these groups, fascinating as it might be for its own sake, would add little to the thesis presented here, since they were largely passive objects of the forces of change in the regional economy.

The Guadalajara region evolved a particular historical identity of its own, and it is also the aim of this study to delineate that identity in some measure. The Guadalajara region has traditionally been considered to be a part of that ranchero Mexico embracing the Altos de Jalisco area, the northwest, and the north of Mexico.[9] Largely this has been due to a certain

9. See, for example, Luis Pérez Verdía, *Historia particular del estado de Jalisco* (1951); Jean Meyer, "Perspectives de l'analyse socio-historique de l'influence de Guadalajara sur sa ré-

analytical blurring between the Guadalajara region and areas to the north and east which center on Zacatecas and the Bajío. The image of the sturdy yeoman farmer portrayed convincingly by a number of historians for the Altos area in particular, and which has been generalized for the rest of western Mexico does not seem to hold for much of central Jalisco, the core area of the old Intendancy of Guadalajara and the even older Kingdom of New Galicia. This area was by the close of the eighteenth century clearly dominated by the great hacienda. It also sustained a complicated social and economic structure including the urban center, a dense if unevenly distributed Indian population, a numerous but largely dependent group of small landowners and renters, and the great rural estates themselves. In fact, one modern writer's image of the rancheros standing resolutely amid the smoking ruins of the hacienda system is not borne out by the evidence.[10] The Guadalajara area lay just to the south of the traditional Chichimec line, and this justifies regarding it as a transitional zone, in some senses, between Indian and ranchero Mexico. If Louis XIV could say that Africa began at the Pyrenees, then the north may be said to begin at Guadalajara. But that the area under study here lay fully within the tradition of the hacienda-dominated, irrigated and mixed dry-farming, central-Mexican core area, both in its economic and social characteristics, will become clear from the chapters that follow.

The geohistorical entity referred to in these pages as the Guadalajara region extended from the edge of Los Altos de Jalisco in the east to the Ameca-Cocula Valley in the west, and from Lake Chapala in the south to the great gorge (*barranca*) of the Río Grande de Santiago in the north. It has a long-recognized identity enduring to the present day. This study concerns itself primarily with the region thus defined as the supply area for the city of Guadalajara at its center. But of course the city had a number of other functions within its region, and within western Mexico as a whole, in the colonial period. It served not only as a market for its hinterland, but also as a political, commercial, and cultural center, and indeed these functions spread its influence well beyond the limits of its role as a consumer of foodstuffs.[11] In a certain sense, therefore, it is artificial to look at one subsystem and ignore the others, since they mutually influenced each other. But the historical and theoretical importance of the regional agricultural economy, and its cohesiveness, justify its separate study here.

---

gion," in Centre National de la Recherche Scientifique, *Villes et régions en l'Amérique Latine* (1970); and for the trans-Chapala area, Luis González, *Pueblo en vilo* (1968).

10. Meyer, "Perspectives."

11. For a more detailed discussion of the geographical and historical boundaries of the region, see Chapter 1 below.

The eighteenth century defined here is a historian's century, like a baker's dozen. It extends from the last decades of the seventeenth century (1675) through the first decades of the nineteenth (1820). There are good reasons for considering the mid-eighteenth century, 1750 or 1760, as one of the great watersheds of Mexican, as of world, history. Great changes in demographic, political, and economic development begin, or at least become obvious to the historical observer, from that point. This is just as true of the Guadalajara region as of other areas of colonial Mexico or of Latin America as a whole. The year 1820, the very end of the Spanish colonial period in Mexico, is not a watershed date of equivalent significance to 1750 or 1760, at least in terms of social and economic development. A good case can be made, for example, that the cycle of rapid change initiated in the mid-eighteenth century carried over until sometime in the mid-nineteenth century, whatever direction one considers the movement to have taken.[12] In the Guadalajara region, the turnover in landownership and the increasing capital investment and value of large agricultural properties obvious in the late eighteenth century seem to have continued at least through the Wars of Independence and the 1820s.[13]

Nonetheless, the cut-off point of 1820 for this investigation is justified in order to limit the field of inquiry. By focusing our attention on the late eighteenth century, in contrast to the late seventeenth, we will be able to observe the important changes in the agrarian regime which altered the face of the Guadalajara countryside toward the end of the colonial period. It is this contrast between the old regime of an extensive economy, low labor utilization, small markets, and low capital investment, and the post-1760 regime of rising land values, intensifying use of land and labor, expanded markets, and increasing capital investment, which will concern us here.

12. The period after 1800 or so seems to correspond to a downward trend in national and per-capita incomes for Mexico; see John H. Coatsworth, "Obstacles to Economic Growth in Nineteenth-Century Mexico," *American Historical Review* 83 (1978), pp. 80-83. An interesting recent discussion on the value of periodization in Mexican history is Woodrow Borah, "Discontinuity and Continuity in Mexican History," *Pacific Historical Review* 48 (1979).

13. See Richard Lindley, "Kinship and Credit in the Structure of Guadalajara's Oligarchy, 1800-1830" (1976), passim.

PART I. THE HUMAN

AND NATURAL ENVIRONMENT

CHAPTER 1

The Guadalajara Region in
Time and Space

The Region Defined

Virtually since its definitive foundation in 1542, Guadalajara has been one
of the dominant cities of western Mexico. Its cultural, economic, and politico-administrative hegemony took time to develop and has not gone un-
disputed by other urban centers, of course. Nor has the development of
Guadalajara been uniform or without interruption—it has experienced
stagnation, slumps, and depressions. But by 1810 the city was clearly in its
heyday of splendor and influence. Its judicial authority covered all of western Mexico and stretched up the Pacific coast to the Californias. The Intendancy of Guadalajara embraced a huge chunk of western central Mexico
with a population of around 600,000, the third-most-populous entity in
Mexico (after the Intendancies of Mexico and Puebla).[1] Guadalajara's economic influence, however, extended far beyond the administrative boundaries of the Intendancy, and the city itself was strongly tied in to the
imperial and extra-imperial commercial network by means of the flow of

1. On population and the evolution of administrative entities, see Alexander von Humboldt, *Ensayo político sobre el Reino de la Nueva España* (1966), pp. 99-106; Edmundo
O'Gorman, *Historia de las divisiones territoriales* (1968), pp. 1-29; and Ramón María Serrera Contreras, "Estado económico de la Intendencia de Guadalajara a principios del siglo
XIX," in *Lecturas históricas sobre Jalisco* (1976), pp. 200-201.

goods and credit.[2] The cultural efflorescence of the city in the late colonial period made it a desirable place to live for those with the means and social background to enjoy urban cultural life, a lodestone for the provincial elites of western Mexico.

In many different ways, then, the city of Guadalajara was the center of a far-flung region: it functioned as a political capital, a bank, a market, a hub of commercial distribution, and an intellectual center and point of reference. This study deals with Guadalajara as the center of a specific regional system defined not only by certain types of places with similar intrinsic characteristics, but by location as well: a spatial relationship to the city.[3] But of course regions may be based upon any number of criteria, alone or in combination: there are physiographic regions, cultural regions, politico-administrative regions, and economic regions. Conceptually speaking, the functions of Guadalajara as a central place can be visualized as a series of concentric rings, the most inclusive of which was its judicial authority, followed in successively declining size by its financial and commercial influence, its political and ecclesiastical jurisdiction, its market area, and the immediate urban zone itself.[4] Of these overlapping systems, the subject of the present work is that region defined by the market area of Guadalajara, and the influence exerted upon that area during the eighteenth century by the expanding urban demand for meat, grain, and other foodstuffs.

The area so defined was preeminently an economic region, yet it was not coextensive with the zone of Guadalajara's economic influence, or even the major part of it. Nor was it the whole of the agricultural area from which the products eaten and processed in Guadalajara were drawn: the city received tropical products (cotton, dyestuffs, luxury food items) from a very large area embracing not only what is now central Jalisco, but extending to the Pacific coast.[5] The region that concerns us here—which might be called central Jalisco or, broadly speaking, the Guadalajara Valley—was the major supplier of those mundane products without which the urban inhabitants could not have survived, and whose availability underwrote the growth of the city: primarily meat and grain. The term "area of primary

2. See particularly Lindley, "Kinship and Credit," passim; and Chapter 8 below.
3. This definition of specific regional system is based upon that in Ronald Abler, John S. Adams, and Peter Gould, *Spatial Organization* (1971), p. 183 ff.
4. On the notion of the market area, see Brian J. L. Berry, *Geography of Market Centers* (1967), pp. 15-16. A closely related idea in location theory is the hierarchy of central places, which includes the interrelations of secondary towns and their functions with regard to (in this case) the regional metropolis.
5. For some statistics on the production of tropical goods in the Intendancy of Guadalajara at the beginning of the nineteenth century, see "Provincia de Guadalajara: Estado que demuestra los frutos y efectos de agricultura, industria y comercio . . ." in Jesús Silva Herzog, comp., *Relaciones estadísticas de Nueva España* (1944), pp. 99-121.

supply" more or less conveys this meaning, as does the more technical concept of "food-shed." The major distinguishing characteristics of Guadalajara's area of primary supply were that it was closest to the city, with a degree of physiographic unity and therefore accessibility, and that producers within it therefore enjoyed a much greater and more regular frequency of contact with the urban market.[6]

In the last years of the colonial period, the agricultural region of Guadalajara embraced an area roughly oval in shape, of about 100 by 200 kilometers, bounded on the south by Lake Chapala, on the north by San Christóbal de la Barranca, on the east by Tepatitlán and Atotonilco el Alto, and on the west by Ameca (see map 1).[7] That the region has a physiographic identity has long been recognized by geographers, though they differ on its precise boundaries.[8] The basic unifying feature of the area is that most of it lies within the basin of the Lerma River, after it emerges from Lake Chapala re-christened as Río Grande de Santiago. Guadalajara and its region lie in a kind of western extension or bulge of the great central mesa of Mexico, whose northern boundary follows the meandering of the Santiago just above the city itself. The relatively complicated topography of the region results from its location on the northern margins of the transverse neovolcanic range which bisects Mexico from east to west, at the junction of this range with the Sierra Madre Occidental.[9] Within this general physiography, the region consists of a number of intermontane valleys transected by ridges and ravines, all interconnected and all easily accessible to the city of Guadalajara. These valleys, of which the major ones are the Atemajac (the site of the city itself), La Barca, Ameca, Tequila, and Tlajomulco, are flat-floored, ancient lake basins which have historically been the sites best suited for agriculture and human habitation.[10] The several valleys vary in altitude from 1,400 to 1,600 meters (the

6. Lindley, in "Kinship and Credit," p. 75, applies similar criteria: the frequency with which residents of the region visited or lived in Guadalajara, and the frequency and volume of produce shipments by haciendas within the region.

7. Lindley, in "Kinship and Credit," pp. 75-84, discusses the same area, though for different purposes; see his interesting subdivision of the ellipse into zones based on differing agricultural production.

8. José Vicente Negrete, in *Geografía del estado de Jalisco* (1926), pp. 42-43, refers to the Guadalajara region as the "región media en la alta planicie de Jalisco"; Angel Bassols Batalla, in *Recursos naturales* (1969), p. 79, and *La división económica regional de México* (1967), pp. 1-48, considers it to be a well-defined area within the major zone "centro-occidente" of Mexico; and Hélène Rivière d'Arc, *Guadalajara y su región* (1973), p. 26, designates it as the Valley of Guadalajara, though she would extend its eastern limit as far as Pénjamo, in the Bajío.

9. Robert C. West, ed., *Environment and Early Cultures,* vol. 1 of Robert Wauchope, gen. ed., *Handbook of Middle American Indians,* passim.

10. *Ibid.*; Negrete, *Geografía,* pp. 45-47; Sévero Díaz, *Geografía general y física del estado de Jalisco* (1946), pp. 35-36. These major valleys all go by other names and are often

Map 1.

The Guadalajara region, state of Jalisco

city itself is at 1,560 meters), declining from about 2,000 meters in the northeast, around Aguascalientes and Lagos, to 1,250 meters at Ameca, and thence to the tropical lowlands of the coast.

One of the most striking geographical features of the Guadalajara region is the lack of major watercourses aside from the Santiago River. The two other important rivers in the area are the Río Verde, a major affluent of the Santiago which meets it just northeast of the city, and the Río Ameca, which originates on the very western margin of the region and flows into the Pacific. The other affluents of the Santiago are ephemeral or intermittent streams (Ayo el Chico, Laja, Ixtlahuacán, etc.), seasonal in flow and uneven in depth.[11] Rainfall in the region is not abundant, averaging about

---

subdivided by names according to local usages. Thus, the Atemajac Valley can be broken down into the valleys of Atemajac, Toluquilla, and Tonalá, all geographically contiguous but set off by topographical features such as single hills or ranges of hills. See, for example, Mariano Bárcena, *Ensayo estadístico del estado de Jalisco* (1888), p. 21.

11. Díaz, *Geografía general*, pp. 13-21; Bassols Batalla, *Recursos naturales*, p. 66; and Robert West, vol. 1 of *Handbook*, passim.

800 millimeters annually. This means that a prosperous *temporal* (non-irrigated) agriculture is very difficult, and that irrigation in some form is vital.[12] The pervasive climate in the region, from the foot of the Altos region in the northeast to the Ameca Valley in the southwest, is of the temperate-highland type, with a rainy season from June to mid-October and a dry winter—a one-crop regimen. In general, the central Jalisco valleys fall into the category of black soil (chernozem) areas, similar to the lacustrine basins of the Mesa Central, such as the Valley of Mexico and the Bajío, which are admirably suited for agriculture. This rich agricultural potential is complicated by problems of erosion, however, and by the eighteenth century the long and intensifying human occupation had begun to tell on the land.[13]

Cortés remarked that Mexico resembled "a crumpled sheet of paper" ("un papel arrugado"), and in some measure the Guadalajara agricultural region shares this jumbled topography. At the beginning of the seventeenth century, Alonso de la Mota y Escobar wrote that there was much good, fertile land in New Galicia, but that it was all "splashed in different spots and valleys" ("salpicada en distintos lugares y valles").[14] The limited extent of arable lands meant that commercial agriculture was necessarily limited to the relatively small valley-bottoms, separated from each other by formidable ranges of hills. The lack of rivers and streams and the semi-arid climate of the region made for a scarcity of water for agricultural purposes. These two factors in combination gave rise to an intense competition for arable land and water, necessitating a considerable investment of capital for the production of European cereals such as wheat.

It is easier to define the physiographic region of Guadalajara than the historical or human region, though the two are intimately related. Within the region, Guadalajara tended to function as the center of gravity politically, socially, and economically. We are dealing here with the notion of a sphere of influence mediated by the market area of the city and its area of primary agricultural supply. The city government itself in the late colonial period was well aware of its area of supply and even tried specifically, with some success, to assign responsibility for the sustenance of the urban population to agricultural producers within its environs ("ocho leguas de contorno"). But human contacts in the region naturally tended to center on

12. Guadalajara, Ayuntamiento de, "Estudios del régimen anual de lluvias en Guadalajara," p. 7; Bassols Batalla, *Recursos naturales*, p. 66.

13. Robert West, vol. 1 of *Handbook*, passim; Bassols Batalla, *Recursos naturales*, p. 162. Local variations in soil quality and other conditions have created special problems historically. The Atemajac Valley, in which Guadalajara stands, is characterized by a particularly thin topsoil and a notable tendency toward erosion.

14. Alonso de la Mota y Escobar, *Descripción geográfica de los Reynos de Nueva Galicia* . . . (1966), p. 27.

Guadalajara, particularly in economic matters. Outside the region, people's economic activities gravitated toward other centers. Jalostotitlán, and to some degree Tepatitlán, were drawn toward Lagos and the Bajío; Teocaltiche fell within the orbit of Aguascalientes; the towns beyond La Barca lay within the sphere of Valladolid (later Morelia); and the southern trans-Chapala towns centered around Sayula.[15] This is not to say that in periods of crisis things did not change, or that in normal times these distinct regions were totally unarticulated, nor even that the situation remained static over the long run, but simply that the direct economic influence of Guadalajara tended to be concentrated within the region defined above.

Pre-Conquest Indian Culture

If the Guadalajara region was marginal, or transitional, in a geographical sense, it was even more so in a human sense. In terms of the major culture areas of Middle America in about 1500, the region lay just on the northern limit of the high cultures. The same boundary which located the region just within the Mesa Central defined it culturally: the Santiago River.[16] To the north of this line lay the so-called Chichimec area, populated by fierce nomadic Indians whose subjection cost the Spanish settlers so much effort in the mid-sixteenth century. To the south of the Santiago, however, in the Guadalajara region, the Indian culture shared in the sedentary agricultural tradition of the central Mexican and Tarascan areas.

The Spaniards who conquered western central Mexico encountered a less densely populated and less complex Indian culture area than those in New Spain or the Tarascan zone.[17] The region lacked the monumental architecture, marked urbanism, and theocratic socio-political structure characteristic of central Mexico. Irrigation seems to have developed in the west only in the post-Classic period (after A.D. 600), and never reached the complexity of the irrigation systems in the Valley of Mexico. The use of calendars and codices was also late in coming.[18] Although the region never fell under the hegemony of either Aztecs or Tarascans, the dominant cul-

15. See the discussion in Lindley, "Kinship and Credit," p. 84.
16. Robert West, vol. 1 of *Handbook*, p. 360.
17. Domingo Lázaro de Arregui, *Descripción de la Nueva Galicia* (1946), p. xxv; Rivière d'Arc, *Guadalajara y su región*, pp. 18-21; Woodrow Borah, "Los tributos y su recaudación en la Audiencia . . . en el siglo XVI," in Bernardo García Martínez, ed., *Historia y sociedad en el mundo de habla española* (1970), p. 37; Otto Schondube B., "El territorio cultural de occidente," in Instituto Nacional de Antropología e Historia, *Lecturas Históricas sobre Jalisco* (1976), p. 20.
18. Schondube, "El territorio cultural de occidente," pp. 20-24, and "La evolución cultural," in Instituto, *Lecturas*, p. 25.

tural influence was Nahua.[19] The area seems to have maintained a tenuous political independence through its position as a buffer zone between the Tarascans and the Toltecs and Aztecs. The zone embracing the modern states of Jalisco, Colima, Nayarit, Aguascalientes, and part of Zacatecas has been designated by some historians as Chimalhuacán, or the Chimalhuacán Confederation. In fact, in political terms it was no more than a loose group of independent seigneuries or small city-states (*señoríos*) which joined together in time of war.[20] Ethnically the region was hopelessly jumbled, a Coca and Coca-mix area extending from Sayula in the south to the Santiago River in the north, with admixtures of Tecos, Purepechas (Tarascans), and others.[21]

Economically and agriculturally, the Guadalajara region of the pre-Conquest period was not nearly as complex as the areas to the southeast. There were, however, centers of sedentary agriculture with pockets of denser population and irrigation systems. Several of the Indian towns which were important in the period just before the arrival of the Spanish, or which became important subsequently, were associated with irrigation, even though many of them were of fairly late foundation.[22] Within or near the Guadalajara region proper, the *Suma de Visitas* of 1548 listed a number of pre-Spanish towns where irrigation works had existed (see map 2):[23]

Ajijic
Amacueca
Atiztaque (near Tonalá)
Chapala
Cocula
Cuistlán (near Matatlán)
Cuyutlán
Jocotepec
Mascuala (northeast of Guadalajara, near Acatic)
Matatlán
Mexticacán (near Nochistlán)
Oconahua (near Etzatlán)
Poncitlán

19. Jean-Pierre Berthe, "Introduction à l'histoire de Guadalajara," in Centre National de la Recherche Scientifique, *Villes et régions* (1970), p. 69; Luis Topete Bordes, *Jalisco precortesiano* (1944), pp. 96 and 109.

20. Topete Bordes, *Jalisco precortesiano*, pp. 101-103.

21. José López Portillo y Weber, *La conquista de la Nueva Galicia* (1935), pp. 21 and 26; Topete Bordes, *Jalisco precortesiano*, p. 109.

22. José Ignacio Dávila Garibi, *El pequeño cacicazgo de Cocollán* (1918), p. 9; Jesús Amaya, *Ameca* (1951), p. 41; López Portillo y Weber, *La conquista*, p. 49.

23. Angel Palerm, "Distribución geográfica de los regadíos prehispánicos," in Angel Palerm and Eric R. Wolf, eds., *Agricultura y civilización en Mesoamérica* (1972), passim.

Quitzeo
Talapoçol (possibly in Tonalá Valley)
Techaluta (near Amacueca and Zacoalco)
Teocuitatlán (near Zacoalco)
Tlacotlán (Tacotlán)
Zacoalco

Certainly the scale of these irrigation works and the human concentrations associated with them do not compare with the hydraulic organization of central Mexico or the central Andes, but they did have relatively dense, nucleated populations. The major point here is that although Chimalhuacán and, within it, the Guadalajara region, may have been considerably less complex culture-areas than either the Aztec or Tarascan heartlands, they were in no sense primitive. In terms of the reductionist tendencies of the Spanish economy which was to be developed in the colonial period, the difference between the Indian cultures of central and western Mexico was not so much qualitative as quantitative.

Conquest and Early Development

The Indians of the Guadalajara region itself, if not of New Galicia as a whole, succumbed easily to the Spanish, though the conquest was exceptionally brutal in its middle phase, under the captainship of Nuño de Guzmán, from 1530 to 1532.[24] The conquest of western Mexico had started with initial explorations by Alvarez Chico, Cristóbal de Olid, Gonzalo de Sandoval, and Francisco Cortés, but the real exploration and subjugation of the west began only with the advent of Nuño de Guzmán in 1529. Nuño, hoping to make himself independent of Hernando Cortés, carve out an empire in his own name, and redeem himself from the malfeasances of the first Audiencia period, went as far up the Pacific coast as present-day Sinaloa, reaching Culiacán in 1531. He established a number of towns, gave out a few encomiendas (including a very rich one to himself), and in 1533 was named governor of New Galicia, as he had christened his conquests (after his native province in Spain). The lack of control by the central Mexican authorities over all this movement led to a high degree of autonomy for the newly established kingdom.[25]

In the meantime, Nuño de Guzmán had founded Guadalajara in 1531, in what was to become central Jalisco. The most obvious site was in the

24. Berthe, "Introduction à l'histoire de Guadalajara," p. 69.
25. *Ibid.*; Cornejo Franco, *Testimonios*, p. ix; Arregui, *Descripción de la Nueva Galicia*, p. xxvi; Borah, "Los tributos," p. 29.

area of Tonalá, the seat of one of the major Indian *tlatoanazgos* of Chimalhuacán. But since Nuño pretended to the title of Marqués de Tonalá (reminiscent of Cortés as Marqués del Valle) and held an encomienda there, he blocked the location of the city and it was initially founded at Nochistlán instead. The fledgling settlement did not fare well there, moving first to Tonalá itself in 1533, to Tlacotlán in 1535, and finally to the Atemajac Valley in 1542. By 1539, before its move to its permanent site, the city had officially received its coat of arms from Emperor Charles. At its foundation in the Atemajac Valley there were only 20 Spanish *vecinos*, and by 1548 there were only 35. The city eventually absorbed the several nuclei of Indian settlements existing in the Valley. By 1550 the Bishop of New Galicia had established his residence in the city, and in 1560 it became the capital of New Galicia when the Audiencia transferred its seat there from the coastal town of Compostela.[26]

Over and around these events eddied and swirled the turbulent advance of the Spaniards into the near north of Mexico. The early 1540s, in particular, were a period of crisis and triumph for the Spanish effort. In the nearer areas of New Galicia, the silver strikes at Compostela, Etzatlán, and Guachinango, as well as other smaller *reales*, afforded some relief for the economic decline caused by Indian depopulation. Although these strikes themselves tended to play out rather quickly, they provided a base for the permanent settlement of New Galicia.[27] Roughly coincident with these events, and with the final foundation of Guadalajara, there occurred the Mixtón War of 1541. This desperate uprising by the Indians of the near north for a time threatened to expel the Spanish from New Galicia, and after costing the redoubtable Pedro de Alvarado his life, brought Viceroy Antonio de Mendoza out to the west to command the Spanish forces in person. Despite its disruptive and destructive effects on the Spaniards, as well as upon the Indians, the end of the war paved the way for effective Spanish penetration into the Chichimec area, and the resulting discovery of Zacatecas in 1546.[28]

The silver mines of Zacatecas were to change the political and economic geography of New Galicia permanently. Paradoxically, this development was to have the dual effect of elevating Guadalajara and depressing it at the same time. The northward military advance which eventuated in the discovery of the Zacatecas mines was in large measure supported with men

26. Cornejo Franco, *Testimonios*, p. x; Arturo Chávez Hayhoe, "El establecimiento de Guadalajara," in Instituto, *Lecturas*, pp. 102-103; Rivière d'Arc, *Guadalajara y su región*, pp. 26-27.

27. Peter J. Bakewell, *Silver Mining and Society in Colonial Mexico* (1971), p. 6.

28. Lesley Byrd Simpson, *Many Mexicos* (1967), pp. 39 and 56; Berthe, "Introduction à l'histoire de Guadalajara," p. 70; Enrique Florescano, "Colonización, ocupación del suelo y 'Frontera,'" in Alvaro Jara, ed., *Tierras nuevas* (1969), passim.

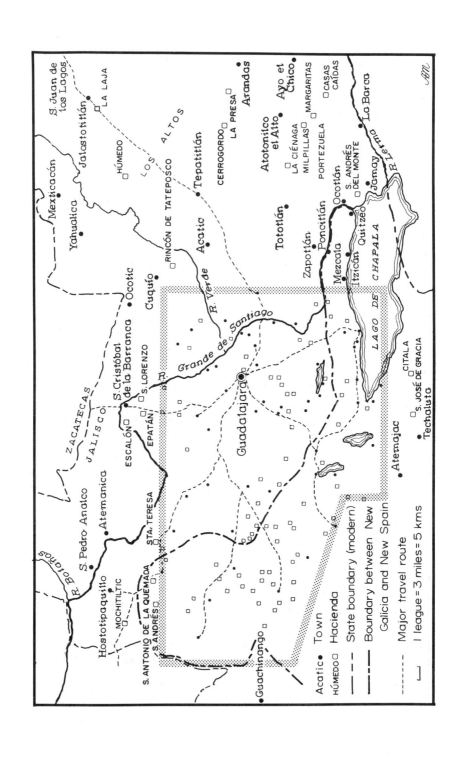

S. Juan de los Lagos

LA LAJA

Jalostotitlán

HÚMEDO

Mexticacán

Yahualica

RINCÓN DE TATEPOSCO

LOS ALTOS

Acatic

Tepatitlán

CERROGORDO

LA PRESA

Arandas

Ayo el Chico

MARGARITAS

CASAS CAÍDAS

Atotonilco el Alto

LA CIÉNAGA

MILPILLAS

PORTEZUELA

S. ANDRÉS DEL MONTE

Ocotlán

La Barca

R. Lerma

Jamay

Itzicán Quitzeo

LAGO DE CHAPALA

Tototlán

Zapotlán

Poncitlán

Mezcala

Ocotic

Cuquío

R. Verde

R. Grande de Santiago

S. Cristóbal de la Barranca

S. LORENZO

R.

EPATÁN

ESCALÓN

Guadalajara

CITALA

S. JOSÉ DE GRACIA

Techaluta

ZACATECAS

JALISCO

S. Pedro Analco

Atemanica

STA. TERESA

Atemajac

R. Bolaños

Hostotipaquillo

MOCHITILTIC

S. ANTONIO DE LA QUEMADA

S. ANDRÉS

Guachinango

Acatic ● Town
HÚMEDO □ Hacienda
- - - State boundary (modern)
━━━ Boundary between New
Galicia and New Spain
- - - - Major travel route
⌐ 1 league = 3 miles = 5 kms

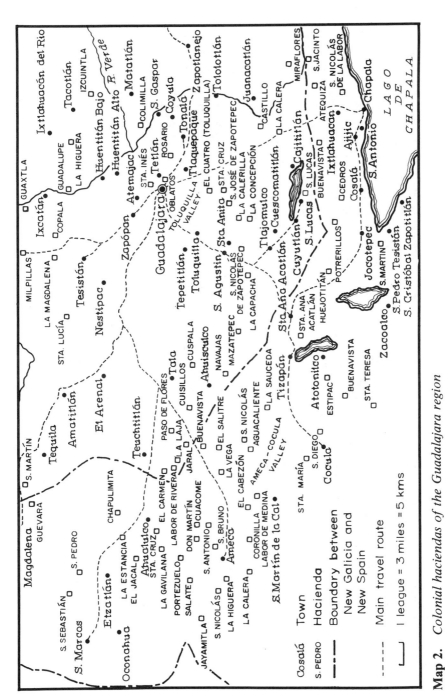

Map 2. Colonial haciendas of the Guadalajara region

and money from Guadalajara.[29] The ensuing ascendancy of the mines in the near north shifted the economic center of gravity of New Galicia from the west to the east. The Audiencia and Bishopric of New Galicia, both established in Compostela in 1548, were officially transferred to Guadalajara in 1560 (where the bishop had unofficially resided since 1550). The definitive rise of Guadalajara coincided with the decline of Compostela, which had only six Spanish vecinos by 1560. Guadalajara was better located than the coastal town for communication with the interior, was closer to Mexico City (by some 200 kilometers), and had greater possibilities for Spanish agriculture. It functioned as a rendezvous point for merchants dealing with the mining camps, and for a while served as an agricultural supplier for Zacatecas, until the major supply area, at least for wheat, shifted to the Bajío.[30] Based upon Zacatecas, the Spanish occupation of the north proceeded apace, eventually leading to the discovery of more silver deposits at San Martín, Sombrerete, Fresnillo, Nieves, and other locations. The silver route to Zacatecas and its northern sister camps was protected by the Crown policy of establishing garrison-towns and presidios, planned by Viceroy Mendoza and carried out by his successors. Among these towns were San Miguel el Grande (1555), Lagos (1563), Fresnillo (1567), Jérez (1570), Celaya (1575), and Aguascalientes (1576).[31]

While Guadalajara was in the ascendant politically, it was suffering the effects of the northward movement through loss of manpower. The tremendous population influx to Zacatecas in 1549-1550, and the subsequent military expeditions to the north, in part involved a draining of Spanish vecinos from the more southerly towns of New Galicia, among them Guadalajara itself. Of the nearly 1,800 Spaniards who had come to New Galicia with the various military and exploratory expeditions during the conquest period, only about 200 remained in the kingdom proper by 1550, because of the poverty of the area, the limited commercial opportunities, and the pull of the mines and near north.[32] The city of Guadalajara had only about 250 Spanish people of all ages in 1554, about 300 in 1586 (at the same date, Zacatecas had roughly four times as many), and barely 500 Spaniards by the beginning of the seventeenth century.[33] Further, despite the fact that the boundaries of New Galicia were clearly established by

29. Philip Wayne Powell, *Soldiers, Indians, and Silver* (1969), pp. 11-12.

30. Bakewell, *Silver Mining and Society*, pp. 17, 19, and 61; Berthe, "Introduction à l'histoire de Guadalajara," p. 70; Arregui, *Descripción*, p. xxviii; Cornejo Franco, *Testimonios*, p. xi; J.H. Parry, *The Audiencia of New Galicia* (1948), p. 29.

31. Arregui, *Descripción*, p. xxviii; Florescano, "Colonización, ocupación," passim.

32. Powell, *Soldiers, Indians, and Silver*, p. 13; Bakewell, *Silver Mining and Society*, p. 15; Antonio Gutiérrez y Ulloa, "Ensayo histórico-político del Reino de la Nueva Galicia" (1816), fols. 49v-50.

33. Berthe, "Introduction à l'histoire," p. 71.

about 1580 (its limits with Nueva Vizcaya and Nuevo León were recognized in 1562 and 1579, respectively), the kingdom's political integrity and semi-autonomy were constantly under attack from New Spain.

Guadalajara in 1600 and in 1800

Guadalajara, in its early development and until the recent past, was preeminently a commercial and administrative center. It was not itself a primary producer of wealth in the form of industrial goods or minerals, although it did develop a good deal of light industry toward the end of the colonial period. Its function was mainly that of a broker: commercial, financial, political, cultural. The city continued to grow despite the mid-century reverses, and by the late sixteenth century it was firmly established in its role of intermediary in the west. A description of the city in about 1600, particularly of its economic life, will help to set the background for its subsequent development. From 1600, we will jump forward in time two hundred years to briefly describe the same city in about 1800, thus establishing something of a framework for the discussion of the region's evolution between 1675 and 1820.[34]

In the early years of the seventeenth century, Guadalajara was neither rich nor populous, nor particularly pretty. Until 1600 and after, the importance of its administrative activity somewhat outweighed its commerce, though the balance began to shift in favor of the latter after the turn of the century. About half of the 500 Spaniards living in the city at that time were officials of some kind (judicial, administrative, fiscal), or their dependents, and the Audiencia was complaining to the Crown that it required more.[35] The seventeenth-century observers Alonso de la Mota y Escobar and Domingo Lázaro de Arregui agreed both that the richest men in the city were merchants (though they varied considerably in their fortunes) and that there was a disproportionately high number of merchants in the population. In Mota y Escobar's time, there were 22 merchants in the city, all trading through Mexico City, ranging in their capital from about 4,000 to 20,000 pesos, with the three wealthiest men possessing upwards of 100,000 pesos each. In addition, there were a number of itinerant merchants (*mercaderes viandantes*). Twenty years later, Guadalajara had some 40 *tiendas* (stores)—though Arregui is less clear in his terminology than Mota y Es-

34. Hardly anything has been published on the seventeenth century as yet (certainly for the Guadalajara region), though a substantial mass of documentary material still reposes in Mexican archives. There is considerable discussion of several aspects of seventeenth-century economic life in subsequent chapters, regarding the structure of agricultural production (Chapter 9), rural labor (Chapter 10), and the formation of landed estates (Chapter 13).

35. Parry, *The Audiencia of New Galicia*, p. 83.

cobar. According to Arregui, most Spaniards who were not merchants at least dealt in livestock for export out of the region.[36] Aside from the somewhat limited opportunities for acquiring wealth through public office, large-scale commerce, or the livestock trade, there were simply no alternatives. By 1600 or so, there were only 26 *encomenderos* in all of New Galicia, and their grants were already in the second and third life. Indeed, Mota y Escobar attributed the retarded condition of the city to the dying-out of the Indians (and therefore of the *encomiendas*) and the decline of various local silver mines. This had led to the emigration of many of the city's "familias principales" and their replacement by European and other immigrants.[37]

The city had fine rectilinear streets lined with unprepossessing, low adobe houses, but no gardens or fountains because of the lack of water. The old cathedral was constructed of "humble adobe, narrow and ruined" ("adobe humilde estrecha y arruinada"), but an ambitious new building was under construction. There was no seminary or university, only a modest Jesuit *colegio*. An urban cultural life was almost completely lacking, and one of the chief attainments and entertainments of the city's Spaniards was their expert horsemanship. Guadalajara was so countrified that the vecinos ran hares through the streets with their hunting dogs.[38]

Already by 1600, however, the relationship of the urb to the surrounding agricultural region was organized along the lines so evident in the eighteenth century. The city drew most of its wheat supply from the irrigated *labores* (farms) immediately surrounding it or located in favored areas not too far away. The four major labores lay in the Zapotepec Valley (later called the Toluquilla Valley) and in the valleys of Mazatepec and Santa Ana Acatlán, their grain being ground in the city's four flour mills. But wheaten bread was in short supply because of the lack of labor to cultivate it, and so the Audiencia (sometime before 1620) ordered the owners of the existing labores each to supply the city with a yearly fixed quantity of grain at a fixed price.[39] Maize production was almost totally in the hands of the Indians of the region. The decline of the indigenous population, combined with the disruptive effects upon labor of the early efforts to introduce the agricultural *repartimiento*, had resulted in a precipitous rise in the price of this staple grain between 1550 and 1600 and a chronic shortness of supply, or at least a fear of it.[40] The city was supplied with fowls,

36. Mota y Escobar, *Descripción geográfica*, p. 25; Arregui, *Descripción*, pp. 66-67.

37. Mota y Escobar, *Descripción geográfica*, pp. 24-25.

38. *Ibid.*, pp. 24-26; Arregui, *Descripción*, pp. 62-63.

39. Mota y Escobar, *Descripción geográfica*, pp. 27-28; Arregui, *Descripción*, pp. lxv, 65, and 69.

40. Mota y Escobar, *Descripción geográfica*, p. 28; Parry, *The Audiencia of New Galicia*, p. 86.

fish, vegetables, and a variety of other produce by the local Indians at a weekly market in the central plaza.[41]

Agriculture was relatively unimportant compared to livestock-raising, however. New Galicia as a whole, especially the southern and western portions, but also the Guadalajara region, was characterized in 1600 by vast tracts of abandoned, uncultivated land. This was not entirely due to the recession of the Indian population, since the Indians had never been numerous enough to exploit all the available land before the advent of the Spaniards, but to the lack of labor, mostly Indian, to support Spanish agricultural enterprises, and to the lack of internal markets. In the Guadalajara region, for example, there was nothing between Tala and Guachinango but cattle *estancias*—no population settlements, no cultivation. Mota y Escobar believed this to be potentially good maize and wheat land, but it had gone unworked because of the scarcity of agricultural labor. These enormous empty spaces were quickly filled with rapidly multiplying herds of feral cattle in the latter half of the sixteenth century, and an entire economy grew up around their haphazard exploitation.

An extensive, wasteful livestock economy developed, not dissimilar to that of the Argentine pampas in the days before the advent of the *saladeros*. Animals were slaughtered for their hides and tallow, the meat left to rot on the carcasses. The long-distance livestock trade to central Mexico began to assume a great deal of economic importance. The city of Guadalajara, chronically subject to shortness of supply for maize and wheat, was amply provided with inexpensive meat. While grain prices rose during the period 1550-1600, meat prices remained stable. Under the impact of the export trade, the natural stabilizing tendency of the livestock population, and the overkilling of the herds, however, meat prices showed an inclination to rise around 1600. Mota y Escobar remarked that the Guadalajara region, previously vastly overstocked with cattle, was understocked by 1605. The herds soon recovered, however, and a more disciplined exploitation of this cheap natural resource made it the mainstay of the region's farming economy until well into the eighteenth century.[42]

The Guadalajara of 1800 was in some ways similar and in other ways very different from what it had been two centuries earlier. The city was still preeminently a mercantile and administrative center. Its official life was dominated by the Audiencia and the Intendancy (established in 1786) and all the protocol attendant upon their functioning. The city was thronged with lawyers and notaries, but despite the great importance of Guadala-

41. Mota y Escobar, *Descripción geográfica*, p. 26.
42. Arregui, *Descripción*, pp. lvii and lxv-lxvii; Mota y Escobar, *Descripción geográfica*, pp. 28 and 36; Parry, *The Audiencia of New Galicia*, p. 85; Berthe, "Introduction à l'histoire," p. 73; Bakewell, *Silver Mining and Society*, p. 72.

jara's politico-administrative function, its life-blood was still commerce. There were upwards of 500 merchants in the city (including 50 or more large wholesalers), the third-largest occupational grouping after laborers and textile workers. After 1790 a movement in the direction of import-substitution in cotton and woolen textiles stimulated the growth of industry.[43] Even if the Guadalajara of 1800 was a small town by modern standards of urbanization, the city had grown tremendously since 1600, reaching a population of about 35,000 in 1803, compared to some 25,000 a decade earlier.[44]

The modest, almost desolate city of 1600 had been transformed by 1800 into a handsome urban center with some 350 city blocks and a large suburban area. The three Indian pueblos of Mesquitán, Analco, and Mexicaltzingo had been absorbed into the city physically, if not yet legally.[45] The adobe buildings of 1600, though they still filled in most of the city's landscape, had been displaced for the most part in the urban center by stone structures dominated by the Cathedral. The suburbs of Tlaquepaque and Tonalá, though still artisanal villages, served as the summer retreat of the city's wealthy, their picturesque villas displaying lovely ornamental gardens and orchards. The institutional and cultural life of Guadalajara had blossomed along with the increase in its population, especially after 1790. The year 1791 saw the establishment of the University and the first printing press; 1795 the *consulado*; 1800 the new Alcalde market; and 1803 the magnificent Cabañas orphanage.[46]

The agricultural support structure of this notable urban growth had developed in a parallel fashion. Population recovery in the countryside had provided an ample labor force for the more intensive agriculture of the late colonial period. The empty spaces in the countryside so obvious in the time of Mota y Escobar and Arregui were now occupied by human settlements and cultivated fields. The large, free-roving herds of cattle and other livestock had been reduced somewhat and contained within a more finely-tuned farming regime. The rustic hacienda houses of the years before 1750 had been replaced on the most important rural estates with the handsome, rambling, but often spartanly decorated country houses of the end of the eighteenth century, some of considerable beauty and even architectural pretension (El Cabezón, Huejotitán, Atequiza). Guadalajara as a market drew in a huge and constant stream of grain, meat, and other foodstuffs, as

43. AHMG, caja 15, 1793 (summary of census data); Berthe, "Introduction à l'histoire," p. 73. See Chapter 8 below for a more detailed discussion of the city's commercial life in about 1800.

44. Berthe, "Introduction à l'histoire," p. 71; AHMG, Caja 15, 1793.

45. José Cornejo Franco, "El paseo del pendón," in *Lecturas históricas sobre Jalisco* (1976), p. 141; Lindley, "Kinship and Credit," p. 37.

46. Berthe, "Introduction à l'histoire," p. 73; Rivière d'Arc, *Guadalajara y su región*, p. 30.

well as cotton and wool for its *obrajes*, tallow and potash for its soap-making establishments, and hides for its tanneries. Although a good deal of livestock was still exported from the region, and from New Galicia as a whole, a much larger share of it than ever before was staying in the west.

In a historical sense, the most important raw material for the processes of rural change was not land, or capital, or cattle, or stalks of wheat or maize, but people: they made the economic decisions, consumed the products of agriculture, and supplied the labor for tilling the fields and running the herds. More specifically, the relative numbers of people involved in these activities, given an almost changeless technology, governed the importance of the urban market, the mix of production factors in farming, and the productivity of agriculture.[47] The changes in the numbers of people living in Guadalajara and its region are therefore of great importance for this study, and the next chapter will sketch in the main outlines of those changes.

47. For a general discussion of the significance of population size, see E. A. Wrigley, *Population and History* (1969), chap. 2.

CHAPTER 2

Demographic Change—
Rural and Urban

The most important social fact in the history of the Guadalajara region in the late colonial period was the increase of population in the countryside, in rural hamlets, villages, and towns, and in the capital of New Galicia itself. The main factor in this movement was the recovery of the Indian population from its catastrophic decline in the sixteenth century. The nadir was reached in about 1650, and thereafter the indigenous population began an increase which continued into the early nineteenth century and beyond. The total population of the region rose even faster, however, and by the last decades of the colonial era non-Indians constituted about half of the whole.[1] The general regional trend was reflected and even surpassed by the growth of Guadalajara, particularly after the mid-eighteenth century. Nor was the demographic growth of the region unique in this regard, within either Mexico or Latin America as a whole. The last century of Spanish colonial rule in the Indies was characterized nearly everywhere by a general and massive population increase which exceeded that in any other part of the world except North America.[2]

1. Sherburne F. Cook and Woodrow Borah, *Essays in Population History*, vol. 1 (1974), pp. 300-375.

2. Nicolás Sánchez-Albornoz, *The Population of Latin America* (1974), p. 86. For the world in general, but particularly for Europe, see Wrigley, *Population and History*, chaps. 5 and 6; T. H. Hollingsworth, *Historical Demography* (1969); and B. H. Slicher Van Bath, *The Agrarian History of Western Europe* (1963), pp. 77-97. For Latin America, see Richard Morse, "Patrones de la urbanización latinoamericana," p. 12, and the other essays in the work edited by him, *Las ciudades latinoamericanas*, vol. 2, *Desarrollo histórico*, especially

Demographic change interacted in important and complicated ways with changes in economic structure. The country districts around Guadalajara not only sent their agricultural products into the city, but their sons and daughters as well; and on its part, the development of the city was underwritten not only by the food supplies available in its hinterland, but also by the broadened local market for its goods and services. In this chapter, therefore, we will sketch briefly the major changes in the numbers of people living in the Guadalajara region and the rhythms of population growth.

The Growth of the City

Guadalajara grew from a small, dusty town of about 1,500 people in the late sixteenth century to a flourishing city of some 40,000 by 1813. The city's growth was strikingly concentrated, however, in the eighteenth century. While Guadalajara's population roughly doubled between 1600 and 1700, it increased sixfold in the century 1700-1800. The number of people living in the city increased by almost 50 percent in the two decades from 1793 to 1813, and continued to rise during the next ten years. Table 1 and Figure 1 present the available data on the size of Guadalajara at various dates from its definitive foundation in 1542 until 1830.

There are some difficulties with these figures which have significance not only for the population counts of colonial Guadalajara but for other colonial cities as well. First, and most obvious, is the gap of almost ninety years between the mid-seventeenth century and the frequent counts of the latter part of the eighteenth century. Second, all the counts before 1760, except for those of 1651 and 1738, are stated in terms of families or vecinos (not necessarily synonymous), while those from 1760 onward are stated in terms of total inhabitants. This makes the earlier counts less reliable than the later ones, even where a reasonable conversion factor is applied consistently. Closely related is the problem of arriving at some reasonable estimate for the number of non-Spanish inhabitants of the city in the pre-census era. The question here turns not only upon the absolute numbers of people living in the city, but upon the changing relationship of the Spanish population to other ethnic groups and the changing role of what may be called the support population, which supplied the labor to keep the Spanish polity going.[3] Where in the pre-census counts are the free blacks, mu-

the one by Alejandra Moreno Toscano, "México," pp. 172-196; and Jorge E. Hardoy, "Two Thousand Years of Latin American Urbanization," in Hardoy, ed., *Urbanization in Latin America* (1975), pp. 1-32.

   3. See the discussion in Cook and Borah, *Essays*, vol. 1, pp. 123-137.

Table 1.

Population of Guadalajara, 1542-1830

Year	Number of People	Comments
1542	63 Spanish vecinos	About 200 people total
1544	20 Spanish vecinos	
1548	35 Spanish vecinos	
1554	80 Spanish families	About 500 Indian families in immediate environs of city
1560	2,500	
1570	50 Spanish vecinos	
[1572-1574] [a]	150 vecinos	Spanish?
1575	60 Spanish families	About 3,000 Indians in immediate environs of city (too high?)
1586	100 Spanish vecinos	
1602	173 Spanish vecinos	Total Spanish population more than 500, with additional 500 mulattos and slaves, not counting free blacks; about 1,200 Indian families in nearby villages
1621	200 Spanish vecinos	About 500 additional non-Spanish people in city and nearby villages; 762 Indian tributaries (representing an approximately equal number of families) in immediate area
1637	600 Spanish vecinos	
1651	5,000-5,500	*Padrón eclesiástico* of parish of Guadalajara gives 3,357 people of all ages and ethnic groups, in 449 families, not including religious or their servants, Indians of city barrios, or laborers on nearby haciendas and ranchos
1713	2,000 vecinos	Spanish?
1738	8,018	From communion lists; does not include monasteries or convents, their domestics, children, or Spaniards living in Indian barrios
[1744] [a]	8,000-9,000 families	Spanish, mestizos, mulattos; does not include Indians of barrios or nearby pueblos
1760	11,294	

Table 1. (continued)
Population of Guadalajara, 1542-1830

Year	Number of People	Comments
1770	22,394	People above the age of two years; from a *padrón eclesiástico*
1777	22,163	Includes Mezquitán, Analcos, Mexicaltzingo, Tetán
1793[b]	28,250	Census summary adjusted to include Indian barrios
1803	34,697	Humboldt's figure of 19,500 people for the same year appears much too low
1813	39,624	
[1815][a]	60,000	An estimate by the city cabildo
[1817-1819][a]	60,000-70,000	An estimate by the city cabildo
1823[c]	46,824	A figure for the same year in AHMG, caja 48, gives 40,272 people
1829	39,894	
1830	40,404	

SOURCES:
1542–Luis Páez Brotchie, *Guadalajara; su crecimiento* (1951), p. 19; the 200 figure is from José R. Benítez, *Conquistadores de Nueva Galicia* (1942), p. 49. 1544–Hélène Rivière d'Arc, *Guadalajara y su región* (1973), p. 31. 1548–Luis Pérez Verdía, *Historia particular del estado de Jalisco* (1951), vol. 1, p. 210. 1554–Jean-Pierre Berthe, "Introduction à l'histoire de Guadalajara et de sa région" (1970), p. 71. 1560–Benítez, *Conquistadores*, p. 49. 1570–Páez Brotchie, *Guadalajara*, p. 36 (quoting an *informe* of the *cabildo eclesiástico* of that year); also Pérez Verdía, *Historia particular*, vol. 1, p. 105. 1572-1574–François Chevalier (ed.) in Domingo Lázaro de Arregui, *Descripción de la Nueva Galicia*, p. lxii, quoting Juan López de Velasco, *Geografía y descripción universal de las Indias* (1894). 1575–Pérez Verdía, *Historia particular*, vol. 1, p. 241. 1586–Berthe, "Introduction," p. 71. 1602–Alonzo de la Mota y Escobar, *Descripción geográfica* (1966), p. 25; figure on Indian families from Berthe, "Introduction," p. 71. 1621–Arregui, *Descripción*, p. 62; figures on others and Indians from Berthe, "Introduction," p. 71. 1637–Páez Brotchie, *Guadalajara*, pp. 65-66, quoting Antonio Vásquez de Espinosa, *Compendium and Description of the West Indies* (1948). 1651–Berthe, "Introduction." p. 71, an estimate based on the *padrón eclesiástico*. 1713–Berthe, "Introduction," p. 71. 1738–Páez Brotchie, *Guadalajara*, p. 75, quoting Matías de la Mota Padilla, *Historia del Reino de Nueva Galicia* (1973); and Berthe, "Introduction," p. 71. 1744–José Antonio Villaseñor y Sánchez, *Teatro americano*, vol. 2, p. 206. 1760–Sherburne F. Cook and Woodrow Borah, *Essays in Population History*, vol. 1 (1974), p. 181, quoting an *informe de curatos* by the Bishop of Guadalajara. 1770–Berthe, "Introduction," p. 71. 1777–Páez Brotchie, *Guadalajara*, pp. 85-87. 1793–AHMG, caja 15; also in Páez Brotchie, *Guadalajara*, pp. 115-119. 1803–Páez Brotchie, *Guadalajara*, p. 127; Alexander von Humboldt, *Ensayo político* (1966), p. 169. 1813–AHMG, caja 41. 1815–Ramón María Serrera Contreras, "Estado económico de la

Table 1. (continued)

Intendencia de Guadalajara" (1976), p. 202. 1817-1819–Serrera Contreras, "Estado económico," p. 202. 1823–Páez Brotchie, *Guadalajara*, p. 185; the 40,272 figure is from AHMG, caja 48. 1829–AHMG, caja 50, leg. 240, exp. 2. 1830–ibid.

NOTES:

[a]Figures for bracketed years were deemed unreliable for various reasons.

[b]It is clear from comparison with the census data for 1777 in Páez Brotchie, *Guadalajara*, pp. 85-87, that the generally cited summary of the 1793 census, giving 24,249 inhabitants, does not include the Indians living in the Indian barrios of the city. I have therefore adjusted the city total for 1793 upward by 4,000, relying on the ratio of 1:1 for city Indians to barrio Indians as reflected in the 1777 census. The adjusted figure appears in this table, in Table 2, and in Figure 1. In subsequent discussion, the more traditional figure of 24,249 is used.

[c]Use of the higher figure seems justified, despite its inconsistency with the 1829 and 1830 counts, because Páez Brotchie, *Guadalajara*, p. 185, gives a breakdown by civil status for that year consistent with the higher number.

lattos, slaves, and *mestizos* who lived in the city? Such problems of essentially social rather than statistical definitions make it necessary to project rough estimates of what by the later sixteenth century had already become the larger part of the city's inhabitants.[4]

Third, there is the difficulty caused by the changing notion of what actually constituted the urban area for census purposes. The contiguous urban area of 1800 was several times larger than that of 1600.[5] Part of this increase in size was due to the continuous physical growth of the city outward from its center, and part to the absorption within the city of the outlying Indian villages.[6] But to assume that the city of 1700 or 1800 embraced its modern boundaries would be an anachronism. By 1602, Mota y Escobar clearly considered outlying Indian villages part of what we might call "greater Guadalajara." But how big an area did this proto-urban zone embrace? These difficulties aside, the import of the figures on Guadalajara's population growth between 1542 and 1830 is clear. If it were a matter of looking at the first forty or fifty years of the city's life alone, the data would be equivocal. But the long-term trend is unmistakably one of growth, particularly after the mid-eighteenth century.

Before the beginning of the eighteenth century, Guadalajara's population increased quite slowly by any yardstick. For the first 30 or 35 years of

4. On these fascinating issues of ethnic identity and social marginality, see Jonathan I. Israel, *Race, Class and Politics* (1975), esp. pp. 60-66.

5. Rivière d'Arc, *Guadalajara y su región* p. 31.

6. Rivière d'Arc, *ibid.*, p. 28, puts the absorption of the Analcos and Mexicaltzingo in the mid-seventeenth century. San Sebastián de Analco and Mexicaltzingo retained at least their titular identity until 1821, when they were formally declared *barrios* of the city and their *cabildos* (town councils) were suppressed. In the same year, Tetán, formerly a *sujeto* of Analco, was elevated into an independent pueblo (together with San Andrés de Analco), with its own *ayuntamiento* (*Colección de acuerdos, órdenes y decretos sobre tierras...*, vol. 2, pp. 10-11).

Population (thousands)

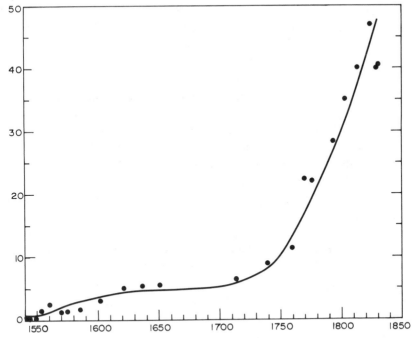

Figure 1.
Population of Guadalajara, 1542-1830

NOTE:
The populations for the years 1542, 1544, 1548, 1554, 1570, 1575, 1586, 1602, 1621, 1637, 1713, and 1738 are estimates based upon the data for those years in Table 1. Where necessary, I have taken other estimates into account (e.g., those of Jean-Pierre Berthe, "Introduction à l'histoire de Guadalajara y de sa région," in Centre National de la Recherche Scientifique, *Villes et régions en Amérique Latine*, 1970), made allowances for non-Spanish elements, and used appropriate multiplying factors to convert vecinos or families into individuals. For the conversion factors, see Sherburne F. Cook and Wood-row Borah, *Essays in Population History*, vol. 1 (1974), pp. 119-200.

the city's existence, the number of permanent Spanish householders— those vecinos upon whose presence the political and institutional identity of the Spanish city depended—hovered at around 50.[7] An unequivocal increase in the number of Spanish vecinos becomes obvious only with the count of 1586. Despite modest growth, the city remained relatively small

7. We have already recounted the early history of Guadalajara to some extent in Chapter 1, noting that until late into the sixteenth century the city was subject to a drain on its Spanish population to the northward exploration and conquest in general, and the discovery and settlement of Zacatecas in particular. The sharp upward jump in the city's population count between 1548 and 1554 was due to the kind of counting inconsistency discussed above, resulting in the inclusion in 1554 of nearby Indian villages which had not been included in 1548. The apparent drop in the total population of the city between 1560 and 1570 is hard to

during the seventeenth century, at least in comparison with Mexico City, Puebla, or Zacatecas.[8]

The real growth of Guadalajara began in about 1750, though the period of greatest increase in the *rate* of growth of the city seems to have been from 1710 to 1770 or so. After 1770 the increase in the absolute number of the city's inhabitants may have been quite striking, as it was to contemporaries, but the rate of growth was linear. By mid-century, José Antonio Villaseñor y Sánchez, in his encyclopedic survey of New Spain, commented on the size of Guadalajara, with its eight handsome plazas and its numerous convents and monasteries, that "the city is made populous by its large number of permanent residents (compared to that of other capitals)."[9] By the 1760s, the population of the city had grown to such a degree ("a flourishing republic, today very large") that the food supply was already of some concern to the city government.[10] The decade of strongest growth was 1760-1770, when the population doubled. By the time of the 1792-1793 census, Guadalajara's population of over 28,000 put it fourth among the major cities of New Spain, as is shown in Table 2. Given its small size in the sixteenth and seventeenth centuries and the substantial growth which it was still to undergo before the end of the colonial period, Guadalajara probably had a relatively higher growth rate than other Mexican cities during the eighteenth century.[11]

It is clear from even the roughest calculations that at least in the period after 1760 much of the city's growth was the result of immigration rather than natural increase, primarily from the rural areas within the Guadalajara region. Even at the reduced rate of growth in the decade 1793-1803,

---

explain. The 1560 figure may well be too high. In any case, what we are seeing in the sixteenth century is the intersection of the trend lines of Spanish and Indian population, the former remaining relatively stable and the latter declining, at first rapidly and then more slowly. The 1575 figure of 3,000 Indians (Pérez Verdía, *Historia particular*, vol. I, p. 241) seems far too high, given the lower figure for 1554, as does the Indian population count for 1602.

8. Berthe, "Introduction à l'histoire," p. 71. Zacatecas had roughly four times as many Spaniards as Guadalajara in 1586. Hardoy, in "Two Thousand Years of Latin American Urbanization," pp. 23-24, states that the relative growth index of urban population within the jurisdiction of the Audiencia of Guadalajara between 1580 and 1630 (2.81) was about the same as that for Spanish America as a whole, but less than that for New Spain proper (3.33). The figures for Guadalajara in this period are unfortunately not reliable enough to permit a test of Hardoy's hypothesis, nor are his raw data—given the nature of the Guadalajara numbers—likely to be accurate enough to sustain close scrutiny.

9. José Antonio Villaseñor y Sánchez, *Theatro americano*, vol. 2 (1952), p. 206. Villaseñor's mid-1740s estimate of the city's non-Indian (Spanish, mestizo, and mulatto) families at 8,000-9,000 (about 25,000 people) is too high to be credible, given the fact that the city's total population some thirty years later (1777) was 22,000.

10. AHMG, caja 3, exp. 16, 1768; caja 3, 1767.

11. Berthe, "Introduction à l'histoire," p. 71.

Table 2.
Population of Major Mexican Cities, 1793

City	Population
Mexico City	112,926
Puebla	52,717
Guanajuato	32,098
Guadalajara	28,250
Zacatecas	24,495
Antequera (Oaxaca)	19,069
Valladolid (Morelia)	17,093
Durango	11,027
San Luis Potosí	8,571
Tlaxcala	3,357

SOURCES:
Humboldt, *Ensayo político*, p. 38; AHMG, caja 15, 1793.

the city must have hosted a constant stream of immigrants. Some of this immigration came in intense bursts and was of a temporary nature. Such was the case with the thousands of destitute people who flooded into the city during the famine years of 1785-1786, and whose presence critically compounded the strains on the city's food supply, economy, and municipal services.[12] Yet this immigration was not of a permanent nature, and the census of 1793 hardly shows a ripple reflecting the intense movement of 1785-1786. The effects of the Rebellion of 1810 and subsequent guerrilla activity in the countryside may have been somewhat more permanent, but this is hard to establish.[13] More important than such fortuitous events was the constant stream of immigrants entering the city in search of work and better living conditions in the late colonial period, and which continues even today.[14] It is clear that immigration from overpopulated country districts into the city was a major source of the city's growth. At the very end of the colonial era, in 1822, almost exactly one-third of Guadalajara's inhabitants (34 percent) were immigrants to the city. What is more, the principle of inverse distance was at work, with the districts closest to the city contributing the most people. The major contributing areas outside the

12. AHMG, caja 10, 1786. For a detailed discussion of the events of 1785-1786, see Chapter 5 below.
13. AHMG, caja 24, 1811; caja 18, 1815.
14. See, for example, Rivière D'Arc, *Guadalajara y su región*, passim; and Sherburne F. Cook, "Las migraciones en la historia de la población mexicana," in García Martínez, ed., *Historia y sociedad* (1970), pp. 367-377.

state of Jalisco were the states of the *meseta* to the north and east.[15] On the basis of the available data, it appears that the ethnic composition of the city's population did not change substantially in the late colonial period, despite the effects of immigration from the countryside.[16]

Population Growth in the Countryside

The moderate growth of the city of Guadalajara during the seventeenth century, and the slow pace of economic development in the region, must be seen within the context of the changing demographic situation in western Mexico. It is by now one of the commonplaces of historical inquiry on Mexico that the diseases and the socio-economic dislocation brought by the Conquest caused a vertiginous drop in the aboriginal population, a catastrophe which profoundly affected the subsequent development of the country.[17] The Indian population reached its lowest point in the middle decades of the seventeenth century and then began a period of steady recovery lasting for the remainder of the colonial period. The resurgence of Indian numbers, in combination with an even stronger relative growth in the non-Indian sectors of the population, made the eighteenth century an era of rapid demographic increase. This scheme for colonial demographic history, with many nuances and regional variants, has chiefly been developed in the work of Sherburne Cook and Woodrow Borah.[18] With a few qualifications, it can be applied to west-central Mexico in general and to the Guadalajara region in particular.

Figure 2 gives an idea of the relative movement of total population in the Guadalajara region during most of the colonial period. It is important to stress the *relative* nature of the curve in Figure 2, which takes in a much larger area than the Guadalajara region. In fact the population of the Guadalajara region itself at the terminal date of the graph, 1793, would have been rather less than half of the 465,000 total indicated, or just over 200,000 people, including the city itself.[19] In terms of rates of change, the size of the

15. Cook, "Las migraciones," pp. 365-367; *Noticias geográficas y estadísticas del Departamento de Jalisco* (1843), p. 31.

16. Humboldt, *Ensayo político*, p. 38; AHMG, caja 15, 1793.

17. For the general acceptance of this thesis, see, for example, Sánchez-Albornoz, *The Population of Latin America*, pp. 39-66; and William H. McNeill, *Plagues and Peoples* (1976), p. 199 ff.

18. The major works are Woodrow Borah and Sherburne F. Cook, *The Population of Central Mexico in 1548* (1960) and *The Aboriginal Population of Central Mexico on the Eve of the Spanish Conquest* (1963); and Cook and Borah, *The Indian Population of Central Mexico, 1531-1610* (1960); *The Population of the Mixteca Alta, 1520-1960* (1968); and *Essays in Population History* (1974-1980).

19. Lónginos Banda, *Estadística de Jalisco* (1873), p. 35. Banda's figures apply to 1793. To

Population (thousands)

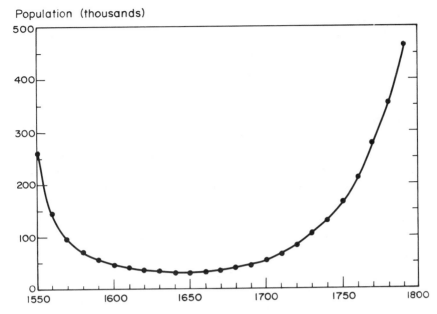

Figure 2.
Relative population movement in the Guadalajara region, 1548-1793

NOTE:
This graph and most of the following discussion are based upon Cook and Borah, "The Population of West-Central Mexico (Nueva Galicia and Adjacent New Spain), 1548-1960," in *Essays in Population History*, vol. 1, pp. 300-375. The figures in the graph are taken from Cook and Borah's Table 40a, p. 310; they are the aggregate of the columns headed "Early Colonial Nueva Galicia," "Southwestern Jalisco," and "Ávalos." These colonial regions, all parts of the area designated by Cook and Borah as west-central Mexico, are not congruent with the Guadalajara region as discussed in this study, but all overlap it to some extent. The resulting aggregate figures are much larger than for the Guadalajara region alone, and should be viewed only as a relative index of population movement within the region. The omission of Colima and the Motines, the two other regions included by Cook and Borah, hardly makes much difference statistically (about 0.04% of the 1793 total for west-central Mexico).

Indian tributary group dropped at a rate of about 5 percent per year between 1548 and 1560, and thereafter continued its decline, but at a diminishing rate, until about 1650. The recovery of the Indian population, coupled with the growth of Spanish and mixed-blood groups, pushed the overall rate of increase to about 1 percent yearly in the last decades of the

arrive at the estimate for the overall population of the Guadalajara region in 1793, I have aggregated the figures for the *subdelegaciones* which lay wholly within the region—Guadalajara, 64,215; Tonalá, 9,814; Cuquío, 17,241; San Cristóbal de la Barranca, 6,693; Tequila, 9,984; Tala, 6,882; Ahualulco-Etzatlán, 14,321; Tlajomulco, 14,924—and added to them half of the totals for La Barca (49,250) and Sayula (65,798), two districts which lay partially within the region. See the note with Figure 2 for further explanation.

seventeenth century, and to more than 2 percent by 1710-1720. The strong demographic upswing continued until about 1800 and then lost its momentum at the end of the colonial period, dropping to 0.7 percent in the decade 1800-1810 and recovering somewhat to 1 percent in the decade 1810-1820. Other areas in New Spain showed the same general upsurge during the seventeenth and eighteenth centuries, and the same tendency to reduce their rates of growth in the last decades of the colonial era.[20]

The major question with regard to the scheme outlined above is not the total number of people within the Guadalajara region at the end of the colonial period, but the distribution within that population of the major ethnic groups which made up colonial society. Put in another way, how can we overcome the averaging function of the aggregate figures set forth in Figure 2 so as to find out where population growth actually occurred? Without detailed micro-historical demographic studies conducted at the town or village level, there is really no way of providing complete answers for these questions.[21] Nonetheless, it is possible to assert in a general way that the concentration of Indian population as compared to other ethnic groups was proportionally higher in the Guadalajara region than in many other areas of west-central Mexico or the Intendancy of Guadalajara. The significance of this fact for the economic changes of the eighteenth century will become clear when we come to speak of the rural labor force and the access of country dwellers to land.

It is certainly true that the upsurge in the total population of New Spain in general, and of the Guadalajara region in particular, was in large measure due to the relatively stronger demographic push exerted by non-Indian groups in the population—which had begun on a smaller base—compared to Indians. By 1700, native Indian tributaries constituted only a fraction of the total population of west-central Mexico, the other component groups being Spaniards and mestizos, free tributary Negroes and mulattos, and displaced but tributary *indios laboríos*. The black and mulatto population, both tributary and nontributary, was particularly fecund, constituting a

20. Cook and Borah, *Essays*, vol. 1, pp. 355 and 375, and *The Population of the Mixteca Alta*, p. 57; and David A. Brading and Celia Wu, "Population Growth and Crisis: León, 1720-1860," *Journal of Latin American Studies* 5 (1973), p. 2.

21. For examples of this kind of micro-historical study—often, but not exclusively, demographic in nature—see Luis González, *Pueblo en vilo*; David A. Brading, "Grupos étnicos, clases y estructura ocupacional en Guanajuato, 1792," *Historia Mexicana* 21 (1972); Brading and Wu, "Population Growth and Crisis: León, 1720-1860"; Marcelo Carmagnani, "Demografía y sociedad: La estructura social de los centros mineros del norte de México, 1600-1720," *Historia Mexicana* 21 (1972); Claude Morin, *Santa Inés Zacatelco*; and Morin's general discussion on colonial parish registers in "Los libros parroquiales como fuente para la historia demográfica y social novohispana," *Historia Mexicana* 21 (1972).

much higher proportion of the total population in the western and northern provinces of Mexico than in the central and southern provinces.[22]

The dilution of the aboriginal population notwithstanding, the proportion of Indians within the Guadalajara region was probably more on the order of half the total, as opposed to one-third in west-central Mexico as a whole. In colonial Mexico, the resurgence of Indian population was strongest, and its share of the total population at the close of the colonial period greatest, in those areas of densest aboriginal settlement at the time of the Spanish Conquest. In western Mexico as a whole, excepting the Tarascan areas (of which Chimalhuacán was in some senses a marginal extension), the Guadalajara region seems to have had the densest pre-Conquest population. Tonalá, Ameca, and the numerous Indian settlements in the area of Lake Chapala did not compare in density of occupation to the Valley of Mexico or to Oaxaca, but for the west they were heavily populated. In quantitative terms, the trend of Indian population within the Guadalajara region during the eighteenth century would have been more like that of the Ávalos area, where the native tributary population constituted something like half the total near the end of the colonial period.[23] This pattern stood in marked contrast to that of regions with sparse Indian populations, such as the Altos and parts of the coast, where the demographic increase in the late colonial period was dominated by Spanish and mixed-blood groups.

In the context of a strong Indian population recovery relative to other groups within the population, the economic and social tensions in the Guadalajara region in the late colonial period become more readily understandable. As the Indian population began to increase and continued a strong growth during the eighteenth century, the pressure on economic resources in the countryside, particularly land, also increased. At the same time, the growth of Guadalajara created an urban market for food and primary materials which required the more intensive use of greater quantities of land and labor. The inevitable strains of adjusting to the new importance of commercialized agriculture included an increasing competition between the peasant and commercial sectors over the ownership and uses of land and other resources.

22. Black tributaries accounted for some 33.9% of all tributaries in the northern and western provinces of Mexico by about 1810, a figure about ten times that for central and southern Mexico at the same time (Cook and Borah, *Essays*, vol. 1, pp. 338-339 and fig. 33, p. 320). The mulatto population of Guadalajara in 1777 was about a third of the city's total (32.5%); by the time of the 1793 census, this proportion had slipped to 23%, suggesting either an inconsistency in ethnic classification or the increasing importance of ethnic intermarriage, or both (Luis Páez Brotchie, *Guadalajara, Jalisco, México* (1951), pp. 86 and 115).

23. Cook and Borah, *Essays*, vol. 1, p. 314, fig. 25.

PART II. GUADALAJARA

AS A MARKET: URBAN DEMAND

AND PUBLIC POLICY

CHAPTER 3

Meat

The city of Guadalajara required ever-increasing quantities of foodstuffs during the eighteenth century. The most basic among these, and representing by far the greatest part of the value of agricultural produce marketed in the city, were meat and grain. The grain and meat trades were mediated by various institutional arrangements whose ostensible goal was to allow government regulation of these vital sectors and to insure a constant food supply for the city. Through a study of these means, therefore, we can trace the commercialization of agriculture which took place in the course of the eighteenth century.

These institutional arrangements—the city meat monopoly, the public granaries for maize, and the wheat trade—are interesting in themselves and reflect the ideas of the time on economics and social utility. It was widely accepted that government agencies were justified in regulating the market in the interest of the public good; the Crown attorney (*fiscal real*) of the Guadalajara Audiencia remarked in an opinion of 1747, apropos of the city meat monopoly, that "although anyone may do as he likes with his own property, in the things necessary for the sustenance of life sellers should not be at liberty to set and raise prices freely."[1] The exclusive study of such institutions in their ideal or formal aspects, however, may lead to a

1. AHMG, caja 34.

kind of tunnel history, the mistaking of form for substance, which ignores such latent processes as the interplay of public and private interest.[2]

Nowhere is this interplay clearer than in the history of the city's meat monopoly, the *abasto de carnes*. Under this system, which prevailed in Guadalajara at least from the early seventeenth century until its abolition at the end of 1816, the exclusive right to supply the city with beef and lamb was leased out by contract to individuals for a specified term of years under competitive bidding. When there was no private bidder, as frequently occurred, the cabildo itself directly administered the abasto. The ostensible justification for this system was to provide the city with a constant supply of meat at a reasonable price by making one individual completely responsible and thereby eliminating as much as possible the random play of market forces. The city government also sought in this way to regulate the sale of meat in the city and to realize an income from the premiums which contractors paid under the terms of their bids. In fact, the goals of the system were realized to a considerable extent. The city was never without the supply of at least some meat, though consumption tended to be concentrated among those with high incomes. Prices were stabilized to a degree, and under the longer contracts were not subject to fluctuation, since the contractor had to supply meat at an agreed-upon price throughout his term.

But the forces of the market, chiefly at the supply end, did come into play, since meat prices rose substantially during the latter part of the eighteenth century (see Figure 3), and the number of animals slaughtered in the city during any given year varied considerably. Furthermore, the abasto system was used to advantage by the greatest stock-raisers of the Guadalajara region to insure their unimpaired access to the largest local market. The great landed magnates, many themselves city officials, frequently obtained the abasto contracts either directly or through their agents. The primary object of the entire institution, on the part of both the municipal government and those stockmen who obtained the contracts, was to eliminate risk. In this policy, as in other aspects of rural economy in the eighteenth century, the spirit of the age shines through.

Patterns of Supply and Consumption

We cannot trace with certainty the development of the urban demand for meat during the eighteenth century. The irregular but notable increase in the consumption of grain in Guadalajara during this period does not have

2. See the interesting remarks by James Lockhart in "The Social History of Colonial Spanish America," *Latin American Research Review* 7 (1972), esp. pp. 6-12.

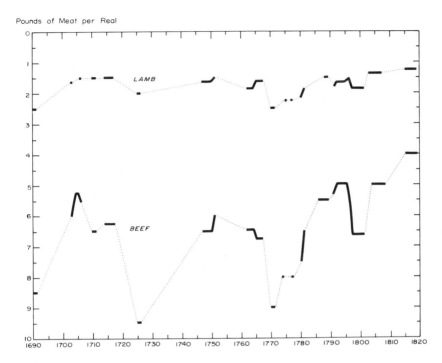

Pounds of Meat per Real

Figure 3.
Meat prices in Guadalajara, 1690-1820

SOURCE:
AHMG, various cajas.

a counterpart in the figures on cattle and sheep butchered in the city. Such figures as can be reconstructed from the existing documents are given in Table 3. The most one can say on the basis of these data is that the level of meat consumption in Guadalajara remained roughly stable, or perhaps increased slightly, during the latter half of the eighteenth century.

The question arises as to why meat consumption in the city remained basically stable while maize consumption doubled and wheat consumption quadrupled during the same period. The probable explanation for this lies in a number of factors. First, the consumption of meat and other animal protein in the city was not precisely equivalent to the number of cattle and sheep slaughtered under the auspices of the abasto de carnes. There was a good deal of contraband livestock coming into the city at all times, and especially during the late colonial period, when prices rose. In addition to contraband, pigs, goats, and chickens were not subject to the abasto monopoly. These forms of animal protein, in addition to dairy produce, were marketed by small independent producers, many of them living on the edges of the city and occupying pieces of land rented from the city itself, or

Table 3.

Number of Livestock
Butchered in Guadalajara, 1750-1812

| | Number of Livestock | |
Year	Cattle	Sheep
1750-51[a]	3,000	—
1770-71[b]	3,477	7,287
1780-81	4,080	8,129
1788-89	2,447	2,477
1811-12	5,666	1,258

SOURCE:
AHMG, caja 34 (1750-51); caja 6 (1770-71);
caja 8 (1780-81); caja 12 (1788-89); caja 24
(1811-12).

NOTES:
[a]Estimate based upon projection from partial
figures.
[b]The figures for 1770-71 are an estimate
derived by dividing the total weight each of
beef and lamb for that year by the average
dressed weight of animals for the year 1780-81.

by Indians or small *rancheros* living farther away from Guadalajara. A variety of fish came from Lake Chapala, including the dried *charales* typically used as a condiment, and were especially important during the Lenten season.

Second, the price of meat—especially of beef, which constituted the major share of the meat consumed in the city—rose considerably during the last quarter of the eighteenth century, as indicated in Figure 3. Except for the period 1797-1801 (during which the abasto contractor may have gone bankrupt because of his low price bid), beef prices, as reflected by the abasto contracts, rose steadily from about 1770 until 1820. Lamb prices showed a similar tendency to rise during the same period, though not quite as drastically. Urban consumers, particularly those in lower income groups, had to curtail their consumption of abasto-supplied beef and lamb. Nor were the abasto prices artificially high: they simply reflected the general rise in the price of live cattle evident from about 1780 or so (see Figure 4).[3]

3. Figure 4 is based upon very heterogeneous sources, including inventories, account books, private livestock sales recorded in notarial registers, and prices quoted randomly in municipal documents. The price quotations are those for *toros*, mature male animals, and *reses* and *ganados*, more general terms applying to cattle as a whole, including female animals. Prices for cows were generally higher, those of younger animals lower. The area represented covers most of central New Galicia.

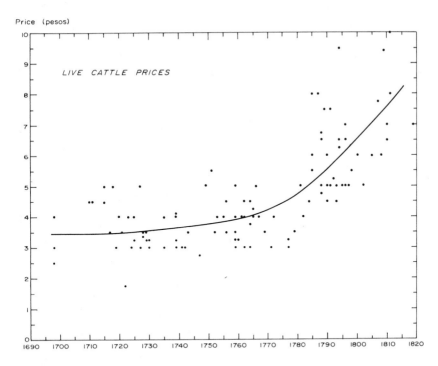

Figure 4.
Live cattle prices in the Guadalajara region, 1698-1819

SOURCES:
Various.

The major reason for these rising livestock and meat prices was a change in the pattern of agricultural production. The extension of grain cultivation had by the last third of the eighteenth century displaced livestock production as the dominant form of rural economic activity among large production units. Live cattle exports to New Spain from New Galicia as a whole declined significantly after midcentury. The exact situation in the Guadalajara region is not clear, but its earlier substantial livestock exports to New Spain probably declined along with its livestock production as a whole.[4] Meat quite literally lost ground in its competition with cereal pro-

4. For a somewhat different view of the trend in livestock exports from the region, see Serrera Contreras, *Guadalajara ganadera*, pp. 84-93 and passim, who asserts that the livestock export trade was growing in this period. Serrera's data do not cover a sufficiently long span of years to represent the secular trend in the stock-raising sector, though he does acknowledge an overall decline in the numbers of cattle, particularly, all over New Spain in the late colonial period. In fact, livestock exports out of the region and from New Galicia as a whole appear to have been much smaller at the beginning of the nineteenth century than at the beginning of the eighteenth. Serrera would ascribe this to the overkilling of cattle herds and a racial degeneration of livestock rather than to shifts in the pattern of rural economy.

duction, though the demand of the urban market was sufficient to keep both grain and meat prices rising throughout the late colonial period. In the face of rising prices, city dwellers cut back their consumption of the relatively more expensive animal protein in favor of wheaten bread and maize.

A basic and intriguing question arises with regard to urban consumption patterns and the demand these created for agricultural and livestock products. Specifically, if meat prices were rising in the late eighteenth century, why didn't local producers take the opportunity to profit from this trend by reconverting arable land to pasture, or increasing their meat production in other ways? At least a partial explanation lies in the limited elasticity of most urban consumers' budgets, so that they would not have been able to afford much meat even at the slightly lower prices resulting from an increased supply. Under the conditions of the late colonial years, meat was too expensive a form of nourishment. That the Guadalajara of 1800 could return to its protein-rich diet of 1600 was simply not possible. Given the possibilities for farming in the region, and the lack of transport facilities, there was not enough decent land to sustain a city of meat-eaters.

The pattern of the city's meat consumption demonstrated a marked short-term or seasonal fluctuation. A particularly rigorous dry season could reduce the overall supply of meat in the city severely, since large numbers of livestock died on the range under such conditions. In a normal year, however, the city population, at least those who could afford the high prices, embarked on a veritable orgy of meat-eating in the spring. Most cattle came into the city to be slaughtered in the spring, before the rainy season began, since it was easier to round them up before the rains. In the 1780s and 1790s, in the few months after Easter the city sometimes consumed 200 cattle and even larger numbers of sheep every week. During the week March 31 to April 6, 1780, for example, the combined weekly per-capita consumption of beef and lamb in the city was about 1.5 pounds, but by the last week of the accounting year, in April 1781, the figure had declined to about a half-pound.[5] In actuality, of course, the consumption of beef and lamb was terribly skewed in favor of the better-off inhabitants of the city.[6]

For a somewhat more detailed discussion of this matter, see my "Review of *Guadalajara ganadera*," *Agricultural History* 53 (1979). For a third view, based on data for colonial Cuernavaca, that abasto meat prices were influenced most strongly by weather cycles, see Ward Barrett, "The Meat Supply of Colonial Cuernavaca," *Annals of the Association of American Geographers* 64 (1974).

5. AHMG, caja 8. This is a very rough estimate based upon an assumed total population for the city of some 20,000 people.

6. AHMG, caja 34, 1789. It is interesting to note that in the middle of the abasto year, as city consumption was leveling off, the dressed weight of the average butchered carcass was generally at its highest, since the rains had by then improved the pasturage greatly.

Analysis of the geographical origin of the livestock purchased by the abasto points to the role of the predominantly creole landowning oligarchy as the city's meat suppliers. By its very nature, the meat monopoly was more concentrated than the grain trade, and a very few haciendas normally kept the city supplied with meat. In the year 1780-1781, of the 4,080 cattle legally slaughtered in Guadalajara, nearly a third (32 percent) came from the Hacienda de San Clemente, near Autlán, owned by the city's *regidor alférez real*, Ramón Fernández Barrena, son-in-law of the great silver baron Francisco Javier Vizcarra, the Marqués de Pánuco. The Hacienda de Huejotitán, of the Villaseñor family, supplied some 12 percent. The Hacienda de Toluquilla, owned by Vizcarra himself, provided 11 percent of the live cattle butchered in the city; Miguel Portillo's neighboring Hacienda de Santa Cruz 9 percent; the Hacienda de Santa Lucía 7 percent; and an assorted group of other estates the remaining animals. Thus five haciendas contributed over 70 percent of the beef consumed in the city in that year. The supply of sheep was, if anything, even more concentrated, with the great Hacienda de Mazatepec sending in 37 percent, the Hacienda de la Sauceda 20 percent, and Atequiza and a limited number of other estates the remainder.[7] Accounts for the years 1750-1751 and 1811-1812 indicate basically the same pattern of origin.[8] In the last four decades of the colonial era, however, there occurred a tendency toward outward displacement of the supply area to more peripheral districts. This was primarily due to the ascendancy of grain production in the environs of the city, and after 1810 to the theft and destruction to which the livestock of these haciendas had been subjected by the recent insurgency.[9]

Abasto Administration and Its Problems

In theory completely open to public bidding, the abasto contract was effectively limited to those large landowners who could themselves supply the necessary livestock or to those individuals who had sufficient capital and connections to purchase what they needed. The dominance over the city's abasto de carnes exercised by the elite group of important hacendados is clearly seen in Table 4, which sets forth information about the holders of the meat monopoly contracts between 1700 and 1820. Despite some gaps, the general drift of the information is clear enough. Until the middle of the eighteenth century, the most important local haciendas generally supplied by themselves the meat consumed within the city in any given year. After the midcentury, however, the great landowners appear

7. AHMG, caja 25.   8. AHMG, caja 34.
   9. AHMG, caja 24. On the destructive effects of the insurgency in the Bajío, see Brading, *Haciendas and Ranchos*, passim.

Table 4.

Contractors for the Meat Monopoly of Guadalajara, 1687-1815

Year	Contractor and *Fiador* (Guarantor)	Hacienda Associated with Contract	Term of Contract
1687	Alonso Rodríguez Vidal	Various holdings near city	——
1703	Cap. Juan de la Mota Padilla	Miraflores	——
1704-1705	Mota Padilla	Miraflores	2 years
1706	Juan Ibáñez, owner of a tannery in city	——	——
1710-1711	Juan Francisco de Urquiza	Atequiza	2 years
1712	Br. Juan Pérez Maldonado	El Cabezón-La Vega	4 years
1714	Cap. Antonio de Vizcarra	Miraflores	4 years
1716	José de Arebillaga (fiadores: Fernández de Ubiarco, Miranda y Villayzán)	El Cabezón-La Vega	——
1719-1722	Francisco Javier Berrueco, city lawyer; early transfer to Miranda y Villayzán	El Cabezón-La Vega	4 years
1723	Pedro Pérez de Tagle	Cuisillos	1 year
1724	Francisco de Soto Ceballos	Atequiza	1 year
1725-1726	Pedro Martínez Martaraña	Cedros	2 years
1727-1728	Cap. Esteban de Larreburu (for Martínez Martaraña)	Cedros	2 years
1738	Bernardo Apolinar Miranda y Villayzán	El Cabezón-La Vega	——
1740	Francisco Porres Baranda; transferred to Miranda y Villayzán	Mazatepec; El Cabezón-La Vega	——
1747	City		1 year
1749-1751	City		——
1759-1761	Miguel de Sierra	Navajas	3 years

Table 4. (continued)

Contractors for the Meat Monopoly of Guadalajara, 1687-1815

Year	Contractor and *Fiador* (Guarantor)	Hacienda Associated with Contract	Term of Contract
1762	Joaquín Fermín de Echauri (fiador: his son, regidor Agustín de Echauri y Panduro)	Various, Sayula area	—
1765	José Clemente Velasco, alcalde ordinario, city (fiador: Miguel del Portillo)	Santa Cruz, in Toluquilla Valley	1 year
1768	Juan Antonio de las Cuevas	—	1 year
1769	Juan Antonio de las Cuevas	—	1 year
1770-1772	Manuel Calixto Cañedo	El Cabezón-La Vega	3 years
1773-1774	José Duval del Valle	—	2 years
1775	Manuel Calixto Cañedo	El Cabezón-La Vega	1 year
1777-1790	Directly administered by city—no bidders	—	—
1791-1795	Diego José Moreno	—	—
1796	Nicolás Henríquez del Castillo	Rancho, Tonalá	—
1797-1801	Francisco Javier Pacheco	—	5 years
1802	Rafael Santos	—	1 year
1803-1807	Miguel López del Rivero (fiador: Juan Alfonso Sánchez Leñero)	Santa Lucía	5 years
1809	City	—	—
1810	Pablo Gutiérrez Higuera (fiador: Miguel del Portillo)	Santa Cruz, in Toluquilla Valley	—
1811-1815	Miguel del Portillo	Santa Cruz, in Toluquilla Valley	—

SOURCES:
AHMG, various cajas; AIPG, prots., various notaries, and LG, various; BPE-BD, various legajos.

much less frequently as holders of the monopoly, and the formal lease of the abasto, when it went to private individuals at all, was much more likely to go to city merchants or other men who were not themselves landowners. This separation of the functions of production and marketing strongly suggests that hacendados were reluctant to assume the legal responsibility of themselves supplying all the city's meat. The reason for this lay in the relative decline of stock-raising which began to be manifest sometime after the midcentury. Single great landowners who before 1750 had no difficulty committing themselves to supply two or three thousand cattle per year could by the last quarter of the century no longer meet such needs, with rare exceptions. Surely it is not coincidental that the fall in live cattle exports from New Galicia to New Spain dates also from the middle of the eighteenth century.

The vexing problem of an irregular meat supply was already in evidence by the midcentury. Within the general trend of inelastic supply and rising prices, there were of course seasonal and yearly variations attributable to weather and other natural conditions such as epidemic outbreaks among the animals.[10] Yet the main causes of the long-term trend in the city's meat supply were economic. As early as 1747 the cabildo was forced to prorate fixed yearly livestock contributions for the major stockmen of the area, since none of them would assume the abasto contract.[11] Two years later, with the city still directly administering the monopoly, the compulsory supply area was extended beyond the haciendas of the Toluquilla Valley, Santa Lucía, Huejotitán, Mazatepec-Santa Ana, Atequiza, and El Cabezón-La Vega, to include all those within a thirty-mile radius of Guadalajara, reaching as far as Sayula and Tepatitlán.[12] And still there were indications that some cattle-raisers had trouble in meeting their assessments.[13]

At the high prices of the latter part of the century and into the 1820s there was really no question of profitability: demand was not the problem. In fact, the abasto de carnes itself continued to be a desirable economic plum, but toward the end of the century individual contractors were unwilling to accept the entire responsibility for the city's meat supply all by themselves. In 1790, there being no bidder for the contract for the entire city but only individual bids for a number of subordinate butcher shops (*tablas*), the *fiscal* of the city suggested permanent division of the abasto contract to facilitate its rental. He pointed to the continued profitability of the meat trade despite the "lack of cattle, of which the most recent example is the present year."[14] The real problem was the insufficiency of livestock from which to meet the urban demand—given the continuation, at a much

---

10. AHMG, caja 15, 1787.   11. AHMG, caja 34, 1747.   12. *Ibid.*, 1749.
13. AHMG, caja 1, exp. 100, 1750.   14. AHMG, caja 13.

reduced level, of the export trade to New Spain, and the retention of live-stock in the rural districts for consumption by the local populace.

A revealing lawsuit of the time clearly indicates that the reason for this situation lay in the shift in land-use patterns within the hacienda economy. In an intra-family suit of 1803 involving the disposition of the Porres Baranda entail, centering on the estates of Mazatepec and Santa Ana Acatlán, the lawyer for the current holder of the entail disputed the opposing party's claim that the rent charged for the Hacienda de Santa Ana could be significantly raised through an extension of its cultivated lands. He dismissed the suggestion as patently foolish, since the supply and price of grain for the city were already reasonable, while the price of meat had risen ridiculously, precisely because grain cultivation had been extended at the expense of stock-raising.[15]

In an effort to circumvent this problem by casting its net more widely, the city government attempted after about 1800 to open the bidding for the abasto to stock-raisers outside the immediate area of Guadalajara. The traditional districts in which the *pregones* (publicly cried notices) of the abasto bidding had been given were La Barca, Sayula, Ahualulco, and Cuquío.[16] At the beginning of the nineteenth century the area of notice was extended to include Puebla, Zacatecas, Mexico City, Querétaro, Valladolid, Lagos, Zamora, Colima, Tepatitlán, Autlán, and Zapotlán el Grande.[17] There is no evidence to indicate that this solved the problem. Nonetheless, the sale of meat in the city continued to be profitable, as indicated by the facility with which the subordinate leases were made. Even in 1790, when the municipal government was forced to continue its direct administration of the abasto within the city for lack of private bidders, it had no difficulty at all in renting out the monopoly in the "pueblos subalternados," and even in raising the premiums paid to the city by the lessees.[18]

It was definitely in the best interests of the city government for the abasto to be leased out to a private contractor, since in that case the contractor assumed the entire risk and costs of the operation and provided the necessary capital.[19] Such an arrangement was not always possible, however, and on numerous occasions the cabildo, overseen by the Audiencia, was forced to assume the administration of the meat monopoly itself for want of private bidders. Direct city administration entailed the formation of a *junta*, or commission, whose appointees were drawn for the most part from among the regular members of the cabildo.[20]

15. BPE-AJA, 235:2:3080.   16. E.g., AHMG, caja 34, 1779.

17. E.g., AHMG, caja 20, 1803.   18. AHMG, caja 13.

19. AIPG, prot. Blas de Silva, 4:171-173; AHMG, caja 34, 1751; caja 4, 1777; caja 15, 1789; caja 23, 1808.

20. AHMG, caja 4, 1777.

In the very nature of things, the landed interest was always prominently represented in the cabildo, and so it was natural that major hacendados like Fernández Barrena, Tomás Ignacio Villaseñor (1789 junta), and José Ignacio Basauri (1790 junta) should take their places on the junta del abasto as city officials and as members of the landowning group. Nor was this apparent conflict of interest of recent origin. Early in the seventeenth century, the six or seven *regidores perpetuos* of the city, all of them prominent hacendados, were fixing abasto prices for their own profit, and the situation remained unchanged despite repeated *real çédulas* forbidding such dealings.[21] The irony is that the *fiscal real* of the Audiencia, in recommending the formal establishment of the junta in 1777, had argued for it on the grounds that private contractors were traditionally interested only in their own profits as opposed to the interests of the public.[22]

The junta, then, was at least in part intended to moderate the influence of stock-raisers on the urban market for meat. Under such circumstances, setting men like Fernández Barrena, Villaseñor, and Basauri to regulate the meat monopoly was like setting the cat to watch the mouse. That this conflict of interest was often resolved in favor of profit to the landowner is demonstrated by a junta transaction of 1789, in which Tomás Ignacio Villaseñor, a junta member and owner of the magnificent entailed estate of Huejotitán, sold several hundred head of cattle to the city at suspiciously elevated prices.[23] Such dealings were probably viewed by the junta members as the legitimate perquisites of office, inasmuch as administration of the meat monopoly involved the expenditure of a great deal of time and money on the part of the commissioners.[24]

In March of 1791, on the eve of the first private abasto contract in the city in some fifteen years, the *fiscal* of the Audiencia reviewed the performance of the junta del abasto in very negative terms. The city government had lost considerable amounts of money in administering the meat monopoly, as in the year immediately past (1790). The meat supply was plagued by chronic scarcity and high prices because of the "excesivo valor" of livestock and the junta's carelessness about buying up sufficient stocks ahead of time.[25] Yet in all fairness to the municipal government, it appears that when the meat supply of Guadalajara was returned to private hands in many of the years after 1790, things did not improve. The Libro de Cabildo of 1799, for example, is filled with references to fines levied against the meat contractor for his repeated failure to supply meat at the various tablas in the city.[26]

21. Chevalier, *La formation*, pp. 214-215.   22. AHMG, caja 4, 1777.
23. AHMG, caja 25.   24. AHMG, caja 12, 1789.
25. AHMG, caja 21, 1791.   26. AHMG, caja 19, 1799.

Contraband and Other Problems

One obvious solution to the chronic scarcity of meat within Guadalajara was the consumption of contraband beef, lamb, and goat meat. It was of course easier for those engaged in this illegal trade to get sheep and goats past the city customs-houses than cattle, so the contraband trade was almost entirely limited to these animals. Complaints of such practices, and attempts by the city government to control them, appear from early on in the eighteenth century. In 1738, for example, the holder of the abasto contract, Bernardo Apolinar de Miranda y Villayzán, owner of the great haciendas of El Cabezón and La Vega, stated that his sales of meat were being undercut in the city by the introduction of animals which had either been stolen or purchased outside the monopoly at less than the prevailing prices.[27] Twenty-two years later, the *abastecedor* was still making the same complaint.[28]

A much more circumstantial account of 1784 described the contraband trade in goat-meat and mutton. Goats and old sheep were being brought into the city in large numbers by several notorious women known to be the kingpins of the trade: María Manuela, La Zúñiga, La Albina, La Chacuala, Juana Méndez, La Sorda, Prudencia Méndez, la mujer de Rivas, and La Jacinta. The animals were slaughtered and the meat purchased at lower than market prices by the city's cooks with the money given them by their employers to buy abasto-supplied beef and lamb, thus providing the cooks with small but tidy sums. The practice very often led to illness in those who ate the meat, and encouraged livestock thefts. The cooks blamed the low quality of the meat on the abasto itself, a face-saving device which apparently nonetheless had some truth to it.[29] In 1800 a number of the subordinate *tablas* were found to be illegally selling meat from bulls which had been killed in the ring (*toros lidiados*). Much of this meat was rotten and dangerous in the extreme. The city physician stated:

... the meat of bulls which die agitated with the furor of the bull ring, without the blood being let, but remaining in all parts of the animals' bodies, can generally only be digested by persons with very strong stomachs, robust and completely healthy; especially the broth given to the sick is dangerous, and perhaps fatal, to those with fever.[30]

The size of the contraband meat trade is open to question, but it must have been substantial. In 1800 one smuggler alone was caught with sixty to seventy sheep.[31]

27. AIPG-LG, 55:290v-291v.   28. AHMG, caja 12, 1760-1761.
29. AHMG, caja 35.   30. AHMG, caja 19.   31. *Ibid.*

Even the meat butchered and sold legitimately within the restrictions of the monopoly, however, was of notoriously poor quality. In 1804 the president of the Audiencia, José Fernando Abascal (later to be Viceroy of Peru), discovered that the meat for his table had been especially set aside for him, and that other meat commonly sold to the city's inhabitants was of low quality or even unsafe. He therefore requested the cabildo to make random daily checks of meat being sold.[32] The following year, 1805, saw a rather more detailed indictment of the quality of abasto meat by the new Intendant of Guadalajara, Roque Abarca. He stated that the quality of the meat sold in the city was bad and even harmful (*nociva*). Carcasses were being butchered so that the better cuts were sold to the wealthier inhabitants at higher prices, while the poor got whatever was left (". . . and the poor must buy bad meat at high prices.") Repeated executive orders dating from at least 1798 had had no effect, so Intendant Abarca issued a decree stipulating the way in which meat was to be butchered and establishing stiff fines for illegal sales practices.[33] The same problems occurred with salted meat, which was not subject to the official monopoly but was sold publicly in the city's plazas along with other foodstuffs brought in from the countryside. Some of this meat was of such low quality that it could only have been presumed to have come from animals which the owners were afraid of losing because of disease or lack of pasture. Many cases of illness and even death were claimed to have resulted from the consumption of this tainted meat. As also with bread, the city's poorer citizens paid high prices for low quality: "since commonly those that use it are of the lower orders, it is rare that illness or death owing to it is noticed, but that does not make it less tragic."[34]

A good deal of livestock entered the city of Guadalajara legally outside the structure of the meat monopoly. Some of this was in the form of sheep purchased privately from major haciendas by the various convents and monasteries in the city.[35] More important even than the limited commerce in sheep outside the abasto was that in pigs, which were used for their fat as well as their meat. Pigs were introduced into the city on an unrestricted basis by private individuals who paid a small tax to the municipal customs according to the size and weight of the animals: *ramo de cerdos* receipts indicate a yearly introduction of about 8,000 animals around 1780, not including the substantial numbers which were raised within the city itself and which caused a health hazard and damaged streets and buildings.[36] *Tapatío* (typically Guadalajaran) cuisine relied heavily on pig lard (*man-*

32. AHMG, caja 20. 33. AHMG, caja 21. 34. *Ibid.*
35. BPE-AJA, 154:12:1736; 155:1:1736.
36. BPE-AFA, vols. 305 and 444, 1780; AHMG, caja 13, 1791.

teca) as the major cooking oil, which several times was the object of restrictive marketing arrangements made by the major dealers in the pig trade.[37]

The End of the Abasto

The last years of the abasto de carnes were clouded with the unsettled conditions caused by the Hidalgo insurgency of 1810 and the chaos resulting from the increasing tendency to lease the monopoly in bits and pieces. The last contractor to hold the monopoly was Pedro Gutiérrez Higuera, a city merchant acting as agent for the perspicacious and eccentric Miguel del Portillo, owner of the important Hacienda de Santa Cruz in the Toluquilla Valley. Gutiérrez fled to San Blas in November of 1810, "fearful of the insurgent fury," leaving the hapless Portillo to fulfill the contract. Portillo balked at this, but his claims were not admitted by the *junta de propios*; and under the threat of having his property legally embargoed, the reluctant Portillo finally agreed to assume the remainder of the contract, which was to run through 1815.

By the end of July 1811, Portillo was claiming that he had lost some 15,000 pesos in addition to the costs and city taxes involved in running the monopoly. The normal requirement for meat within the city had been increased by the many refugees who had flocked in from the countryside because of the unsettled conditions, and by the soldiers garrisoned there. The year 1811 was exceedingly dry, and the cattle supply was therefore so scarce that Portillo had been forced to overslaughter his own herds in order to meet his obligations in the abasto. Live cattle prices were "extremely high" (*subidísimos*)—due not only to unfavorable weather, but also because of the "horrible and deplorable destruction which the haciendas, and especially their livestock, have suffered on account of the insurrection." The roads around the city were "infested with villainous people," so that normal communications and transport were interrupted. It was very risky to bring livestock from any distance, and Portillo cited no less than four separate incidents early in the year involving the beating or murder of herders and robbery of the livestock they were transporting to the city. In order to prevent Portillo's bankruptcy, the cabildo somewhat reluctantly agreed to increase the price of meat in the city over the original contracted price.

Early in 1814, Portillo again sought to renounce the abasto contract, claiming huge financial losses and that recent *reales cédulas* had abolished

37. AIPG, prot. Berroa, 5:363v-365v; AHMG, caja 23, 1808.

such monopolistic arrangements. His administration of the abasto apparently lasted through 1815, and the city government itself assumed the monopoly during the following year.[38]

At the end of 1816, the meat trade in Guadalajara was declared by the
Intendant, General José de la Cruz, no longer subject to the monopoly. By
the middle of the following year, beef was selling in the city for as much as
a *real* (an eighth of a peso) for forty ounces, and the "libertad de abasto de
carnes" was purported to have led to numerous abuses in the marketplace.
One prominent merchant-hacendado, Captain Alfonso José Sánchez Leñero, testified that there were so many independently run butcher shops
that effective inspection was impossible, that meat was scarce and expensive, and that robberies of livestock were increasingly frequent. In the latter part of 1817, a committee of regidores was designated to formulate
regulations for the meat trade, but the concrete outcome of this commission is not known.[39]

The history of the city meat monopoly is peculiarly fraught with inde-
cision, ad-hoc administrative arrangements, and crises. The same was true
of the trade in maize and wheat, but not to such a great degree. Two facts
emerge fairly clearly from a study of the abasto de carnes. The first is that
the system functioned effectively as a conduit for the livestock of the area's
major haciendas. The individuals who made city policy regarding the abasto
were very often landowners themselves, or had strong links with the landowning elite. The system insured a monopolistic access to the urban market, although there is no particular evidence that it kept meat prices artificially high. Second, the change in the rural economy in the late eighteenth century, characterized primarily by increasing commercialization
and a shift in favor of cereal production, put new strains on the old monopolistic system and turned it from an asset for the great landowners into
a liability. In the last years of the colonial period, the abasto de carnes had
become a tar-baby which few wished to embrace.

38. AHMG, cajas 24 and 27.   39. AHMG, caja 23.

CHAPTER 4

Wheat

Guadalajara as a Market for Wheat

A number of sources, including hacienda inventories, commercial correspondence, and city records, indicate the growing importance of Guadalajara as a market for wheat after about 1750. Not all locally produced
wheat was consumed in the city in any given year. Substantial amounts of
it appear to have been sold in the *tierra dentro* and the coastal area.[1] But
the growing population and prosperity of Guadalajara in the later eighteenth century encouraged capital investment in many landed estates, particularly for irrigation works and storage facilities, in order to increase
their production of wheat and flour for sale in the city. Table 5 presents
figures for the total entries of wheat and flour into Guadalajara in the last
years of the eighteenth and the first years of the nineteenth century. The
numbers are represented graphically in Figure 5.

The yearly flow of wheat and flour into the city of Guadalajara increased
from around 2,000 cargas[2] at midcentury to about 8,000 cargas in the
1780s and some 15,000 cargas in the years just before the outbreak of the
Independence movement. All in all, the figures indicate a seven- to eightfold increase in the wheat and flour consumption of the city of Guadala-

1. As can be seen, for example, in the commercial correspondence between the Hacienda
de Cuisillos' administrator and its factor in Tepic, 1800-1806 (AHMG, caja 20).

2. AHMG, caja 3, 1760-1762.

Table 5.

Total Entries of Wheat and Flour into Guadalajara, 1753-1818

Year	Number of Cargas[a]	Year	Number of Cargas
1753[b]	1,089	1798[d]	6,708
1766	5,195	1799[d]	9,148
1779	9,615	1801[d]	8,328
1780	7,772	1803[d]	10,532
1781	10,447	1804[d]	15,036
1783	8,375	1805[d]	13,680
1784	7,662	1806[d]	12,652
1788[c]	8,000	1807[d]	15,392
1789[c]	8,500	1808[d]	14,712
1790[c]	8,500	1809[d]	16,664
1791	8,481	1813[d]	16,108
1794[d]	8,097	1814[d]	16,236
1795[d]	5,276	1816[d]	9,516
1796[d]	4,692	1817	7,748
1797[d]	5,516	1818	8,665

SOURCES:

AHMG, cajas 10, 12, 24, 31, and 35; BPE-AFA, vols. 57, 305, and 444; BPE-AJA, 200:6:2457 and 203:1:2525.

NOTES:

[a]A *carga* was two *fanegas*, or roughly 200 pounds.

[b]The figure for 1753 covers the months May to December only; but since the wheat crop was not harvested until May, the total for this year is probably not above 2,000 cargas at the most.

[c]The totals for the years 1788-1790 are rough estimates based upon conversion of a three-year total for *derechos* collected by the city on entering wheat and flour, cited in AHMG, caja 24.

[d]The figures for the years 1794-1816 are estimates based upon summary accounts of the city's *propios*, or municipal income, found in a series in AHMG, caja 31. See the text for a discussion of the reliability of these figures.

Cargas (thousands)

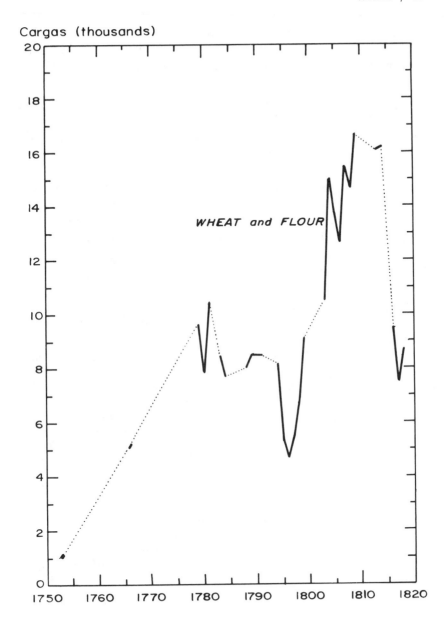

Figure 5.
Wheat and flour entering Guadalajara, 1753-1818

SOURCE:
AHMG, various cajas.

jara between 1750 and 1815.[3] The precipitous drop in entries into the city in the years 1816-1818 may have been due to a combination of weak harvests and the renewal of insurgent activity in the countryside. The rise in the urban consumption of wheat can be attributed to the increase in the population of the city and the prosperity in the years around the turn of the century. But the increase in the city's population alone after 1800 is insufficient to explain the rise in demand during the period if the same level of per-capita consumption continued into the new century.

In the documents of the time, there are intriguing if all-too-brief hints at who ate wheaten bread and in what quantities. In 1786 the *procurador síndico general* of the cabildo estimated that the city's convents accounted for about 40 percent of the wheat consumed every year.[4] While this may be an exaggeration, it is certainly reasonable to assume that people of means and European background were the ones who ate wheaten bread most regularly and in the largest quantities.[5] According to the census of 1793, the portions of the city's population classified ethnically as "European" or "Spanish" amounted together to nearly 10,000 people.[6] In fact, the consumption of wheaten bread extended surprisingly far down into the lower social strata of the city.[7] It was acknowledged by the city's bakers on several occasions that their profit margins were greatest on white bread of the highest quality sold to "persons of means," though they sold much of the cruder sort of bread known as "de segunda clase."[8] As early as 1751, how-

3. AHMG, caja 12, 1788; caja 3, exp. 16. The totals for the years 1794-1816 are derived from peso values of the taxes collected by the city on entering wheat and flour. The effect of a tax differential favoring grain and flour originating in certain areas close to the city ("las haciendas y lugares del contorno"), as opposed to more distant areas, has been corrected for on the basis of known proportions for several years. The general accuracy of the derived figures is confirmed by direct figures by weight for several years in the early nineteenth century.

4. AHMG, caja 11, exp. 2.

5. The high consumption of the religious establishments, if it was so high, is not easy to explain. Certainly the regular clergy ate well—but even so, the few hundred monks and nuns in the city could not have consumed so much wheat and wheaten bread. It seems likely that they exercised some sort of welfare function, disposing of large quantities of bread simply by giving it away to the urban poor.

6. AHMG, caja 15.

7. The yearly per-capita consumption of wheat and flour by the European-Spanish population of 1793 would have been about 160 pounds. The consumption of bread would have been somewhat higher, of course, since the weight of bread is made up of other elements besides flour. Assuming the European proportion of the population to have remained constant (about one-third), the yearly per-capita consumption would have risen to about 280 pounds by 1810, or nearly a pound a day of bread, small by contemporary European standards but still considerable. At the population of 1810 (about 35,000), the yearly per-capita consumption of the city as a whole would have been about 100 pounds. It must be borne in mind, however, that the diet of the vast majority of the urban population was supplemented with the cheaper and more plentiful maize.

8. AHMG, caja 21, 1806; caja 6, 1771.

ever, bakers were engaged in sharp practices in selling bread to the urban lower classes. At that time they were accustomed to divide half-loaves into four "pedacillos muy pequeños" normally sold at five for a half-real, but sold them at only four per half-real to the poor and Indians.[9] By 1806, the bakers were asking that a separate pricing scale (*calicata*) be established for the "pan de segunda clase" relied upon by the city's poor. In this same year the síndico of the cabildo noted the general rise in bread consumption in the city.[10] It seems likely that in these years the per-capita consumption of bread was growing, apparently across a broad social range.

Areas of Supply

Detailed records of wheat and flour entries for the years 1779, 1784, 1791, and 1818 indicate that the major haciendas within a forty- to fifty-mile radius of Guadalajara consistently supplied about 60 percent of the city's consumption needs. Table 6 shows the percentages by area of origin for grain coming into the city for these four years. Except for the year 1791, in which their total share dropped to 5 percent, the principal wheat-growing haciendas nearest Guadalajara supplied a very consistent one-fifth to one-quarter of all the wheat consumed in the city. The major haciendas of the Toluquilla Valley, forming a rough semicircle to the south of the city, were that of Toluquilla itself (called El Cuatro after the turn of the century), Santa Cruz, San José, San Nicolás, and La Concepción (see Map 2). With the addition of the great estate of Santa Lucía, which lay to the north of the city, these haciendas formed the group which has been designated as "close-in" in Table 6. Even more stable in its share of the city's wheat supply was the group of haciendas located somewhat farther from the immediate environs of the city, designated as "other local haciendas" in Table 6. The dominant producer among this group was the entailed estate of the Porres Baranda family, Mazatepec, with its sister establishment Santa Ana Acatlán, which between them supplied a remarkably consistent 12 percent of the city's wheat and flour in all four of the years for which detailed information exists. Also accounting for large entries of grain in at least three of those years were the haciendas of Cedros, Atequiza, Miraflores, El Cabezón-La Vega, Huejotitán, and Cuisillos, with substantial quantities from a number of other local estates as well.

The role of the Altos and Bajío regions as wheat suppliers for the city was clearly of increasing importance in the late years of the eighteenth and the first years of the nineteenth century. These two producing areas

9. AHMG, caja 1, exp. 52, 1752.   10. AHMG, caja 21, 1806.

took up the slack in local production in the year 1791, and continued to make an important contribution through the first decades of the following century, though their share had declined somewhat by 1818. The decrease in the share of smaller and unidentified Guadalajara-area producers is very notable in the last years of the century, and this slack was also taken up by increased reliance upon the Altos and Bajío regions.

It is not clear why the share in the total wheat supply of "other local haciendas" increased slightly in 1791, the year in which that of the Toluquilla Valley haciendas and local small producers declined. But certainly with the return of the close-in estates to their formerly strong position in the years before 1820, the proportion of grain coming from smaller local producers in the area around the city remained at a much reduced level. This suggests that the major wheat-growing haciendas had garnered a proportionally larger share of local output at the expense of smaller producers, thus concentrating the benefits of an increasing commercialization of agriculture in the hands of fewer people. This same tendency is evident in the production of maize, but was even more pronounced in the case of wheat, since wheat was preeminently a cash crop whose production depended upon the mobilization of greater capital resources.

Such an interpretation is corroborated by detailed evidence from the entry books themselves. Whereas at midcentury much of the wheat and

Table 6.

Geographic Origin of Wheat and Flour Entering Guadalajara, 1779, 1784, 1791, 1818

	1779	1784	1791[a]	1818[a]
Close-in haciendas	21%	22%	5%	24%
Other local haciendas	37	41	44	36
Subtotal	58%	63%	49%	60%
Guadalajara area and other unidentified local	32	31	15	14
Altos and Bajío	10	6	30	23
Other	––	––	5	4
Total	100%	100%	100%	100%

SOURCE:
AHMG, various cajas.

NOTE:
[a]The totals for 1791 and 1818 do not add up exactly to 100% because of rounding.

flour introduced into the city came from small producers, primarily from the area of Jocotepec and Santa Ana Acatlán, by the late years of the century this group had almost completely disappeared from the urban grain market.[11] The same is true of those producers of wheat specifically designated as Indians. Nor is the change over the course of the century due merely to a change in the classification of those who introduced grain into the city, since the categories were consistently applied throughout the century. It is true that the participation of smaller producers in the market may have been masked to some extent by the fact that certain haciendas (among them Mazatepec-Santa Ana and Atequiza) characteristically had much of their wheat output produced by renters.[12] Nonetheless, the increasing share of large producers, mostly from what may be termed "demesne farming" (direct exploitation of home farms), is clear during the latter part of the century.

Further evidence confirming the trend toward concentration of wheat production relates to the city's flour mills in the early decades of the nineteenth century. There were four major mills ("the four mills of this city"), all regarded as local landmarks and all in or near the city along the Río de San Juan de Dios, from which they drew their power. From the documentation, it appears that mill-owners most frequently realized income from their mills by leasing them out to others to operate. The most complete records of leasing transactions exist for the two mills belonging to the Colegio de Niñas de San Diego de Alcalá, a religious establishment. Table 7 gives available information on the leasing histories of these two properties for the eighteenth century.

With the price of wheat and flour generally rising in the city, and the total urban consumption having grown eightfold between 1750 and 1810, one would expect the rents charged to lessees of the city's mills to have increased considerably during the course of the eighteenth century. Judging by the figures in Table 7, however, rents remained roughly stable, at about 400 pesos per year, and if anything showed a tendency to decline in the last quarter of the century. Nor was this decline due to any deterioration in the condition of the mills, since leases demanded maintenance of the plant and equipment and were renewed frequently enough to insure this condition. The decline in rental of the mills relative to the enormous increase in overall urban consumption suggests that the mills were not receiving their proportional share of the grain coming into Guadalajara. This was related to the increasing concentration of local wheat production in the hands of haciendas nearer the city, to the disadvantage of smaller

11. AHMG, caja 35, 1753; BPE-AJA, 203:1:2525; AHMG, caja 10, 1784; caja 31, 1791 and 1818.
12. BPE-AJA, 203:1:2525.

Table 7.

Rental of Flour Mills Las Beatas and Sierra in the Eighteenth Century

	Molino de las Beatas			Molino de Sierra (Piedras Negras)	
Year	Rent per Year (in pesos)	Number of Years	Year	Rent per Year (in pesos)	Number of Years
1721	300	3	1741	450	5
1730	300	3	1745	500	2
1740	300	4	1748	500	2
1744	300	4	1765	500	3
1748	300	4	1774	361	2
1757	400	2	1776	450	2
1761	400	6	1790	350	9
1794	350	— —			

SOURCE:
AIPG, prots., various notaries.

producers. Most important wheat-growing haciendas had their own mills, or milled their grain at neighboring estates, while most small producers could not afford such substantial capital outlays. The only year for which there exist data that allow a discrimination between shipments of unmilled grain and flour entering the city is 1779. Even at this early date, before the dominance of the hacienda in wheat production became obvious, most wheat coming into Guadalajara was in the form of flour, and most of this flour originated on the important wheat-producing estates.[13]

Another fact which emerges from the study of grain entries into Guadalajara is that the city relied relatively less on the regions of the Altos and the Bajío for its wheat supply than for its maize supply. Whereas the city's dependence upon nonlocal sources for maize reached 41 percent in 1817 (all of it from the Altos), it relied upon nonlocal suppliers of wheat for 27 percent of its consumption needs at the same time. Even in apparently difficult years for some local producers, such as 1791, the Altos and Bajío areas (including Zamora) accounted for only 30 percent of the city's wheat, while the reliance upon all outside sources was some 35 percent of the total supply.

13. AHMG, caja 27, 1814. With the exception of the Molino del Batán, all were mentioned by Matías de la Mota Padilla in his *Historia del Reino de Nueva Galicia* of 1742 (1973), pp. 196-197. Figures for Joya are in AIPG-LG, 31:29-30v; for Batán, in AIPG-LG, 4:172-175v. (AIPG, prot. Mena menor, 4:148-156v; prot. de Silva, 3:15-20; prot. Berroa, 4:340-341v and 22:73; prot. Vargas, 13:167v-169v, 1741; prot. Mena mayor, 32:101v-103v, 1745). Inventories for Las Beatas for 1730 and 1757 are in AIPG, prot. García, 29:364-366v, and prot. Berroa, 1:17v-19v, respectively (BPE-AJA, 203:1:2525; AHMG, caja 27, 1814.)

This contrast between the wheat and maize supply suggests that wheat occupied an increasingly advantageous competitive position relative to maize in terms of the amount of land and capital devoted to its production. This is especially true when we consider that while maize consumption in Guadalajara hardly doubled in the seventy years between 1750 and 1820, wheat consumption increased almost eightfold during the same period. Accordingly, the amount of land put down to wheat, assuming reasonable yields, would have increased four times as much as that in maize.[14] Moreover, wheat cultivation, since it depended on irrigation, would have to some degree displaced maize from the most favored, level soils which composed only a small proportion of most haciendas. It thus becomes clear that the development of an urban demand for wheat exerted considerable pressure on the economy of maize production and was tending to displace maize from its earlier primacy in terms of land use, even while maize production was itself increasing in absolute terms.

Bakeries and Granaries

Wheat and flour, after their entry into the city of Guadalajara, were distributed to urban consumers by means of a marketing system at once more complicated and chaotic than that which existed for maize. Because of its comparatively high value (the price of wheat was roughly ten times that of maize, though the relationship varied constantly) and the number of hands through which it had to pass before it reached the consumer, wheat never came effectively under the control of the city government, despite periodic efforts to regulate the trade. The attempts of the city government to manage the wheat trade took two forms: the control of bakeries and bread prices, and the establishment of a public granary for wheat and flour, neither of which succeeded very well.

Most wheaten bread consumed in the city was made by bakers in commercial establishments of varying size, though the convents and monasteries probably baked their own breadstuffs. The exact number of commercial bakeries in Guadalajara was said to be 27 in 1786 and 19 in 1810.[15] But these numbers must have applied only to the largest establishments, since in 1788 it was noted by an *oidor* of the Audiencia investigating abuses in the production of bread that bakers were so numerous, many of them

14. The data on the Guadalajara region do not permit calculations on seed and acreage yields for wheat and maize such as those made by Charles Gibson in *The Aztecs*, pp. 309 and 328, and David Brading in *Haciendas and Ranchos*, pp. 65-67. From the scanty data which do exist, Brading's estimates, adjusted for the local differences in agricultural land measurements, seem applicable to the Guadalajara region. On seed yields, see Chapter 10 below.

15. AHMG, caja 11, exp. 5, 1786; caja 24, 1810.

being unknown, that the trade was impossible to regulate.[16] Government efforts to control the bread and wheat trades stemmed not only from a concern over the wheat supply, but also over abuses perpetrated by bakers and the many shopkeepers who bought from them and resold to the public. Although the concern of the Audiencia and the city cabildo with bread prices dated back at least to the beginning of the eighteenth century, it was only from the 1760s that active government intervention was particularly notable.[17] Attempts at such regulation took on a positively obsessive tone after the famine year of 1786, and it was surely no accident that the establishment of a bakers' guild (*gremio*), with elaborately detailed ordinances for the production and sale of bread, dated from 1786.[18]

Throughout the late eighteenth century, despite all attempts at regulation by city and royal governments, there were renewed "clamores públicos" about the high price and low quality of bread. In part this was due to the very structure of urban commerce and consumption themselves, and to the credit arrangements they relied upon. The city's smaller stores, the *tendejones* and *pulperías*, despite explicit prohibitions, continued to sell a large part of the bread on the market. It was from these small stores "that the poor generally supply themselves, and even others in emergency situations." These establishments sold on credit and in small amounts and demanded a large profit in return for their trouble and risk. The bakers, on their side, sold to the *tendejoneros* on a regular basis at a discount, thus gaining in the security of the outlet what they lost in immediate profits. The public was being gouged not only by this custom, but also by the low quality of the bread itself. Bakers, in order to cut their losses or to save themselves money to begin with, often used rotten flour in their bread, adding large quantities of lard in an attempt to hide the poor quality of the flour.[19] The problem was compounded by the duplicity of the local flour mills in short-weighting the bags of flour which they sold to the bakers. The general high cost and low quality of bread were ascribed by the president of the Audiencia to the bad faith of the bakers, and to their "immoderate profits, or to say it more properly, the robbery they perpetrate and have always perpetrated upon the public."[20]

Aside from the relatively late formation of the bakers' guild, the most consistent effort made by local and royal government to regulate the bread trade within Guadalajara was the *calicata*, a sliding scale which pegged the price of bread to the price of wheat in a fixed ratio. The first calicata was made up by the municipal government at the behest of the president of the Audiencia in 1701. The price of flour had risen precipitously between December 1700 and the end of January 1701, and it was felt by both local and

16. AHMG, caja 12.   17. AHMG, caja 3, 1767; caja 6, 1771.
18. AHMG, caja 14, 1792.   19. AHMG, caja 12, 1788.
20. AHMG, caja 21, 1804-1818.

royal officials that pegging the price of bread to that of flour would prevent immoderate increases in the price of bread, thus both protecting the public and insuring a reasonable return to the bakers. The city government carried out a series of experiments and made observations on the costs and proportions of flour, lard, salt, and other ingredients necessary to produce a given weight of bread, and also the costs of materials such as wood and candles. The wages of bakers' apprentices and helpers were also taken into account, and later in the century rent was even included in the cost calculations. With the final addition of a reasonable profit margin for the baker, a sliding ratio of ounces of bread per real to the price of one carga of wheat was settled upon.[21] The 1701 calicata was apparently not revised until 1752, although subsequent adjustments occurred more frequently, if irregularly. In this and subsequent calicatas, the experiments made used flour from the haciendas of Santa Lucía and Mazatepec, two of the major suppliers of wheat and flour to the city.

The experiments became increasingly complex and the observations increasingly detailed as the century progressed, but the city lacked the means of enforcing the elaborate regulations it established. The next revision of the scale occurred in 1768 and reflected the considerable rise in wheat and flour prices which occurred in the 1750s and 1760s. In recognition of the broadened and increased consumption of bread in the city, lower-quality bread, called *pan vasso*, was for the first time included in the price scale.[22] Continued periodic revisions of the calicata take on considerable irony in the face of universally acknowledged noncompliance with them. Indeed, the efforts of the city government to regulate the price of wheat and bread increasingly partake of an air of unreality, with the calicata of 1786 the same as that for 1774.[23] This same pattern of rising production costs, extremely variable wheat prices, complaints and sharp practices by bakers and tendejoneros, intransigence and complicated proposals for regulation by the city government, and sporadic and generally ineffective attempts at enforcement, continued into the new century with the calicatas of 1806, 1809, and 1814.[24]

The second means by which the city government attempted to regulate the prices of wheat and bread, the establishment of a public granary (*alhóndiga*) for wheat, was an even more conspicuous failure than the calicata system. The project first came up in 1751, when the city's cabildo applied to the Audiencia for license to use the lower, vacant rooms of the *casas reales* for the central deposit and public sale of wheat. The current practice was for producers (*labradores*) to bring their grain or flour into the city, store it in privately owned buildings, and sell it at their conve-

21. AHMG, caja 1, 1701.   22. *Ibid.*, exp. 52; caja 3, exp. 16.
23. AHMG, caja 14, 1774; caja 11, exp. 5.
24. AHMG, cajas 21 and 27.

nience. This made enforcement of the calicata virtually impossible and the collection of taxes very difficult.[25] This proposal apparently never came to fruition, since in 1764 the same considerations of the public good led the city government to apply to the Audiencia for another license, this time for the construction of an alhóndiga in the centrally located *plazuela* of the Convent of San Agustín. The license was granted by the Audiencia in July 1764, but the plan came to nought, since four years later the same proposal was again under consideration.[26]

The elaborate but short-lived project of 1768 set forth in typical detail the way in which the granary was to be run, its officials, their duties and emoluments, the rules governing the calicata, and such prohibitions as the bearing of arms in the building. Standing out particularly strongly from the new granary regulations was the cabildo's almost rabid fear and condemnation of the practice of illegally reselling wheat and flour. This was referred to as "the abominable practice of regrating (*regatonería*) and resale in which many engage to the detriment of their consciences and to the intolerable offense of the public good." Large fines were to be levied against anyone selling or storing grain or flour anywhere in the city except at the granary. Muleteers and other carriers were to bring written testimony from the magistrates of their districts as to where the grain had originated, or from whom and at what price they had purchased it. Other measures reinforced these rules, such as the prohibition against the purchase of wheat and its resale as flour by the owners or renters of the city's handful of flour mills. The cabildo was clearly concerned with the vulnerability of the city's grain supply to speculation and profiteering by persons other than the original producers.[27] By 1789, however, the previous situation still prevailed, the practice being to store and sell grain in private homes or warehouses.[28] In 1804 the president of the Audiencia noted that there was still no public granary for the sale of wheat and flour, and this continued into the 1820s.[29] As with the city's unsuccessful attempts to enforce the calicata, the various alhóndiga projects failed, probably for much the same reasons.

Two points of interest emerge from this general account of the calicata system. First, it was not so much the price of wheat as the price of other primary materials and the rising costs of production which were most often cited by bakers in their complaints about the injustice of city regulations.[30] The price of wheat and flour had always varied greatly, even at the beginning of the century when the calicata was first instituted. The wheat prices on the sliding scale almost always ranged between 5 and 20 pesos per carga, all during the century. Thus, although wheat prices showed some tendency to increase during the eighteenth century, it was a modal increase

25. AHMG, caja 1, 1751.   26. AHMG, caja 3, exp. 1.   27. *Ibid.*, exp. 16.
28. AHMG, cajas 6 and 12.   29. AHMG, caja 21.   30. E.g., AHMG, caja 27, 1814.

within an already well-established range of variation, and it was not as sharp a relative increase as that experienced by maize prices during the same period. This suggests that the supply of wheat to the city was more elastic than that of maize, and reinforces the view that the cultivation of wheat was displacing that of maize during the eighteenth century in the area around Guadalajara.

Second, it is clear that the supply and price of bread in Guadalajara was a more or less constant preoccupation of both municipal and royal government. Yet there is an obvious ambivalence present, especially on the part of the city officials, who often proposed elaborate regulatory schemes, only to drag their feet when it came to enforcing them. Furthermore, there are hints of conflicting policy aims between the city government and the Audiencia, and the latter often reproved the former for its laxity.[31] The prominence of major landowners in the city government all during the late colonial period suggests that there may have been a very real conflict between the avowed goal of the city government, in attempting to regulate the prices of foodstuffs, and the interests of individuals who stood to benefit from the development of commercialized agriculture and rising prices.

The Grain Trade

In actual fact, the city's supply of wheat and flour depended upon a confusing tangle of marketing arrangements which were intimately linked to the system of rural credit. Thus the functions of market distribution and credit mobilization (banking) were in some measure interdependent, mediated by city merchants by means of two basic arrangements, direct sales and commission sales. Of these two systems, the latter appears to have been the more important throughout the eighteenth and early nineteenth centuries. Direct sales were quite straightforward and tended to involve relatively limited quantities of grain, though this was not always the case. Often the seller was required to post a bond of some kind to insure delivery of the grain.[32] Major wheat-producing haciendas occasionally dealt in this way, even when their owners had commercial relationships of long standing with city merchants.[33] Some major hacendados were themselves important merchants and sold the grain produced on their properties directly to other city merchants or to bakers.[34]

The characteristic volatility of wheat prices often made for problems in direct sales, however, since prices agreed to at the time of the sale might

31. E.g., AHMG, caja 21, 1804-1818.   32. AIPG, prot. Berroa, 8:203v.
33. AIPG, prot. Sandi, 2: no page no.   34. AHMG, caja 11, exp. 2.

have dropped or risen substantially by the date of actual delivery.[35] A kind of subcase of the direct-sale system occurred when the city of Guadalajara itself purchased substantial quantities of wheat from the producers for sale to the public, though this practice was apparently never engaged in before the famine year of 1785-1786 and only once thereafter.[36] Certainly the city never developed a system of regular intervention in the wheat trade, as it did for the maize trade with the *pósito*.

In contrast to these ad-hoc arrangements for the direct sale of wheat in the city stood the system of *encomienda*, or commission sales, very often only one aspect of more inclusive commercial relationships of long standing between hacendados and city merchants. The earliest reference to such an arrangement specifically for the sale of wheat is from the early 1760s, when Patricio de Soto (who himself later came to be an important landowner on the strength of his mercantile wealth) was acting as encomendero for Lic. José Manuel de la Garza Falcón, an *oidor* of the Audiencia of New Galicia and owner of the important wheat-producing estate San José de Tolu-quilla.[37] But such commercial relationships involving the marketing of other crops, most notably sugar, were already common at the beginning of the century, and there is no reason to suppose that encomenderos were not also dealing in wheat from very early on. Typically, such merchants as De Soto had their own stores in Guadalajara, with their own warehouses (*bodegas*), and received the wheat or flour directly from the producer for resale. Their commission was charged at the rate of 3 percent.[38]

The responses of hacendados to the cabildo's circular inquiry of 1786, occasioned by the critical food shortages of that year, reveal in consider-able detail the structure of commission grain sales in the city. Most of the great wheat-producing haciendas of the area around the city were repre-sented by encomenderos who were either holding or expecting large quan-tities of grain. Juan Abendaño handled the wheat of the "casa de Basauri" (the Basauri family owned the haciendas of Atequiza and Miraflores); Juan María Martínez that of the Hacienda del Cabezón of Manuel Cañedo; and Mariano Pedraza that of the "casa de Echauri" (another major landhold-ing family). Calixto Cháves was the agent of Rafael María Villaseñor, owner of the Hacienda de Cedros, and was reselling wheat from the 1786 harvest to the city's bakers in small lots. José de Trigo had already dis-posed to bakers of most of the 565 cargas of wheat he had received from Miguel Portillo, owner of the important Hacienda de San José in the To-luquilla Valley. Ignacio de Estrada (later to marry the heiress to the Porres Baranda fortune) had sold most of the wheat remitted to him from the

35. BPE-BD, leg. 73, exp. 10; AIPG, prot. Sandi, 2: no page no., 1818.
36. AHMG, caja 11, exp. 2; caja 12, 1789; caja 18, 1790.
37. BPE-BD, leg. 109, exp. 1, 1764.   38. BPE-AJA, 138:9:1489.

Porres Baranda entail, Mazatepec. Juan de Dios Egón, the encomendero of Tomás Ignacio Villaseñor, was awaiting the milling of a small quantity of grain remaining from the harvest of the great Hacienda de Huejotitán.[39]

The commission sale of wheat (or of other agricultural produce) was often only one element in a complex matrix of commercial transactions. Such relationships were generally of more or less long standing and were reinforced by friendship, kinship, or *compadrazgo*. This personalistic aspect of an economic relationship is illustrated by the commercial correspondence between the administrator of the Hacienda of Cuisillos and his factor in the city of Tepic just after the turn of the century. In a letter of June 1802, Ordóñez, the administrator, commented to Mestas, the Tepic merchant, "even though several people in that town [Tepic] have asked me to sell to them on commission, I have confidence only in you; and you should remember that Asturians from the town of Llanes should keep on good terms with those from Cabrales."[40] Closer to home, Ignacio de Estrada's long relationship with the Porres Baranda family illustrates the same kind of thing. Within such relationships, wheat sales were often tied into the system of *avíos*, the working capital supplied by urban merchants to landowners. Balancing commercial accounts through the consignment of all or part of the wheat harvest by a producer was not the same as the sale of grain on a commission basis and the payment of the principal price to the producer, less commission, but both practices were characteristic of such commercial relationships.[41] On a grander scale than most were the dealings of Manuel Calixto Cañedo, a former miner and owner of the rich estates of El Cabezón and La Vega near Ameca, with the Guadalajara merchant Eugenio Moreno de Tejada. Cañedo's 1793 testament stated that Moreno de Tejada was holding some 31,000 pesos of Cañedo's money, in addition to an as-yet unspecified sum from the sale of wheat produced upon the haciendas.[42]

Not all of the wheat and flour which entered the city of Guadalajara from the major grain-producing haciendas remained there. In fact, the more or less continual leakage of wheat from the city periodically became a concern of the royal and municipal authorities, again with little effect. A number of estate owners, most prominent among them Juan Alfonso Sánchez Leñero, habitually brought large quantities of wheat into the city for milling, only to re-export it to other areas for sale. In 1784, for example, Sánchez Leñero sent into the city almost 350 cargas of wheat from his Hacienda de Santa Lucía, had it ground at the Molino del Batán, and sent all but twenty cargas of the flour out of the city, mostly to Tepic, Rosario,

39. AHMG, caja 11, exp. 2.   40. AHMG, caja 20.
41. AIPG, prot. Mena mayor, 2:141-144; prot. Ballesteros, 8:118-120.
42. AIPG, prot. Ballesteros, 18:80-91v.

and Compostela.[43] If the grain was declared at the customs houses, ground in a city mill, and re-exported, as Sánchez Leñero did, there appears to have been nothing wrong in the practice, but in the famine year of 1786 many hacendados were accused of selling wheat directly from their haciendas and their own mills furtively, outside the jurisdiction of the city, thus driving up prices in Guadalajara.[44]

The most striking fact which emerges from this discussion of the place of wheat in the economy of late colonial Guadalajara is the magnetic effect upon production of the growing population of the city. Whatever distortions, changes, or difficulties may have arisen in the agricultural sector due to the growth of urban demand for wheat, it is clear that this demand was largely met through an expansion of traditional agriculture rather than through any revolutionary transformation. The increasing commercialization of agriculture during the late colonial period was primarily a matter of adjusting the factors of production rather than of changing the technology of farming. The complicated and anarchic commercial system which mediated the city's supply of wheat served well enough, but supply and price levels were subject to fluctuations which were built into the farming and marketing system. This inherent precariousness could not be eliminated, despite the efforts of municipal and royal governments to regulate the grain trade. Indeed, it is ironic that even though government did succeed to a large degree in exhaustively regulating the maize trade, that aspect of the city's food supply remained essentially just as precarious as the wheat supply, and for much the same reasons, as will be seen in the next chapter.

43. AHMG, caja 10, 1784. Why Sánchez Leñero did this is not entirely clear. Probably it was because there was no functioning mill on his hacienda, and no neighboring hacienda at which he could have his grain ground.

44. AHMG, caja 11, exp. 7, 1786. A number of the city's bakers complained about similar practices in 1814; AHMG, caja 27.

CHAPTER 5

Maize

Maize Consumption in the City

The movement of maize into Guadalajara during the second half of the eighteenth century can be traced in some detail through the extant records of the public granary, the *alhóndiga*, which had existed in the city at least since the end of the seventeenth century and was administered directly by the cabildo from 1748. As with the meat monopoly and the wheat trade, the city government attempted to regulate the maize trade not only with an eye toward realizing revenues from it, but also to eliminate sharp practices and to insure at least minimum standards of quality. But beyond this, the city government sought to assure for the urban consumer a steady supply of maize at a reasonable price through the direct purchase and sale by its own granary, the *pósito*. The most striking fact about the yearly flow of maize into Guadalajara after the mid-eighteenth century is that it almost doubled, rising from about 45,000 fanegas per year in the 1750s to some 80,000 in the second decade of the nineteenth century (see Figure 6). During these same years, the population of the city grew from 10,000 to about 40,000.[1] The magnitude of the oscillation between one year and the next also increased after 1805, so that yearly entry totals swing wildly compared to the mild changes in the latter half of the previous century.

1. The discrepancy between population growth and food supply was partially made up by the increased consumption of wheat in the city.

Fanegas (thousands)

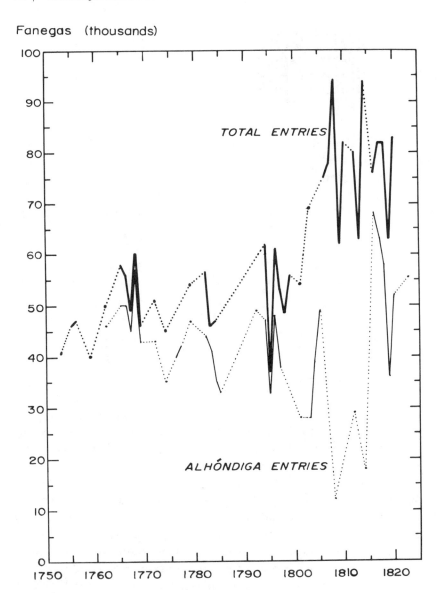

Figure 6.
Maize entries into alhóndiga and pósito of Guadalajara, 1753-1823

SOURCE:
AHMG, various cajas.

Aside from the absolute increase in the amount of maize entering the alhóndiga, there was a notable tendency for the city granary, the pósito, to account for a larger share of the total after 1780. Briefly, the purpose of the pósito was to control the price of maize in the city to some degree and to insure a constant supply throughout the year, moderating the fluctuations of the harvest cycle. Special commissioners from the cabildo annually used city funds to purchase the amount of maize which they estimated would be necessary, given the prospects for that year's harvest, to fill out the city's need in the following year. In a year of scarcity and high prices, pósito grain would be sold at a slightly higher price than privately owned maize, thus tending to stimulate the entry of privately stockpiled grain into the city. Toward the end of the summer, generally beginning in September, pósito maize might be sold to urban consumers in large quantities to make up for the dwindling supply coming into the city from private sellers.

Before 1780, even in years of marked scarcity and high prices, the share of the pósito in the city's maize supply appears never to have risen above 10,000 fanegas (see Table 8). If we eliminate the year 1795, the increasing difference between the maize needs of the city and what could be supplied by the private sector becomes evident after 1780, and especially noticeable after 1800. Beginning in 1801, and continuing until about 1815, there was a huge gap between the consumption needs of the city and the maize available from private sellers in the alhóndiga. This gap was filled by pósito purchases and sales of maize, which in most of those years far outstripped the participation of the private sector. Of the ten out of fourteen years from 1802 until 1815 for which information is available, pósito purchases never dropped below 35,000 fanegas per year, and for six years rose above 50,000 fanegas, accounting for more than 50 percent of all maize sold in the city. This tendency was reversed after 1815, but the proportion of publicly purchased grain remained high.[2]

The increased share of the pósito in urban maize sales simply reflected the increasing urban demand relative to the productive capacity of the agricultural heartland around the city, and indicated that the maize trade had shifted from a buyer's to a seller's market. This is evidenced by the growth of both rural and urban population, by the general rise in prices toward the end of the eighteenth century, and by changes in the market area from which Guadalajara drew its subsistence. As the rural population increased, more grain, especially maize, was retained in the countryside; but at the same time the city of Guadalajara increased its demand through its population growth. With a backward technology and a limited supply of suitable agricultural land, the areas around the city which had tradi-

2. Though in several years there were large residual stocks of maize from the previous year (particularly 1803 and 1810), the figures for pósito entries are quite close to the actual sales.

Table 8.

*Entries of Private and Pósito Maize into Alhóndiga of Guadalajara,
1749-1823 (in fanegas)*

Year	Privately Owned Maize	Pósito Maize	Total Maize
1749	––	4,169	––
1753	––	––	40,849
1755	––	––	46,002
1756	––	(incl. in total?)	47,206
1759	––	(incl. in total?)	40,171
1761[a]	27,488	3,972	31,460
1762	46,127	3,806	49,933
1765	50,061	7,954	58,015
1766	49,899	6,287	56,186
1767	45,197	3,768	48,965
1768	56,808	3,046	59,854
1769	43,353	2,365	45,718
1772	43,401	7,520	50,921
1774	35,264	9,500	44,764
1776	40,401	––	––
1777	41,754	––	––
1779	47,089	6,427	53,516
1782	43,517	12,968	56,215
1783	41,134	5,036	46,170
1784	35,125	11,731	46,856
1785	33,746	––	––
1788	––	15,000 (est.)	––
1789	––	15,000 (est.)	––
1792	48,810	––	––
1794	46,596	15,484	62,080
1795	32,618	4,003	36,621
1796	47,820	12,777	60,597
1797[b]	37,981	15,009	52,990
1798	––	––	49,494
1799	––	––	55,578
1801	28,349	26,019	54,368
1802	––	35,293	––
1803	28,046	40,822	68,868
1804	––	––	39,126
1805	––	––	47,850[c]

Table 8. (continued)

Entries of Private and Pósito Maize into Alhóndiga of Guadalajara, 1749-1823

Year	Privately Owned Maize	Pósito Maize	Total Maize
1806	—	—	75,086
1807	—	51,336	77,846
1808	12,450[c]	81,720	94,170
1809	—	—	61,912
1810[d]	23,664	57,965	81,629
1811	—	46,378	—
1812	29,000	50,822	79,822
1813	—	—	63,460
1814	18,367	75,757	94,124
1815	—	35,616	—
1816	68,000	8,368	76,368
1817	62,700	19,547	82,247
1818	58,312	24,088	82,400
1819	36,367	26,333	62,700
1820	52,247	30,553	82,800
1823	55,500	—	—

SOURCE:
AHMG, various cajas.

NOTES:
[a]February-September only.
[b]January-October only.
[c]Derived from tax figures.
[d]January-August only.

tionally supplied it with its staple grain were unable to meet the larger demand. This situation was exacerbated by the decisions of large agricultural producers to increase their production of wheat and to at least maintain their position as producers of livestock.

Patterns of Price and Supply

The city of Guadalajara embraced an ever-larger supply area from the last years of the eighteenth century, and the records of maize entries into the city granaries reflect this change. The major regional beneficiary of this demand was the Altos, especially Tepatitlán and Arandas. Up until the

last years of the eighteenth century, when Guadalajara was amply supplied with maize at normally low prices, producers in the Altos region
were excluded from a share of this market by their distance from the city.
Tepatitlán lay 45 miles to the east, Arandas some 75 miles. Most of the
traditional major maize-supply areas of the city, on the other hand, lay
within 30 miles, with Ameca located at the greatest distance, 45 miles.
With prices in the city relatively low, it was not profitable for producers at
a greater distance to pay even the marginally higher transport costs for
access to the urban market. With the general rise in prices after the 1780s,
however, producers in the Altos region were enabled to compete more
successfully, and it is in these years that scattered references to maize
shipments from the Altos begin to appear in the alhóndiga records. Certainly Tepatitlán and other Los Altos towns had been relied upon as breadbaskets in emergency situations, as in 1782, 1783, and 1784, when the pósito
commissioners bought substantial amounts of grain there to alleviate
shortages in Guadalajara.[3] But it was only very late in the century that
maize from the Altos began to show up regularly in the city in significant
amounts.

For the period prior to 1808, at which date the records permit analysis
of the city's maize supply by geographic origin, there is little useful information on the origins of maize shipments into the city. Of those producers
which can be readily identified, most were from the area around Guadalajara, whether larger renters, independent rancheros, or hacendados. Some
names prominent up to the 1770s and even into the 1780s are conspicuously absent from the more detailed records after 1808. This may partially
be due to their replacement as direct suppliers by their own renters or
sharecroppers, but in a number of cases they simply drop out of sight as
important sellers of maize in the city. This is true of several of the smaller
but important haciendas of the Toluquilla Valley, for example, as well as
of the important Hacienda de Santa Lucía to the north of the city, which
seems by the end of the century to have turned its productive capacity
almost exclusively to wheat. On the other hand, several of the important
haciendas which were active in the urban maize market in the middle of
the eighteenth century remained prominent as suppliers in the first decades
of the nineteenth, such as Mazatepec-Santa Ana, Huejotitán, and El
Cabezón.

The fact remains that the city's maize supply, until after the 1780s, was
overwhelmingly if not exclusively drawn from its immediate hinterland.
The detailed entry books which exist for the years 1808, 1812, 1817, and
1819 show an important change in this pattern of predominantly local
supply (see Table 9). There was a very clear tendency for grain from the

3. AHMG, cajas 14 and 15, 1782, 1783, and 1784.

Table 9.
Geographic Origin of Maize Entries into Guadalajara,
1808, 1812, 1817, 1819

	1808[a]	1812[a]	1817[b]	1819[b]
Guadalajara area				
Zacoalco	23%	8%	7%	16%
Other (Cocula, Jocotepec, La Barca, Ameca, Atotonilco, Zapotlanejo, Cuquío, etc.)	7	20	13	7
Specific haciendas:				
Mazatepec-Santa Ana	11	11	8	6
Atequiza	3	1	—	—
Miraflores	—	7	—	—
El Cabezón	—	7	2	—
Huejotitán	—	—	2	—
La Sauceda	—	—	—	2
Others	3	7	5	4
Miscellaneous local, un-identified city	33	16	21	31
Subtotal	80%	77%	58%	66%
Bajío	14	4	—	—
Los Altos	6	19	42	34
Total	100%	100%	100%	100%

SOURCE:
AHMG, various cajas, alhóndiga books.

NOTES:
[a]Private maize only.
[b]Private and pósito maize.

Altos region to claim an increasingly large share of the urban market. This is not to say that maize production remained stagnant or totally fixed in quantity in the traditional supplying areas. The area of Zacoalco, for example, doubled its absolute contribution to the city's maize supply between 1812 and 1817, and again between 1817 and 1819. But most of the additional demand for the staple grain of the city's diet was met by shipments from the Altos.

It is altogether more difficult to arrive at a notion of long-term maize prices than of areas of supply. Figure 7 sets forth data on maize prices in the Guadalajara region during the eighteenth and early nineteenth cen-

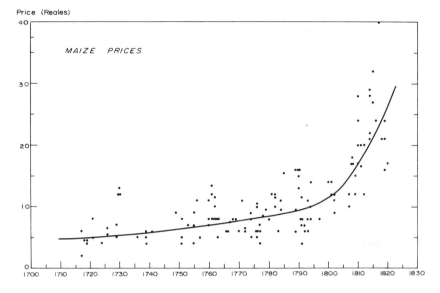

Figure 7.
Maize prices in the Guadalajara region, 1700-1825

SOURCES:
Various.

turies.[4] Despite the heterogeneity of the sources and the discontinuity of the series, it does appear that in general maize prices rose during the eighteenth century, and particularly after about 1780. Before that date, by and large, maize prices infrequently rose above one peso per fanega, and after it they seldom fell below one peso. The sharp upturn in prices after 1810 is clearly marked, and was only initially due to the dislocative effects of the Hidalgo revolt. Certainly prices did not rise steadily during the century and a quarter represented in Figure 7. It is even possible to discern the major cycles discussed by Enrique Florescano—a slight rising trend from 1721 to 1754, followed by a fall from 1755 to 1778, and then another rise between 1779 and 1814.[5] Whatever the shorter cycles may have been, however, maize prices did show a tendency to rise over the course of the eighteenth century.

In shorter-term movements, maize entries into Guadalajara demonstrated a marked seasonality. Behind short-term cycles lay seasonal variations in the price of maize sold in the city, in the share of large and small

4. The data are derived from private sales, accounts, inventories, alhóndiga and pósito sales, and pósito purchases.
5. See the price series in Florescano, *Precios del maíz*, passim, and the discussion of long-term trends on pp. 180-182.

producers in the urban market, and in the participation of Indians in supplying the city with grain. The harvest year was of course not coterminous with the calendar year, since maize was harvested generally during November and began to flow into the city in the following month. The inflow of grain tended to continue strong (depending on the nature of the harvest) through March, then to decline steadily to its nadir in the early summer, in June. The entries picked up again for the months July to October, as previously purchased pósito stocks began coming into the city in large quantities, and as larger producers sought to reap the advantage of the higher prices which prevailed toward the end of the harvest year. The yearly cycle is illustrated in Figure 8, which presents an average based on data for twenty-seven years between 1753 and 1818. In gross terms, the yearly move-

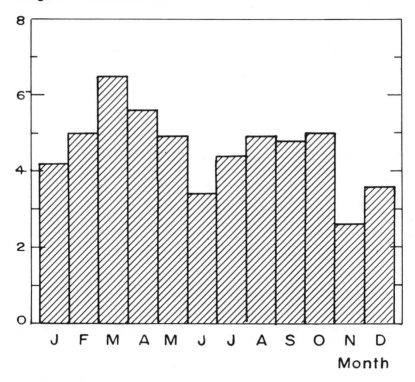

Figure 8.

Total average monthly maize entries into Guadalajara (private and pósito combined), 1753-1818

SOURCE:
AHMG, various cajas.

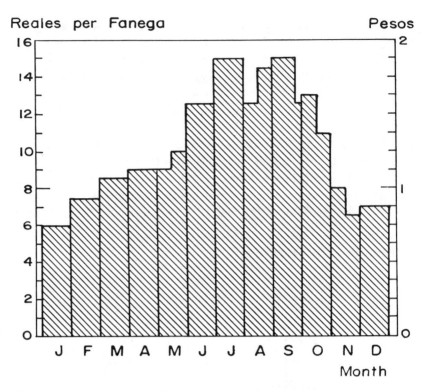

Reales per Fanega   Pesos

Month

Figure 9.
Monthly maize prices in Guadalajara, 1776

SOURCE:
AHMG, caja 5, 1776.

ment of maize prices within the city was the inverse of the supply pattern, as might be expected. Prices tended to peak about the middle of the year or slightly thereafter. For purposes of illustration, monthly prices for the year 1776, quoted in reales per fanega, are given in Figure 9.

Linked to the seasonal movement in the quantity and price of maize was the market position of small versus large producers. There is strong evidence to indicate that smaller producers flooded the urban market with their salable surpluses in the months immediately after the harvest, but that larger producers took over an increasing share of the market as maize became scarcer and prices rose, later in the year.[6] Figure 10 illustrates the changing relationship of small to large consignments of grain over the course of the year, based upon data for selected years from 1753 to 1779.[7]

6. *Ibid.*; and the same author's *Estructuras y problemas agrarios.*
7. The designation of shipments of less than 50 fanegas as "small" and those of more than 50 fanegas as "large" is admittedly somewhat arbitrary; but had a more relevant division been

Percentage

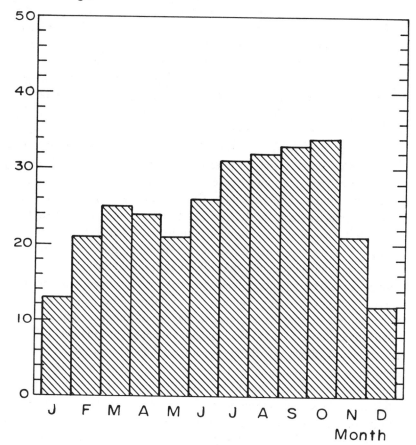

Figure 10.
Average monthly size of maize consignments to Guadalajara alhóndiga, 1753-1779 (shipments of more than 50 fanegas as percentage of total)

SOURCE:
AHMG, various cajas.

Smaller grain producers were under considerable pressure to sell their surpluses as quickly as possible, for two reasons. First, they generally lacked the storage facilities to keep any significant amount of maize protected from the weather for very long. Second, and more important, small agriculturalists needed the cash which they could realize through the sale of their grain immediately after the harvest, and could ill afford to hold their

possible, the changing relationship between the two over the course of the year would probably be even clearer.

maize back from the market until the price rose later in the year. Indians needed to pay their tributes in cash, and renters their rents; local merchants required the payment of debts contracted during the pre-harvest dearth; and often seed, tools, and dry goods had to be purchased for the coming year. Small producers thus typically lacked the capital or credit to await the higher prices which almost inevitably came later on in the year.

Larger producers, on the other hand, possessed ample storage facilities and generally had sufficient capital of their own or access to credit to allow them to wait out the period of low prices which accompanied the flood of grain into the city after the harvest. Thus the share of large producers in the market increased from just over 10 percent in December and January of the typical year to about 33 percent of the total maize shipped into the city in late summer and early fall. The overall share of large producers actually increased significantly from the 1750s to the 1770s. Several times in the late 1760s the share of large producers exceeded 50 percent in some months, and there are scattered indications that this trend continued through the latter part of the century. In addition to the seasonal pattern of maize introductions themselves, the variations in price quotations indicate the tendency of larger producers to speculate in the maize trade. Very often (and this was particularly true in the case of Indians selling their own maize in the alhóndiga), smaller consignments of grain had lower prices set on them. Sometimes this difference amounted only to a *real* or so per fanega, but there was a notable tendency for larger producers to peg their selling price higher than that of their smaller competitors.

Indian maize introductions were characterized by seasonal variations even more marked than the variations of other small producers. The profile of Indian participation in the urban maize market shown in Figure 11 is substantially accurate for the decades of the 1750s, 1760s, 1770s, and 1780s, when it quite consistently amounted to about 25 percent of the total on a yearly basis. The share of urban maize supplied by Indian producers may have been even higher earlier in the century. The yearly pattern of Indian maize shipments into the city was governed by the same rhythms of rural life—the harvest and the need for cash early in the year—as that of other small producers. But long-term forces were at play in the rural economy which, during the last years of the eighteenth century, reduced the Indian share in this grain trade by a very large measure, so that after the turn of the century Indians had almost dropped out of the Guadalajara market. The evidence for this is scattered, but its import is clear enough. For most of the years from the 1750s through the 1770s, the Indian share of the market stood at about 25 percent of total shipments introduced, though only at about half that level in terms of actual maize by weight.

By the early 1780s a certain softening in the market position of the Indian

Percentage

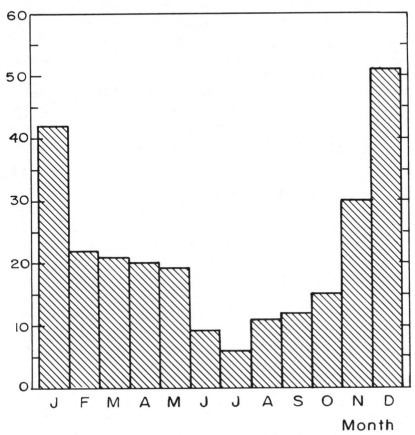

Month

Figure 11.
*Average monthly maize introductions into Guadalajara by Indians, 1753-
1784 (as percentage of total)*

SOURCE:
AHMG, various cajas.

producer was already in evidence. In 1782 the Indian share of total introductions dropped to 5 percent, recovered somewhat in the next two years,
and dropped back to 9 percent in 1785, due largely to the failure of the
maize harvest at the end of that year. Data on this point are unfortunately
lacking for the following years, but a reliable figure for the year 1808 is 1
percent, and for 1812 less than 1 percent. There is no reason to believe that
most Indian producers would have ceased in these years to take advantage
of the traditional exemption from taxes on the introduction of their grain

into the city.[8] It must therefore be concluded that the figures represent a real drop in their participation in the market. It seems probable that up to the 1780s there had been a surplus of maize produced within the Indian economy which was available for consumption in Guadalajara. With the continued growth of the Indian rural population and the increased competition for agricultural land between Indians and others, whatever was produced within the Indian sector came to be needed there for local consumption, and seldom reached the city. With the curtailment of their productive capacity for the urban market, Indians re-entered the money economy largely as sellers of labor or labor-intensive agricultural products.

The Pósito and Public Policy

The persistent and elaborate attempts of the municipal government to regulate the grain trade, in the form of the alhóndiga for maize and the calicata for wheat, were essentially passive. That is to say, they sought to impose some order on the play of market forces, but strictly within the limits set by the already-existing system in which decisions about production, price, and sales were in the hands of private individuals. The existence and legitimacy of these regulatory institutions were accepted from very early on in the history of the city, and they were adjusted after the middle of the eighteenth century to accommodate the growth of urban demand. There were other, more aggressive means, however, by which the municipal and royal governments tried to insure Guadalajara's food supply. The chief among these was the pósito, through which the city government itself actively participated in the provision of maize, the vital staple, to the city's population. This institutional arrangement was present also from a very early period, but it took a quantum jump in importance during the last third of the eighteenth century, in the period when the city's increased population put new strains on the traditional structure of supply. In addition to the growing importance of the pósito, the efforts of the cabildo to insure the city's food supply relied upon a number of ad-hoc measures taken in times of scarcity. Such measures included interdictions against the export of grain from New Galicia, the seizure of private hoards of grain, and the forced sale of privately owned maize and wheat in the city.

The primary avowed purpose of the pósito of Guadalajara was to insure the city's maize supply through the manipulation of prices. This was to be achieved not through direct setting of prices by the municipal or royal government, but by the sale of grain within the city at prices which would

8. AHMG, cajas 10 and 24.

encourage the introduction of stored maize by private individuals. Its secondary function was to directly supply urban consumers while awaiting an adequate volume of private maize, and to smooth out the seasonal variations in supply which occurred even in good harvest years. Yet the attempts of the city government to realize these ostensible goals exposed contradictions inherent in the fundamental opposition between the interests of private agriculturists and those of the consuming public.

The pósito very rarely sought directly to undersell private suppliers in the alhóndiga if the amount of maize available from the private sector was thought to be sufficient for the needs of the city, even if the price was high. It is true that the municipal government was not perfectly consistent in this policy, especially around the midcentury.[9] Even after 1770, however, there is no evidence that the cabildo or the royal government seriously tried to lower urban maize prices in this manner. To do so would have been consistent with the increasingly common moral condemnation of excessive profit-taking in the late colonial period, but inconsistent with the ideal and practical necessity for homeostasis to which the pósito administration was committed. At least until the last quarter of the eighteenth century, the price level of maize per se did not particularly concern the pósito commissioners, since it was generally acknowledged by those in authority that in times of scarcity it was proper that prices rise. Even in the famine year of 1786, one of the commissioners of the pósito remarked that "to the public, the higher or lower price of foods of prime necessity is not important, but having them at all."[10] Indeed, it was this very mechanism upon which the pósito relied to fulfill its function of spurring the flow of privately owned maize into the city. High prices were intended to "attract introducers of grain since, encouraged by the higher profits, they withdraw from their granaries the maize which they had stored for sale at more advantageous times and which they had not introduced into the city because they observed that prices had not yet risen high enough."[11]

Yet the legitimacy of profiting from scarcity was under attack in the last decades of the eighteenth century, particularly after the disastrous year of 1785-1786, and speculation began to be roundly condemned by officials at all levels of government. Certainly the political instability which appeared to be endemic in the world at that time played its part in persuading officials that public unrest, even in the form of grain riots, must be forestalled at all costs. Then, too, the reasons for the rising prices of the last years of the century were imperfectly understood by those making policy. Despite

9. AHMG, caja 1, 1756; cajas 3 and 5, 1760.

10. AHMG, caja 11, 1786.

11. *Ibid.*, 1787. For more on pósito policy, see AHMG, caja 23, 1807, and caja 24, 1810, par. 13.

the obviously expanding orbit of the urban market represented by Guadalajara, and the equally obvious increase in rural and urban population, most city and royal officials acted as if they believed the grain supply to be perfectly elastic and infinitely expansible. The corollary of this assumption was that the price rise which began in earnest after about 1780 was the result of conscious decision-making by large landowners. This, in fact, was only a part of a more complex situation. Nonetheless, the city's pósito policy reflects an increasing concern that urban consumers, particularly the poor, were being gouged by large-scale private sellers of grain.[12]

Under such pressures, what had formerly been the lesser purpose of the pósito—directly to supply the city with maize—became in the last decades of the colonial period its primary purpose. Up until about 1780, when its regulatory function had been dominant, the pósito was simply an appendage of the alhóndiga. That the tail had begun to wag the dog after that date is obvious. By 1810, the alhóndiga regulations refer to the pósito, as opposed to the private sales sector, as the "principal and essential branch" of the urban maize market.[13] This shift in the role of the pósito from that of a regulatory agency to that of the major supplier of Guadalajara in most years is seen very clearly in Figure 6 and Table 8. The city's available local supply of maize was becoming ever more finely tuned to its consumption needs, leaving less and less margin as population increased during the late colonial period. In the view of the municipal and royal governments, at least, this necessitated a more aggressive procurement policy on the part of the city, and the pósito naturally filled this function. Nor was the capital of New Galicia alone in its increasing reliance upon government intervention in securing an adequate maize supply. Late colonial documents refer to the establishment of pósitos in the towns of Zapotlán and Sayula in 1786 and 1802, respectively.[14]

Pósito records permit an illuminating if somewhat sketchy reconstruction of the way the agency worked. Until the period when the pósito came to dominate the city's maize supply, after about 1780, the process by which the designated city commissioners purchased grain seems to have been fairly informal, lacking the standardized contract and accounting procedures which came into use later. Early in the eighteenth century, purchases were small and drawn from a heterogeneous group of modest and medium-sized producers, including Indians.[15] The Indians disappear from the pósito records even sooner than from the records of private maize introductions into the city, and they are not at all in evidence after 1750.

The wholesaling trend in pósito supply is already quite clear by the 1760s.

12. AHMG, caja 11, 1787.   13. AHMG, caja 5, 1769; caja 24, 1810.
14. AHMG, caja 11, 1786; caja 19, 1802.
15. As can be seen, for example, in the accounts for 1730, in AHMG, caja 2.

Entries into the alhóndiga specifically earmarked for the pósito account were generally much larger on the average than entries of privately owned grain, and were concentrated at those times of the year when private maize introductions were at their weakest. By 1810 or so, procurement for the pósito had become concentrated among a very restricted group of producers. In 1814, for example, the city's commissioners made some 47 contracts with as many different individuals to supply the pósito with 50,716 fanegas of maize. Of the sales which can be identified by geographic origin, the Altos region accounted for nearly 20,000 fanegas, including the largest single sale to the pósito, some 7,000 fanegas at 16,625 pesos. But the owners of great estates near Guadalajara did participate in this wholesale trade, and quite heavily, if not every year. Most prominent among these was the master of Huejotitán, Tomás Ignacio Villaseñor, who frequently supplied 12,000 to 15,000 fanegas of grain, as in the years 1802, 1808, and 1815.[16] Once contracted for, pósito maize entered the alhóndiga in dribs and drabs, as it was intended to do, so as not to overstrain the limited storage facilities at the disposition of the city commissioners. Often there were substantial remainders of pósito maize from one year to the next, somewhat complicating the business of buying for the following year—a problem never satisfactorily resolved by the city administration. Sales from the pósito stocks were effected by direct orders from the cabildo, with prices tending to reach their peak near the middle of the harvest year, about June or July.

Supplementing the role of the pósito were the more sporadically applied, ad-hoc measures used in times of sharp scarcity, when failures in the maize crop subjected Guadalajara to the danger of starvation. These periods of extreme dearth occurred in a roughly cyclical pattern about every ten years —1741, 1750, 1761-1762, 1770, 1785-1786—and their effects were felt throughout colonial Mexico.[17] The most notorious of these cyclical disasters was that of the years 1785-1786, the famous "año de hambre," in which the entire panoply of available responses was called into action to relieve the famine conditions which developed in the city and surrounding countryside. The most frequently employed method was for commissioners from the cabildo, either personally or by letter, to canvass local haciendas in order to ascertain the supplies of grain held at each and urge the owners to send it into the city for sale. Very often hacendados appeared to succumb to this kind of moral pressure, but made excuses for their tardiness in remitting grain to the city and succeeded in forcing prices up anyway.[18] On occasion the Audiencia threatened hacendados with punishment if they

16. AHMG, caja 1, 1802; caja 37, 1808; and caja 15, 1815.
17. See Florescano, *Precios del maíz*, pp. 111-139.
18. E.g., AHMG, caja 4, 1776.

did not send their stored maize into the city for sale, but this was fairly rare. A more extreme measure, resorted to by the Audiencia only when other methods had obviously failed to dislodge grain from its owners, was the prohibition of grain sales outside New Galicia, or the immediate district of Guadalajara itself. In the early 1770s, for example, the high prices of maize in Mexico City drew grain from New Galicia like a magnet, causing local shortages in Guadalajara. Under these circumstances, the Audiencia forbade any exports of grain to New Spain except under specific license, as it was to do again in 1785-1786.[19]

The various components of cabildo and Audiencia grain policy—the calicata and alhóndiga for wheat, and the alhóndiga, pósito, and ad-hoc policies applied to maize—all point to one enduring and fundamental feature of the urban grain market: its vulnerability to speculation. Regulate as they would, neither city nor royal officials ever succeeded in eliminating this vulnerability. That the grain supply of colonial cities and towns was prey to the speculative manipulations of large agricultural producers emerges clearly from eighteenth-century documents, and was a matter of much concern at the time.[20] Large grain producers did not speculate in the classic sense of buying up quantities of grain and gambling on windfall profits from anticipated price rises, but rather by holding their grain off the market until prices had risen during the normal course of the harvest year. Alternatively, they could hope for conditions of scarcity resulting from a poor crop, which might push prices up even beyond the peaks associated with ordinary yearly fluctuations. It is arguable that such profit-maximizing behavior was essential in an agricultural economy characterized by a backward technology, meager surpluses, and precarious profitability. In any case, such a policy was universally practiced by hacendados of the period, and was even considered legitimate as long as it remained within reasonable limits. Certainly the pattern of private maize entries into the Guadalajara alhóndiga illustrates this.

The distinction between such large producers and the small producers who found themselves at a competitive disadvantage in terms of the urban market was clearly made by the *oidor fiscal* of the Guadalajara Audiencia in 1799:

Farmers may be reduced to two classes: some sow considerable quantities, from which they not only supply their annual cash expenses but also, from the sale of large surpluses, increase their fortunes; and others sow small quantities, in proportion to their very limited resources, without having any other property, business, or

19. AHMG, caja 15, 1771.

20. For a general discussion of this phenomenon in eighteenth-century Mexico, see Florescano, *Precios del maíz* and *Estructuras y problemas agrarios*, passim; for the Valley of Mexico, see Gibson, *The Aztecs*, pp. 324-327.

means with which to support their families and provide them with other necessities. From their limited sales they supply themselves with the indispensable food, shelter, rents, and clothing which often they would lack, thus subjecting themselves to further hardship, if they held back the harvesting of their small crops.[21]

The group of large producers, on the other hand, did not need to rush their grain into the city immediately after the harvest (the oidor's comments were apropos of a suggested measure prohibiting the harvesting of maize before it was fully matured). Because of the greater variety of their production and their substantial capital, they generally harvested their maize well ripened (*bien sasonado*), retaining it even for years at a time in their granaries to sell when maize was at its most scarce and prices at their highest, or sending it outside the area to places where prices were more favorable. Both practices were to play a part in aggravating the famine of 1785-1786.

The second major form of speculation to which the city's grain trade was subject was classical regrating, involving the purchase of maize or wheat from the primary producer by a middleman, who then sold it to the consumer at a considerably higher price than he had originally paid. This practice was universally condemned by consumers, government officials, and landowners, since both producer and consumer stood to lose by such an arrangement. Complaints about *regatones* (regraters) were endemic throughout the eighteenth century, and they were apparently involved with virtually every kind of foodstuff. The number of these "wasters of the republic," as an outraged regidor referred to them in 1808, was almost daily on the increase in the last years of the eighteenth century, resulting in unprecedentedly high prices.[22] Laws and police officials multiplied, but largely without effect. Two additional constables (*alguaciles*) were employed by the municipal *junta de policía* in 1805 to combat this menace. The police commissioners spoke of the "public outcry about the multitude of regraters in this capital, so that it is a rare day when food is bought from its producer, since the speculators travel far with the object of buying on the roads whatever is coming to supply the city."[23]

Both wheat and maize were subject to regrating practices, though it was probably somewhat easier, as the century wore on, for regraters to buy and sell in commodities other than cereals (chickens, vegetables, fruit, pottery, etc.). There is evidence that some individuals of real but modest economic

21. AHMG, caja 19, 1799. This constitutes a quite explicit distinction between capitalist farmers and peasants; see Eric R. Wolf, *Peasants* (1966), passim.

22. AHMG, caja 23, 1808; caja 15, 1795; caja 16, 1798. It seems entirely likely that the number of small-scale regraters increased directly with the increase in the city's population in the latter part of the eighteenth century. The increase in the city's food supply meant that people who had no jobs or who were underemployed could participate in the market with very limited capital through buying and reselling in small quantities.

23. AHMG, caja 22, 1805.

resources actually went about the countryside buying up grain crops for storage and later resale. In 1808, for example, a number of witnesses testified that one Lorenzo Ruíz, a "residente" (renter?) on the Hacienda de Mazatepec, was buying up maize locally before the harvest (*en verde*) in the prospect of reselling it later in the year at a substantial profit. More common was the buying up of grain on its way into the city from its point of origin, and then reselling it in the city, with the regatón assuming the guise of the producer. Regatones were also known to establish stalls (*vendimias*) in front of the alhóndiga itself and there to "induce the muleteers bringing maize to exchange it for other kinds of food." On a rather larger scale, individuals occasionally took advantage of the rumor or fear of a shortage in the following season to buy up grain within the city itself. This apparently occurred in July 1814, when the city's bakers complained that such purchases had driven the price of flour up more than five pesos per carga in the space of only a few days.[24] All of these practices, particularly the dealing in grain between its point of origin and the city, were repeatedly outlawed in municipal laws and alhóndiga ordinances (1749, 1762, 1768, 1798, 1810), but to no effect. The trade in foodstuffs in general, and the grain trade in particular, remained vulnerable to this kind of profiteering throughout the colonial period.

The Famine of 1785-1786

The best way to conclude this discussion of the grain trade is with an account of the dramatic events of the great famine year of 1785-1786. The economic dislocation, starvation, and disease that followed upon the loss of the maize crop in the autumn of 1785 were not typical of the late eighteenth century, but the events of these fatal years do throw into relief the vulnerability of the city of Guadalajara as a consumer of grain, particularly of maize, during times of scarcity. An examination of the shortages of these years reveals all the problems inherent in the market side of the expanding commercialized agriculture of the late colonial period, as well as the policies implemented by the municipal and royal governments in dealing with these problems.

The year of 1785 had been unusually dry all over Mexico, the effects of the abbreviated rainy season being compounded by early frosts in May and a second, severe frost on the night of August 27. What would have been a sparse maize harvest in any case was largely destroyed by the August frost, and what remained of the crop was finished off by a third wave of cold

24. AHMG, caja 37, 1808; caja 3, exp. 16, 1768; caja 10, 1762; caja 27, 1814.

weather in September. The harvest of 1783 had been short, with the result that pósito prices had risen to two pesos per fanega for much of the following year, and there was no surplus carried over into 1785.[25] The maize crop of 1784 was also less abundant than usual, and prices were prevented from rising astronomically in the city during the first half of 1785 only by dint of substantial pósito purchases, again with no surplus left over. A canvass of country districts, combined with an Audiencia prohibition of grain exports to New Spain, failed to dislodge the small existing maize surpluses. Shipments of grain from several large haciendas eventually raised the volume of maize supply in the city to about 60 percent of the normal level, with prices correspondingly high all year long.[26]

Coming as it did upon the heels of two short harvests, the maize-crop failure of 1785 was bound to wreak havoc in the city's grain supply. By early November it was obvious to city and royal officials that a disaster of major proportions had occurred. Maize entries into the alhóndiga were at about a third of their normal volume in November and December. The relatively small consignments of maize which normally dominated the urban maize market just after the harvest were conspicuously absent, reduced almost to nothing. By mid-November, maize was selling in Guadalajara at three pesos per fanega, and the poorer inhabitants of the city were already in a desperate situation. To compound the problems of the city's grain supply, hungry emigrants from the country districts began to flow into Guadalajara seeking relief. In mid-November the cabildo deliberations noted "the flow of people and wandering families who, pursued by hunger, are now coming and will inevitably come to this capital as common home of all the towns making up this kingdom."[27] By February 1786, the *fiscal* of the Audiencia estimated that upwards of 12,000 people from small towns and the countryside had swelled the city's population. One regidor suggested establishing a "cordón" along the Río Grande de Santiago to keep emigrants out, as well as issuing an order to local justices to prohibit the movement of families to the city.[28]

The social problems attendant upon such a rapid influx of unemployed and desperate people were already rampant in the city by the beginning of 1786, including the spread of disease encouraged by overcrowding. The city government found itself in a moral dilemma:

To deny lodging to these wandering unfortunates, among them women, children, and the old, is very harsh; to welcome them, risky. Because, the city not having

25. Sherburne F. Cook, "The Hunger Hospital in Guadalajara," *Bulletin of the History of Medicine* 8 (1940), p. 534; Gibson, *The Aztecs*, p. 316; Florescano, *Precios del maíz*, p. 133; AHMG, caja 7, 1784.

26. AHMG, cajas 7 and 10, 1785.   27. AHMG, caja 10, 1785.

28. *Ibid.*, 1785 and 1786.

available the grain which in less sterile years is sufficient to contain the arbitrary prices by which farmers enrich themselves, the demand will double. And [such a situation] will bring with it continual murders, repeated robberies and rapes, and encourage prostitution and the inexcusable acts of violence impelled and provoked by unemployment and hunger.[29]

Nor was this kind of criminal activity the only fear of royal and municipal officials and citizens of means. There was a genuine dread of grain riots and God-only-knew what kinds of movements developing from them. Commenting on a Febrary 1786 proposal that daily maize sales from the alhóndiga and pósito be limited to a total of 200 fanegas, the *fiscal* of the Audiencia stated that:

. . . such a terrible and stern paternal measure might well cause a general uprising . . . and it should not be surprising if the poor people, provoked by hunger, were to throw themselves upon the carts and mules which daily conduct maize and thus begin a riot . . . .

And the same official hinted darkly at a situation which might escape the control of the authorities "because as the wise commentator Bobadilla stated in treating of a similar question, 'Neither armed force, nor magistrates, nor respect for God or man, nor the laws themselves could dominate or restrain a people starving and in need of physical sustenance.'"[30]

Under such circumstances, what would have been a very hard situation in Guadalajara began to take on the proportions of a major disaster. The Audiencia and the municipal government sought desperately to find grain to feed the city. On November 15, the Audiencia ordered the *alcalde mayor* of La Barca to have the tithe administrator of the district open his granaries and sell maize retail until further notice at the price then prevailing in Guadalajara, three pesos per fanega. At least 3,000 fanegas of the old maize were to be sent into the city, and beyond this whatever possible to Zacatecas, which found itself in an equally desperate situation. On November 17, the officials of San Blas were ordered to promote the sowing of "maíz de verano" in the district, and the same order went out to the justices of Aguacatlán, Jala, Tepic, Sentispac, and Mazapil. The jurisdictions of Zapotlán el Grande, Sayula, Autlán, Etzatlán, and Tuscacuesco were canvassed by letter concerning the possibility of sending grain to succor the city, and the *teniente* of Ameca, traditionally a maize-producing center, was dispatched to look for maize on the major haciendas of the area.

At the end of November, a new commissioner appointed by the Audiencia went to Sayula, Zapotlán el Grande, Tuscacuesco, Colima, Autlán, Etzatlán, and Ahualulco to oversee sending into the city some 8,000 fa-

29. *Ibid.*, 1785.   30. *Ibid.*, 1785 and 1786.

negas purchased earlier in the month by cabildo commissioners, but it was discovered that some of the contractors had subsequently sold their grain elsewhere, despite their obligation to the city. Local landowners around the city did the same thing, having initially offered their small quantities to the city but almost immediately selling them to commissioners from Sombrerete instead. At about the same time, in response to a request by the city cabildo, the Dean and cabildo of the Cathedral began to prepare a list of the tithe farmers and collectors in the Bishopric of Guadalajara, with the amounts they had collected from the harvest. Producers in various jurisdictions committed their surpluses to the city during November and December, but were in some instances met with the objections of local officials, especially those in New Spain (much of Sayula was within New Spain), who pointed out that the viceroy had already issued a decree forbidding the export of grain from New Spain to New Galicia. But fortunately, during these two months maize purchased by the various city and royal commissioners began to flow into the city in small consignments.[31]

In many cases, districts or whole provinces which had been looked to as sources of maize to feed the city were themselves in desperate need and were completely unable to supply any surpluses. The district of Tala, for example, which included a number of important haciendas, was repeatedly canvassed for maize and was largely unable to meet even its own needs. Speaking in 1790 of the situation in several Indian pueblos within the district, a witness in a land suit stated:

In that fatal year of '86 hunger and disease left no time to do anything but cry misery and search for food—I do not mention the poor Indians, who by their poverty sustained the worst of it, but even people of more substantial means.[32]

By the beginning of 1786, despite emergency measures by the city government and the Audiencia and some success in dislodging the meager surpluses from the countryside, the situation in Guadalajara was increasingly desperate.[33] What little harvest there had been in the immediate environs of the city had been consumed, largely because buyers from outside the city supplied themselves from the alhóndiga and pósito. The maize in the pósito, normally not sold until June or July, was selling at more than 100 fanegas per day, but it was estimated that the rate of consumption would climb to 300 fanegas shortly.[34] In early January the maize purchased for the current year began to be sold, and by the end of the month the price had risen to 3½ pesos the fanega.[35] The city government requested that

31. AHMG, caja 11, 1786.

32. AIPG, Tierras, leg. 20, exp. 18. Sharp scarcity also prevailed in Guachinango, Mascota, Aguacatlán, and Jala (AHMG, caja 11, 1786).

33. AHMG, caja 11, 1786.   34. *Ibid.*, exp. 26.   35. *Ibid.*

two oidores of the Audiencia be commissioned with plenary powers to canvass the countryside for maize, since producers tended to hide their grain from commissioners who lacked the power to enforce their compliance. Ultimately, what maize did flow into Guadalajara came from the climatically warmer districts to the south of Lake Chapala, or from coastal areas, where there had been normal harvests. Zapotlán el Grande, Tuscacuesco, and Colima, all normally outside the orbit of the Guadalajara market, supplied the city with some 15,000 to 20,000 fanegas of grain during 1786. The big problem here was getting the maize to the city. Transport costs rose tremendously during the year, under the dual impact of abnormally heavy demand and the seasonal lack of pasturage, which had been exacerbated by the dryness of 1785. Most local mule trains (*requas*) and ox-carts were already involved in bringing vital food supplies into the city and therefore could not be requisitioned, as the Audiencia threatened to do. The municipal government was accordingly forced to underwrite the transport costs for many producers in outlying areas, thus contributing to the spiraling price of maize in Guadalajara.[36]

And spiral the prices did. At the end of February, maize was selling at the pósito for four pesos per fanega. After remaining at this level for some time, the price jumped to five pesos in mid-April and hung there through May, June, July, and August, falling only at the end of the year, when the good harvest of 1786 began to flow into the city.[37] The precipitous rise in maize prices was accompanied by rising prices for other foodstuffs of prime necessity. By the end of 1786, the ubiquitous *frijoles* (beans), so much a part of the diet of urban as well as rural dwellers, had risen in price fivefold, to ten pesos per fanega, and lentils and garbanzos experienced similar increases.

With such a critical shortage of maize, urban consumers and those officials charged with keeping Guadalajara fed turned naturally to wheat as a substitute for the normal staple grain. By mid-November of 1785, the municipal government had already begun to canvass the major wheat-producing haciendas of the Guadalajara region by a circular letter in much the same way as they were doing for maize at the same time. The initial replies were hardly optimistic. Most large wheat-producers had already disposed of the greater part of their 1785 harvest, including traditionally important suppliers such as the haciendas of Atequiza, El Cabezón-La Vega, Toluquilla, Santa Cruz, San Nicolás, La Concepción, Huejotitán, Cedros, and Santa Lucía. The availability of wheat was further compromised by labor shortages on most haciendas, the necessity of sowing for the following year with smaller and debilitated working forces, and the

36. *Ibid.*   37. *Ibid.*

need to retain more grain for rations to make up for maize shortages. Despite these difficulties, the city did manage to attract the normal level of wheat entries for the first half of 1786. In addition to efforts to solicit grain from as far away as the Valle de Santiago, Irapuato, Zamora, and Lagos, where the 1785 harvest had been normal, the cabildo itself sought directly to purchase wheat for the succor of the city, primarily from the Conde de la Presa de Jalpa, one of the great landowners of the Bajío region in New Spain. Although wheat and flour entries into the city attained their normal levels in the latter half of 1786, prices stabilized at about double the usual and remained there for the entire year. That the flow of wheat and flour did not exceed their normal quantity was due to a number of reasons, including labor shortages for the 1785 sowing and increased local demand. In addition, however, it seems likely that producers who had enjoyed windfall profits from the scarcity of late 1785 and early 1786 were probably reluctant to lower their profits by overproducing. Such economic behavior was certainly consistent with the policy of low risk-taking practiced by most contemporary agriculturists, large and small.[38]

The sheer human misery caused by the harvest failure of 1785 is substantiated by both contemporary accounts and historical research.[39] Probably there was some mortality due to outright starvation, but it seems unlikely that this was the major cause of death among victims of the *año de hambre*. It must be recognized that famine functions in a socially selective way, and that those city dwellers with sufficient means to weather the worst months of the famine did not suffer from malnutrition or starvation, nor from the disease that accompanied the dearth.[40] The chronology of the series of epidemics which ravaged the Guadalajara area and much of New Spain from 1784 to 1787 is difficult for us to follow with any accuracy. Certainly disease of some kind was present in the Guadalajara area from 1784. By early March of 1785 the city was already in the grip of "malignas fiebres y dolores de costado" which proved fatal within a week to those who contracted them, regardless of age or sex.[41] The famine of 1785-1786, then, struck a population already suffering from the effects of disease, and

38. *Ibid.*, exps. 2 and 7. For details on the Hacienda de Jalpa, see Brading, *Haciendas and Ranchos*, passim.

39. The situation in New Spain has been described by Florescano, *Precios del maíz*, esp. pp. 159-163; Gibson, *The Aztecs*, pp. 316-317; and Brading and Wu, "Population Growth and Crisis," pp. 32-36. For Europe, the "crise de subsistances" has been particularly well studied by French historians. Pierre Goubert provides a fully circumstantial account of the great famine of 1693-1694 in his *Beauvais et le Beauvaisis* (1960) and *Louis XIV and Twenty Million Frenchmen* (1972), pp. 215-219. For seventeenth- and eighteenth-century Spain, see Gonzalo Anes, *Las crisis agrarias en la España moderna* (1970), passim; for Europe in general, Slicher Van Bath, *The Agrarian History of Western Europe*, passim.

40. Goubert, *Louis XIV and Twenty Million Frenchmen*, p. 218.

41. AHMG, caja 10, 1785.

compounded the situation disastrously. The tremendous influx into Guadalajara of people from the countryside created ideal conditions for the recurrence of disease in epidemic proportions: overcrowding, bad sanitation, and the lowered resistance due to malnutrition.[42] Only in 1786 did the situation in the city become really critical, however. The descriptions of the time do not render enough information for definite clinical identification of the diseases in question, but Cook has suggested that there was a combination which included at least typhoid, dysentery, pneumonia, and influenza.[43] Nor was the contagion general but, like the weakening from hunger itself, it seems to have struck mainly the poorer social groups.

By September 1786, the *peste* had been raging within the city for many weeks and showed no sign of abatement, but was even increasing in intensity. The Bishop estimated that since the beginning of March, 25 corpses per day, both adults and children, had been buried in the cemeteries. Almost 5,000 people had died already during 1786, and the prospects for the rest of the calamitous year were frightening. There was no room left for further burials without the risk of opening graves and freeing "vapores pestilentes." The city's churches were making a tremendous effort to bury the dead decently, but "each morning the corpses removed during the night are piled up, most of them entirely naked, with no way of finding out who they are, their civil status, or where they came from. . . ." It was immediately necessary to open another cemetery sufficiently large and distant from the city; in the meantime, however, it was proposed that a large ditch (*vallado*) be opened outside the city in which to deposit the corpses of disease victims until they could be buried.[44] By mid-November, conditions in Guadalajara were just as appalling. "Muchas gentes miserables" were living all over the city in squalid huts. When these people died, as they did in huge numbers, they were left unburied for many hours, and their bedclothes, *petates*, and other belongings were simply left in the street, where they increased the chance of contagion. Bodies were regularly found in the plazas and more removed parts of the city. Beggars roamed the streets "so poor, weak and wasted, like skeletons hardly able to stand on their feet . . . ." The hospitals were discharging patients in mid-cure, leading to still more contagion, and the city's sanitation was terrible.[45]

An overall estimate of the mortality caused in the immediate Guadalajara area by the epidemics of 1784-1787 is impossible to arrive at. In León, which also experienced the dual scourge of famine and disease in these years, the burial rate for 1786 was about four times the average for the

---

42. Cook, "Hunger Hospital," pp. 537-538.   43. *Ibid.*, p. 537.
44. For an account of similar conditions in Mexico City at the same time, see Donald B. Cooper, "Epidemic Disease in Mexico City" (1963), pp. 98-118.
45. AHMG, caja 10, 1786.

three preceding years. This is probably on the low side, since deaths were typically under-registered.[46] There is every reason to assume that in Guadalajara things were worse, since conditions of crowding and sanitation in the much larger city would probably have encouraged a heavier incidence of disease and mortality. Cook estimates that the overall mortality for New Galicia in these years came to 50,000, and that the death-rate in Guadalajara itself in May 1786 was about 100 people per day.[47] Records of rentals of city lands (small house and garden plots) indicate a mortality among the tenants of 25 to 50 percent.[48] All in all, it seems reasonable to assume that during the worst year of the period, 1786, about a quarter to a fifth of the city's normal population died because of the combined effects of starvation and disease.

The relief measures undertaken by the municipal government extended beyond attempts to assure a food supply for the ravaged city. Already by mid-November of 1785, it was obvious that social conditions in Guadalajara would become intolerable if the mass of emigrants entering from the countryside could not find some kind of gainful employment. The city fathers were not willing to establish a dole, but did propose a variety of relief measures. Among these were the formation of work-gangs from able-bodied poor, the planting of potatoes and *camotes* on public lands around the outskirts of the city, and an elaborate scheme for a yarn factory (*fábrica de hilados*)—though what became of these projects is not certain.[49] Eventually a poorhouse and a number of infirmaries were established by the city government, supported by subscriptions from people of means and the Church, as well as by royal and city officials.[50] The poorhouse (*hospicio*) also cared for those of its inmates who fell ill, though what the recovery rate was it is impossible to say. In late 1786 the hospicio administrator, Troncoso, himself died of a "maligna fiebre."[51]

Even though the maize harvest of 1786 was apparently somewhat below average, the flow of grain into Guadalajara which began after November of that year eased the situation considerably, and prices dropped quickly from their exceptionally high levels of the previous months. By April of 1787, there were fairly abundant stocks of maize in the pósito, and these were selling at two pesos the fanega to "attract the introducers of these grains." By early May, private entries of grain showed signs of slackening, so the pósito raised its price to 18 reales, higher than normal but still less than half the price of the preceding May. By the beginning of June, maize

46. Brading and Wu, "Population Growth and Crisis," p. 34.
47. Cook, "Hunger Hospital," p. 538.
48. AHMG, caja 14, 1792.   49. AHMG, caja 10, 1785.
50. See Cook's interesting article, "Hunger Hospital."
51. AHMG, caja 11, exp. 26, 1786.

had climbed to 19 reales the fanega in the city, but fell again to about two pesos in July because of abundant private introductions, and remained at this level through most of the summer. In September, maize began to enter the city in large quantities from La Barca and the Altos region, and prices dropped to 14 reales and continued to fall during the rest of the year. By the end of September, the pósito commissioners were sufficiently worried about losing the maize purchased for 1787, because of strong private sales, that they were empowered by the cabildo to set prices on a daily basis. As to the *hospicio de pobres*, it had ceased to exist in January 1787, by which time conditions in the city had improved to the point that its relief efforts were no longer considered necessary.[52]

The disastrous years of 1785 and 1786 clearly demonstrate Guadalajara's vulnerability as a consumer of grain, and its ultimate dependence upon large producers of both maize and wheat. This trend became accentuated during the remainder of the colonial period, although small and medium-sized producers continued to play an important part in supplying the urban market. The vigorous action of the city and royal governments presaged a period in which the purposeful interference of the state was seen as essential in mobilizing food resources for the support of Guadalajara. There was no longer such a degree of elasticity in the agricultural economy that the fate of the urban consumer could be left entirely to the free play of market forces.

It remains to assess the place of the crisis of 1785–1786 in the overall development of the Guadalajara area in the eighteenth century. Did those years of famine, epidemic, and death in fact constitute a crisis of some kind? Certainly they conform to the model of the classical subsistence crisis developed in recent years by French and English social and economic historians.[53] Several years of mediocre cereal harvests were followed by a disastrously bad year. Prices rose; the poorer groups of laborers and peasants in both town and country were afflicted with severe malnutrition, if not actual starvation, on a massive scale. There occurred a tremendous influx of rural inhabitants into the city in search of food and relief. The weakened state of the population, combined with the increased geographical movement of large numbers of people and the breakdown in public services, created the conditions for epidemic disease. Brigandage and crime of all sorts flourished amid the social and economic dislocation attendant upon famine and sickness. The shortage of labor and the temporary slack-

52. *Ibid.*, 1787.

53. See, in particular, the works of Pierre Goubert cited above (n. 39); Emmanuel LeRoy Ladurie, *Les paysans du Languedoc* (1966); George Rudé, *The Crowd in History* (1964); and Peter Laslett, *The World We Have Lost* (1965). For Mexico, see the suggestive work of Florescano, *Precios del maíz*.

ening in the purchasing power of most consumers affected manufacturing output ruinously.[54]

Thus all of the elements of the subsistence crisis were present in the Guadalajara area, as well as in most of New Spain, during the episode of 1785-1786. But the crisis of 1785-1786 was not unique: similar episodes occurred in a cyclical pattern, as Florescano has pointed out, albeit with less intensity, such as the harvest failures of 1749-1750 and 1809-1810.[55] Maize prices had begun to show a tendency to rise before 1785, and continued to do so afterward. The development of the urban market for foodstuffs, and the changes in the agricultural sector which these brought about, also antedated the famine of 1785-1786, and proceeded during the remaining years of the colonial period. The mortality of the years 1785-1786, though severe, certainly was no Malthusian demographic disaster on the scale of the Black Plague or even of some of the smallpox epidemics which attacked New Spain in the eighteenth century. Indeed, demographic figures for the León area indicate that marriage, baptism, and death rates had returned to their normal levels by 1788,[56] and more detailed demographic research on the Guadalajara region would probably yield similar results.

The desperate years of 1785-1786 did not constitute a crisis, then, in the sense that they caused any basic structural change in the rural economy or in the relationship of the city and the surrounding countryside. While it is true that the terrible conditions of these two years reinforced the determination of the municipal and royal governments to assure the food supply of the city, such a trend was already evident before 1785. No other term appears adequate to describe the kind of situation which has been called a "subsistence crisis." Nonetheless, it is important to place the dramatic events of 1785-1786 in their appropriate context, and to see that they were a symptom of a certain type of pre-industrial economic structure and the strains which wracked it.

54. This type of secondary effect upon industry, particularly textiles, is described by Goubert in *Beauvais et le Beauvaisis*. Inasmuch as Guadalajara possessed a thriving textile manufacture, later to rival Puebla's in importance, industrial output probably dropped during 1785-1786, but the available data do not as yet permit a detailed description of this (Florescano, *Precios del maíz*, p. 153).

55. Florescano, *Precios del maíz*, passim.

56. Brading and Wu, "Population Growth and Crisis," p. 34.

PART III. THE FLOWERING

OF THE HACIENDA SYSTEM

CHAPTER 6

The Late Colonial Hacienda— An Introduction

This chapter and those that follow will deal with the functions of the hacienda within the rural economy of the Guadalajara region in the eighteenth and early nineteenth centuries. Not only was the great estate the most highly visible social and economic institution in the late colonial countryside, but it dominated the factors of agricultural production—land, labor, and capital—and supplied the city with most of its staple foodstuffs. Late colonial observers knew intuitively what an hacienda was, in contrast to other types of agricultural holdings. Fray José Alejandro Patiño, the Franciscan curate of the parish of Tlajomulco, provided an interesting if somewhat vague definition of both haciendas and ranchos in his "Relación geográfica" of Tlajomulco, written in 1778:

Haciendas, in these American realms, are country houses belonging to people of more than average means, with lands for cattle, horses, and sheep, breeding pastures, and agricultural lands on which, more or less according to the capabilities of each owner, are produced various grains and livestock. Ranchos, in these realms of the Indies, are country houses of little pomp and small value occupied by men of modest means, or the poor, who cultivate the small parcels which they own or rent according to their available resources, and on which they raise domestic animals and livestock.[1]

1. BPE-MC, leg. 50, vol. 3, exp. 3.

Table 10.

Haciendas and Ranchos in the Intendancy of Guadalajara, 1791

Jurisdiction	Number of Haciendas	Number of Ranchos	Ratio of Ranchos to Haciendas
San Cristóbal de la Barranca	15	21	1.4:1
Tonalá	3	6	2:1
Tlajomulco	7	22	3:1
Tala	4	18	4.5:1
Santa María de los Lagos	45	295	6.5:1
La Barca	18	684	38:1
Cuquío	1	85	85:1
Tepatitlán	3	1,528	509:1

SOURCE:
BPE-MC, leg. 42, vol. 2, 1793.

Patiño's definition points to the amount of capital investment, the size of the landholding, and the variety of agricultural and livestock production as the most important criteria in distinguishing between haciendas and ranchos. Also strongly implied in Fray Alejandro's discussion is an association between a given landowner's socio-economic status and the designation of his property.[2]

In addition to the economic and social dimensions pointed up by Patiño's definitions of hacienda and rancho, it was widely recognized that certain geographic areas were characterized by the dominance of either large or small landholdings. The "Noticias varias de Nueva Galicia" of 1791, for example, was prepared on the basis of information remitted to the capital of the Intendancy by provincial magistrates, which included a count of the haciendas and ranchos in various jurisdictions. Table 10 gives this information, with the jurisdictions ranked in ascending order of the ratio of ranchos to haciendas.

2. Thus, the property of a wealthy individual ("personas de más que mediano caudal") might automatically be considered an hacienda, while that of a person of the rural middle or lower groups ("hombres de mediano pasar, o pobres") would be classed as a rancho. This curious inversion, so strange to our eyes, would seem rather unlikely were it not for the fact that rural properties did, in fact, change their designations from rancho to hacienda on occasion, and that such changes were sometimes related to the ascendancy of socially mobile individuals. For example, the sitio Los Sauces, near Tala, was referred to in one generation as a rancho and in the following generation as an hacienda, even though it remained the same size (AIPG, Tierras, leg. 41, exp. 17, 1796). Similarly, the Rancho de Tetán, a small but rather intensively farmed

One of the difficulties with the kind of material presented in Table 10 is that a precise definition of the term "rancho" is nowhere explicitly given. Its many distinct referents included small hamlets or other rural population concentrations, independently owned small properties, and rented holdings which could be organic parts of larger properties or only loosely annexed to them.[3] In the "Noticias varias," the distinguishing feature of the rancho, whether owned or rented, seems to have been its independent existence as a landholding, based upon what may be termed titular identity (land titles or accepted usage). The jurisdictions of San Cristóbal, Tonalá, Tlajomulco, and Tala, relatively close to Guadalajara and strongly tied to the urban market for grain and meat, contrasted markedly with those areas lying farther to the east and northeast—La Barca, Cuquío, and Tepatitlán—which were less strongly connected economically to the city, with sparser populations scattered around the countryside on numerous smallholdings.

With the exception of Santa María de los Lagos, which constituted something of an anomaly, the apparent quirkiness of some of the figures in Table 10 can be accounted for fairly easily. La Barca embraced a large area, including part of the Altos of Jalisco, as well as the rich belt of mixed-farming haciendas stretching along the northern margins of Lake Chapala (e.g., Cedros, Atequiza, Buenavista, etc.). Its high proportion of ranchos thus corresponded more closely to the Altos pattern of a multitude of small, independent units of production, while its large number of haciendas put it squarely within the agricultural heartland of the Guadalajara region. San Cristóbal de la Barranca, not particularly noted for its agricultural richness, had the lowest ratio of ranchos to haciendas (1.4:1), explained largely by the fact that there was much sugar-growing in this district because of its proximity to the Río Grande de Santiago. Since sugar production required a relatively high degree of capital investment, even if done on a fairly small scale, the sugar-producing properties in this area were generally designated as haciendas.

Moving beyond such phenomenological descriptions, one of the earliest, and still the most systematic, modern attempts to build a model of the Latin American hacienda was that of the social anthropologists Eric Wolf and Sidney Mintz in an article which appeared over twenty years ago.[4]

---

property near the pueblo of Analco on the outskirts of the city, was originally owned by an Indian cacique woman of Analco, who married a Spaniard named Villamayor. By 1746 the property was referred to not as a rancho but as an "haciendita," apparently on the strength of some capital investment and the status of the owners (BPE-BD, leg. 94, no exp. no., 1749). Manuel Payno satirized this kind of thing in his great *costumbrista* novel, *Los bandidos de Río Frío* (1959).

3. Jan Bazant points to the difficulty of concretizing the terms "hacienda" and "rancho"; see his "Una tarea primordial de la historia económica latinoamericana" (1972), p. 113.

4. Wolf and Mintz, "Haciendas and Plantations in Middle America and the Antilles."

They chose to deal not with a historical analysis of the classical Mexican hacienda as it had emerged from the pages of François Chevalier's pioneering work,[5] or from that of Woodrow Borah on the seventeenth century,[6] but with a set of important variables which, though held in common with the lowland plantation, set the hacienda apart from it: capital, labor, land, markets, technology, and social sanctions. Their view was basically that the hacienda as a type of rural economic and social organization should be studied as a nexus of relationships among these variables, and not as a static model.[7] Indeed, more recent studies of rural economic and social structures have stressed the multiplex character of the Latin American great estate and the difficulty of generalizing about its nature, despite the constancy of the major variables through time and space.[8]

The most useful approach, therefore, is to look at the hacienda as a nexus of relationships whose equilibrium was determined by the ecological, social, and economic context. If we take this view of the matter, the problem of identifying an hacienda then becomes both a question of function and a matter of degree. In terms of the major variables of capital, labor, land, markets, technology, and social sanctions, haciendas performed certain economic functions in ways that were different from, or not available to, smaller units of production. In the Guadalajara region, as elsewhere in central Mexico, however, there was so much overlap in these variables among haciendas, and between haciendas and less developed holdings, that rigid criteria for the establishment of models are not appropriate. In terms of the land variable, for example, larger ranchos and smaller haciendas overlapped. The relatively small but important grain-producing haciendas on the outskirts of Guadalajara included Nuestra Señora del Rosario, Oblatos, and San Nicolás de Toluquilla, all ranging between four and five thousand acres in size.[9] It was not at all unusual for mixed-farming ranchos, such as El Potrero (Tonalá), Casas Caídas (Poncitlán), and Los Curieles (Colimilla-Matatlán), to be in the same size range.[10] On the other hand, no hacienda was ever as small as some of the two-to-five acre

5. Chevalier, *La formation.*

6. Borah, *New Spain's Century of Depression.*

7. Wolf and Mintz, "Haciendas and Plantations," p. 408.

8. See, for example, Gibson, *The Aztecs*; William Taylor, *Landlord and Peasant in Colonial Oaxaca*, which discusses a variety of Spanish landholdings all referred to as haciendas, but which differed from each other in many ways; and Mörner, "The Spanish American Hacienda," pp. 185-186, on the difficulty of definitions.

9. Rosario, 1744—AIPG, prot. Mena mayor, 31:255v-266v. Oblatos, 1784—BPE-AJA, 131:2:1384. San Nicolás, 1705—AIPG, prot. Ayala Natera, 3:45v-49. San Nicolás was referred to around 1700 as San Nicolás de Zapotepec, and the Toluquilla Valley, in which it was located, as the Zapotepec Valley.

10. El Potrero, 1767—AIPG, prot. Berroa, 10:390-391. Casas Caídas, 1720—AIPG, prot. Mena mayor, 10:356-363. Los Curieles, 1747—AIPG, prot. Mena mayor, 33:110-112v.

parcels rented out on the city *ejidos*—also called ranchos—or even of the numerous ranchos in the under-1,000-acre range; and nothing called a rancho ever attained the dimensions of the great haciendas of El Cabezón-La Vega, Atequiza, or Cuisillos. Thus while the size of the landholding was not the sole determining factor in assigning the unit to one category or the other, there was a definite tendency for haciendas to be large, in terms of acreage, and ranchos small.

Similarly, most of the other variables differed in some degree or other across the entire spectrum of property types. Ranchos and *labores* (grain farms) were tied into the rural credit system through the supplies and working capital they received from city or provincial merchants (*aviadores*).[11] Small properties of various designations (*ranchos, labores, sitios*) employed wage labor, though they generally did not have substantial populations of resident laborers.[12] By the same token, properties of all sizes and types of organization, from Indian communal holdings to great haciendas, could produce wheat, as well as maize, for a market, be it that of provincial towns or of Guadalajara. The technology employed by small and large production units was about the same. But where more capital was invested and production was geared to a larger market, a greater amount of the available technology, especially irrigation, was in use.

If the late colonial hacienda in the Guadalajara region had any uniquely distinguishing features as a unit of rural economic and social organization, they were its resident labor force, the status aspirations of its owners, and the tendency of those owners to be absentees.[13] This is not the *reductio ad absurdum* it might at first appear to be, since a strong case can be made that labor use and relationships constituted the core variable around which the classical Spanish American hacienda evolved.[14] Indeed, the accessibility of labor and the ways in which it was recruited and held were

11. E.g., *avíos* by a Guadalajara merchant to an unnamed rancho in Tlajomulco, 1758 (AIPG, prot. Leyva Carrillo, 1:362-363), among numerous examples.

12. E.g., AIPG, prot. García, 14:104-118, 1717.

13. Regarding the status aspirations of large landowners, see Wolf and Mintz, "Haciendas and Plantations," p. 387, and the discussion in Mörner, "The Spanish American Hacienda," pp. 192-193. Most of the major landowners of the Guadalajara region were absent from their properties during all or part of the year, though they did tend to return at critical times of the planting and harvesting cycles, as it was generally accepted that they should. In 1792, for example, the *mayorazgo* Joaquín Ignacio de Echauri refused to accept his election as a regidor of Guadalajara on the grounds that his extensive properties in the Sayula district required his personal attention (AHMG, no caja no., 1792). The subdelegado of Aguascalientes had some sharp comments on the absenteeism so prevalent among the important hacendados of the area (AHMG, caja 28, 1813, *censo* of Aguascalientes).

14. On the role of labor relationships in hacienda social and economic organization, see Wolf and Mintz, "Haciendas and Plantations," pp. 389-393. In their view, however, it is the availability of capital rather than labor which is the "strategic initiating condition" in the emergence of the hacienda, as opposed to the plantation type of organization (p. 390). See

one of the two necessary factors in the development of the hacienda economy of the Guadalajara region during the eighteenth century, the other being the growth of the urban market.

Necessary, but not sufficient. And it is here that the interrelatedness of the several variables mentioned above becomes clear. Without sufficient and fairly lavish use of capital and labor, the availability of land, the development of an urban market, and an appropriate technology, the changes in rural economic organization described in these chapters would never have come about. It was precisely the great rural estate as a unit of production which was most profoundly affected by the trends of the late colonial period. All these variables in combination, then, with the added dimension of size (greater amounts of land, numbers of laborers, fixed capital investments, connections to the urban market, use of available technology), constitute a definition of what an hacienda was, and what it did. The great rural estate of the late colonial period was thus more a set of interlocking relationships, or systems, than an entity with fixed and exclusive characteristics. Each of the major variables discussed above is therefore dealt with in a separate chapter in this study, except for technology, which is subsumed in Chapter 10 under changes in the nature of agricultural production, and social sanctions, which are dealt with only in passing.[15]

It has become increasingly apparent over the past twenty years or so that the most meaningful point of view for the study of Latin American agrarian history, particularly for the colonial period, is from the region or subregion, often centering on a city or important town. This is no accident, considering the crucial role which regionalism—economic, social, and political—has played in the evolution of Latin America. It is true that the view outward from a single great estate—the view from the *mirador*, as it were—has produced and will produce in the future many valuable studies which provide innumerable insights into the social and economic life of the countryside.[16] Nonetheless, the single-estate perspective makes for a cer-

---

also Mörner, "The Spanish American Hacienda," pp. 199-203; Borah, *New Spain's Century of Depression*, p. 39; and Jan Bazant, "Peones, arrendatarios y aparceros en México, 1851-1853," *Historia Mexicana* 90 (1973), p. 332.

15. The interaction between the social functions of the hacienda and its economic functions is one of the most interesting questions to be asked about Spanish American rural history, and is touched upon in Chapters 8 and 11.

16. In addition to the works cited above in the Introduction, examples of this kind of basically entrepreneurial history include Edith B. Couturier's doctoral dissertation, "Hacienda of Hueyapán: The History of a Mexican Social and Economic Institution, 1550-1940" (1965), and James D. Riley's article, "Santa Lucía: desarrollo y administración de una hacienda jesuíta en el siglo XVIII," *Historia Mexicana* 23 (1973); while Bazant's article, "Peones, arrendatarios y aparceros," examines a more specialized question, that of the labor system, from the perspective of a single estate. See also the large number of studies cited by Mörner in "The Spanish American Hacienda."

tain solipsism in the study of agrarian structures which obscures some of the most important aspects of their history.

The relationships which made up the colonial rural economy are more easily understandable if we look at an area large enough to minimize the particular characteristics of a single estate, but sufficiently well-defined that all of the major variables can be delimited in some form. The geographical concept of the region seems to fit these criteria, and it is studies of regions, of valleys, or of valley systems, which have so far been the most productive in explaining how haciendas functioned in Latin America. This study on the rural economy in general, and on the hacienda system in particular, is therefore based on a fairly large region, corresponding to the agricultural hinterland of Guadalajara. Having looked at the development of the city as a market, and in part at the response of various sectors of the agricultural economy to that development, we will now examine the nature of the changes brought about in the late colonial countryside by this confluence of events.

CHAPTER 7

Hacienda Ownership— Stability and Instability

The General Trend in Hacienda Turnovers

In recent years, the development of the great landed estate in Latin America has been investigated in a number of essentially entrepreneurial histories, such as those of Richard Pares, Ward Barrett, and Charles H. Harris.[1] Yet despite their enormous value, these studies, by their very nature, have contributed to the notion that the great estate in Latin America was a stable, if not changeless, institution which at all times and places partook of a patriarchal, even feudal, character. The concomitant of this picture is that great rural estates were stable in their ownership—that they belonged to the same families for generations or even centuries at a time. The value of entrepreneurial history, of course, is that it attempts to study one enterprise over a significant period of time on the basis of continuous data. And it is a fact that those bodies of data which allow such intensive studies of a single enterprise are generally pre-selected by the very survival of that enterprise, often within one family, as a stable concern for a very long time-span. For colonial Mexico, the stereotypical view of the great landed estate held in one family for many generations has been stated by François Chevalier:

1. Pares, *A West-India Fortune*; Barrett, *The Sugar Hacienda of the Marqueses del Valle*; Charles Harris, *A Mexican Family Empire*. For a survey of literature, see Mörner, "The Spanish American Hacienda."

In the seventeenth century, the true owners of haciendas were families and lineages, rather than individuals. Some estates were owned jointly by a number of relatives and, therefore, could not be divided; many others were entailed, so that individual owners could not dispose of their property, which remained indissolubly linked to a family name, a pedigree, or, sometimes, to a title.[2]

Entailed estates, primogeniture, and noble titles were certainly important in the colonial land-tenure system, but they by no means dominated the land- scape even in the eighteenth century, the heyday of the Mexican aristoc- racy.[3] David Brading's work indicates that there was a much greater degree of social mobility into and out of the elite stratum in the late colonial period than had previously been thought; Doris Ladd and François Che- valier have also described the mechanisms by which great aristocratic for- tunes were made, preserved, and sometimes ennobled.[4] But fortunes of all sizes were dissipated as well as accumulated, and the *latifundia* which formed so important a part of most colonial fortunes were lost to individ- uals and families with great frequency. William B. Taylor's study of ha- ciendas in colonial Oaxaca indicates that, in fact, most non-entailed estates changed hands more frequently by sale than by inheritance, and that Spanish landownership became increasingly unstable in the late colonial period.[5]

A study of land transfers during the eighteenth century for the Guada- lajara area testifies to the endemic instability of Spanish land ownership. Figure 12 presents a compilation of 375 land sales and other transfers spanning the years 1700 to 1815 and covering about 80 haciendas, almost all of them in central New Galicia.[6] Each of the properties in the sample changed hands by sale an average of 4.68 times during the 115 years, or

2. Chevalier, *Land and Society*, p. 299.

3. On the titled aristocracy, see Doris Ladd's doctoral dissertation, "The Mexican Nobility at Independence" (1972); and David A. Brading, *Miners and Merchants in Bourbon Mexico* (1971).

4. See also the article by John M. Tutino, "Hacienda Social Relations in Mexico," *Hispanic American Historical Review* 55 (1975).

5. William Taylor, *Landlord and Peasant*, pp. 140-141.

6. The vast majority of the transactions represented in Figure 12 are sales, whether private or at public auction resulting from some type of bankruptcy proceeding. Included also are cessions of property by one individual to another, but not within the same family. Transfers by inheritance are specifically excluded. The source of the information on these properties is in almost every case the notarial registers in the AIPG, with a scattering of data from land suits and other judicial proceedings, tax records, and municipal records. The geographical coverage corresponds to the Guadalajara region as defined in Chapter 1 above. In the nature of things, not every sale or other transfer of all the 80 or so rural estates covered in the sample found its way into the compilation. For a few properties, there are conspicuous gaps in the data on the history of their ownership; in general, however, the coverage of the properties in the sample is fairly complete. This is borne out by the close correspondence between the

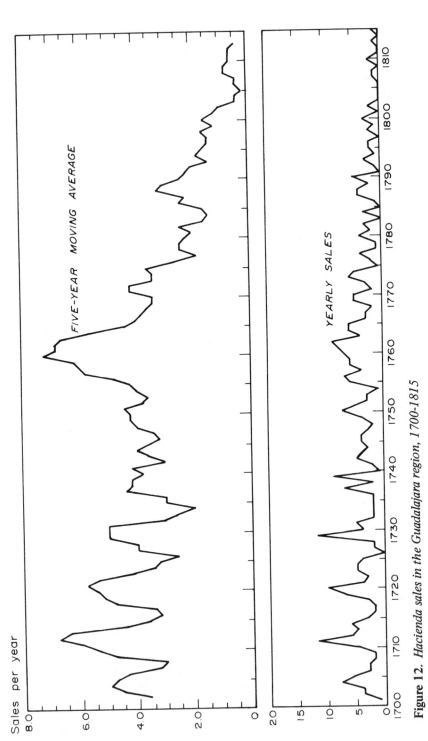

Figure 12. *Hacienda sales in the Guadalajara region, 1700-1815*

SOURCE: AIPG, prots., various notaries.

about once every 25 years. The overwhelming majority of these transfers took the properties out of one family and into another. Although the average possession for a quarter-century hardly indicates that properties changed hands rapidly for speculative purposes, neither does it bear out the image of great seigneurial establishments kept within one family for generations.

A second striking characteristic about these land transfers is their marked periodicity, made particularly clear by the graph of yearly sales. The peaks, representing seven to twelve sales, occur with regularity every decade up to the midcentury: 1711, 1720, 1729, 1739, and 1750. These ten-year cycles are still evident in the graph of the five-year moving average of sales over the same period, though because of the averaging function they are not so precisely centered on the decades. After 1760, the magnitude of the yearly fluctuation decreases and the ten-year cycle all but disappears in both graphs. Interestingly enough, the cyclical pattern of sales corresponds very closely to maize prices and meteorological data presented by both Enrique Florescano and Charles Gibson.[7] Even though price data for the Guadalajara area do not permit the kind of reconstruction of long-term movements possible for central Mexico, contemporary testimony does indicate that the years in which hacienda sales were most numerous were those of bad harvests, scarcity, and high prices. This means that haciendas, far from being always in a position to benefit from scarcity and rising prices in hard or disastrous years, were subject to ruin, bankruptcy, and unavoidable or even forced sale. The reasons for this are complex, but the fact remains that the great rural estate seems to have been in a quite precarious position during the first half of the eighteenth century, and that it was extremely vulnerable to financial collapse and resulting sale. This certainly undercuts the notion of stability of ownership.

The situation in the Guadalajara area changed markedly in the latter third of the eighteenth and the first years of the nineteenth century. After a flurry of sales from about 1755 to 1765, the yearly average number of sales declined from four per year to two per year in 1780 and less than one per year after 1800. Put another way, the 80 or so haciendas composing the sample were sold more than twice as often from 1700 to 1760 (3.2 times) as

---

cumulative sales history of the 35 haciendas for which virtually complete information is available, and the larger sample of some 80 estates. And lest it be thought that the drop in the average frequency of sale after 1760 is due to a lack of information, it should be noted that notary coverage for the latter part of the eighteenth century is, if anything, more detailed and more complete than that for the first part of the century. Thus, if there is any error stemming from inadequate data, it is more likely to produce a lower sales-rate for the first half of the eighteenth century than for its second half and the early years of the nineteenth century.

7. Florescano, *Precios del maíz*, p. 113; Gibson, *The Aztecs*, pp. 455-459.

they were from 1760 to 1815 (1.5 times). Aside from the midcentury flurry of selling there is one other obvious reversal in the half-century decline in hacienda sales, during the years between 1785 and 1790 or 1792. What factors may have accounted for the resurgence of sales in the decade 1755-1765 is not clear. Inasmuch as this notable increase in the frequency of sales is much more obvious in the graph of the five-year moving average, some of its magnitude may be due to the anticipatory nature of the moving average as a statistical technique.[8] Then again, the years just after 1760 were not good for producers of grain in the Guadalajara area, and a succession of abnormally small harvests may have accounted for some of the sales in these years. Finally, it may be that the resurgence of hacienda sales in the decade 1755-1765 represented a response to economic strains attendant upon the development of commercialized agriculture, obviously in full swing by the end of the 1760s, winnowing out landowners who were without sufficient capital resources to respond to the increasing needs of the urban market. As to the increase in the number of sales between 1785 and 1790 or so, this was almost certainly due to the subsistence disaster and associated hardships of the years 1785 and 1786.

The decline in the frequency of hacienda sales in the last third of the eighteenth century indicates that landowners were able in this period to hold onto their estates longer. Independent confirmation of this trend comes from another area of Mexico as well. William Taylor found that in the area around Oaxaca, sales were especially frequent between 1699 and 1761, falling off somewhat thereafter.[9] Furthermore, maize-price series for central Mexico indicate that after about 1780 the ten-year cyclical pattern of prices broke down, movement in general became more capricious, and oscillations were more intense.[10] If we can reasonably assume that grain production and prices in the Guadalajara region underwent the same kind of movement during the eighteenth century as that in central Mexico, it is evident that the ownership of rural estates in central New Galicia was becoming increasingly stable at the same time that grain production and prices were becoming less stable. This suggests that the hacienda as an economic enterprise was becoming more profitable and better able to withstand the fluctuations in weather, productivity, and the demands of the market. The increased viability of the rural estate in the late eighteenth century was due in large measure to an increase in (primarily urban) demand for agricultural products, an elastic labor supply, and what may be

8. Paul G. Hoel, *Elementary Statistics*, 2nd ed. (1966), p. 292.

9. Taylor, *Landlord and Peasant*, p. 141. It is interesting to note that for the eighteenth century, Taylor's average frequency of sale for properties with complete transfer histories was once about every 25, the same as the average for the sample in Figure 12.

10. Florescano, *Precios del maíz*, p. 118.

called the recapitalization of many of the haciendas of greatest productive potential.

A more restricted sample of 35 important haciendas for which virtually complete transfer records exist illustrates more precisely the nature of property sales, and will serve as a springboard for a more detailed discussion of why and how rural estates changed hands during the period. Table 11 lists these properties by district, together with the dates of sale during the eighteenth century.

In general, the information concerning these estates confirms the trend of the larger sample set forth in Figure 12. The total number of sales for the smaller sample is 150, which means that over the 115-year period under discussion each property in the sample was sold 4.28 times. This accords reasonably well with the 4.68 average for the larger sample. Furthermore, the long-term trend for the eighteenth century is very similar among the haciendas of the smaller sample. If the century is divided into quarters, with the years to 1815 added onto the last quarter, the results look like this:

	Sample of 80 Haciendas		*Sample of 35 Haciendas*	
	Total number of sales	Percentage of total	Total number of sales	Percentage of total
1701-1725	114	30.4%	52	34.67%
1726-1750	90	24.0	26	17.33
1751-1775	114	30.4	46	30.67
1776-1815	57	15.2	26	17.33

The 35 properties which make up the smaller sample were the most important haciendas of the Guadalajara region. The characteristics they had in common were their relatively centralized location with respect to the city of Guadalajara, their high degree of orientation to the urban market for foodstuffs, and their relatively high capital value. With the single exception of Cerrogordo, which lay formally within the huge administrative jurisdiction of La Barca but actually on the margins of the Bajío, all 35 properties were located in the immediate environs of the city, in the depression of the Santiago River to the near north, on the basin and margins of Lake Chapala, or in the Ameca-Cocula Valley. All these estates thus had relatively easy access to Guadalajara, close enough that transport costs to the city were not prohibitively high. Virtually without exception they produced maize and cattle, some of them in sufficient quantities to be major suppliers of the urban market, some of them only to meet their own or purely local needs. A surprisingly large number of them produced wheat, especially in the latter part of the eighteenth century, which they marketed in Guadalajara. An even more specialized cash crop was sugar, produced primarily on the estates to the north and northwest of the city, near San

Table 11.

Sales Histories of 35 Selected Haciendas in the Guadalajara Region in the Eighteenth Century

---

San Cristóbal de la Barranca
  Copala–1697, 1702, 1707, 1716, 1732, 1758, 1763, 1773, 1777, 1791
  Epatán–1728, *1780
  San Antonio de Guastla–*1760, 1762, 1768, 1777, *1790, 1794, *1804
  La Magdalena–1727, 1760, 1788, 1793, 1796, 1808
  Santa Lucía–1722, *1736
  Martel–1727, 1760, 1793

Toluquilla Valley
  La Capacha–1712, 1713, 1714, 1714, 1750, 1760, 1762, 1765
  La Concepción–1705, 1720, 1739, 1755
  Nuestra Señora del Rosario–1712, 1715, 1744, *1770, *1810
  Los Oblatos–1701, 1711, 1715, 1724, 1725, 1755, 1784, *1810
  San José de Zapotepec–1707, 1716, 1737, 1760, 1764, 1765, 1767, 1768
  San Nicolás de Zapotepec–1705, 1712, 1718, 1751, 1755, 1759
  Santa Cruz–*1700, 1704, 1781
  Toluquilla (also known as El Cuatro)–1770, 1817

Tequila
  San Martín–*1700, 1717, 1729, 1756, 1758, 1786

Cuquío
  Izcuintla–1712, 1713, 1724, 1735, 1760, 1761, *1780, 1802
  Miraflores–1693, 1702, 1712, *1725, 1755, 1782

La Barca
  (e)Cerrogordo–*1720, *1740

Chapala
  Atequiza–1725, 1751, 1784, 1819
  San José de Buenavista–1760, 1770
  San Nicolás de Buenavista–1787, 1795
  Cedros–1711, 1742

Jocotepec
  (e)Huejotitán–1733
  Potrerillos–1712, 1714, 1729, 1739, 1739

Tlajomulco
  San Lucas–1757, 1762, 1767, *1773

Table 11. (continued)
*Sales Histories of 35 Selected Haciendas in the Guadalajara Region
in the Eighteenth Century*

Tala

(e)Cuisillos—*1700, 1710
Cuspala—1751, 1765
(e)Mazatepec-Santa Ana Acatlán—none
Navajas—1704, 1708, 1710, 1711, 1727, 1736, 1745, 1750, 1767, 1769,
1773, *1780
Salitre—1712, 1712, 1732, 1734, 1747, 1751

Ahualulco

La Gavilana—*1700, *1730, 1774
Paso de Flores—1743

Ameca-Cocula

Buenavista—1739, 1774
(e)El Cabezón-La Vega—*1697, 1725, 1747, 1769
Estipac—1769

SOURCE:
AIPG, prots., various notaries.

NOTES:
The same year appearing twice in succession indicates two sales in that year. An asterisk
indicates an approximate date; an "e" in parentheses before a name indicates that it was
entailed from the last date of sale.

Cristóbal de la Barranca, where water was relatively abundant. Sugar in
more limited quantities was also produced, however, around Tequila (San
Martín and a number of smaller properties), Tala (Cuisillos), and Ameca
(El Cabezón). All of these estates, especially during the latter part of the
eighteenth century, were characterized by a relatively heavy capital investment in their buildings, storage facilities, and irrigation works, and large
inventories of livestock. When they were sold, their prices tended to be
higher than outlying haciendas, even those of larger size, and when they
were leased out (a fairly infrequent occurrence), they fetched higher rents.

Aside from these three common characteristics—location, market orientation, and capital value—the 35 haciendas in the sample cover an extremely broad range in terms of their individual histories, size, and structure. Indeed, it is this *sui-generis* quality about colonial rural estates which
makes it so perilous and difficult to generalize.[11] In size these 35 haciendas

11. See Mörner, "The Spanish American Hacienda," pp. 185-186.

ranged from the enormous Cuisillos (the largest hacienda in central New Galicia) at more than 100,000 acres (22 *sitios de ganado mayor*, 6 *sitios de ganado menor*, and 68 *caballerías*), to the diminutive Oblatos at about 4,000 acres (2 sitios de ganado menor and other small parcels). Because of high land values, there was, to be sure, a certain tendency for the larger haciendas to be located farther from the city, but within districts which shared similar endowments in terms of topography, soil quality, and water, diversity in size was the rule rather than the exception. The natural resources available in these production units, and the different decisions made by their owners at various times about the way in which to utilize them, made for a quite varied product mix among these 35 estates.

The history of ownership among these rural estates reflects the diversity of their natural and economic circumstances as well as those manifold accidents and quirks effected by human agency. As we have seen, each of the 35 haciendas was sold an average of 4.28 times during the period 1700-1815. The difference between properties in the actual number of sales, however, is quite striking. Some were sold with fair regularity, such as the Hacienda de los Oblatos, near the city (1701, 1711, 1715, 1724, 1725, 1755, 1784, 1810). Still others were sold in peculiar, manic bursts, like La Capacha, a small but fertile estate in the Toluquilla Valley near the city (1712, 1713, twice in 1714, 1750, 1760, 1762, 1765). Nor is there, apart from the general century-long trend characteristic of the estates as a group, any discernible pattern of transfers by sale relating to location or size of property. In the area of San Cristóbal de la Barranca, for example, the Hacienda de Copala, in the latter part of the century an important wheat producer, changed hands some ten times between 1697 and 1791, while the nearby sugar-producing Hacienda de Epatán was sold only twice during the eighteenth century. The small but rich estates of the Toluquilla Valley, in the grain belt describing a crescent from the southeast to the southwest of Guadalajara, changed hands with remarkable frequency, though their ownership showed a definite tendency to stabilize after the 1760s. However, two important grain-producing estates in this area, Toluquilla (later known as El Cuatro) and Santa Cruz, enjoyed virtually uninterrupted ownership during the eighteenth century, by the Jesuits and the Portillo family, respectively. The key in these cases seems to be in the efficiency of management, which was notoriously high by contemporary standards.

If many even potentially rich rural estates changed hands six or eight times during the period 1700-1815, mostly because of the financial problems of their owners, no other single property can match the rueful history of the Hacienda de Navajas. This estate, in the Tala area, was sold twelve times between 1704 and 1780, or once every nine years over the period 1700-1815, as opposed to the general average of once every twenty-five years. Navajas, which changed hands a number of times in the quarter-century before 1700, was subsequently owned by a number of city and provincial merchants, at least two religious (a priest and a nun), and two ecclesiastical corporations. It was embargoed for debt and sold at public auction on at least three occasions, had its sale rescinded once, and was twice involved in protracted probate litigation. The Hacienda de Navajas was a victim of what might be called the revolving-door syndrome, but several factors emerge from the history of this property which can be found in the histories of other haciendas, and which point to a number of important changes characteristic of the eighteenth century.

First, Navajas was sold rather more often during the first sixty years of our extended century (eight times) than during the last sixty years—in this it conforms to the normal behavior as demonstrated in Figure 12, even if the frequency of its transfer makes it an unusual case. Second, Navajas was always heavily encumbered with liens of various sorts against its capital value, and the cumulative weight of these mortgages increased during the eighteenth century. This high level of indebtedness greatly facilitated the rapid turnover of the property in 1711, 1727, 1736, 1745, 1750, 1767, 1769, 1773, and 1780, since the buyer had only to make an acknowledgment (*reconocimiento*) of the existing mortgages and put up a small amount of cash to consummate the sale. This practice meant that men without sufficient financial resources to make necessary capital improvements, to meet operating expenses, or to ride out periods of low prices for agricultural products could fairly easily acquire large properties, something which occurred with Navajas on a number of occasions. In such a situation, low productivity and bankruptcy were virtually inevitable, and the frequency of sale of most haciendas during the early part of the century reflects this. Also, interest payments themselves (at an annual 5 percent) created a substantial drain on the resources of such undercapitalized owners, with the result that a seemingly safe and easy investment could turn into an albatross that sank many a modest fortune into the murky waters of litigation, judicial embargo, and liquidation. Finally, the latter half of the eighteenth century saw Navajas increasing its capital value considerably, despite its reverses—not just through the natural process of inflation, but through active investment, primarily by its last owners, the Portillo family.

Nor was Navajas an isolated case, as we shall see, for most rural estates underwent the same evolution during the eighteenth and early nineteenth centuries. Though in many cases the capital improvements of the late eighteenth century were also financed with borrowed money, rural estates were in a much better financial position at that time to pay the charges of this borrowed capital as well as to provide some margin of profit to the entrepreneur. As far as rural estates were concerned, therefore, the early eighteenth century was a buyer's market, and the later eighteenth century a seller's market.[12]

Entails and Ownership Stability

One very salient difference does emerge from a comparison of the transfer histories of the haciendas for which complete records exist: this is the effectiveness of entailment—the foundation of a *mayorazgo*, an estate inheritable only by the eldest heir, and which could not legally be alienated —in keeping property within the same family for a number of generations. A glance at Table 11 demonstrates this. The great haciendas which were held in entail remained within the same families after the entails were created. Thus the ownership histories of these important estates most closely approximate the traditional model of stability over several generations or even (in the case of the Porres Baranda mayorazgo) centuries.

It is difficult to arrive at an exact figure for the number of mayorazgos existing in central New Galicia in the eighteenth century. Certainly there were a number of large entailed estates on the periphery of the region, including the immense Hacienda de la Ciénega de Mata of the Rincón Gallardo family in the Lagos area, and that of the Marquéses del Villar del Aguila, a huge chunk of which (some 100,000 acres) lay in the jurisdiction of La Barca and was disentailed and sold in 1766.[13] Several were founded during the course of the century, among them the Gómez de Parada entail in Autlán, in 1723,[14] and the Canal entail in Tecolotlán, in 1750.[15] Closer to Guadalajara, there was a small miscellany of minor mayorazgos based upon a mixture of rural and urban holdings, such as those of the Puga y Villanueva family around Atotonilco el Alto, and the Mota entail (at one time held by the lawyer and chronicler of New Galicia, Matías de la Mota Padilla), based primarily upon urban property in Guadalajara, both dating from the seventeenth century.[16] Perhaps the most striking thing about

12. Navajas, 1704—AIPG, prot. Morelos, 2: no page nos. 1708—AIPG, prot. Ayala Natera, 6:280-282v. 1710—AIPG, prot. Ayala Natera, 6:295-299; AIPG, prot. Morelos, 3:40-47. 1727—BPE-BD, leg. 63, exp. 12. 1736—BPE-BD, leg. 108, exp 4. 1745—AIPG, prot. Mena mayor, 32:237v-240v. 1750—AIPG, prot. Mena menor, 8:106v-162v. 1767—BPE-BD, leg. 8, exp. 4. 1769—AIPG, prot. Berroa, 12:290-293v. 1773—AIPG, prot. Berroa, 16:176-177. BPE-BD, leg. 63, exp. 12.

For a more detailed discussion of the role of both private and ecclesiastical capital in this development, see Chapter 9 below. Specifically on the role of the Church as an investor, see Michael P. Costeloe, *Church Wealth in Mexico* (1967), chap. 4; and Arnold J. Bauer, "The Church and Spanish American Agrarian Structure," *The Americas* 28 (1971).

13. AIPG, prot. Berroa, 9:14-31v.   14. AIPG, prot. García, 20:308v and 36:313v-316v.
15. AIPG, prot. Berroa, 25:254.
16. AIPG, prot. Maraver, 16: no page nos.; and prot. Mena mayor, 11:251.

the few but important entailed estates of the Guadalajara region was the lateness of their foundation. In the Oaxaca area, for example, most mayorazgos emerged between 1550 and 1650.[17] In central New Galicia, with the single exception of the Porres Baranda entail, mayorazgos were the product of the eighteenth century, almost all after 1725.[18]

The century's earliest foundation of an entail involved the huge Hacienda de Cuisillos, purchased in 1710 by Pedro Sánchez de Tagle, governor of the Marquesado del Valle de Oaxaca, regidor of Mexico City, Knight of Calatrava, and Marqués de Altamira as husband of the second Marquesa, Luisa Sánchez de Tagle. The global value of the hacienda in 1730, more than 125,000 pesos, compares quite favorably with the values of other late-eighteenth-century noble entails, if one allows for the inflation of property values characteristic of the years after the midcentury.[19] The fifth Marqués de Altamira inherited the hacienda after a period of administration by his brother-in-law and legal guardian Domingo de Trespalacios y Escandón, a former oidor of the Audiencia of Mexico and a member-elect (1763) of the Council of the Indies.[20] The later ownership of the hacienda, after 1800 or so, is cloudy. Apparently it was disentailed at some point, and by the first years of the nineteenth century it had come into the possession of the Marqués de Santa Cruz de Inguanzo.[21]

The histories of the other major entails founded during the eighteenth century are rather less problematical than that of Cuisillos, and all begin in a cluster in the 1750s and 1760s. The first was formed by the González de Castañeda family on the haciendas of Milpillas, Margaritas, and Cerrogordo, all in the La Barca area, dating from about 1750.[22] The next mayorazgo was established in 1757 by Joaquín Fermín de Echauri, a Spanish Navarrese merchant of Guadalajara, based upon four haciendas in the province of Ávalos, in New Spain.[23] Five years later, the patriarch Lorenzo Javier de Villaseñor founded an entail on the magnificent Hacienda de Huejotitán, near Lake Chapala.[24] The substantial wealth and prestige of the Villaseñor family, which lasted through the nineteenth century and beyond, was underwritten by one of the few genuinely agricultural for-

---

17. Taylor, *Landlord and Peasant*, p. 153.

18. For a comprehensive treatment of Mexican noble entails, see Ladd, "The Mexican Nobility," chap. 4.

19. AIPG, prot. García, 29:395-417v; and Ladd, "The Mexican Nobility," p. 134.

20. For the genealogy of the Marqueses de Altamira, see Ladd, "The Mexican Nobility," p. 325.

21. BPE-AJA, 265:5:3617.

22. BPE-AJA, 260:10:3532; Ladd, "The Mexican Nobility," pp. 84 and 313.

23. On the San José de Gracia area, see Luis González, *Pueblo en vilo*; and AIPG, prot. Echasco, 1:66-68v. For the actual instrument of foundation, see AIPG, prot. Mena menor, 19: no page nos.

24. AIPG, prot. Mena menor, 23:59v-61v.

tunes of the region. The last major foundation of the century was the Cañedo entail in 1790, based upon the haciendas of El Cabezón, La Vega, Buenavista, and La Calera, all in the Ameca area. The founder of the mayorazgo, Manuel Calixto Cañedo, had made his initial fortune in the silver mines at Rosario, in the province of Sonora, in partnership with Francisco Javier de Vizcarra, the first Marqués de Panuco (1772), and had converted his assets into a string of rich haciendas besides continuing as a merchant and financier.[25] The holders of the González de Castañeda, Echauri, Villaseñor, and Cañedo entails formed a quartet of disappointed aspirants to noble titles when they were all nominated for the honor by the Ayuntamiento of the city and the Intendant of Guadalajara in 1804, but failed to receive patents.[26]

The foundation of entails, then, could and most often did preserve substantial fortunes within single families for several generations. The essential purpose of the mayorazgo was to underwrite an aristocratic style of life, and in the cases of the Sánchez de Tagle, González de Castañeda, Echauri, Villaseñor, Cañedo, and Vizcarra families it did just that, with varying degrees of grandeur. The establishment and maintenance of a fortune on the basis of agricultural holdings was an inherently risky venture, however, even when insured by the legal provisions of an entail, and the prosperity of the family fortune required luck and perspicacious management in ample proportions. Even when commercial agriculture began to show signs of profitability in the late eighteenth century, large rural estates might require the constant injection of capital from other family resources (e.g., commercial or mining wealth) or the assumption of loans. Where such resources were not available to the landholder, large-scale commercial agriculture was hardly feasible. This appears to have been the case with the great entail of the Porres Baranda family, the Hacienda de Mazatepec, which was the oldest major rural estate in the Guadalajara region to be retained within a single family prior to Independence. The Porres Baranda mayorazgo conforms quite prettily to the stereotype of the once-grand but largely impoverished entail described by both Taylor and Ladd.[27] The decline in the fortunes of the Porres Baranda family is worth some attention, both because of its inherent interest and because it points up some of the problems of landownership in the eighteenth century which will be discussed in more detail below.

25. AIPG, prot. Ballesteros, 13:173v-184v; Cañedo's *memoria de testamento* of 1793 is in *ibid.*, 18:80-91v. For an exhaustive history of the Cañedo family, see Jorge Palomino y Cañedo, *La casa y mayorazgo de Cañedo de Nueva Galicia* (1947); and Ladd, "The Mexican Nobility," p. 342. It is not clear whether the estates held by the ennobled Vizcarra and his heirs were entailed or owned as non-entailed properties (*bienes libres*).

26. Ladd, "The Mexican Nobility," p. 313.

27. Taylor, *Landlord and Peasant*, pp. 152-158; Ladd, "The Mexican Nobility," chap. 4.

The Porres Baranda Entail

The family fortune and the mayorazgo which sought to preserve it were founded by Diego de Porres, *alcalde mayor* of Sombrerete, and later *tesorero real, alférez mayor,* and *alcalde ordinario* of Guadalajara. Porres' wealth was apparently based upon the trade in mules to Zacatecas, San Luis Potosí, and Sombrerete. By 1611 he was reputed to be one of the wealthiest men of New Galicia, with property valued at 360,000 pesos, including agricultural holdings and urban property in Guadalajara. Through his first marriage, Diego de Porres became related to Juan González de Apodaca, the master of Cuisillos, one of the greatest estates of western Mexico, and by his second to Santiago de Vera, long-time president of the Audiencia of Guadalajara.[28] Other dynastic links included the De la Mota family (of the entail of the same name), and the Robles family, for a number of years important landowners in the rich Valley of Toluquilla. Diego de Porres had acquired his first lands in the Cocula Valley about 1580, and by the first decade of the seventeenth century he was one of the major suppliers of foodstuffs of all kinds to the small city of Guadalajara. The patriarch died in about 1620, but not before he founded a vast entail embracing lands between Tala and Zacoalco, to the west of Lake Chapala, as well as a number of tracts in the area to the east of Guadalajara, extending as far as Tepatitlán.

The exact size of the Porres Baranda entail is difficult to determine. As late as 1701, the extent of the mayorazgo lands in the jurisdictions of Colimilla-Matatlán and La Barca was still unknown. During the eighteenth century, the successive holders of the entail were embroiled in almost continual litigation with other landowners and Indian communities in the Zacoalco area over the legal boundaries of the haciendas of Mazatepec and Santa Ana Acatlán, the heart of the entail. Despite the confusions and ambiguities, however, it appears that the actual entailed holdings to the east of Guadalajara amounted to about 80,000 acres in a jumble of bits and pieces (20 sitios de ganado mayor), and that the two major haciendas accounted between them for something on the order of 110,000 acres (19 sitios de ganado mayor, 11 sitios de ganado menor, and 55½ caballerías).[29]

The mid and late seventeenth century was clearly the heyday of the family fortune, though the actual details of its finances during this period are fuzzy. It is clear enough that the wealth of the Porres Barandas was almost entirely based upon the landholdings accumulated early in the century by Diego de Porres, and not upon large-scale commerce or mining or the

28. Chevalier, *La formation*, pp. 213-214; Jesús Amaya, *Los conquistadores Fernández de Híjar y Bracamonte* (1952), pp. 115-118.
29. AIPG, prot. García, 13:226-229v, 1717; AIPG, Tierras, leg. 41, exp. 17, 1796.

holding of government office. Income seems to have been derived almost exclusively from renting out the entailed lands, including the Hacienda de Mazatepec itself, and its sister establishment Santa Ana Acatlán.[30] On occasion all the mayorazgo lands, the two haciendas as well as the holdings to the east of Guadalajara, were leased out together to a single individual.[31] When this happened, all the lands were used together for sheepraising on a large scale, with the flocks pasturing in the Zacoalco area during the drier winter months and passing to the Colimilla-Matatlán area during the rainy season. Such rental agreements were necessarily rather complicated, since they invariably overlapped the leases of numerous small tenants already occupying pieces of agricultural and pasture land, as well as those areas occupied by the livestock of the Porres Baranda family itself. Generally, however, the entailed lands to the east of Guadalajara were all rented out in more-or-less small parcels to individual renters. Indeed, for some years of the early eighteenth century, the registers of those Guadalajara notaries favored by the Porres Baranda family's business virtually teem with lease agreements for small ranches. This style of rentier exploitation continued to be the policy of most of the holders of the family entail right through the colonial period and into the early decades of the nineteenth century.[32]

Owing to the absence of representative accounts for the Porres Baranda properties for any length of time, it is impossible to say to what degree the holders of the entail participated directly in agriculture and stock-raising themselves, or what may be called demesne farming. In fact, they must always have done so to some extent, since the Hacienda de Mazatepec was always considered to be an important supplier of maize, wheat, and meat (predominantly lamb) to Guadalajara. The major question concerns the balance in the income from the entail between rents and direct production, and on this only the most impressionistic evidence is available.

To some degree the Porres Baranda estates followed the general trend of the eighteenth century, at first dependent for direct income upon livestock-raising and shifting more toward demesne farming of cereals in the last decades of the century. The haciendas of Mazatepec and Santa Ana supplied large amounts of maize to the city in the mid-eighteenth century and maintained their position as important suppliers into the first two decades of the nineteenth century, though their relative contributions declined after 1812. The two estates also produced substantial quantities of wheat and

30. The leases are in AIPG, prot. Ascoide, 1:156, 1683; prot. Morelos, 1:115-117v, 1699; AIPG, Tierras, leg. 33, exp. 37, 1701; prot. García, 27:49, 1728.

31. AIPG, prot. García, 13:226-229v.

32. The leases for Mazatepec and Santa Ana Acatlán are in AIPG, prot. Sandi, 19: no page nos., 1825; and prot. Altamirano, 6:73-74 and 6:114-115v, 1833.

flour, supplying the city of Guadalajara with a remarkably consistent 12 percent of its consumption in the years for which complete records are available. Much of this, however, as with the maize, was produced and sent into the city by renters. In 1786, for example, in response to an urgent inquiry from the cabildo of the city, the tithe administrator for the Cocula area stated that he had collected from Mazatepec's *arrendatarios* about 102 cargas of wheat from that year's harvest, which would yield a total production figure of about 1,000 cargas. The Hacienda de Santa Ana produced some 200 cargas from its harvest, all belonging to a renter, and the direct production on Mazatepec, belonging to the then-holder of the entail, María Francisca Porres Baranda, amounted to about 600 cargas.[33] The relatively small share of demesne production in the total is obvious, then, with the dominant role being played by a number of renters with resources of varying size.

As to livestock production, the Porres Baranda properties were apparently never very important producers of cattle, but during the entire late colonial period they did participate heavily in the market for sheep. During 1780, for example, the Hacienda de Mazatepec itself directly supplied the urban market, through the abasto de carnes, with some 3,500 sheep, accounting for over a third of the total consumed in the city in 1780-1781.[34]

Despite the increasing importance of direct farming by the Porres Baranda family, due in large measure to attempts to recapitalize the haciendas during the last years of the eighteenth century, the role of renters in the production structure of the estates and of rents in the total makeup of entail income is obvious. In this policy, the Porres Baranda estates were something of an anomaly in the late colonial period, since with few exceptions renters appear to have been less important on other large haciendas. In 1803, writing to the court-appointed *depositario* of the entail, the administrator of Mazatepec commented on the necessity of rental income to supplement demesne farming.[35] Certainly other local haciendas had renters and sharecroppers on them, but none was as dependent on them for income as the Porres Baranda entail. Indeed, an effort by the husband of the *mayorazga* María Francisca to reverse this dependence is in part responsible for some of the financial problems suffered by the estate in the years around 1800.

The decline in the family fortunes of the Porres Barandas seems to have begun definitively in the 1750s, during the life of the mayorazgo Francisco Porres Baranda. In the early decades of the century, Francisco's wealth seems still to have been substantial, since he frequently made loans to Guadalajara merchants during the 1720s.[36] His troubles seem to have be-

33. AHMG, caja 11, exp. 2, 1786.   34. AHMG, caja 25, 1780.
35. BPE-AJA, 235:3:3080.   36. AIPG, prot. García, 18:120.

gun with a perhaps too prodigal use of his money and the assumption of a bad debt of several thousand pesos for which he had been a friend's guarantor. Out of this incident grew a protracted lawsuit and claims against the entail for a number of other outstanding debts.[37] By the early 1750s Francisco Porres Baranda, at that time a *regidor perpetuo* on the Guadalajara cabildo, had no non-entailed property other than a few buildings in the city which he could give as a dowry to his eldest daughter by his second marriage. In 1754 the entailed properties were under an embargo for debts, and a court-appointed interventor was collecting two-thirds of the rents on leased entail lands.[38]

Francisco Porres Baranda died in 1763, and his will of the preceding year adds some details to the picture of financial reverses. The dowry of his first wife, María Francisca de Tenorio, he had spent on "reparos" to the entailed properties, since these had been somewhat in decline when he inherited them. However, this limited attempt to revive the flagging family fortunes was wiped out by bad harvests and other reverses, resulting in the embargo of the mid-1750s and still-pending litigation. Francisco said in his testament that he had fully satisfied all claims against the estate by the children of his first marriage (one of whom, Bernardo, succeeded his father as holder of the entail after the death of his elder brother Miguel), but was unable to provide dowries to any of his three daughters by his second marriage. He claimed never to have received 5,000 pesos of his first wife's dowry, and his second marriage brought him only 700 pesos. He had been sued by one of his sons-in-law and had had to pay a settlement of more than 5,000 pesos. He had renounced his office of *regidor alférez real* in favor of another son-in-law, but the sum of money he had received in return had been consumed in legal expenses. Francisco was owed 1,000 pesos back rental on the entailed *obraje* in Guadalajara, but a number of other small debts in favor of his estate were deemed uncollectable. The bequests he could afford to make were all small, and at his death there were a number of outstanding claims against the estate by his children. Apparently to satisfy these and other liabilities, Francisco's Hacienda de Cuspala, in the Tala area, which he had purchased largely on credit in the late 1740s and owned outside the Porres Baranda entail, was sold in 1763.[39]

For the twenty-three years between the death of Francisco Porres Baranda in 1763 and the accession of his daughter, María Josefa, to the entail

---

37. A suit brought against the owner of a rural estate by one creditor, not infrequently a convent holding a lien against the property, often resulted in eventual bankruptcy proceedings and forced sale to satisfy the debts. Creditors tended to act much like piranhas—the sight of blood drove them into a frenzy.

38. AIPG, prot. García, 18:120; prot. Mena mayor, 32:16-17v; prot. Leyva Carrillo, 2:97; prot. de Silva, 5:182; prot. Mena menor, 13:369-370.

39. AIPG, prot. Berroa, 5:189v-192v and 6:396-397.

in 1786, the family fortunes seem to have declined slowly but steadily. No major capital investment was undertaken during this period, and Francisco's son Bernardo, while maintaining his position in Guadalajara society and politics, did not advance the value of the family properties, but lived the sybaritic existence of a genteel rentier. During Bernardo's lifetime, the fortunes of the Porres Baranda family became inextricably entwined with those of a Guadalajara merchant, Ignacio Francisco Solano de Estrada, who married into the family and dominated its economic fate for the period between 1786 and 1805. Estrada was a man of social connections, ambition, and reasonable if not outstanding business acumen, whose career in many aspects typifies that of a number of merchants, landowners, and city officeholders of the last decades of the colonial period. Indeed, a broader, prosopographical view of the elite of late colonial Guadalajara would bear out many of the patterns evident in his career—his social origins, his marriage, his economic activities, his civic life—for a large group.

Ignacio de Estrada was born in Mexico City in 1734, the son of a merchant whose father had emigrated from Spain late in the seventeenth century. His family had some kind of kinship and/or mercantile links with Antonio de Colazo Feijoo, one of the most important Guadalajara merchants and landowners (two haciendas in the Toluquilla Valley) of the mid-eighteenth century. By the 1760s young Estrada was in Guadalajara serving as the assistant and general factotum for Colazo Feijoo. He rapidly acquired a modest fortune from his commercial dealings, which included silver-banking, maize-dealing, and a partnership in a wholesale establishment (*tienda de grueso*) with the Rosario miner-turned-hacendado, Mañuel Calixto Cañedo. In 1777, upon his marriage to María Josefa de Porres Baranda, his personal fortune amounted to just over 40,000 pesos. About half of this was tied up in his venture with Cañedo, a small amount consisted of the value of personal possessions, and 18,000 pesos were owed to him in debts. His close association with Cañedo suggests that his silver-banking activities had been on behalf of the Rosario miner.[40] After his marriage, Estrada took an active part in civic affairs, including a long tenure as *alcalde ordinario* (elected 1779) and *regidor*, and a captaincy in the provincial militia. Estrada's marriage brought him the comparatively modest dowry of 3,000 pesos, and three children, the eldest of whom, Francisco Manuel Victorio Ramón Porres Baranda de Estrada, succeeded to the entail around 1804. To himself become the co-holder of the entail with his wife, Ignacio de Estrada legally assumed the surname Porres Baranda, so that in documents after 1790 or so he is styled Porres Baranda de Estrada.[41]

40. E.g., BPE-AFA, vol. 472, *platas de azogues*, 1764.
41. BPE-AJA, 101:2:1086. Testament of 1785—AIPG, prot. Ballesteros, 4:100-105.

Ignacio de Estrada's wife, María Josefa, succeeded to the entail in 1786, upon the death of her father Bernardo, as a result of the exclusion of her own elder sister because of a marriage which incurred Bernardo's disapproval.[42] After about 1790, most of Estrada's energies seem to have centered around reviving the flagging magnificence of the entailed estates of his wife's family. In the 1780s Estrada's commercial interests had suffered some reverses, though the nature of these is not clear. In addition to this, the rentier mentality of his deceased father-in-law had helped to debilitate Mazatepec and Santa Ana, so that considerable investment, long deferred, became necessary in the early 1790s. To accomplish this, Estrada was forced to turn to outside sources for large loans. Already by 1790 he was seeking a 25,000-peso loan from José Joaquín Basauri, owner of the magnificent Hacienda de Frías, near León, "for the development of his business interests and repair of the losses he has suffered." At that time his wife's property and her dowry, totaling some 30,000 pesos, were tied up in his business ventures.

By 1793 Estrada was entangled in a real financial imbroglio. His creditors were pressing him, and he was owed large sums which he could not realize to pay his own debts. His own capital consisted of about 10,000 pesos in commercial goods and an equal amount in personal property. The necessary shoring up of the entailed haciendas had still not been accomplished. During the next two or three years he borrowed almost 20,000 pesos, some of it from the estate of his former partner, Cañedo, and some of it in the form of livestock from the merchant and hacendado Miguel Portillo. When refinancing these loans in 1796, Estrada was compelled by Portillo to promise not to spend any entail income on anything other than the payment of his debts and the development (*fomento*) of his haciendas. Other loans for the resuscitation of Mazatepec and Santa Ana followed in 1798 and 1801. In the latter year, Estrada rented the Hacienda de Mascota, belonging to the Colegio de San Agustín of Guadalajara, in an attempt to underwrite with its income from livestock production his efforts to revive the entailed estates.[43] With his personal business activities in such a precarious situation, Estrada was hardly able to achieve the revival of the family's entailed properties which he had so ardently sought. Rental of the Hacienda de Mascota proved to be an unmitigated disaster, eventuating in considerable financial loss for Estrada and a partner who subsequently abandoned the enterprise, leaving Estrada to fend for himself.[44]

These several difficulties were compounded by the acrimonious suit car-

42. Bastardy and bad marriages seem to have been fairly frequent occurrences in the Porres Baranda family, as these things went.

43. AIPG, prot. Ballesteros, 13:228v-230v; BPE-AJA, 101:2:1086; AIPG, prot. Sandi, vols. 4, 3, and 6: no page nos., for 1799, 1798, and 1801, respectively.

44. BPE-AJA, 101:2:1086.

ried on from the mid-1790s until about 1805 by Estrada and his wife (she died about 1796) with his wife's elder sister, María Francisca Porres Baranda, who had been excluded from the succession due to her first marriage. Her claim to the succession was eventually disallowed, but not before the costs of litigation and payments to her (*alimentos*) drained much of Estrada's resources and energy. In the late 1790s, the major portion of the income from the entail was in the form of rents from the rancheros of Mazatepec and Santa Ana and those in the Cuquío area, which brought in the not-inconsiderable sum of about 10,000 pesos per year, aside from direct farming income earned by Estrada. But despite recent increases in rentals, income barely covered the expenses of the entail. Expenses included 400 pesos per year to a *capellanía*, repairs, administrative costs, about 1,000 pesos per year in legal costs, and some 5,000 pesos per year paid out to María Francisca, by that time remarried and living in Mexico City. Income from rentals was extremely variable from year to year because of vacancies, deaths, absences, and lateness. Even so, had it not been for María Francisca's claims and the costs of litigation, the entailed properties would have provided a modest income for Estrada and his son and successor. In 1803 the entail was put under judicial embargo, an interventor being appointed to collect the rents, and remained so until at least 1807, even though Estrada's son succeeded him in 1804. By 1805, Estrada had been reduced to the condition of a renter, albeit the major one, on his son's embargoed estates, and in that year a land suit before the Audiencia drew attention to the much-decayed condition of the mayorazgo.[45]

The career of Ignacio de Estrada illustrates a number of important themes which we will have occasion to discuss again in succeeding pages. These themes—mining or mining-connected and commercial wealth, social aspiration and mobility through marriage, landownership, problems of capital accumulation and debt—recur in the careers of many late colonial men of affairs, even if in different variations and without the unhappy fate which overtook Estrada. Some of Estrada's difficulties were purely fortuitous (his legal problems with his sister-in-law), some were apparently the result of his own ineptitude (his business reverses and his losses in the rental of the Hacienda de Mascota), and some (the necessity for a fairly heavy capital investment to make commercial agriculture profitable) were characteristic of the late colonial period and not subject to individual control. The main factor in his decline and fall, however, appears to be that he overextended his limited resources in an attempt to revive the Porres Baranda family fortunes, and that in this effort he was sucked into the vortex of debt and bankruptcy.

45. AIPG, prot. Ballesteros, 22:369; BPE-AJA, 101:2:1086, 61:7:780, and 235:2:3080; AIPG, Tierras, leg. 41, exp. 2.

Patterns of Inheritance

If entails and rapid turnovers by sale represent the two extremes in the spectrum of land transfers, it is nonetheless important to remember that inheritance played a major role as well. Although the most common method of property transfer from one person to another appears to have been by sale, some properties stayed within the same family for a number of generations and were passed on by inheritance without recourse to legal encumbrances.[46] The most stable of these rural estates, in terms of ownership, were those which were well enough situated and managed to provide a consistent income so that they would not fall into debt. Usually the owners of such properties had to have access to outside sources of capital as well, in order to sustain the heavy operating expenses and periodic heavy investment required to make a success of agriculture on a commercial basis. In fact, the non-entailed haciendas conspicuous for the stability of their ownership were frequently linked to commercial fortunes, some of them of long standing, and were involved in the production of a cash crop for the urban market. Examples of this kind of enterprise were the Hacienda de Epatán, in the San Cristóbal area, owned by the merchant and long-time regidor Pablo Delgado Coronel, which produced sugar; the Hacienda de Santa Lucía, to the west of the city, belonging for several generations to the prominent mercantile family of Sánchez Leñero, which produced wheat; and the Hacienda de Santa Cruz, in the Toluquilla Valley, which belonged for most of the eighteenth century to the Portillo family, and which also produced wheat in substantial quantities, as well as cattle.

Generally speaking, the principle which governed the passing on of real, as of other, property was that of primogeniture, the right of the first-born child to inherit. Although in non-entailed estates this was not legally binding, a strong impression emerges from the documents on land transfers that hacienda owners favored this method.[47] In fact, landowners most often tried to provide for their other children and their widows. Substantial debts could gobble up an estate quickly, and this overlay of extra-family interests could confuse matters considerably. The conflicting legal claims of co-heirs and creditors embroiled many quite valuable estates in endless and expensive litigation which consumed their substance and eventually left little or nothing for either heirs or creditors. The major points to keep in mind are that landowners most often tried to keep their

46. The dowries brought by women into their marriages were an important form of inheritance, but major rural landholdings almost never changed hands in this way. Among the wealthy, however, dowries could be a source of capital. Dowries in the form of livestock or small amounts of cash were important to small property-holders and Indians.

47. This contrasts with Taylor's statement in *Landlord and Peasant*, p. 140, that Spanish landowners in the Valley of Oaxaca did not particularly favor primogeniture.

property within their families, and that this had to be accomplished consistent with children and widows (or, occasionally, widowers) getting enough out of the estate so that their condition did not decline. The methods used in testamentary dispositions allowed the owners of property to settle equal shares on their heirs or to favor some of them over others, points to keep in mind are that landowners most often tried to keep their within limits. These methods involved a complicated legal terminology (*quintos, hijuelas, tutelas,* etc.) and provided fertile ground for the cavilings of notaries and lawyers, but they did not change much over the course of the eighteenth century and warrant only passing attention here. The various ways of passing on property by inheritance did create problems, however, which played into the broader economic currents of the age, and it is for this problematical potential that certain forms of inheritance are worth looking at briefly.

A fairly typical estate settlement, if one may venture to use the word, was that made among the heirs of Miguel del Portillo y Zurita upon his death in 1726. Portillo, a native of Antequera, in old Castile, came to the Guadalajara area about 1675 or so and established a respectable fortune as a merchant. In 1704 he purchased the Hacienda de Santa Cruz, in the Toluquilla Valley, and devoted the last two decades of his life to building it up and overseeing what remained of his commercial interests. His son and grandson continued to be merchants and hacendados to the very end of the colonial period, and were respected men of affairs in Guadalajara. Portillo had married Isabel Gallo Navarro, who died before him. Their elder son, José Portillo y Gallo, was a canon of the Guadalajara Cathedral; three daughters had married prominent local merchants, producing a number of grandchildren (two of the daughters died before the settlement), and Miguel del Portillo y Gallo, the second son, was a young bachelor who managed his father's business interests. All five co-heirs (the three living children and the two sons-in-law for the grandchildren) agreed to make an extrajudicial division of the property in order to avoid the loss of time and money which almost invariably occurred in civil suits over estate divisions.

The total assets of the estate amounted to 105,368 pesos. The most important single asset was the Hacienda de Santa Cruz, evaluated at nearly 40,000 pesos, a very valuable property considering its size and the date. Other major assets included almost 5,000 pesos in the value of some 25 black slaves; 12,000 pesos for the family's main residence and several smaller houses in Guadalajara (including the elder Portillo's store); 2,500 pesos in merchandise; 1,500 pesos in worked silver; another 1,500 pesos in jewelry and gold; nearly 3,000 pesos' worth of furniture, clothing, etc.; and some 40,000 pesos received by the various heirs during their lifetimes, both in goods and cash. Outstanding debts payable by the estate as a whole came to just under 30,000 pesos, including a mortgage on the main Guadalajara house, the 2,000-peso capellanía held by José, and 11,000 pesos owing to the elder Portillo's former business partner. Once the debts had been subtracted from the assets, the remaining 75,000 pesos were divided into five equal shares, each coming to about 15,000 pesos. From these shares were again subtracted what each heir (or group of heirs) had received during the lifetime of the patriarch, and the remaining amount was charged against the estate. The liquid assets were divided up to satisfy the claims of the heirs, and the difference was settled on each heir as an annuity charged against the hacienda, which was to be owned and administered by the son Miguel.[48] A remarkably similar, and similarly amicable, arrangement was made among the co-heirs of Portillo y Zurita's grandson, Miguel del Portillo y Navarro, with the eldest son inheriting the two haciendas of Navajas and San José de Zapotepec and obligating himself to pay the settlements of his co-heirs.[49]

The reason that the Portillo property division of 1726 left the family hacienda in the hands of the second-born son seems to have been a tacit agreement among the heirs that, since the eldest son was a churchman and would not be able to have children, the property should go to the heir who would be able to carry on the family name. This same preoccupation with keeping property within the family crops up again and again in testaments of the eighteenth century and suggests one of the most important motives for the acquisition of land: the preservation of a fortune and the linking of a family name to a rural estate. Pedro Alvarez Cantón, a former miner of Bolaños and master of the important Hacienda de Atequiza, near Lake Chapala, himself embroiled in a bankruptcy suit in 1784, still hoped to end his days "in the peace he desires, and without having his property, especially land, leave the family (which to him would be the most painful thing)."[50]

Another method of estate division was the outright purchase of an hacienda by one heir from the co-heirs. This differed technically from the kind of settlement on heirs discussed above, but in actuality amounted to the same thing. Occasionally this happened with entailed properties, as when José María González de Castañeda purchased the haciendas of Milpillas and Cerrogordo from his father and his father's brothers in the late 1780s.[51] This technique was rather more common, however, among heirs to non-entailed estates. Such was the case, for example, when José Luis de Siordia purchased outright the Hacienda de San Nicolás de la Labor de Rivera, in the Tequila area, from his co-heirs in 1756, with 5,000 pesos

48. AIPG, prot. Mena mayor, 16:531-538.   49. AIPG, prot. Altamirano, 1:187-192.
50. AIPG, prot. Ballesteros, 2:1-12.   51. AIPG, prot. Ballesteros, 14:182.

payable in cash and 5,400 pesos payable within five years.[52] The purchase of a non-entailed property directly from a parent or grandparent also sometimes occurred, as with the sale by Francisca Velásquez Morelos of her Hacienda de Atequiza to her grandson Francisco de Soto Ceballos y Aranguren in 1725. Of the total sales price of Atequiza (20,000 pesos), some 13,000 pesos, the amount of Francisca's equity in the hacienda, remained charged upon the property without interest, to be disposed of at her will.[53]

One problem with all such arrangements, of course, was that for the sake of insuring retention of the property within the same family, liens were created upon the property which drained the income from it and reduced the possibility of capital accumulation. Another problem was that although most divisions of property among co-heirs appear to have been friendly, there were cases in which the arrangements did not satisfy one or more of the heirs, with the result that the families were rent by bitterness and interminable litigation. We have already examined one such case, that of the Porres Baranda entail. A similar judicial conflict, involving the interests of minor heirs, arose over the establishment of the Cañedo mayorazgo in the late 1780s.[54] With non-entailed estates, divisions among heirs could also be delayed for years by litigation, as occurred with the Medina family and their Hacienda de la Labor, in Cocula, in the 1790s,[55] or the Fernández Partida family's Paso de Flores, in Ahualulco, in the 1740s.[56]

The most bitter of such internecine struggles over property occurred when widows and their children fought over the estate of a deceased husband and father. It is true that this did not happen very often, but the fact that it happened at all indicates the dangers of inheritance. Examples of this kind of conflict are the protracted suits between the children of José de Ocampo and their widowed mother over the ownership of the Hacienda de San Lucas in the early 1760s,[57] and the conflict of two of the cadet line of the Villaseñor family with their mother, María Josefa Gómez, over the ownership of the Hacienda de Cedros, in 1776.[58] These problems were compounded by questions of the dowry and the increase of an estate's value during the period of a marriage (*gananciales*). During litigation, haciendas were often placed under some kind of interim administration, and they suffered from the slipshod management which almost invariably characterized such arrangements. Such bad administration, coupled with legal costs and the bad feeling which accompanied the conflicts, could weaken both the family and the rural estate being fought over.

52. AIPG, prot. Leyva Carrillo, 1:5v-10.   53. AIPG, Mena mayor, 19:7-11v.
54. AIPG, prot. Ballesteros, 13:173v-184v.   55. AIPG, prot. Ballesteros, 20:201v.
56. AIPG, prot. Mena mayor, 29:279v-283.   57. BPE-BD, leg. 107, exp. 2.
58. BPE-BD, leg. 123, no exp. no.

The basic institutional aspects of landownership—sale, inheritance, entail, credit arrangements, bankruptcy proceedings—changed hardly at all over the course of the eighteenth century. What changed in a major way were the economic dimensions—the value of rural estates, the modes of agricultural production, and the general economic environment. The increasing stability of hacienda ownership after 1760 suggests that commercial agriculture had become more profitable than earlier, and that it therefore attracted more capital than before the midcentury. Access to capital was a vital factor in the success or failure of large-scale agriculture, as we have seen in looking at the career of Ignacio de Estrada. It is to the question of the sources and uses of agricultural capital that we will turn our attention in the following chapter.

CHAPTER 8

Hacienda Ownership— Sources of Capital

The most interesting questions about hacienda ownership are: Who owned them, and why? If we want to know how social and economic institutions interact, the question becomes a matter of describing the mechanisms by which individuals were induced to invest in large-scale farming. Specifically, why did people buy rural estates? What accounts for the almost obsessive familism which surrounded the ownership of rural property? What economic sectors supplied the capital used for investment in agriculture? Was the great rural estate used primarily to underwrite the social aspirations of an elite group or to produce a profit by participation in a market economy, or both? Did the social and economic function of the hacienda change over the course of the eighteenth century?

Status and Profit

Direct evidence on the motives of individuals or social groups in buying rural estates is extremely rare, because the unarticulated assumptions of the age were subscribed to by almost everyone and never became an issue. Certainly the seigneurial ideal still held much power for landowners in the eighteenth century. As Magnus Mörner and other recent writers have pointed out, however, behavior which may be construed as non-economic —the attempt to monopolize land, for example—made a good deal of economic sense in the eighteenth century, even though the reason for such a policy may have changed during the course of the century.[1] Still, in an overwhelmingly agrarian society, in which most of the population lived in the countryside and many lived in a condition of economic, social, and political dependence upon landowners, the possession of a rural estate also conferred a degree of social power and legitimacy which was unmatched by any other calling. The eighteenth century was a mercantile age, yet most merchants of substance sought to consolidate their social position and preserve their fortunes through judicious investment in land. The sons of men who had made money in trade often disdained commerce in favor of living on their rural estates, or as absentee rentiers. Thus, for example, when Luis Fernández de Ubiarco, the son of a prominent Guadalajara merchant, came into his inheritance in 1759, he chose to take it in the value of the Hacienda de la Calera, near Lake Chapala, "because it is not to his liking to devote himself to the exercise of trade."[2]

Not the least of the gratifications attendant upon the ownership of a landed estate must have been the deference and loyalty owed to the owner, and generally paid, not only by retainers and dependents of the property itself, but by other local inhabitants as well. The communications and petitions of local Indian pueblo-dwellers to neighboring hacendados were nearly always couched in the most deferential, even obsequious terms. The Indians of the pueblo of Tizapán, for example, in addressing a letter to Francisco de Porres Baranda over an invasion of their village lands in 1761, implored that ". . . you will look upon us as your children who are always at your disposition, obeying the precepts and orders of Your Grace."[3] In the same vein, when the mayorazgo José María González de Castañeda had dealings over land rentals with the pueblo of Atotonilco el Alto, the Indians agreed "when he comes down to the village to receive him with the appropriate recognition and demonstrations, taking care also to aid his administrators."[4] The loyalty of the resident labor force and renters on colonial haciendas seems to have been very real. Land conflicts between neighboring estates, for example, were occasionally punctuated by verbal abuse and violence between their respective groups of retainers. And in the emergency situation of late 1810, Audiencia officials requested that hacendados recruit their own *gente*, under arms, to fight the rebels. The sight of a landlord or his administrator riding out at the head of an armed band of the estate's retainers was apparently not a rare one during the early stages of the rebellion, and it has a positively feudal flavor about it.[5]

1. Mörner, "The Spanish American Hacienda," pp. 192-193.
2. AIPG, prot. Berroa, 2:242v-246v. 3. AIPG, Tierras, leg. 33, exp. 38.
4. AIPG, Tierras, leg. 8, exp. 1. 5. AHMG, caja 24, Sept. 24, 1810.

The line between investing in land to legitimate a family's social aspirations, and making the same investment in order to preserve a fortune made in commerce or mining with a small but regular return, is admittedly a fine one. In fact these two motives overlapped in inducing individuals with capital to become landowners. Commercial agriculture itself was looked upon as a good investment, especially in the late eighteenth century, when the conjunction of cheap labor in the countryside and increasing urban demand improved the margins of profit which might reasonably be expected. In 1760, for instance, José de Joaristi, renter of the royal salt monopoly at Peñol Blanco, between San Luis Potosí and Zacatecas, *alcalde mayor* of the district, and vecino of Zacatecas, asked his agent in Guadalajara to purchase for him "alguna bonita hacienda" near the city which he could give as a dowry to his daughter on her marriage to oidor Garza y Falcón of the Guadalajara Audiencia. The hacienda purchased was San José de Zapotepec, in the Valley of Toluquilla, a grain-producing estate of some importance. Joaristi wanted his daughter and her husband to have the hacienda not only for a country retreat (*recreo*), but also because of the potentially high profitability of irrigated wheat so near the city.[6] Haciendas, when properly managed, could provide handsome annual incomes for their owners. The entailed properties of Joaquín Fermín de Echauri in the Sayula area, for example, yielded some 10,000 pesos per year around 1760, a not inconsiderable sum and by no means rare among major landowners.[7] A rarer economic motivation for landownership was the construction of a vertically integrated enterprise in which agricultural and livestock production served as a support for other kinds of economic activity, most notably mining. This was the case with the string of haciendas near Guadalajara owned by the Marqués de Pánuco, whose economic interests are discussed in more detail below. In this the Marqués was exceptional, however, since few colonial landowners in the Guadalajara area maintained such diversified establishments.

These brief direct glimpses of the motives behind landownership are ultimately only suggestive, and do not really tell us anything new about the way the agricultural sector interacted with the rest of the colonial economy. The nature of the interface between economic and non-economic motives in the accumulation and preservation of agricultural capital can really only be inferred from the actual behavior of a large number of landowners over a long period of time. We have already seen that the stability of ownership of rural estates increased notably during the latter part of the eighteenth century, and at the same time the increasing urban demand for foodstuffs created new opportunities for profit among large-scale agricul-

6. AIPG, prot. Leyva Carrillo, 2:154-160v.
7. AIPG, prot. Mena menor, 19: no page no.

tural producers. The relation between these two circumstances is not accidental, and points to a successful response by large rural estates to the
changing market conditions of the late colonial period. This new situation
altered the economic function of the hacienda in the late eighteenth century, even if the traditional social aspirations attached to landownership
remained largely the same. The last half-century of the colonial period saw
new infusions of capital into the agricultural economy from both new and
old sources. It is to the nature of the changing function of agriculture and
the recapitalization of the agricultural sector that we now turn.

Commerce and the Regional Economy

The largest single reservoir of landowners and agricultural capital during the eighteenth century was the mercantile economy centering in and
around Guadalajara, with its connections to the northern mining districts,
the coast, and Mexico City. Certainly not all merchants became landowners on a large scale during the eighteenth century, and indeed during
the last years of the colonial period there is some evidence of an increasing
social and economic differentiation between the two groups. Still, the overlap between major entrepreneurs in commerce and agriculture was always
significant, and the movement within the mercantile sector of the economy
had a strong influence on the capital available for the development of
agriculture. Commerce also reached out into the countryside to provide
credit to agriculturists, large and small, who themselves had no mercantile
sources of wealth, and supplied the rural laboring population with those
things it could not make itself. In the largely pre-industrial economy of the
eighteenth century, commerce was the glue which held society together
and the nexus which integrated the various sectors of the economy.[8] It is
therefore appropriate at this point to digress briefly and discuss the general
nature of Guadalajara as a mercantile center and its development during
the eighteenth century.

That Guadalajara, because of its geographic location, was and is predominantly a commercial and administrative center for western and north-
western Mexico has long been recognized. At the beginning of the seventeenth century, Alonso de la Mota y Escobar commented on the disproportionately high number of merchants who dealt in cloth and other goods
imported from Spain and the Philippines.[9] Even more circumstantial in his
description of the city's mercantile life was Domingo Lázaro de Arregui,
who wrote some twenty years later that out of a Spanish population of 200

8. See Gideon Sjoberg, *The Preindustrial City* (1960), pp. 199-203.
9. Mota y Escobar, *Descripción geográfica*, p. 25.

householders in the city, some 40 or 50 were merchants, with inventories ranging from 2,000 to 20,000 pesos each. Commerce dominated the life of the city, according to Arregui, and "outside of the merchants, there are few wealthy men. . . ."[10] By the beginning of the eighteenth century, there were 80 or 90 commercial establishments in the city, including both wholesalers and grocers.[11] By 1791, there were 50 major wholesale establishments, an equal number of large grocers, and about 150 small stores (*pulperías*) which dealt primarily in locally produced goods.[12] The census of 1793 lists some 431 individuals directly involved in trade (*commerciantes* and *tratantes*), a number exceeded only by the occupational categories of laborers (*jornaleros*) and textile workers (*fabricantes de algodón* and *obrajeros*).[13] While these figures mean little or nothing in themselves, they do indicate in a very rough way the importance of commerce in the city's economic life, and the growth which the commercial sector experienced during the colonial period. This commercial function was the primary factor accounting for Guadalajara's development as the center of a far-flung region and, with the addition of banking, has also spurred its tremendous modern growth.[14]

Though Guadalajara occupied a strategic position as the center of its own region and the entrepôt for most of western Mexico, the opposite side of the coin was its almost total financial and commercial dependence upon Mexico City, lessened to a degree only at the very end of the eighteenth century. The stranglehold of the Mexico City merchants on the substantial trade in goods imported from Europe and the Philippines was obvious already in the early seventeenth century, when Mota y Escobar noted that no Guadalajara merchants, however large their capital, traded directly with Spain.[15] In the 1750s oidor Antonio Gutiérrez y Ulloa complained bitterly and at length about Guadalajara's dependence on Mexico City, despite its own pivotal position with regard to the *provincias subalternadas* of New Galicia. By means of its commercial monopoly:

Mexico City gains all the profits and has made of itself a bottleneck through which everything must pass. It is for this reason that in the two centuries since the conquest of the kingdom, only Mexico City has grown, and the other parts of the realm suffer such a notable debility. In the center of the country there are hardly any towns which outlive their mining bonanzas, and always the profits go to Mexico City; no one desires to remain permanently where he makes his fortune, be-

10. Arregui, *Descripción*, pp. 66-67.
11. AHMG, caja 1, exp. 3, 1705.
12. Rubén Villaseñor Bordes, *El mercantil consulado de Guadalajara* (1970), p. 7.
13. Páez Brotchie, *Guadalajara*, p. 119.
14. Rivière D'Arc, *Guadalajara y su región*, p. 41. See also Berthe, "Introduction à l'histoire," passim.
15. Mota y Escobar, *Descripción*, p. 25; Rivière D'Arc, *Guadalajara y su región*, p. 42; Berthe, "Introduction à l'histoire," p. 73.

cause he must resort to Mexico City for everything: for the education of his children, for the conveniences of life . . . Mexico City is the source to which all must turn, and all turn to it because it is the center which monopolizes all profits. . . .[16]

Although this statement was exaggerated even in the 1750s when it was made, certainly the commercial restrictions imposed by the dominance of Mexico City had begun to chafe badly by the end of the century. The prices of imported goods were inordinately high, and their quantities restricted (though this was probably as much in the interests of Guadalajara merchants as it was for those of the capital). All the major mercantile houses of Guadalajara had connections with the great wholesalers (*almaceneros*) of Mexico City. Lorenzo Javier de Villaseñor, for example, had a commercial relationship of long standing with Joaquín Dongo, one of the most prominent Mexico City merchants.[17] The Sánchez Leñeros, Colazo Feijoos, Basauris, Cañedos, and other merchant families (all landowners, by the way) had similar connections. The commercial credit system, though less centralized than access to merchandise itself, frequently employed drafts (*libranzas*) written by Guadalajara merchants against wholesale establishments in Mexico City.[18]

This situation began to change somewhat during the last decades of the colonial period, due to the growth of Guadalajara itself and of the Intendancy of which it was the administrative center. A number of mining booms (most notably those of Bolaños and Rosario), combined with the development of light industry both in the city and in provincial towns, provided the economic demand for an increased flow of goods into New Galicia. In addition, the Bourbon commercial reforms of the late 1770s and after, and the unsettled conditions of the Napoleonic period, contributed to the freeing-up of trade. Although commercial profits may have dropped somewhat after the loosening of trade restrictions in 1778, commerce in western Mexico remained brisk through the 1780s, and there is little sign of a massive flight of capital into either agriculture or mining.[19] The value of European goods entering the city of Guadalajara, for example, increased from about 500,000 pesos to about 1,200,000 pesos between 1779 and 1791.[20]

The immediate effect of this increase in commercial prosperity was the foundation of the *consulado* (merchants' guild) of Guadalajara in 1791,

16. Gutiérrez y Ulloa, "Ensayo histórico-político," f. 67r-v.
17. AIPG, prot. de Silva, 8:238-246v, 1755. This same Joaquín Dongo, along with most of his household, was in 1789 the victim of a spectacular robbery and murder described in gruesome detail by Fanny Calderón de la Barca, *Life in Mexico* (1966), pp. 483-486.
18. E.g., AHMG, caja 20, letter of Aug. 17, 1802.
19. On such a possible shift in investment patterns, see David A. Brading, "La minería de la plata," *Historia Mexicana* 18 (1969), p. 319.
20. BPE-AFA, vols. 181, 161, and 426, *alcabalas*.

which considerably weakened the Mexico City consulado's commercial monopoly on the overseas trade.[21] But while the monopoly was weakened, it was not broken, and most Guadalajara merchants continued to deal through Mexico City houses, since they had neither the means nor the connections to trade directly with Spain. One of a limited number of exceptions to this rule was Juan Alfonso Sánchez Leñero, among the greatest merchants of Guadalajara, who at his death in 1793 left an estate amounting to nearly 500,000 pesos, consisting of wholesale establishments in Guadalajara and Tepic and the important Hacienda de Santa Lucía.[22] But the outer limit of most commercial fortunes in the late colonial period, or at least of those which were not based initially upon mining wealth, was more on the order of 100,000 to 200,000 pesos, so that credit from Mexico City merchants with greater resources was still necessary.

By 1814, the Guadalajara consulado had deputations in a number of important cities and towns, including Zacatecas, Durango, Aguascalientes, Chihuahua, Sombrerete, Bolaños, Saltillo, Rosario, Fresnillo, Tepic, Colima, Sayula, and San Juan de los Lagos. Aside from its specifically mercantile functions, the consulado especially undertook to improve the notoriously poor roads both within and outside of the Intendancy. Its road- and bridge-building activities were primarily concentrated in the immediate vicinity of Guadalajara after 1800, but occasionally extended as far north as Fresnillo, Durango, and Rosario. In 1794, largely through the agency of the consulado, a regular stagecoach service (the trip took two weeks) was established to Mexico City. The organization also subsidized the building of permanent structures to house the famous trade fair of San Juan de los Lagos in the late 1790s.[23] While the activities of the consulado undoubtedly helped to some degree to consolidate Guadalajara's position as a major mercantile center in the last three decades of the colonial period, and to stimulate trade in general, it was probably more notable as an effect than as a cause of commercial prosperity.

Another contributing factor in the late colonial commercial prosperity of Guadalajara was the increased use of the port of San Blas after the early 1790s.[24] The real commercial importance of the port for the merchants of Guadalajara did not begin until after 1812, when Intendant José de la Cruz

21. Villaseñor Bordes, *El mercantil consulado*, p. 6 ff.; José Ramírez Flores, *El real consulado de Guadalajara* (1952), p. 16; Rivière D'Arc, *Guadalajara y su región*, pp. 43-44.
22. AIPG, prot. Ballesteros, 20:68-71.
23. Ramírez Flores, *El real consulado*, pp. 52-74; Rivière D'Arc, *Guadalajara y su región*, p. 43. For a vivid account of the annual fair, dating from the early decades of the nineteenth century, see Payno, *Los bandidos de Río Frío*, pp. 559-563.
24. Michael E. Thurman, *The Naval Department of San Blas* (1967), pp. 35, 50, 239; *Noticias varias de Nueva Galicia* (1878), p. 17; Miguel Lerdo de Tejada, *Comercio exterior de México* (1967), pp. 21, 115, 124.

opened the port without restriction because of the closing of the road from Mexico City to Guadalajara. In 1813, a royal *cedula* suppressed the entry of Asian goods through Acapulco in favor of the entrepôt at San Blas, and this decree was reconfirmed in 1816. In fact, so heavy was the currency outflow from New Galicia to pay for the imports coming through San Blas that it aggravated the chronic money shortage in the Intendancy of Guadalajara.[25]

The years 1812 to 1817 were apparently ones of unparalleled prosperity for the merchants of Guadalajara.[26] The fragmentary information available on late colonial sales taxes confirms this. For the entry of European goods, sales tax (*alcabala*) receipts in the city of Guadalajara itself recovered from a slump in 1810-1811 and reached new heights by 1816. Receipts for the entry of Asian goods also experienced a recovery in this same period, though they did not attain the levels of the first few years of the century.[27]

The great mercantile houses of Guadalajara profited greatly from the mining prosperity of the latter part of the eighteenth century.[28] This association, of course, was not a new one. Guadalajara merchants had been involved since the sixteenth century in the finance and supply of mining enterprises, from the great complex at Zacatecas to the tiny mining camps scattered all over New Galicia. For example, when Captain Juan García de Castro, a Coruña-born merchant and hacendado of Guadalajara, died in 1707, his testament enumerated among outstanding debts several thousand pesos owed to him for merchandise, cash loans, and mercury by miners of La Magdalena, Etzatlán, Jala, Acaponeta, Rosario, the Real de los Frailes, and San Sebastián.[29] In fact, the testaments, inventories, and other documents relating to early eighteenth-century merchants indicate that virtually all of them were more or less heavily involved in financing miners.

The most conspicuous example of such financial involvement was the redoubtable Miguel del Portillo y Zurita, one of the great city merchants of the early eighteenth century. Portillo, Spanish-born like his contemporary García de Castro, left upon his death in 1726 nearly 50,000 pesos' worth of debts payable to him by miners of Mascota, Guachinango, Hostoticpac, Rosario, and the Real de los Alamos, in addition to an equal or greater amount deemed uncollectable. Portillo had invested part of his

25. AHMG, caja 23, letter of Oct. 10, 1803; CG-ACE, Diezmos, leg. 3, 1806; Leopoldo I. Orendain, *Cosas de viejos papeles* (1968), vol. 1, p. 13.

26. *Noticias geográficas de Jalisco*, p. 27.

27. BPE-AFA, vols. 306, 307, 478, 228, *alcabalas*.

28. On the interaction between the mining and mercantile sectors, see Brading, *Miners and Merchants*, esp. pp. 95-128.

29. AIPG, prot. Ayala Natera, 5:178v-185v.

substantial profits from financing miners in purchasing the fertile Hacienda de Santa Cruz, in the Toluquilla Valley (1704); he himself was never directly involved in mining.[30] This same pattern of association of big merchants with silver-mining continued throughout the rest of the colonial period. By the closing years of the eighteenth century, such important merchants as Juan Alfonso Sánchez Leñero, Juan Manuel Caballero, and Juan Francisco de Corcuera were prominently involved in mining finance.[31]

The mining bonanzas of Rosario and Bolaños, both in the latter part of the eighteenth century, were sustained largely through capital originating with the great merchants of Guadalajara. The silver district of Bolaños, north of the city, was discovered in 1736 and was producing at full tilt by the late 1740s. During the following decade it accounted for some 15 percent of total Mexican silver production. The Villa de Bolaños had a population of about 16,000 people in the late 1750s. The two decades from 1757 to 1775 saw the playing-out of the initial rich strikes, massive flooding of the mines, virtual abandonment, and a precipitous drop in production, followed by a brief but spectacular recovery in the late 1770s and a renewed decline from the late 1780s until the end of the colonial period. Even by the 1790s, when despite a slight recovery the long-term trend in silver production was downward, Bolaños still represented an important outlet for commercial capital from Guadalajara, and its much-reduced population remained a significant market for merchandise distributed through Guadalajara.[32]

As to the role of Guadalajara mercantile capital in financing the mid-century boom, one has only to look at the lists of names of those paying taxes on silver in the Real Caja of Guadalajara to reconstruct a veritable Who's Who of city merchants.[33] A description of the mines in 1791 stated, perhaps with some exaggeration, that they "notoriously sustain the larger part of New Galicia"; the district "produces only silver, scorpions, cockroaches, and a variety of poisonous animals; its commerce is completely passive, since all supplies of prime necessity must be brought in from outside; the town finds itself abundantly supplied with everything. . . ."[34]

A particularly piquant illustration of the way in which mining, commercial, and agricultural capital were intertwined in the development of Bolaños (and of other mining centers as well) involves the miner Pedro Alvarez Cantón, who settled in the Guadalajara area in the 1750s. Alvarez

30. AIPG, prot. García, 24:99v-109v.

31. AIPG, prot. Sierra, 7: no page no., 1783; BPE-AJA, 154:12:1736.

32. Brading, "La minería de la plata," pp. 319-322.

33. BPE-AFA, vols. 10, 472, *platas de azogues.*

34. BPE-MC, leg. 42, vol. 2, "Noticias varias de Nueva Galicia, Intendencia de Guadalajara," 1793.

Cantón, who had made a moderate fortune in the mines of Bolaños, sold his mining interests in about 1750 to Francisco Javier de Uribarren, a resident of Guanajuato. Uribarren had borrowed part of the money for this purchase, some 20,000 pesos, from Francisco de Soto Ceballos y Aranguren, a merchant and landowner of Guadalajara, who about this same time was making a multitude of loans to other Guadalajara merchants and Bolaños miners. The capital for Ceballos' spurt of financial activity had come in part from the sale of his Hacienda de Atequiza, a grain- and livestock-producing estate near Lake Chapala, to Pedro Alvarez Cantón.[35]

The midcentury mining bonanza in the area of Rosario, on the Pacific coast southwest of Durango, was financed in much the same way as Bolaños. A good many of Guadalajara's wealthier merchants lent money to Rosario's miners and supplied them with the cash and merchandise necessary to carry on mining operations.[36] By the late 1780s, the Caja Real of Rosario, which collected receipts from the subordinate cajas of Rosario, Cosalá, Copala, and Alamos, received more taxes on silver than the combined receipts of the cajas of Guadalajara, Pachuca, Bolaños, Sombrerete, and Zimapán.[37] Even more than Bolaños, Rosario contributed directly to the accumulation of capital in the Guadalajara area by generating a number of large fortunes (those of the Vizcarra and Cañedo families, most prominently, but also a number of associated names) which were largely converted into local agricultural and mercantile wealth. As a market for the sale of goods, Rosario increased in importance into the last decades of the century. Between 1780 and 1800, the gross consumption of goods of all kinds in the Rosario area doubled (from about 110,000 pesos to about 230,000 pesos), with Guadalajara merchants heavily involved in the trade.[38]

Another key factor in the commercial prosperity of the late eighteenth century was the growth of small-scale light industry in the Intendancy of Guadalajara, spearheaded by the expansion of textile production, especially after 1770. The Intendancy had previously functioned primarily as a supplier of cotton and wool for the distant textile-producing centers of Puebla, Mexico City, Querétaro, and San Miguel el Grande, whence it received back finished goods in the form of inexpensive cloth.[39] This situ-

35. AIPG, prot. Mena mayor, 35:177; prot. Leyva Carrillo, 1:110v.

36. The pivotal role of mercantile capital in both Rosario and Bolaños is clearly seen in "La minería en la Nueva España a postrimerías del siglo XVIII" in *Documentos*, vol. 12 (1938), pp. 24-25.

37. Miguel Othón de Mendizábal, *La evolución del noroeste de México* (1930), p. 110.

38. BPE-AFA, vols. 181, 210, 426, 314, *alcabalas*.

39. "Noticias geográficas, políticas, militares . . . de la Provincia de Guadalajara. . . ," in Jesús Silva Herzog, comp., *Relaciones estadísticas* (1944), p. 20.

ation began to change in the last quarter of the eighteenth century due to growing local demand, the availability of labor, and, from the 1790s, the need for import-replacement due to interruption of the trans-Atlantic trade. By the early years of the nineteenth century, the global value of cotton goods produced in the Intendancy of Guadalajara rivaled that of Puebla, the principal cotton textile center of Mexico. Woolens were also an important product.[40]

The textile industry was apparently organized on a fairly small scale. Village production was substantial, with various pueblos specializing in certain types of textiles or articles of clothing. The 457 textile workers listed in the 1793 census comprised the largest single occupational grouping in the city after unspecified workers and day laborers. By 1803, in the Intendancy of Guadalajara as a whole some 20,000 people were working in various forms of textile production, and the city of Guadalajara had a number of large establishments manufacturing woolens and cottons. The exact size of *obrajes* (cotton textile mills) within the city is not clear, but Manuel Puchal's, on the western outskirts, employed a "considerable número de gentes," and the Porres Baranda family's obraje was also substantial and employed convict labor. Contemporary statements note a certain decline in textile production, both in the city and in the countryside, due to the unsettled conditions following the Insurrection of 1810.[41] Two other industrial activities which contributed to the increasing commercial traffic of the late eighteenth century were tanning and soapmaking.[42]

Commercial Wealth and Agriculture

The increase in both urban and rural population, the mining booms in Bolaños and Rosario, and the development of textile and processing industries all helped to generate commercial activity during the latter part of the eighteenth century. The merchants of Guadalajara, though restricted

40. Serrera Contreras, "Estado económico de la Intendencia de Guadalajara," p. 203; Robert A. Potash, *El Banco de Avío de México* (1959), p. 18; Humboldt, *Ensayo político*, p. 451.

41. AHMG, caja 15, 1793; caja 13, 1791; BPE-BD, leg. 90; AHMG, cajas 28 and 41, 1813. The 1793 census figure is probably more valuable as a relative indication of the importance of textile manufactures in the city economy than as an absolute count, given the fact that over 20,000 of the city's inhabitants were not identified as to occupation.

42. "Provincia de Guadalajara: Estado que demuestra los frutos y efectos de agricultura, industria y comercio, . . . 1803," in Herzog, comp., *Relaciones estadísticas*, pp. 1 and 3; AHMG, caja 23, 1808; AIPG, Tierras, leg. 51, exps. 8, 11, 1797; AHMG, caja 10, 1785; inventory of Hacienda de la Sauceda, 1790—BPE-AJA, 154:12:1736; of Cuisillos—AHMG, caja 22, 1806.

in certain respects by their dependence upon Mexico City for access to European goods and for credit, were nevertheless in a position to dominate the trade of most of western Mexico. They provided goods and capital for the mining centers, organized rural and urban industries, and brokered the industrial and craft production of the region. Although the general price inflation of the late eighteenth century canceled out some of the apparent rise in mercantile earnings, the larger merchants of Guadalajara and the more important provincial towns were able to reap large profits from their dealings. Some of these profits were reinvested in commercial enterprises, but much went into buying and developing landed estates around Guadalajara. This offered a surer, if lower, rate of return on capital, especially if the commercial enterprise was maintained as a source of income with which to ride out years of agricultural scarcity. Furthermore, the investment in land helped to preserve commercial fortunes which might otherwise, because of the institutional context of Spanish colonial society, dissolve after the first generation.[43] Many merchants, of course, never bought any land at all. Still others, who sought to preserve their wealth in this fashion, saw it dissipate nonetheless. But the relationship between commercial and agricultural capital is strong enough to warrant our examination of the nature of mercantile fortunes and the way in which they were converted into the ownership of great estates.

One of the best-documented of eighteenth-century commercial-agricultural fortunes is that of the Basauri family, which was prominent in the economic and social life of Guadalajara from about 1750 until the end of the colonial period. A number of the patterns that we have seen in the careers of Miguel del Portillo y Zurita, at the beginning of the century, and of Ignacio de Estrada, at its end, are evident in greater detail in the history of the activities of the Basauri family, which can be traced over several generations. The patriarch of the family was Tomás Basauri, born in 1720 of a Basque father and a creole mother in the town of Piedragorda (the modern Manuel Doblado) on the western edge of the Bajío. Tomás' father, Gregorio, was apparently a merchant who left a very modest estate at his death sometime before 1747. The first really hard information about Tomás' fortune dates from that year, when he contracted a marriage with María Magdalena de Iriarte, daughter of a notary and customs administrator of Guadalajara. Tomás' capital at this time, which included his inheritance from his father, consisted almost entirely of the value of the Hacienda de Frías (52,500 pesos) and a bequest of 8,400 pesos from his deceased sister in Mexico City. Where he had acquired Frías, later one of the major haciendas of the western Bajío, is not certain, but he probably

43. Brading, *Miners and Merchants*, pp. 102-103.

bought it himself and developed it. María Magdalena brought Tomás a dowry of some 4,000 pesos, bore him one son, José Tomás Mauricio, and died prematurely in 1749.[44]

In the early 1750s Basauri's fortune flourished, mostly through astute management of the Hacienda de Frías, which sold large amounts of wheat in Zacatecas and other mining centers, and through his commercial interests in Guadalajara. In 1749, 1753, and 1756, Tomás Basauri entered into commercial partnerships with three different merchants of Guadalajara for the management of wholesale establishments in the city, Basauri supplying the lion's share of the capital, about 30,000 pesos, in each case.[45] The 1756 agreement with José Zarobe, a city merchant of modest capital, was formalized not by Tomás himself, who apparently preferred to maintain his residence on the Hacienda de Frías, but by a proxy. The two men agreed to purchase a large shop in the Portal de la Fruta, in Guadalajara. Basauri's capital of 30,000 pesos consisted primarily of over 15,000 pesos in merchandise (left after the dissolution of the 1753 partnership) and 13,500 pesos in silver, and Zarobe's of 1,800 pesos' worth of merchandise then on its way from Puebla. The labor of administering the enterprise was all to be that of the junior partner, with the profits divided equally. The partnership prospered and was dissolved by Tomás' widow only in 1781, by which time Zarobe was a wealthy merchant and *alcalde ordinario* of the city.

In 1756 Tomás Basauri contracted a second marriage, with María Magdalena Cid de Escobar, a creole woman of Aguascalientes. At that time his entire estate, consisting of the Hacienda de Frías and his property in Guadalajara, amounted to a very substantial 190,000 pesos, or roughly triple its value a decade previously. Since his second wife brought him no dowry he settled 11,600 pesos on her, and his son from the first marriage received half the increased value of Tomás' estate during the period 1747-1756, plus the value of his mother's dowry. Subtracting some other minor liens against his property, this still left Tomás Basauri with a personal fortune of over 100,000 pesos free and clear upon his second marriage.[46]

The next glimpse of the Basauri interests comes some thirty years after Tomás' second marriage. The patriarch had died in 1780 or 1781, leaving his widow and three children from that marriage, José Joaquín, José

44. AIPG, prot. Mena mayor, 19: no page nos., 1757.

45. AIPG, prot. Berroa, 13:66; prot. Mena mayor, 34: no page no., 1749; prot. Mena menor, 12:164, 1753; prot. Mena menor, 17: no page no., 1756. Basauri's first partner, Agustín de Arzubialde, had only 5,000 pesos capital available to invest in the concern. Later Arzubialde married into the Porres Baranda family, was active in city government (as *alférez real* and regidor), and gave a daughter in marriage to the first Marqués de Pánuco; he died in 1776.

46. AIPG, prot. Mena menor, 19: no page no., 1757.

Ignacio, and María Josefa, who had married the holder of the González de Castañeda entail, José María de Castañeda y Medina. The family had dissolved the partnership with Zarobe in 1781 and continued to administer the commercial enterprises as a group, but had decided in the formal division of Tomás' estate (Mexico City, 1787) to liquidate the business and divide up its assets. The total value of the *tienda* and its merchandise was something over 47,000 pesos, including a shop in Tepic. The debts owed to the mercantile house were considerable; those current amounted to 27,252 pesos, including sums owed by the administrators, tenants, and *peones* of the Hacienda de Frías, inherited by José Joaquín, and the haciendas of Miraflores and Atequiza, acquired after Tomás' death, belonging to José Ignacio and his mother. There were in addition a huge number of small debts owing by small farmers of the Guadalajara area—Los Altos, Acaponeta, Cuyutlán, Chapala, Santa Cruz, Ameca, La Barca, Ahualulco, and Jocotepec—as well as a host of urban craftsmen (shoemakers, blacksmiths, cigar-makers, tailors, etc.). Ancient debts owed to the commercial house amounted to more than 75,000 pesos, most of them deemed uncollectable. Outstanding debts owed by the house came to over 40,000 pesos, 25,000 pesos of which were owed to merchants of Mexico City and Vera Cruz.[47]

The 1787 division of Tomás Basauri's estate left one son, José Joaquín, in possession of the Hacienda de Frías, and another son, José Ignacio, in joint possession with his mother of the haciendas of Miraflores and Atequiza, purchased after Tomás' death. The daughter, María Josefa, had her inheritance in the form of an annuity charged upon part or all of her co-heirs' holdings. José Joaquín lived a more or less retired life on his hacienda, passing it on to his children.[48] María Magdalena lived on for some years as the matriarch of a great landowning family with branches in León and Guadalajara, and saw her children and grandchildren marry into some of the best and oldest creole lines. She herself converted part of her share in her late husband's estate into landholdings by purchasing, sometime in the 1780s, the haciendas Izcuintla and La Higuera, in the Cuquío area. These properties she generally rented out, living on this and other income. She sold the two haciendas for 25,000 pesos in 1802 and died shortly thereafter.[49]

The real luminary of the family in the generation after Tomás Basauri

47. AIPG, prot. Ballesteros, 9:398v-432v.

48. Two of his daughters in succession married José María Echauri, heir to the Echauri entail and member of one of the great landowning families of the late colonial period (AIPG, prot. Altamirano, 6:117-120, 1833).

49. AIPG, prot. Ballesteros, 13:123v-125v, lease of 1790; prot. Sandi, 7: no page no., 1802. The co-purchasers of the haciendas were Felipe de Guinea, her husband's former head cashier, and Dionisio Ruíz de Cabañas, a brother of the Bishop of Guadalajara.

was his second son by his second marriage, José Ignacio. Beginning with a considerable fortune—he inherited from his father, by the family property division of 1787, about 135,000 pesos (some of this must have been part of the value of the Hacienda de Frías, retained by his brother José Joaquín)—but no landed property, he converted his cash assets into one of the most important of contemporary landed fortunes, based primarily upon the great Hacienda de Atequiza, near Lake Chapala. Sometime in the early 1780s José Ignacio married Mariana Villazón, the granddaughter of Pedro Alvarez Cantón, the former Bolaños miner who had liquidated his mining interests in about 1750 and purchased the Hacienda de Atequiza. In 1783, Alvarez Cantón was declared bankrupt because of debts of some 125,000 pesos, much of it in the form of mortgages with unpaid interest on his hacienda. Before the old man's death in 1784, José Ignacio Basauri had agreed with Alvarez Cantón and his son (Basauri's uncle by marriage), a Jesuit priest, to buy the hacienda for 100,000 pesos (its actual evaluation stood at 90,000 pesos), as well as some other property of Alvarez Cantón's in Guadalajara (a house, some merchandise, and personal belongings). Thus it was that José Ignacio Basauri acquired the Hacienda de Atequiza, which, a decade later, had doubled in value to about 160,000 pesos.[50]

In the meantime, José Ignacio had purchased at public auction in 1782, as the result of yet another bankruptcy action, the substantial remaining portion of the once-great Hacienda de Miraflores, which lay to the east of Guadalajara, in the Cuquío district. During the 1780s, by dint of several small property sales, Basauri rationalized his holdings east of the city and accumulated some capital for the refurbishing of Miraflores. Thereafter, Miraflores was most often leased out for very respectable rents (2,000 pesos per year), and seems to have remained in the Basauri family until the end of the colonial period. Other investments in landed estates during the 1780s were the attempted purchase of the small Hacienda de Santa Clara (also known as Los Curieles) in the jurisdiction of Colimilla-Matatlán, to the east of Guadalajara, which fell through because of the insecurity of the title; and the purchase in 1790, again at a bankruptcy proceeding, of the small but important Hacienda de la Huerta, in Poncitlán, neighboring Atequiza, for 9,000 pesos.[51]

The early 1790s saw the apogee of José Ignacio Basauri's fortunes and the first signs of strain. About 1790 or so he became a *regidor perpetuo* of the city, but in 1794 his wife died and he took holy orders (a not uncommon practice for widowers with grown children). At that time, a schematic inventory of his property looked very good on paper, amounting to a total

50. AIPG, prot. Ballesteros, 2:275-278v and 1-2.

51. AIPG, prot. Ballesteros, 2:419-420v; 1:44r-v; prot. Zapotlanejo, 1: no page no., 1787; prot. Ballesteros, 9:21-22v; prot. Zapotlanejo, 1: no page no., 1798; BPE-BD, leg. 152, exp. 5.

of 324,968 pesos. Most of his actual worth was in the Hacienda de Atequiza, in which he had invested considerably and which was evaluated at 162,456 pesos. The Hacienda de Miraflores was valued at 35,579 pesos, and La Huerta at 10,702 pesos. Besauri's house in Guadalajara was worth a very substantial 28,562 pesos, and other property accounted for about 3,000 pesos. A large chunk of his gross worth was in the form of 85,478 pesos in debts owed to him, some of it lent out by him at interest, but a good part of it remaining from the division of his father's estate in 1787. His properties were charged with a 30,000-peso debt he had guaranteed for José Antonio Rincón Gallardo, as well as some 20,000 pesos in annuities and *capellanías* held by members of his own family, including his son José Rodrigo, a priest (José Ignacio had had eight children altogether by his late wife). Although Atequiza produced a large yearly income, Basauri was definitely short of cash, and his resources were stretched rather thin. In 1795, for example, in order to repay a loan of 17,000 pesos to the Seminario de San José of Guadalajara, he had to borrow a like sum from José Zarobe, his father's former junior business partner, by then a wealthy merchant.[52] Dr. Don José Ignacio Basauri, as he was known in his last years, lived to see some of his children well-married and died at about the same time as his mother, around 1804. The Hacienda de Atequiza, the linchpin of Basauri's fortune, passed to his minor heirs after his death in 1804, and was purchased and taken out of the family in 1819 by a Panamanian merchant, Pedro de Olazagarre.

Not all merchant families liquidated their commercial enterprises from one generation to the next in favor of becoming rentiers or gentleman farmers, like the Basauris. A handful of families did manage to make and maintain considerable fortunes solely on the basis of agricultural wealth under the more profitable conditions of the late eighteenth century, but this was a fairly rare occurrence. Most of the major landowners who made a go of commercial agriculture needed to have an external source of capital available to them, or else they almost inevitably overextended themselves financially and their estates became burdened with debt. This appears to have been the case with José Ignacio Basauri, whose numerous heirs, under the weight of their own number and the precariousness of the fortune left them by their father, eventually lost the Hacienda de Atequiza to a newer commercial fortune. Continued involvement in commerce by an hacendado, however, was in itself no guarantee that agricultural property would remain in the family or that, if it did, it would not accumulate a crushing burden of debt.

52. AIPG, prot. de Silva, 35: no page no., 1794; prot. Ballesteros, 24:53.

One late colonial merchant-hacendado who made a resounding success of his enterprises and used his commercial and agricultural resources in a mutually supportive fashion was Juan Alfonso Sánchez Leñero, one of the greatest Guadalajara merchants of the latter part of the eighteenth century. Juan Alfonso, a native of the Villa de Tembleque, in Toledo, Spain, seems to have emigrated to Guadalajara with a small amount of capital in the 1750s. His entering wedge into business in the city was his uncle, Gabriel Sánchez Leñero, also a native of Tembleque. Gabriel's father had been alcalde mayor of Aguascalientes in the early years of the century, and Gabriel himself became a successful merchant in Guadalajara. He had a cousin in Mexico City, Juan Antonio, who was an important wholesale merchant. Gabriel married well, in the late 1730s, to a local creole heiress, Angela de Amesqua y Gamboa, who had inherited the Hacienda de Santa Lucía from her father. Gabriel Sánchez Leñero was an important merchant of wide-ranging interests, including the supply and financial backing of mines and haciendas, and the marketing of the livestock and other produce of his wife's hacienda in Guadalajara. He was at various times alcalde ordinario of the city cabildo and financial administrator (*mayordomo*) of both the important Convent of Santa María de Gracia and the Cathedral of Guadalajara. He died in about 1760.[53]

Juan Alfonso Sánchez Leñero arrived in Guadalajara and went to work for his uncle, probably in the time-honored capacity of a *cajero* (clerk). His brother Miguel was also a Guadalajara merchant and later married into a wealthy mercantile family. By the time of his aunt's death in the early 1760s (she had outlived Gabriel by a few years), Juan Alfonso had a small capital of some 4,000 pesos tied up in a store which he owned in partnership with her. He purchased the Hacienda de Santa Lucía from her estate for some 37,000 pesos, and developed the property considerably during the ensuing years. Over the next three decades, Juan Alfonso Sánchez Leñero accumulated a very large commercial fortune by dint of silver-banking, large-scale trading in livestock to Puebla and Mexico City, and a brisk trade with the coast in general merchandise.[54]

Santa Lucía itself yielded a handsome yearly income, and from at least the 1770s through the rest of the colonial era it was one of the city's major suppliers of wheat and an important source for cattle and sheep as well. Juan Alfonso not only used his commercial profits to develop the hacienda, but used the hacienda to underwrite his commercial ventures. Thus in 1772, for example, when he needed 25-30,000 pesos in cash for the

53. AIPG, prot. Mena mayor, 27:341r-v; prot. Mena menor, 6:140; prot. Tapia Palacios, 2:62-65v.
54. AIPG, prot. Berroa, 3:241-245, 1760; prot. Sierra, 7: no page no., 1783; prot. Berroa, 8:372v-374, 1765; 19:439, 1775-1776; 4:172v-174.

upcoming Jalapa trade fair, he borrowed this amount from the *juzgado de capellanías* in Guadalajara with the security of the hacienda, his house in the city, and the guarantees of his brother Miguel and Francisco Javier de Vizcarra, soon to be the first Marqués de Pánuco. A 50,000-peso loan from the same source five years later was probably taken out for the same reason, and was also secured with the hacienda (the previous loan having by that time been repaid).[55] Juan Alfonso's wealth continued to grow during the 1770s and 1780s, and at some point he acquired an interest, and later control, of a mercantile establishment in Tepic. Of his five children, one son went into the Church, another became very active in civic affairs, and a third managed and later inherited the Hacienda de Santa Lucía. His two daughters married the Moreno de Tejada brothers, Spanish merchants from La Rioja, the sons of a former alcalde mayor of La Barca.[56]

When Juan Alfonso Sánchez Leñero died in May 1793, the overall value of his estate was something on the order of 500,000 pesos. About 100,000 pesos represented the value of the Hacienda de Santa Lucía, which had tripled in value over the thirty years since he had acquired it. In the immediate division of the estate, not including debts and a somewhat confused situation regarding a large quantity of goods recently purchased in Spain, each of the ten heirs received free and clear 31,000 pesos. Aside from the hacienda, the estate included houses and other buildings in Guadalajara and Tepic, stores and large stocks of merchandise in both cities, and common debts payable to the estate.[57] The Hacienda de Santa Lucía was inherited by a son, Alfonso Sánchez Leñero, and continued to thrive until the end of the colonial period.

Even though the great merchants of Guadalajara effectively dominated the commercial life of New Galicia, there were commercial-agricultural fortunes based on provincial towns. The possibilities for the accumulation of sufficient mercantile capital to allow the purchase and development of a landed estate were admittedly smaller in towns outside Guadalajara, but men of initiative and perspicacity did manage to acquire important landholdings, even if their social status never matched that of the great hacendados who lived in the provincial capital. The most outstanding instance of a small merchant from a provincial town who built a substantial enough fortune to underwrite an aristocratic lifestyle for his heirs was Lorenzo Javier de Villaseñor, apparently a descendant of one of the conquerors of New Galicia, who began as a merchant in the town of Cocula in the early decades of the eighteenth century.[58] Rare as such cases

55. AIPG, prot. de Silva, 16:62-65, 1772; 20:5-8, 1777.
56. AIPG, prot. de Silva, 35: no page no., 1794; prot. Mallen, 1:124; prot. Berroa, 14:76.
57. AIPG, prot. Ballesteros, 20:68-71; 22:191v.
58. Francisco A. de Icaza, *Diccionario autobiográfico* (1969), vol. 1, p. 188. Simón Mainar

were, they do nevertheless indicate that the economic structure of the region encompassed more elements than just the city at the center and the groaning peasant masses in the hinterland.

In fact, there was an important group of individuals living in provincial towns and in the countryside—merchants, hacienda administrators, royal officials (*corregidores, alcaldes mayores*, and later *subdelegados*)—who performed an important intermediary function in the relationship of the urban and rural economies. These men were intimately involved in the complex operation of rural credit, whose web embraced independent farmers, hacienda laborers, market towns and their inhabitants, and city merchants. One of the most interesting of such late-colonial middlemen was José Prudencio de Cuervo, of the town of Tequila, who left a remarkably large fortune at his death in 1811. His activities are particularly interesting because of his pivotal involvement in the distilling industry. While the size and scope of his fortune were something of an anomaly among provincial merchants, a brief description of his business interests points up many of the ways in which such men contributed to the integration of the city and the town with the countryside.

José Prudencio de Cuervo's family background is not clear. It seems probable that his father, José Antonio de Cuervo, emigrated to Tequila from Spain in the early decades of the eighteenth century. Ildefonso Luis Cuervo y Valdés, possibly José Antonio's brother or cousin, was *tesorero juez oficial* of the Real Hacienda and Caja of Guadalajara before 1730, when he died. José Prudencio's mother was a member of the Montaño family, local landowners of middling importance in the Tequila-San Cristóbal area. José Prudencio seems to have begun his career modestly enough as a merchant in the town of Tequila in the early 1770s, and naturally extended his mercantile activities into credit operations and small-scale money-lending. By the late 1770s he was beginning to acquire land in the Tequila area through small purchases.[59] Cuervo's economic dealings emerge in some detail from his 1787 testament and the inventories of his estate made after his death in 1811. Sometime in the early 1780s, if not before, he had begun to be heavily involved in growing and marketing sugar—important in both Tequila and San Cristóbal de la Barranca—first as an aviador, and later on small pieces of rented land. Before 1785, he purchased the small sugar-producing Hacienda de Guadalupe, near Tequila, which by the end of the decade was yielding some 300 cargas of sugar per year, a small but respectable output. In 1786,

---

Paniagua, a merchant of Atotonilco el Alto, had a similar history (AIPG, prot. Mena menor, 2:85v; prot. Mena mayor, 10:134-135).

59. AIPG, prot. Mena mayor, 12:279; prot. García, 15:45v-49; prot. Berroa, 21:226-227v.

he purchased one of the major properties in the area, the Hacienda de San Martín, consisting of nearly 30,000 acres. The purchase price of 18,000 pesos was composed primarily of mortgages which Cuervo assumed, and the purchase was consummated for only 6,000 pesos in cash. By 1790 all the mortgages had been paid off. Aside from the land in these holdings, he owned numerous heads of livestock, some 50,000 mescal plants distributed among all his properties, and two houses in the town of Tequila.[60] Including his commercial establishment in Tequila, Cuervo's net worth in 1787 was about 50,000 pesos.

The growth of José Prudencio de Cuervo's wealth during the following two decades, based essentially upon the same holdings described in the 1787 testament, was very striking. As the insurgents approached Tequila, in late 1810, Cuervo fled to Guadalajara, taking with him as much cash, jewelry, and personal property as he could manage. He died in the city in December of 1811, and his estate was left entirely to his brothers and their numerous children (Cuervo himself never married). While the inventories, made at the beginning of the following year, and the accounts of the interim administration of the estate are rather confused, it is clear that Cuervo's net worth at the time of his death was around 200,000 pesos. Table 12 gives a schematic idea of the composition of his personal fortune, described in considerable detail in the 1812 inventories.

The detailed list of the debts owed to Cuervo's estate gives an insight into his activities as a merchant-agriculturist. Cuervo's debtors included two former parish priests of the town of Tequila, for unspecified goods; the former subdelegado of Tequila, for an advance to pay Indian tributes, and a quantity of mescal plants sold to him; the current subdelegado, for various expenses; the former brandy monopolist (*estanquero*) of Ahualulco, for tequila (*vino*) sold to him on credit; the teniente of the pueblo of Santa Ana for tequila on credit; and Cuervo's *compadre*, the administrator of the royal posts of Tequila, for 1,300 pesos lent to purchase mescal plants. In addition, there were a multitude of small debts owed by local rancheros and Indians, primarily for mescal plants, sugar, merchandise, and livestock (mules and oxen).

Cuervo's agricultural holdings produced maize and livestock in substantial amounts, and the inventories describe huge plantings of sugar cane. But the most obvious source of his wealth was his involvement in the distilling industry centering on the town of Tequila. The estimated 50,000 mescal plants on all his properties in 1787 had increased by 1812 to nearly 400,000, and the list of his commercial debts indicates that he dealt heavily in plants for the expanding industry and in the finished product from his

60. AIPG, prot. de Silva, 28:217-223v; CG-ACE, Diezmos, leg. 12, 1788; prot. Ballesteros, 6:269v-272.

Table 12.

The Estate of José Prudencio de Cuervo, 1812

In Guadalajara:	
House	2,486 pesos
Cash	1,335
Other funds	9,461
In Tequila:	
House (with store)	3,910
Merchandise	30,000
Debts owing to him	8,000 (appr.)
Personal belongings	2,093
Hacienda de Guadalupe	54,363
Hacienda de San Martín	64,877
Rancho lo de Guevara	6,271
Miscellaneous property	13,950
Total	196,746 pesos

SOURCE:
AIPG, Tierras, leg. 41, exp. 1.

own lands. He did his own distilling and barreling. His heavy investment in the Hacienda de San Martín had more than tripled its value in the years after its purchase, and the Hacienda de Guadalupe had experienced a similar increase in value.[61]

The association of mercantile capital with landownership was so general that it would be superfluous to continue detailing specific instances. Of course not all commercial fortunes were as large as that of Juan Alfonso Sánchez Leñero, and there were few landowners who held as much prime property as José Ignacio Basauri. The history of the Basauri family in the later eighteenth century also demonstrates that commercial wealth (in this case, combined with early landownership) could be used as a springboard to enter the creole landed aristocracy. Yet even those commercial fortunes which eventually underwrote much economic and social mobility were not in themselves proof against progressive indebtedness, even in the relatively profitable conditions for commercial agriculture which obtained at the end of the colonial period. The history of Juan Alfonso Sánchez Leñero shows us that a substantial commercial fortune could be tapped for the development of a rural estate, and that such an estate could in turn be used to further the mercantile activities of

61. AIPG, Tierras, leg. 41, exp. 1.

its owner. That of José Prudencio de Cuervo demonstrates that the accumulation of considerable capital and its conversion into agricultural wealth was possible in provincial towns as well, and that commercial agriculture (in this case coupled with the tequila-distilling industry, admittedly something of an anomaly) could be profitable. These histories, of course, are simply permutations of the same basic phenomenon. Perhaps the main point is that, economically speaking, the mobility of capital was almost always originally from commerce into agriculture, and not the other way around. There is no single case in late colonial documentation of any major landowner's converting a landed fortune into a mercantile fortune, but the number of cases of the opposite movement is legion.

Mining Wealth and Agriculture

The second great source of agricultural capital was the mining economy of western Mexico. Indirectly, of course, such mining centers as Rosario, Bolaños, Etzatlán, Asientos de Ibarra, the Real del Mesquital, Hostotipaquillo, Guachinango, Mascota, and a host of smaller mining strikes stimulated the accumulation of capital by merchants who lent money to miners, banked their silver, and supplied the reales with merchandise.[62] We have already noted that a number of commercial-agricultural fortunes were linked to this kind of activity. But there were also many great landowners during the course of the eighteenth century who drew their wealth directly from mining enterprises. The names of Alvarez Cantón and the Marqués del Castillo de Aiza are associated with Bolaños, those of Miranda Villayzán and Fernández de Ubiarco with Rosario, and those of Sánchez Calderón and Robles with Etzatlán, to mention but a few. But these mining-based fortunes cannot for the most part compare in size with those of the great silver barons of the central Mexican mining districts, such as the legendary Pedro Romero de Terreros, the Conde de Regla.[63] The conversion of vast mining wealth into agricultural fortunes on the scale of the Condes de Regla, Casa Rul, or Pérez Gálvez was virtually unknown in the Guadalajara region, for the simple reason that most of the mines of western Mexico did not produce on a scale comparable with Zacatecas, Guanajuato, Pachuca, or

62. The 1788 petition for the establishment of a *casa de moneda* in the city ("Qué la situación de ésta ciudad es immejorable . . . se demuestra por los muchos minerales que la rodean . . .") in AHMG, caja 10, exp. 3, gives a list of the far-flung mining centers regarded as dependent in some degree on the city of Guadalajara.

63. Manuel Romero de Terreros, *El Conde de Regla* (1943). For a discussion of mining wealth, see Brading, *Miners and Merchants*; and Ladd, "The Mexican Nobility."

Sombrerete. Then, too, men who made their fortunes in central Mexico tended to remain there and buy their chains of rich agricultural properties there; there was no particular reason for them to venture out into the provinces, and they preferred the life of Mexico City.

But there were two conspicuous exceptions to this pattern in the late eighteenth century—the great age of Mexican silver—both originating in the same mining partnership in the Real del Rosario: the twin fortunes of Manuel Calixto Cañedo and Francisco Javier de Vizcarra, both of which approached or exceeded 1,000,000 pesos in the last years of the century. Millionaires were certainly not common in late colonial Mexico; and even if the wealth of Cañedo and Vizcarra was small by comparison with some of the fortunes of central Mexican miner-hacendados, it was huge by the standards of New Galicia.[64] These fortunes were unique in the Guadalajara region, and were not representative of the lesser mining wealth which provided a constant dribble of capital into the agricultural economy during the eighteenth century. Nonetheless, they were so important in and of themselves, and their histories of such inherent interest, that they deserve to be examined here in some detail.

Manuel Calixto Cañedo was born into an old creole family in the Real del Rosario in 1727. From the early 1750s, at least, he was involved in a mining enterprise at the nearby Mineral de Pánuco, close to Mazatlán, with another creole native of Rosario, Francisco Javier de Vizcarra. In the late 1750s, apparently, the two partners hit a rich lode and subsequently became very wealthy from the silver their operations produced. The partnership was amicably dissolved in 1766; Vizcarra, who for some time had been administering Cañedo's mining interests, paid his partner 125,000 pesos over three years for his share in the enterprise.[65] Cañedo's involvement in mining did not end with the Vizcarra partnership, however, for in 1797, four years after his death, his children were still working the Santa Gertrudis mine, employing 120 workers.

In 1763, Manuel Calixto Cañedo moved to Guadalajara, bought a house, and began to engage in large-scale commerce. Around 1775, Cañedo's mercantile establishment in Guadalajara was worth some 80,000

64. For a list of the putative millionaires of New Spain, 1770-1830, with estimates of their assets, see Ladd, "The Mexican Nobility," pp. 317-319; she does not include Vizcarra in her list.

65. Palomino y Cañedo, *La casa y mayorazgo de Cañedo*, vol. 1, p. 42n, cites a 1765 description of the Real del Rosario which states that the mines were almost totally decadent by that time, and that the main economic activity of the area was stock-raising. This does not square with Mendizábal's assertion, cited in n. 38 above, that by the 1780s the area was still a major silver producer, or with Vizcarra's continued heavy involvement in mining there. It may be that the description of Rosario does not strictly apply to the Real de Pánuco, or that production revived subsequently. This paragraph is drawn in the main from Palomino y Cañedo, vol. 1, pp. 40-45.

pesos, aside from the nearly 20,000 pesos tied up in it which belonged to Ignacio de Estrada, whose career we have examined in some detail above.[66] The two decades between 1763 and 1783 saw Cañedo heavily preoccupied with his commercial activities, with money-lending to local landowners and merchants, and building up his agricultural holdings. His first wife, María Andrea Ciprián, the great-granddaughter of the discoverer of Rosario and a descendant through her mother's family of Nuño de Guzmán, died in 1773, leaving Cañedo with six daughters, all of whom subsequently entered Guadalajara convents. In 1774, Cañedo married María Antonia Zamorano de la Vega, the daughter of a mining family of Hostoticpac, who counted at least two conquistadores on her mother's side of the family. She died in 1787 while giving birth to their ninth child, and Cañedo himself died in 1793, at the fairly advanced age of 66 years.[67]

Cañedo had begun to acquire land in the Ameca area in 1767. The first and most spectacular of his purchases were the haciendas of El Cabezón and La Vega (for the two estates really constituted one unitary holding, administered together since the early years of the century). These he acquired at a bankruptcy proceeding against Lic. Antonio Miranda y Barreda, a priest who had managed in turn to salvage the properties by a legal trick from the bankruptcy of his father, Bernardo Apolinar de Miranda y Villayzán, a landowner, miner, and merchant of Guadalajara. The haciendas, which comprised about 35,000 acres of prime agricultural and pasture land in the fertile Ameca Valley, had been decaying slowly since the 1730s or so, due to the absenteeism and progressive indebtedness of the Mirandas, father and son. Cañedo was able to acquire the estates for just 60,000 pesos, a large part of which (over 26,000 pesos) was in the form of outstanding mortgages held by the Guadalajara convent of Santa María de Gracia.[68] During the nearly thirty years of his careful management, El Cabezón-La Vega developed into one of the great rural estates of Mexico, despite its relatively small size in terms of land area. Cañedo and his successors supplied the city of Guadalajara with huge quantities of maize, and indeed the hacienda produced "a maize that was famous and held the highest position in the grain trade."[69] The hacienda also produced substantial amounts of wheat, consumed in the city. With an eye "to facilitate the sale of the livestock of the said estates," Cañedo held the contract for the city's meat monopoly for four years during the 1770s, and the hacienda was a

66. AIPG, prot. Berroa, 19:293; prot. Ballesteros, 4:100-105.
67. Palomino y Cañedo, *La casa y mayorazgo de Cañedo*, vol. 1, passim; Amaya, *Ameca*, p. 32.
68. AIPG, prot. de Silva, 14: no page no., 1769.
69. Manuel Romero de Terreros, *Antiguas haciendas de México* (1956), p. 115; Orendain, *Cosas de viejos papeles*, p. 52.

major contributor of cattle to the urban market in other years as well. Between 1798 and 1800 alone, José Ignacio Cañedo, Manuel Calixto's son, sold some 15,000 head of cattle to private buyers, for a total price of about 90,000 pesos.[70] A rough estimate of the value of El Cabezón-La Vega at Manuel Calixto's death in 1793 would be about 250,000 pesos.

Manuel Calixto Cañedo's acquisition of property in the Ameca Valley did not stop with El Cabezón-La Vega, however. In 1774 he purchased at auction, again for a very low price (13,000 pesos), the small (about 9,000 acres) but fertile Hacienda de Buenavista in the same general area. This was followed in 1780 with the acquisition, again at auction, of the Hacienda de la Calera, contiguous to the other properties, and with the purchase in the meantime of a miscellany of small parcels and fragments of other properties. All this agglomeration brought the total of Cañedo's holdings in the Ameca Valley to perhaps some 60,000 acres of pasture and cultivated land, which were managed with the utmost attention to balanced development and the maximizing of productivity.[71]

Cañedo's will of 1793 gives a general, if very sketchy, picture of his fortune at that time. In 1790 he had founded a mayorazgo based upon the haciendas El Cabezón-La Vega, Buenavista, La Calera, and all additional lands, whose total value must have amounted to something between 200,000 and 300,000 pesos. The first holder of the entail was to be his eldest son by his second marriage, José Ignacio Cañedo Zamorano de la Vega. There had initially been some difficulties with the establishment of the entail, regarding the provision for the non-inheriting heirs, but these had been settled.[72] Cañedo had apparently had considerable amounts of liquid assets at his disposal during the 1780s and early 1790s, since he had lent out very large sums at interest, primarily to other hacendados of the Guadalajara area.[73] A number of these debts were still outstanding at the time of Cañedo's death in 1793, and his heirs continued to lend out huge sums (to Ignacio de Estrada, to the Villaseñor family, and to others) after his death. Although he stated that he had terminated all his commercial connections ten years earlier (in 1783), Cañedo still had nearly 50,000 pesos in the care of a Mexico City merchant, and some 30,000 pesos with the large Guadalajara merchant, Eugenio Moreno de Tejada. Altogether, debts and accounts payable to the estate amounted to over 200,000 pesos in 1793. Not including the value of standing crops, the physical plant, or the land, the

70. AIPG, prot. Berroa, 13:265; prot. Sandi, 3: no page no., 1798; 5: no page no., 1800.
71. Cañedo's *memoria de testamento* of 1793—AIPG, prot. Ballesteros, 18:80-91v.
72. AIPG, prot. Ballesteros, 13:173v-184v.
73. E.g., 20,000 pesos for the purchase of an hacienda in Tepic—AIPG, prot. Ballesteros, 9:74, 1788; 35,000 pesos to Antonio Colazo Feijoo—AIPG, prot. Ballesteros, 14:93-109v, 1787.

value of the livestock on Cañedo's landholdings was about 150,000 pesos. It seems likely that a number of debts outstanding were not included in the 1793 testament, and neither was the value of Cañedo's remaining mining interests. An overall estimate of his gross worth in 1793 would fall between 700,000 and 800,000 pesos.[74]

After the death of the patriarch in 1793, the family continued to prosper, though the heirs for a time fell to wrangling over the fortune left by their father. One of his daughters married, in 1795, the Marqués del Real del Mesquital, Barón de Santa Cruz de San Carlos, Don Guillermo Antonio Caserta Daens Stuart, a gold miner and the holder of a substantial agricultural entail. Cañedo's son, José Ignacio, the first possessor of the entail based upon El Cabezón-La Vega, met an unhappy end in 1815 as a result of his revolutionary sympathies; but José Ignacio's son, of the same name, successfully revived the flagging family fortunes and became governor of the state of Jalisco in the late 1820s.

The other great fortune which came out of the mines of Rosario was that of Francisco Javier de Vizcarra, the first Marqués de Pánuco. Though Vizcarra's wealth was greater than that of his partner Manuel Calixto Cañedo, his activities are less visible in the contemporary documentation and he took a less active role in the life of Guadalajara. Like Cañedo, he was born in Rosario, probably at about the same time (1727). His father, Juan Antonio de Vizcarra, was a native of Guadalajara and was probably related to Captain Antonio de Vizcarra, a prominent stock-raiser (haciendas of Miraflores and La Capacha) of the early decades of the eighteenth century. After making a substantial fortune from a silver strike at the nearby Real de Pánuco in partnership with Cañedo, as we have seen, Vizcarra bought out Cañedo's interest in the mining enterprise in 1766 and continued to operate the mines until his death in 1788. In two shorts spasms of investment in 1769 and 1780-81, Vizcarra purchased five major haciendas, four of them in the Guadalajara area, and realized considerable sums from their production during his lifetime, as did his heirs after his death. Unlike his former mining partner, he did not enter commerce, nor was he conspicuous for his money-lending activities. His first marriage, to Josefa del Castillo y Pesquera, produced three daughters and a son. The son and one daughter entered the Church, while the other two daughters married prominent Guadalajara merchants and landowners. His second marriage, to María Ana de Arzubialde, daughter of a major Guadalajara merchant and member of the city cabildo, produced two sons: Francisco, who became a canon of the Cathedral of Guadalajara and briefly the second Marqués; and José María, who became the third Marqués de Pánuco. For his

74. BPE-AJA, 170:3:1882; AIPG, prot. Ballesteros, 18:80-91v.

payments of silver taxes into the royal coffers, his support of missionary activity in Sonora, and his construction of the parish church of the pueblo of Rosario, Francisco Javier de Vizcarra had been created the Marqués de Pánuco in 1772.[75]

Vizcarra's acquisition of haciendas began in 1769, with the purchase of the great and fertile Hacienda de Toluquilla which had belonged to the recently expelled Jesuits. Toluquilla (known after 1800 as the Hacienda del Cuatro) was already in the seventeenth century, and continued throughout the colonial period, one of the most important suppliers of wheat to the city of Guadalajara. Its 25,000 acres pastured substantial numbers of live-stock, and it participated significantly in the urban market for meat.[76] Vizcarra bought the hacienda for 50,359 pesos in 1769, and its value almost doubled over the next two decades. In the same year, he bought at auction the Hacienda de Estipac, in the Cocula area, for an unspecified amount. This property, amounting to about 30,000 acres (seven sitios de ganado major) was partially parcelled out in rentals during the 1780s, but also produced large quantities of grain and sheep. Sometime around 1780 or slightly earlier, Vizcarra had bought from the Gagiola family the huge Hacienda del Palmito de Verde, near Rosario, for about 15,000 pesos. This estate, which was evaluated at some 100,000 pesos at Vizcarra's death, produced large numbers of livestock which were sold in Mexico City and locally, and provided both livestock and foodstuffs for the Marqués' min-ing enterprise nearby. In 1781, Vizcarra bought the Hacienda de Santa Cruz, in the Toluquilla Valley, after the death of its long-time owner, Mi-guel del Portillo y Gallo. This property was not particularly large (some 15,000 acres, or three sitios de ganado mayor and one menor), but it was an important producer of wheat and, like its sister establishment at Toluquilla, also supplied the city with meat. To pay the purchase price of 68,000 pesos, due immediately, Vizcarra, who was short of cash at the time, was com-pelled to borrow 70,000 pesos on short term (two years) from the wealthy convent of Santa María de Gracia in Guadalajara, giving as security his other properties and the guarantees of his son-in-law, Ramón Fernández Barrena, and his own son, Dr. José Apolinario de Vizcarra.[77] Finally, in this same year of 1781, Vizcarra purchased the ex-Jesuit Hacienda de la Sauceda, a major sheep-raising estate located in the Cocula area. The value of this important property, for which the Marqués paid some 80,000 pesos, increased by about 60 percent in the ensuing decade. These properties, then, along with a few other small holdings, constituted the extensive agri-

75. AHMG, caja 4, 1772; Ladd, "The Mexican Nobility," p. 342; Ricardo Ortega y Pérez Gallardo, *Estudios geneológicos* (1902), p. 76.
76. E.g., about 450 head of cattle in 1780-81, AHMG, Caja 25.
77. AIPG, prot. de Silva, 23:57-61.

cultural empire which Vizcarra acquired by virtue of his profits from the mines of Rosario.

The relative importance of continued mining activity and agriculture within the entire fortune of the Vizcarra family is an intriguing question— but one which cannot, unfortunately, be answered for the years before the death of the first Marqués in 1788. Accounts for the administration of the Marqués' estate during the 1790s, however, shed some light on this. In 1798, the one year for which a clear summary of the income of the estate as a whole exists, the three haciendas of La Sauceda, Estipac, and Toluquilla produced a net profit of 16,695 pesos, and the mining operations 51,557 pesos. The global value of the Vizcarra estate and the relative share in it of mining and agricultural properties is set forth in Table 13, based on an inventory of 1790, the year in which the second Marqués formally assumed the administration of his father's fortune on behalf of all the co-heirs.

The debts against the estate of the first Marqués were primarily in the value of inheritances due the co-heirs and some 115,000 pesos in mortgages, most of them charged to the four haciendas of Toluquilla, Santa Cruz, Estipac, and La Sauceda. Six years later, at the death of the second Marqués, the condition of the estate had improved somewhat through the collection of debts owing to it, liquidation of some of the claims against it by the third Marqués' sisters, and the continued prosperity of the haciendas. The gross value in that year was some 1,140,801 pesos, the debts 232,459 pesos, and the net value of the entire estate 908,342 pesos.[78]

Vizcarra's personal fortune was probably the greatest ever seen in Guadalajara, and his agricultural wealth was the greatest accumulated since the early seventeenth century, when Luis de Ahumada owned virtually the entire Ameca Valley himself. But aside from the scale of Vizcarra's activities, his career had another aspect: the creation or enhancing of a number of lesser but significant fortunes which formed a constellation around his own. Ramón Fernández Barrena, a Spanish merchant who apparently emigrated to Mexico in the 1760s, married Vizcarra's daughter Eusebia in 1770, receiving a large dowry with her (she died in 1779). He later acquired the important Hacienda de San Clemente, near Autlán, and became one of the city's major suppliers of cattle, as well as an important merchant. Fernández Barrena served on the city cabildo in the 1770s and 1780s, and was *prior* of the Consulado in 1798.[79] Another of Vizcarra's daughters by his first marriage wed Lic. Juan Francisco Corcuera, a lawyer and city merchant of obscure origins, probably also a Spaniard, and they eventually inherited the Hacienda de Santa Cruz and a part interest in Toluquilla,

78. BPE-AJA, 154:12:1736.   79. AIPG, prot. Ballesteros, 11:261-264v.

Table 13.
The Vizcarra Estate, 1790

Agricultural:

Hacienda la Sauceda	134,334 pesos
Hacienda de Estipac	61,413
Hacienda de Santa Cruz	60,320
Hacienda de Toluquilla	94,133
Hacienda del Palmito de Verde, with annexes	107,211
Rancho La Magdalena	1,000
Debts owing by peones of Toluquilla and Santa Cruz	3,474
Subtotal	461,885 pesos

Mining:

Real del Pánuco	442,972
Real del Rosario	56,409
Villa de San Sebastián	870
Subtotal	500,251 pesos

Other:

House and goods in Guadalajara	70,376
Miscellaneous	1,996 pesos
Subtotal	72,372 pesos
Total gross value of estate	1,034,508 pesos
Debts	−329,347 pesos
Net value of estate	705,161 pesos

SOURCE:
BPE-AJA, 154:12:1736.

along with Eusebia's son-in-law, Juan Manuel Caballero. Corcuera was also a regidor and an active member of the Guadalajara consulado.

In the next generation, the daughter of Ramón Fernández Barrena and Eusebia de Vizcarra married Juan Manuel Caballero, one of the greatest of late-colonial merchants. He too was a Spaniard who came to Guadalajara in the late 1790s, established himself in both maritime and local trade, and acquired a considerable fortune through his marriage in 1803.[80] From

80. Orendain, *Cosas de viejos papeles*, vol. 2, p. 61.

his father-in-law, Fernández Barrena, he inherited the Hacienda de San Clemente, and also through his wife's family, the Hacienda de Estipac. In 1817, his wife having by then died, he and his aunt sold the great Hacienda de Toluquilla to yet another great city merchant, Manuel García de Quevedo. Caballero served on the cabildo and was prior of the Consulado in 1800, 1809, and 1817.

A fourth in the constellation of fortunes associated with Vizcarra's, though not by marriage, was Manuel Capetillo, who from about 1790 administered the testamentary estate of the first Marqués, including both mining and agricultural properties.[81] Capetillo made a substantial killing in this capacity, turned his hand to commerce in Guadalajara, and married into an old landowning family (Martínez Martaraña). Through his wife, he gained control of the Hacienda de Buenavista, near Lake Chapala, and invested considerable sums in developing it. He also served in the consulado of Guadalajara during the first two decades of the nineteenth century.[82] Yet another name associated with Vizcarra was Isidoro Sarachaga, a Basque miner resident in Bolaños, who was also involved in the administration of the Vizcarra mining interests in Rosario.[83]

The Church and Landownership

A third major group of landowners during the colonial period consisted of churchmen and ecclesiastical corporations. Although the Church was far more important in the Guadalajara region in its role as agricultural financier than as a direct landowner, something should be said here about ecclesiastical landholdings, both corporate and individual. There were very few major haciendas in the region which were not at some time in their history—or even at some time during the eighteenth century—owned by a priest. But except for the problem of inheritance, priests owned land in exactly the same way laymen did. They bought and sold haciendas and smaller properties with the same frequency and ease as other people; they lost landed estates through bankruptcy and foreclosure, sometimes for ecclesiastical mortgages; and they encumbered their properties in the same way non-ecclesiastical landowners did. Most prominent landed families counted priests among their ranks, in the traditional Spanish fashion, and these sons often inherited rural property.

The two things that set priests apart from other landowners were the scale of their land acquisitions and the ultimate disposition of their proper-

81. AIPG, prot. Ballesteros, 13:195v.
82. On consulado membership, see Villaseñor Bordes, *El mercantil consulado*, p. 141 ff.
83. BPE-AJA, 154:12:1736; Brading, *Miners and Merchants*, p. 192.

ties. Generally speaking, priests almost never entered the ranks of the really large landowners. Their landholdings were most often limited to one, very seldom more, and their tenure was likely to be rather short. There were, of course, exceptions; the most notable was Lic. Juan Pérez Maldonado, who owned El Cabezón-La Vega in the first dozen years of the eighteenth century, in addition to the Hacienda de Navajas.[84] As to the sources of capital with which priests purchased rural properties, it seems unlikely that many churchmen managed to become landowners on the strength of the salaries or fees they received. Generally they invested money they had inherited, or they directly inherited property. A few high Church officials used inherited wealth and the emoluments of ecclesiastical office to acquire rural estates which they then donated to convents or other religious institutions.[85] Ultimately, haciendas owned by priests were in large measure outside the ideally family-centered property-transfer system. Since priests had no children to inherit their property, they tended to dispose of their landed estates through donation, bequest to other clerics, or by passing them on to brothers, sisters, nieces, nephews, etc.—though such bequests within the priest's family were rarer than might be imagined. Nor were the landholdings of churchmen exempt from loss by bankruptcy or forced sale for debts.

The religious establishments—convents, monasteries, seminaries, hospitals, congregations, and sanctuaries—of Guadalajara were not directly involved in agriculture to a very great extent during the eighteenth century. This stands in marked contrast to the religious houses of Oaxaca at the end of the colonial period, which were the leading Spanish landowners in the Valley of Oaxaca.[86] What exactly accounts for this difference in attitude toward landowning is not clear, but many of the Guadalajara convents actively shunned the ownership of rural property and got rid of it as quickly as possible when they by chance acquired it. Table 14 (see also Map 2) presents data on the history of eighteenth-century landholding by the several religious houses of Guadalajara.

As can be seen from Table 14, a number of agricultural estates passed through the hands of Guadalajara religious establishments, mainly convents, in the eighteenth century, but few were kept very long. The most active institution in this regard seems to have been the Convent and Hospital of San Juan de Dios (or Belém), which held and then sold five haciendas during the century. The least active were the convents of Santa Teresa de Jesús and San Francisco. But the hospital needed a constant and

84. Pérez Maldonado's activities as a landowner are summarized in Palomino y Cañedo, *La casa y mayorazgo de Cañedo*, vol. 2, pp. 465-466.
85. AIPG, prot. Berroa, 3:194v-196v.
86. Taylor, *Landlord and Peasant*, p. 193.

Table 14.
Landownership by the Religious Houses of Guadalajara
in the Eighteenth Century (property and location; mode and date of
acquisition; subsequent history)

Convento y Hospital de Belém (San Juan de Dios)

Hac. de Calerilla (Tala)—donation?, ca. 1700?; owned throughout colonial
period

Hac. La Capacha (Toluquilla Valley)—donation?, ca. 1650?; sold, 1712

Hac. San Miguel de Buenavista, Estancia de Juanacatlán (Zapotlanejo)—
sold, 1727

Hac. San Nicolás de Guaxtla (Tequila)—purchased, 1747; sold, 1749

Sitio (mayor) de Santa Quitería (San Cristóbal de la Barranca)—purchase,
n.d.; sold, 1783

Hac. Nuestra Señora de la Soledad (San Cristóbal)—donation, 1773

Hac. de San Jacinto (La Barca)—donation, 1801 (for sale); sold, 1802

43 small ranchos, various sizes, near city—various donations and purchases;
rented out

Convento de San Agustín

Hac. de San Andrés del Monte (Ocotlán)—acquired before 1700; sold,
1753; sale rescinded, 1770; thereafter, leased out

Hac. de Mascota (Mascota)—acquired before 1700; leased out

Hac. del Rosario, also known as Rancho del Tránsito (Toluquilla Valley)—
donation, 1666; sold, 1712

Convento de la Merced

Hac. de Copala (San Cristóbal)—donation?, before 1685; reacquired for
nonpayment of interest on mortgage, 1732; sold, 1732

Hac. de Guastla (San Cristóbal)—donation, early seventeenth century;
reacquired because of defaulted mortgage, 1712; sold, 1712

Hacs. Palmarejo, Izcuintla, La Higuera (Cuquío)—donation, 1760; sold,
1761

Hac. de Santa Rosa (Juchipila) — donation, ca. 1770; sold, 1772

Hac. de Navajas (Tala)—purchased at auction, Jesuits, 1767; reacquired by
cancellation of 1769 sale, 1773; sold, ca. 1780

Compañía de Jesús (Colegio de Guadalajara)

Hac. de Costilla (Tepic)—donation, 1671; sold, 1731

Hac. de Guimaraes (Tepic)—donation?, 1671?; sold, 1740s

Hac. de Toluquilla (Toluquilla Valley)—donation, late sixteenth century;
subsequent purchases; confiscated, 1767; sold, 1769

Table 14. (continued)
*Landownership by the Religious Houses of Guadalajara
in the Eighteenth Century (property and location; mode and date of
acquisition; subsequent history)*

Convento de Santa María de Gracia
    Hac. Chilapa (Acaponeta)–in deteriorated condition, leased out, 1711
    Hac. de Cuspala (Tala)–owned hacienda, 1742; sold by 1751
    Hacs. Atistic and Escamilpa (San Cristóbal)–purchased at auction for
        debts, 1749; sold, 1759
    Hac. de Tepushuacán (Guachinango)–purchased at auction, 1755; sold,
        1757

Convento de Santa Monica
    Hacs. La Isla and La Cañada (La Barca)–donation, 1714; 1720 sale abro-
        gated; resold 1739
    Hac. Naguatlán (San Cristóbal)–owned hacienda, 1721

Colegio de Niñas de San Diego
    Owned two wheat mills, Las Beatas and Sierra, in Guadalajara, throughout
        eighteenth century, always leased out
    Hac. Santa Inés (Huentitán, near city)–donation by Bishop of Guadalajara,
        1746

Convento de Jesús María
    Hac. de Papachula (Banderas Valley)–donation?, seventeenth century?; sold,
        1733
    Hac. de la Calera (Cajititlán)–by inheritance, 1756; sold, 1756

Sanctuario de Nuestra Señora de la Soledad (Congregación del Salvador)
    Hac. de Oblatos (near city)–donation, 1701; sold, 1711; repossessed and
        resold, 1724

Convento del Carmen
    Hac. de Miraflores (Ahualulco)–cession, 1731; owned and operated by
        convent for rest of colonial period

Convento de Santa Teresa de Jesús
    Unnamed rancho (Huentitán, near city)–by adjudication, 1739; sold, 1739

Convento de San Francisco
    Unnamed rancho (near city)–rented out, 1698

SOURCES:
Various.

rather high level of expenditure to support its activities, and thus received a great many bequests, while the Franciscan rule, at least, required poverty of its adherents.

Altogether, the regular clerical establishments of Guadalajara owned only five haciendas of any importance for most of the eighteenth century—and only one of these, the Jesuits' Hacienda de Toluquilla, was a major agricultural property.[87] Toluquilla, which dominated the valley of the same name on the outskirts of Guadalajara, was a major producer of livestock and wheat during the eighteenth century, both as a Jesuit property, until 1767, and afterward, when it was owned by the Marqués de Pánuco and his heirs. Under the Jesuits there was a substantial obraje on Toluquilla, from at least the mid-seventeenth century, which produced cloth from the wool of the considerable number of sheep raised on the property.[88] It provided the Jesuit Colegio of Guadalajara with a substantial and regular income, but certainly nothing on the scale of the Hacienda de Santa Lucía of the Colegio Máximo of Mexico City.[89] On the whole, the regular religious orders and other establishments of Guadalajara did not make a very impressive showing as property-owners, compared with those of Oaxaca, for example, or with the Mexican Jesuit colegios of other bishoprics. But the Church was very much involved in agriculture as a source of capital, as we shall have occasion to see. The convent of Santa María de Gracia, for example, which was unimportant as a landowner itself, was the holder of a huge number of mortgages on rural estates around Guadalajara, and was one of the major financiers of agricultural investment.

Patterns of Ownership:
Kinship, Nationality, and Politics

Up to this point, we have examined some of the social and economic dimensions of landownership during the eighteenth and early nineteenth

87. Interestingly, this valuable hacienda does not appear on some lists of confiscated Jesuit properties (Fabián de Fonseca and Carlos de Urrutia, *Historia general de Real Hacienda*, vol. 5 (1852), p. 232; and the list of 1764 in AGN, leg. 107, exp. 14; the AGN list, along with other materials relating to the Jesuits in Guadalajara, was graciously made available to me from his own notes by Lic. Salvador Reynoso of the Universidad Autónoma de Guadalajara). Documents relating to the Hacienda de Toluquilla appear, however, in the list of Chilean Jesuit materials catalogued by Hermés Tovar Pinzón, "Las haciendas jesuítas de México," *Historia Mexicana* 20 and 21 (1971), pp. 603 and 604. The Hacienda de la Sauceda, a major property in the Cocula area, was owned for much of the century by the Jesuit Colegio of Valladolid (Morelia), in the Bishopric of Michoacán. This property, used principally by the Jesuits for raising sheep, possibly in conjunction with other holdings in Michoacán, was confiscated in 1767 and eventually came into the hands of the Marqués de Pánuco, as did Toluquilla. La Sauceda does appear on the lists mentioned above.

88. AIPG-LG, 14:130v-136, April 22, 1698.

89. On Santa Lucía, see Riley, "Santa Lucía"; for Jesuit hacienda administration in general, see François Chevalier, ed., *Instrucciones a los hermanos jesuítas* (1950).

centuries. A salient category of analysis has been the origin of agricultural capital—whether it came directly from the mercantile or mining sectors of the colonial economy, or from the Church. But once invested in landed estates and commercial agriculture, there was effectively no difference in the economic function of capital. Other characteristics of landowners, or of subgroups within the landed elite, do not shine forth unambiguously from contemporary documentation. The variables which might prove important in determining who owned land and why they owned it—such as patterns of kinship, geographical origin (Spanish vs. creole), other sources of wealth, or political participation—do not appear to be particularly significant in this respect.

As to kinship and the way it consolidated or contradicted economic relationships, the pattern among Guadalajara landowners appears substantially to follow that sketched by David Brading in his *Miners and Merchants in Bourbon Mexico*. Landowners per se were not the virtually endogamous caste they have been thought to be. Recruitment from other economic groups into the ranks of hacendados was a continuous process. The fact is that though many great landowners were referred to by their contemporaries, and by themselves, as hacendados, they were also merchants, miners, or professionals at the same time. Indeed, in some respects the designation "hacendado" is meaningless in terms of differentiating among elite subgroups during the eighteenth century. The categories are so blurred, and intermarriage among elite individuals and families was so general, that any attempt to sift out the social characteristics of the land-owning group is hazardous. Elite recruitment patterns led to such frequent intermarriages that the upper class of late-colonial Guadalajara was in some ways simply a huge extended family. In recognition of this tendency, the historian of the Ameca Valley, Jesús Amaya, trying to unscramble the links among the major landowners of the colonial period, referred to the genealogy as an "inextricable family tangle."[90]

The Spanish-creole dichotomy was not a particularly telling way of distinguishing landowners from other groups. Certainly many of the prominent landowners of the late eighteenth century were Spaniards who had come to Guadalajara, made their fortunes (usually in commerce), married into good creole families, and acquired land either by inheritance or purchase. But like the recruitment of landowners in general, this was a continuous process all during the colonial period and does not seem to have accelerated notably during the late eighteenth century. The patriarch of a landed dynasty, if such could be said to exist within the context of the ownership instability discussed in Chapter 7, was more than likely to be a Spaniard, whether at the beginning of the century or at its end. Similarly,

90. Amaya, *Ameca*, p. 270.

there is no particularly striking correlation between landownership and employment in the royal bureaucracy. Men who held high or lucrative office during the seventeenth century were perhaps more likely to use their emoluments and judicial advantage to acquire and develop landed estates, but by the first decades of the eighteenth century this was less and less the case. Certainly during the latter part of the eighteenth century, when the regional economy began to heat up and other sources of wealth burgeoned more and more, office-holding ceased to be any particular advantage.

The relationship of local political power to landholding is an intriguing one, and on this score a discernible pattern may indeed have been emerging during the eighteenth century. Although complete lists of eighteenth-century Guadalajara cabildos are not available, there is nonetheless a sufficiently large sample, spread over enough of the century, to allow us to mark a general trend. In the early decades of the century, city government, as reflected in the composition of the municipal cabildo, was very much dominated by the area's great landowners, both Spanish and creole. Of the seven identified members of the 1716 cabildo, for example, four (Miguel de Amesqua, Pedro Martínez Martaraña, Pablo Delgado Coronel, and José Félix de Escobar) were important local landowners. The cabildo of two years later, in 1718, was even more obviously dominated by hacendados, who held six of the seven positions of alcalde and regidor (Francisco Porres Baranda, Amesqua, Martínez Martaraña, Miguel del Portillo y Zurita, Bernardo Apolinar de Miranda Villayzán, and Delgado Coronel).[91] This situation seems to have obtained through the 1740s.

By the 1750s, at least, the hegemony of landowners in local political affairs, as reflected in cabildo membership, had begun to soften somewhat. The cabildos of the 1760s, 1770s, 1780s, and thereafter were more often numerically dominated by city merchants who cannot for the most part be identified as landowners or even, generally, as allied through kinship or in other ways with landowning families. Landowners were still very much present in city politics, of course, and their influence in some areas of municipal policy led to definite conflicts of interest between their needs as a group and the putative goals of city government (e.g., in the abasto de carnes, as we have seen). Such men as Ignacio de Estrada and Antonio Colazo Feijoo were more or less continuously active in municipal politics in the late eighteenth century, but the great landowners of the area did not cram the lists as they had in the early decades of the century. In a fairly

91. Exactly which of the regidorships were perpetual (i.e., purchased) is not clear, but even these offices apparently changed hands frequently through various means. For an overview of the legal and political development of Spanish-American and Mexican cabildos during the eighteenth century, see Guadalupe Nava Otero, *Cabildos y ayuntamientos de la Nueva España en 1808* (1973).

typical cabildo of the late eighteenth century, that of 1798, the single identified landowner was Miguel del Portillo (the third of that name). There
were some years in which landed magnates were strongly represented, such
as 1801, when Joaquín de Echauri, Juan Francisco de Corcuera, Juan
Manuel Caballero, and Alfonso José Sánchez Leñero (though Corcuera
and Caballero were not yet landowners) accounted for four out of ten identified cabildo positions. Even allowing for a slight resurgence of landowners in municipal government after 1800, however, the cabildos of the last
colonial years were still dominated by major city merchants, a good many
of whom were Spaniards. This situation was the reverse of that which had
prevailed until the middle of the eighteenth century.[92]

The significance of this political slippage on the part of landowners is
very debatable. It seems possible that a schism was developing in the late
colonial period between creole landowners and newly arrived peninsular
merchants. That such a division may have overlaid the traditionally-held
opposition between Spaniards and creoles considerably complicates the
picture of the Independence movement. If such a dichotomy existed, it
raises the possibility of a real conflict in interests between the city and the
countryside. This leads to questions of internal economic and social structure as they developed during the late colonial period and as they subsequently affected the course of Mexican history. The image of a declining
creole landed aristocracy living a sybaritic existence on decaying feudal
estates does not square with what we have seen so far about commercial
agriculture, capital accumulation, elite recruitment, and the functions of
landownership in the late eighteenth century. The picture is certainly too
complicated to allow the application of a simple model from elsewhere,
such as the prototype of rising gentry and declining nobility offered by
R. H. Tawney for sixteenth- and seventeenth-century England. Nonetheless, the decline in political power—or at least participation—of landowners as a group is fairly clear in late-colonial Guadalajara.[93]

92. AHMG, various cajas.
93. R. H. Tawney, "The Rise of the Gentry, 1558-1640," *Economic History Review* 11
(1941); H. R. Trevor-Roper, "The Elizabethan Aristocracy," *ibid.* 3 (1951); see also J. H.
Hexter, *Reappraisals in History* (1961). For a more highly nuanced view of the Mexican
Independence movement than the traditional one, see David A. Brading, *Los orígenes del
nacionalismo mexicano* (1973), pp. 215-221.

CHAPTER 9

Hacienda Ownership—Patterns of Value and Investment

Land Values

The congenial situation for large-scale commercial agriculture which was created by the conjunction of urban demand, the growth of capital resources, and the availability of relatively inexpensive labor had the effect of greatly increasing the value of land in the Guadalajara region during the period between 1760 and 1820. Nor was the general increase in land values and in the value of rural estates simply the product of a general inflationary trend, although such a process was at work during the century. The disparity in increases in value among different rural estates, and the tendency toward greater increase for those haciendas which lay within the effective orbit of the developing urban market, controvert a simply passive, monetary increase in value and point to an active effort at capital investment and the importance of geographical location. In a number of cases, haciendas experienced tremendous increases in value mainly during the final third or quarter of the eighteenth century.[1]

The increase in capital value of many of the haciendas around Guada-

1. A similar rise in inventory values as the result of active capital investment has been noted by David A. Brading for Bajío haciendas in the eighteenth century, in an unpublished paper, "Hacienda Profits and Tenant Farming" (1972), p. 11, and in "La estructura de la producción agrícola en el Bajío," *Historia Mexicana* 23 (1972), and *Haciendas and Ranchos*, passim.

lajara is highlighted by the fact that, even by the middle of the eighteenth century, land was acknowledged to be a relatively plentiful and cheap production factor in agriculture. This was the heritage of the extensive, rather than intensive, production mode of the seventeeth century, concentrated predominantly on the raising of livestock. Elsewhere in Mexico, particularly in the Puebla-Tlaxcala and Mexico City areas, where population density was greater and agriculture more developed and intensive, land values were concomitantly higher. Comparisons in land values between different geographical areas are admittedly difficult, but for purposes of illustration let us make one between Guadalajara and Tlaxcala in the early years of the eighteenth century.

In 1712, the Hacienda de San Juan in the district of Huamantla, near the city of Tlaxcala, consisted of 30 caballerías (about 3,000 acres—a caballería was slightly more than 100 acres) of land, various buildings and equipment, some 300 head of horses, cattle, and mules, and 500 pigs. The overall estimated value of the property was 31,000 pesos, or about 1,000 pesos per caballería.[2] At a slightly later date (1725), the Hacienda de Atequiza, on the northern rim of Lake Chapala—later to be one of the important grain-producing estates of the late eighteenth century in the Guadalajara region—measured altogether about 245 caballerías, or about 25,000 acres and in addition to its buildings had a wheat mill and more than 4,000 head of cattle. If the overall value of Atequiza were equivalent to that of San Juan, it should have been worth about 250,000 pesos. In fact, it was sold in 1725 for 20,000 pesos.[3] Its value per caballería was thus about 83 pesos, or less than one-tenth that of the Tlaxcala property. Of course there were immense differences in property values around Guadalajara at any given time during the eighteenth century, but the low worth of Atequiza's lands was not at all untypical. Even by the early 1760s, when the situation around Guadalajara had begun to change, it was estimated that a caballería of agricultural land near Mexico City was worth more than an entire sitio de ganado mayor (about 4,000 acres) near the capital of New Galicia.[4]

This situation had changed vastly by the end of the eighteenth century. Whether land values increased relatively faster in the Guadalajara area than elsewhere we do not know, but the marginal return on investment in agriculture in the Guadalajara area may have been greater during the course of the late colonial period than in areas where property values were already high at the beginning of the century, or even before, such as Tlaxcala or Puebla. All that we can say for certain is that property values in general,

2. Isabel González Sánchez, *Haciendas y ranchos de Tlaxcala en 1712* (1969), table facing p. 80.
3. AIPG, prot. Mena mayor, 14:78v-82v.   4. AIPG, Tierras, leg. 33, exp. 38.

and the value of large rural estates in particular, increased substantially, and in some cases spectacularly, during the eighteenth century. And this seems to be especially true of those rural estates whose owners had access to substantial amounts of capital for investment, whether it came from commerce, mining, or any other source. Table 15 gives information on the increasing value of several important haciendas during the eighteenth and early nineteenth centuries.

Any attempt to arrive at an average rate of increase would vitiate the most interesting fact which emerges from the data—that previously less-developed estates in favored but formerly marginal areas generally experienced the greatest increases in value during this period. This was most obviously and spectacularly the case with the four haciendas near Lake Chapala—Huejotitán, Cedros, Potrerillos, and Atequiza—and El Cabezón-La Vega, in the Ameca area. And most of the enormous increase in the capital value of these rural estates occurred toward the end of the eighteenth century and in the first decades of the nineteenth. El Cabezón-La Vega, for example, through the heavy capital investment by Manuel Calixto Cañedo, the wealthy Rosario ex-miner, quintupled in value within thirty years, from its purchase by Cañedo in 1763 until his death in 1793. Overall, the most spectacular growth in value was shown by the Hacienda de Atequiza, which increased 800 percent in the near-century 1725-1821. Atequiza, Huejotitán, and El Cabezón-La Vega had all been almost entirely livestock producers at the beginning of the eighteenth century, and while the raising and marketing of cattle remained important for all of them, they became major grain suppliers for Guadalajara as well. Most of the capital investment characteristic of the late colonial period seems to have been in buildings, fencing, and irrigation works, although the enormously increased overall values in the later eighteenth century were also in some cases due to greater numbers of livestock and higher livestock prices.

Generally speaking, the increase in estate values was less spectacular in those areas, such as the Toluquilla Valley, which were already well-developed by the mid-eighteenth century. The Hacienda de Toluquilla, through the investment of Francisco Javier de Vizcarra, the first Marqués de Pánuco, did almost double its value between 1772 and about 1795, and the Hacienda de la Concepción increased its value by almost 300 percent between 1705 and 1822; these were both major grain-producing haciendas.[5] But the Hacienda de San Nicolás had virtually the same assessed value in 1791 as it had forty years earlier, and La Capacha and Santa Cruz did not increase notably in value during the agricultural boom period of the later eighteenth century.

5. That Toluquilla should have increased in value between the expulsion of the Jesuits in 1767 and its sale in 1772 to Vizcarra, its first lay owner, seems unlikely. It is more probable that the 1767 valuation was low and the sale price more closely represented the true value.

Table 15.
Values of Selected Haciendas in the Guadalajara Region, 1697-1823

Property	Year	Value
Toluquilla (Toluquilla Valley)	1767	37,794 pesos
	1772	50,359
	ca. 1795	96,661
La Concepción (Toluquilla Valley)	1705	13,200
	1720	13,246
	1739	20,500
	1755	22,400
	1791	30,000
	1822	58,000
San Nicolás (Toluquilla Valley)	1705	9,000
	1751	30,000
	1755	22,000
	1759	19,000
	1762	24,000
	1791	30,000
Santa Cruz (Toluquilla Valley)	1728	37,350
	1781	68,000
	1804	75,000 (appr.)
La Capacha (Toluquilla Valley)	1711	6,000
	1712	7,000
	1712	10,000
	1714	9,000
	1750	8,241
	1762	15,000
	1765	15,000
	1782	9,400
	1788	10,000
	1798	10,000
	1803	12,000
Huejotitán (Lake Chapala)	1733	26,029
	1754	52,345
	1759	57,704
	1808	200,000
Cedros (Lake Chapala)	1741	32,000
	1754	56,721
	1759	61,235
	1789	100,000

Table 15. (continued)

Values of Selected Haciendas in the Guadalajara Region, 1697-1823

Property	Year	Value
Potrerillos (Lake Chapala)	1714	7,500
	1729	11,000
	1739	7,265
	1751	17,614
	1754	15,143
	1777	18,000
	1823	32,000
Atequiza (Lake Chapala)	1725	20,000
	1751	50,000
	1772	70,000
	1784	89,604
	1794	162,456
	1821	180,000
Izcuintla-La Higuera (Cuquío)	1713	23,000
	1724	11,522
	1761	18,000
	1791	24,000
	1804	46,000
Navajas (Tala)	1704	7,500
	1708	5,535
	1710	6,500
	1711	5,500
	1727	8,343
	1745	5,500
	1750	13,000
	1764	14,065
	1769	16,000
El Cabezón-La Vega (Ameca)	1747	88,596
	1763	50,000
	1769	60,000
	1793	250,000
San Martín (Tequila)	1717	14,200
	1758	22,311
	1786	18,000
	1810	64,877
Copala (San Cristóbal de la Barranca)	1697	4,500
	1702	3,000
	1716	6,000

Table 15. (continued)

Values of Selected Haciendas in the Guadalajara Region, 1697-1823

Property	Year	Value
Copala, *cont.*		
	1732	3,350
	1758	6,500
	1763	6,500
	1773	6,000
	1777	8,000
Santa Lucía (San Cristóbal de la Barranca)	1761	37,124
	1777	50,000
	1791	76,850

SOURCE:

AIPG, prots., various notaries. The majority of the values quoted are from sales of the properties. Some of them are from inventories of estates, global estimates of value for the securing of loans, or leases with the rent capitalized at 5 percent. A very few are careful estimates.

Outside the most fertile and well-watered grain-producing areas, rural estates did increase in value, but not so notably. Navajas and Copala fluctuated a good deal in value in the first half of the century, and achieved 100-percent increases during its later years. Santa Lucía, under the careful management of Juan Alfonso Sánchez Leñero, did double in value between 1761 and 1791, primarily because it became an important supplier of grain for Guadalajara. Izcuintla and La Higuera, on the other hand, remained virtually stable in value during the last three decades of the eighteenth century and only experienced a spurt of investment after 1800, and then primarily as producers of livestock. Outside the grain-producing areas, the most notable growth in value of any agricultural property was that of the Hacienda de San Martín, in Tequila, which increased its worth by about 250 percent in the twenty-five years it was owned by José Prudencio de Cuervo. This is testimony to the lucrative possibilities of the distilling industry, and is in some ways the clearest example of the profitability of commercial agriculture in the late eighteenth century. Thus, although the accidents of individual career and family histories make a comparison regarding agricultural investment very chancy, we may say that those areas with the greatest unrealized agricultural potential at midcentury received the greatest amount of capital investment and increased most notably in value.

Lest it seem that the heterogeneous nature of the data on property values negates its significance, it should be noted here that the available information on hacienda rentals bears out the trend sketched above. Most rural estates were not leased out during the eighteenth century—and for those that were, serial data on their value is not available. Nonetheless, the general increase in the capital value of haciendas is reflected in rising rents. The rent paid for the Hacienda de Santa Ana Acatlán, part of the Porres Baranda entail, increased from 500 pesos per year in 1720 to 2,850 pesos per year in 1833.[6] The Hacienda de San Andrés del Monte near Ocotlán, owned throughout the eighteenth century by the Augustinian monastery of Guadalajara, was almost continually leased out, and many of the leases survive. The rental on this large, livestock-producing property increased from 450 pesos per year in 1713 to 1,200 pesos per year in 1787.[7] And the Hacienda la Capacha in the Toluquilla Valley, which increased in value from 6,000 pesos in 1711 to 12,000 pesos in 1803, fetched a rental of 300 pesos in the former year and 600 pesos in the latter year, exactly matching the change in capital value.[8]

The notable and in some cases spectacular rise in the value of rural estates during the eighteenth century was not simply the result of vegetative growth due to inflation, but was underwritten by an active process of capital investment. Nor was the increase in value, at least in the Guadalajara region, the result of marked territorial expansion of haciendas at the expense of small holdings or corporate Indian villages—as Florescano, among others, has maintained.[9] The great haciendas of the Guadalajara region, especially those closer to the city, were all formed by the beginning of the eighteenth century at least, and hardly altered at all in size thereafter. Much of the investment of the eighteenth century, therefore, was in the form of irrigation works, storage facilities, fencing, and increased areas of tillage. A vital source of this capital was the Church, whose role as investment banker in agriculture can hardly be overstated.[10]

Church Lending in Agriculture

That the Church was an immensely important investor in agriculture, and remained far and away the most important institutional source of capital

6. AIPG, prot. Mena mayor, 10:662v-667v; prot. Altamirano, 6:114-115v.

7. AIPG, prot. Mena mayor, 8:365; prot. Ballesteros, 8:199-202v.

8. AIPG, prot. García, 5:106v-111; prot. Sandi, 8: no page no.

9. Florescano, *Estructuras y problemas agrarios*, chap. 3 and p. 175.

10. The Church as a source of capital for investment differed from the ordinary sources of rural credit, consisting primarily of urban and provincial merchant-*aviadores*. The basic distinction is that between long-term investment of capital and short-term expenditure for operating costs—though in practice the difference is often difficult to determine.

throughout the colonial period, is by now a commonplace.[11] In broad terms, the symbiotic relationship between the Church and large-scale agriculture was very strong. Colonial latifundia provided income for the Church in the form of tithes, gifts, bequests, and annuities, as well as personnel from the elite families whose status was in part based upon landownership. The establishment of a *capellanía* (a chaplaincy, or benefice) which drew its income from a principal invested in a rural estate was a very common practice in the eighteenth century—in many respects equivalent to setting up a trust fund, generally for the son of the owner. The establishment of such liens, or of principals to be devoted to pious works, or of outright gifts to the Church, was—apart from matters of God and conscience—a socially approved form of conspicuous consumption, for such acts of public piety redounded to the credit of anyone who performed them. For its part, the Church provided a degree of social control and acted as a banker to the landowning elite.[12] A vital function of Church investment-banking was to redistribute capital generated in more highly productive but risky economic sectors, primarily mining and commerce, by channeling it into large-scale agriculture. Through this redistributive function, the Church may be said to have aided significantly in the process whereby the commercial and mining sectors of the economy subsidized an agriculture of relatively low productivity.

The universality of Church investment in agriculture in the form of liens and mortgages is unquestioned, and the situation in the Guadalajara region during the late eighteenth century was certainly no different. Virtually every rural estate had charged against its value some principal, whether by donation from the owners or through personal loans from the Church. The most interesting question with regard to this indebtedness—for such it was, regardless of the origin of the Church's claim—is the use to which it was put. In the case of the establishment of benefices or funds for pious works, the answer is fairly straightforward: godly favor, the underwriting of a decent lifestyle for children who went into the Church, and social prestige. But what of the multitude of loans which landowners took from the Church, and which consisted not of liens but of actual liquid Church

11. François Chevalier, *Land and Society* (1966), 253-262; Brading, *Miners and Merchants*, pp. 217-218; Taylor, *Landlord and Peasant*, pp. 141-142; Florescano, *Estructuras y problemas agrarios*, pp. 162-178; Bauer, "The Church and Agrarian Structure, 1765-1865," pp. 79-95; and for an indispensable overview of the institutional aspects of Church lending in agriculture, Costeloe, *Church Wealth in Mexico*.

12. Bauer, "The Church and Agrarian Structure," p. 79. For an interesting recent treatment of Church lending in agriculture, which in general confirms the line of argument laid out in this section, see Linda L. Greenow, "Spatial Dimensions of the Credit Market in Eighteenth-Century Nueva Galicia," in Robinson, ed., *Social Fabric and Spatial Structure* (1979).

assets? Is it true, as the conventional wisdom would have it, that such loans were used either in conspicuous consumption or merely to recoup losses in agricultural income, rather than to increase agricultural productivity?[13]

Before we attempt an answer to this question, it should be noted that there are two technical problems which make any such attempt difficult. In the first place, it is often hard to determine from contemporary documents the origin of charges against a given property. Haciendas were said to "recognize" a certain number of principals charged against their value, on all of which the owner paid the standard 5-percent simple annual interest. But which of these represented liens created by previous owners in the form of benefices or pious works, and which were actual liquid capital borrowed for a certain term from the episcopal *juzgado de capellanías* or from religious corporations, it is often impossible to tell. This difficulty, in fact, may have led to an exaggerated view of the Church's role in the supply of agricultural credit.[14] In the second place, it is extremely difficult to trace the actual use of Church loans for capital improvements in agriculture, assuming that such investment took place at all. Applicants for personal loans from the juzgado de capellanías, convents, lay brotherhoods, or other religious corporations were not obliged to state the purpose of the loan, though in the Archbishopric of Mexico they generally claimed the money would be used to improve their agricultural holdings.[15] In colonial Guadalajara, such declarations, even though they were not strictly binding, were seldom made at all, and the loan was considered strictly on the basis of the security offered. Therefore, the correlation between Church loans and the improvement of agricultural productivity (as reflected, generally, in increasing property value) can only be inferred.

What use, then, did hacendados make of funds borrowed directly from the Church? The evidence strongly suggests that estate owners did, in fact, invest to improve agricultural productivity, and that this investment was partially behind the ability of commercialized agriculture to respond to the increased urban demand created by the growth of Guadalajara. This is not to say that every spurt of heavy investment brought immediate returns in agriculture, or that investment itself could counteract ill-timing or mismanagement, but simply that Church loans were seen as a source of investment capital by landowners. The development of the Hacienda de Santa Cruz in the Toluquilla Valley, for example, was heavily linked to Church

13. Florescano, *Estructuras y problemas agrarios*, pp. 171, 175-176; Costeloe, *Church Wealth in Mexico*, p. 103.

14. The distinction, for example, seems to escape Florescano, in *Estructuras y problemas agrarios*, pp. 166-167. For more on this point, see Bauer, "The Church and Agrarian Structure," pp. 92-93.

15. Costeloe, *Church Wealth in Mexico*, p. 67.

loans, especially those contracted by the second Miguel del Portillo during the period 1729-1780. Table 16 summarizes the history of Portillo's loans over this 51-year period (but does not include liens he may himself have established against the hacienda).

The information on Portillo's Hacienda de Santa Cruz is unfortunately not complete, but it does indicate two interesting things. In the first place, the owner, whatever the use to which he put the borrowed capital, was able to repay the loans on a fairly regular basis. At any given time, the outstanding debt probably amounted to less than 25 percent of the total value of the hacienda. In the second place, the total value of the loans enumerated in the table, 32,200 pesos, is almost exactly equal to the increase in the property's value between 1728 and 1781, the year of Portillo's death. This correspondence is probably somewhat fortuitous, since the information on the loans is incomplete, but it does suggest that Portillo used the loans to develop his estate. In fact, Santa Cruz became a very important supplier of grain and beef for Guadalajara during this period, and continued to be so after the hacienda was acquired by the Marqués de Pánuco in 1781.

Other instances, throughout the eighteenth century, of hacendados utilizing borrowed Church capital to improve the value and productivity of their estates are too numerous to mention here in detail. The formidable

Table 16.
Church Loans to Hacienda de Santa Cruz, 1729-1780

Year	Amount of Loan	Current Indebtedness
1729	3,000 pesos	
1732	7,000 (redeemed 1742)	3,000 pesos
1742	2,500	
1746	2,000 (redeemed 1748)	
1747	2,000	8,450
1748	1,000	
1749	2,750	
1765	950	
1768	4,000	
1769	1,000	
1772	3,000	16,500
1780	3,000	
Total	32,200 pesos	

SOURCE:
AIPG, prots., various notaries

increase in the value of the Villaseñor family's Hacienda de Cedros, between 1754 and 1789, was based largely upon some 20,000 pesos in Church loans assumed during the period.[16] Other examples of such active periods of capital improvement based upon Church loans are: Navajas in the 1750s; the entailed Hacienda de Mazatepec in the 1780s ("para refaccionar y habilitar sus fincas"); El Cabezón-La Vega during the 1720s, 1730s, and 1740s, while it was owned by Bernardo de Miranda Villayzán; the Hacienda la Gavilana, in the Ahualulco area, in the 1770s ("fomento de su hacienda"); and the great Hacienda de la Ciénega de Mata of the Rincón Gallardo family ("obras importantes"; the loan was guaranteed by José Ignacio Basauri, hacendado of Atequiza).[17]

The specific nature of the capital improvements made with borrowed Church funds is not often discussed in the legal instruments relating to personal loans, but on occasion there is information. In 1799, Raphael Hernández y Chacón, a Guadalajara physician, purchased the Rancho el Potrero, near Tonalá, for 4,000 pesos. He immediately borrowed 4,000 pesos from the Dominican monastery in the city and used the money to plant, fence, and irrigate 22 *fanegas de sembradura de trigo* (about 33 acres). In 1805 the property—by then called the Hacienda del Potrero— was worth more than 7,000 pesos, and by 1821 about 17,000 pesos, all by dint of continual investment rather than by expansion of the land area.[18] Earlier in the century, in 1736, Antonio Fernández Chasco, a public notary of Guadalajara, sought a 1,000-peso loan from the Convento de Jesús María for the improvement of his ranchos San Andrés de Buenavista and Torres, in Tonalá. At that time the ranchos had already increased considerably in value since Fernández' purchase in about 1720 because he had invested in new buildings, new plantings of wheat ("de húmedo y riego"), granaries, and a *noria* (irrigating wheel) for his orchard and garden, which contained grapevines, olive trees, and 700 large and small fruit trees.[19] Later in the century, Fernández' two ranchos were known as the Hacienda de Oblatos. It is not accidental that both these small, intensively farmed properties were very near the city—for as urban demand expanded, the zone of intensive agriculture expanded with it.

The picture regarding Church loans to the agricultural sector is of course neither as simple nor as rosy as the evidence cited above suggests. Mismanagement, bad judgment, and climatic adversity resulted in large

16. BPE-BD, leg. 132, no exp. no., 1783.

17. AIPG, prot. de Silva, 27:100-102; prot. García, 14:257v-259v; prot. de Silva, 20:9-11 and 27:155-158.

18. AIPG, prot. Sandi, 4: no page no., 1779; AHMG, caja 9, expedientes on the University of Guadalajara, 1805; AIPG, prot. Sandi, 15: no page no., 1821.

19. AIPG, prot. Mena mayor, 24:350-352.

amounts of capital improvement going down the drain. Heavy investment underwritten by Church loans did not keep Lucas Calderón (Navajas) or Bernardo de Miranda Villayzán (El Cabezón-La Vega) from eventually going bankrupt, even though the incidence of bankruptcy seems to have declined in the later eighteenth century, and the stability of ownership certainly increased. And many hacendados did encumber their properties with debts to the Church without investing the money in capital improvements. This seems to have been the case with La Concepción and San Nicolás, in the Toluquilla Valley, which were acquired by Antonio Colazo Feijoo in 1755. The previous owner, Lic. Sebastián Feijoo Centellas, the *chantre* of the Guadalajara Cathedral, and his heir, also a priest, had encumbered the haciendas with 36,800 pesos' worth of debts—mostly in the form of personal loans from Guadalajara convents and the juzgado de capellanías—which represented almost 80 percent of its 1755 sale price.[20] Colazo Feijoo himself borrowed a tremendous amount of money in the 1780s from Manuel Calixto Cañedo, the former Rosario miner and master of El Cabezón-La Vega, but during his tenure the overall value of the two haciendas did not increase anywhere near as dramatically as their total indebtedness.[21] Nor were all personal loans from the Church redeemed with the alacrity shown by the second Miguel del Portillo. Families could hang onto a rural estate for generations, sometimes, despite the specified terms of redemption included in the original contracts.[22] For example, when Pedro Sánchez de Tagle purchased the great Hacienda de Cuisillos in 1710, it had some 28,000 pesos in outstanding liens and debts on it. Some of these were long-established legacies and capellanías (the earliest dated from 1592), and these were expected to be perpetual. But some were personal loans which dated from the mid-seventeenth century or earlier, and were not redeemed until the late eighteenth century.[23]

Personal loans from the juzgado de capellanías or ecclesiastical corporations were used for a number of purposes aside from conspicuous consumption and capital improvements on rural estates. They could be used to purchase other properties if the borrower could secure them sufficiently on land already owned—as, for example, when the Guadalajara Convent of Santa María de Gracia lent 70,000 pesos to Francisco Javier de Vizcarra, the Marqués de Pánuco, in 1781 to finance the purchase of the

---

20. AIPG, prot. de Silva, 8:104v-110v.   21. AIPG, prot. Ballesteros, 14:93-109v.

22. If the interest had been paid regularly, extension of the loan might be expected indefinitely, since it was in the interest of the juzgado de capellanías, convent, or other religious corporation making the loan to keep the principal secure and generating a steady income (Costeloe, *Church Wealth in Mexico*, p. 73). Later in the eighteenth century, many loans, called *depósitos irregulares*, were made for terms of two years, though extension was possible.

23. AIPG, prot. García, 5:301v-308.

Hacienda de Santa Cruz. This unusually large personal loan was secured by the Marqués' other haciendas and was granted for the short term of two years.[24] Or loans could be used to repay other loans to the Church, or to private individuals, which had fallen due and could not be paid off out of available cash assets—as with José Ignacio Basauri in 1794, when he borrowed some 17,000 pesos from the Colegio Seminario del Señor San José de Gracia, in Guadalajara, to repay other loans which had fallen due.[25] But not all Church loans were on a large scale, nor were they all made to large landowners, as some modern writers insist—though most credit does seem to have been granted to large rural estates.[26] Small ranchos which were intensively cultivated, though of low value, might provide security for small-scale loans from the Church—as with the ranchos Los Ameales and Tochincalco, in Ameca, and Nuestra Señora de Guadalupe, in the Tlajomulco area.[27]

Although the litigation involved in a judicial embargo against properties whose owners did not meet interest payments was invariably protracted, expensive, and messy, the juzgado and the ecclesiastical corporations of Guadalajara did not hesitate to initiate such actions.[28] Just one missed interest payment entitled the ecclesiastical lender to seek embargo of the security. And since nonpayment of interest was generally related to economic reverses to the borrower, and there were likely to be other debts involved, both lay and ecclesiastical, such embargoes generally eventuated in judicial free-for-alls in which the assembled creditors tore at the remaining assets of the debtor like piranhas scenting blood, in a frenzy to recover as much of their money as possible. Generally these proceedings resulted in the bankruptcy of the debtor and the sale at judicial auction of the property in question.

There are so many examples of this process in the eighteenth century that it would be fruitless to do more than mention a few of the most notorious: the embargo of the important Hacienda de Miraflores in 1722; Navajas in 1726 and 1762; San Martín, in Tequila, in 1755; San Lucas, in Cajititlán, in 1759; and the Hacienda San Nicolás de las Fuentes, in Tala, in 1773.[29] Not all these actions involved such large amounts as were claimed against the estate of Bernardo de Miranda Villayzán, the owner of El Cabe-

---

24. AIPG, prot. de Silva, 23:57-61.   25. AIPG, prot. de Silva, 35: no page no., 1794.

26. Costeloe, *Church Wealth in Mexico*, p. 102; Florescano, *Estructuras y problemas agrarios*, p. 170.

27. AIPG, prot. de Silva, 3:36-37, 1750; prot. Maraver, 1:81-83, 1733.

28. For a contrary view, see Costeloe, *Church Wealth in Mexico*, pp. 73, 78-79; and Bauer, "The Church and Agrarian Structure," p. 94; both state that the judicial recovery of ecclesiastical loans was difficult and rarely attempted.

29. AIPG, prot. García, 19:434v-449; AHMG, caja 1, and BPE-BD, leg. 108, exp. 4, 1762; AIPG, prot. de Silva, 8:78v-79v and 11:97-101; prot. Berroa, 16:315.

zón-La Vega, who died in 1747: the Convento de Santa Monica claimed 19,139 pesos, the Convento de Santa María de Gracia 19,000, the Convento de Santa Teresa de Jesús 12,700, and the Sanctuario de la Soledad 4,000 pesos, mostly for personal loans made to Miranda.[30]

It is interesting to note, however, that the frequency of such judicial actions seems to have decreased considerably during the course of the eighteenth century, even while the term of personal loans was increasingly often set at two years. The resulting decline in bankruptcies contributed materially to the increased stability of landownership, and suggests as well that the more profitable situation for agriculture in the latter part of the century made it easier for landowners to service their debts,[31] despite a continued high rate of borrowing to finance capital improvement in agriculture. But this increased stability of landownership was the result of economic, and not of institutional, factors. The contention of nineteenth-century Mexican liberals, such as Mora and Lerdo de Tejada, that the high rate of investment of Church capital in the form of loans kept landed property from circulating, is not borne out by the facts, at least in eighteenth-century Guadalajara. If anything, in fact, the establishment of capellanías and borrowing from various Church lenders encouraged the circulation of property, since it meant that the potential purchaser of a rural estate had only to pay the difference between the assessed value and the total indebtedness of the property.[32] In many cases, as we have seen, this facilitated the rapid turnover of ownership especially characteristic of the first part of the eighteenth century.

As to the broader patterns of Church lending activity—how it changed over time, where Church loans went, geographically, or how much capital the Church injected into the agricultural economy of New Galicia during the eighteenth and nineteenth centuries—the evidence is insufficient for us to draw any conclusions. Concerning such specific questions as the *consolidación de vales reales* of 1804-1809—the forced redemption of ecclesiastical loans with the royal government, which had such a drastic political and economic effect on the rest of New Spain—there is virtually no information for the Guadalajara region, though there is no reason to suppose that it did not affect New Galicia in the same way.[33] Nonetheless, some information does exist which throws light on the general impact of Church lending in agriculture.

30. AIPG, prot. Maraver, 12:185-186v. See also BPE-AJA, no box or document nos., 1708.

31. Taylor suggests, in *Landlord and Peasant*, p. 142, that in Oaxaca in the early eighteenth century the growth of hacienda mortgages was related to an economic decline.

32. Bauer, "The Church and Agrarian Structure," p. 88; and especially, Costeloe's critique of Mora and Lerdo de Tejada, in *Church Wealth in Mexico*, pp. 86-107.

33. Brading, *Miners and Merchants*, pp. 340-341; Romeo Flores Caballero, "La consolidación de vales reales," *Historia Mexicana* 18 (1969).

The records of Blas de Silva, a prominent notary of Guadalajara of the 1780s and 1790s, provide some data with regard to the overall rate of Church lending to agriculturists. Blas de Silva was apparently the major, and perhaps the only, notary used by the Cathedral Chapter of Guadalajara and the episcopal authorities in making loan contracts with agricultural borrowers. The broad geographical range of the loan contracts in his registers, as well as the variety of lending institutions (including the juzgado, the various Guadalajara convents, brotherhoods from the city and provinces, etc.), suggest that his records may well embrace all personal loans made by the various Church lenders during the period of his activity. Table 17 shows the total volume of ecclesiastical loans for each of the years 1787-1794. To say that nearly a half-million pesos invested in agriculture is "substantial" is not very meaningful, but certainly this represented a major injection of capital into the agricultural economy. Aside from the figures themselves, two things are worth noting. First, the low level of loans in 1787, when the agricultural economy was still reeling from the effects of the great harvest failure of 1785-86, tends to belie the notion that large landowners borrowed from the Church in bad years in order to make up their losses. During an agricultural crisis, the juzgado and the ecclesiastical corporations would in fact be in the least advantageous position to make massive loans, for the very reason that the redemption of capital through the paying-off of old loans would be slower. Second, the contracts indicate that most of the lending was done to agriculturists in areas lying outside the Guadalajara region, including such far-flung districts as Charcas, Aguascalientes, Sierra de Pinos, Tuscacuesco, Fresnillo, and Lagos, and this widespread lending policy was equally true of the decade of the 1770s.[34]

The greatest ecclesiastical lenders in the Guadalajara region seem to have been the convents located in the city of Guadalajara itself, although the episcopal juzgado de capellanías was a very important source of borrowed capital, and the lay brotherhoods also made personal loans. It is virtually impossible for us to estimate the amounts of liquid capital which the major convents and monasteries of Guadalajara had available at any time during the eighteenth century. The 1792 *libro de censos* of the Convento de Santa Monica, one of the major conventual lenders, shows some 190,000 pesos in loans extant in that year, though this figure may not represent all or even the major part of the convent's liquid assets. At an interest rate of 5 percent, this amount of outstanding principal would have yielded an annual income of almost 10,000 pesos.[35] The greatest institutional lender of the eighteenth century in Guadalajara was unquestionably the Convento de Santa María de Gracia, the wealthiest convent in the

34. AIPG, prot. de Silva, vols. 15, 21.   35. BPE-MC, Conventos, 1792.

Table 17.
Agricultural Loans Made Within
the Bishopric of Guadalajara,
1787-1794

1787	14,000 pesos
1788	94,773
1789	82,600
1790	20,000
1791	95,823
1792	26,830
1793	68,650
1794	74,140
Total	476,816 pesos

SOURCE:
AIPG, prot. Blas de Silva, vols.
28-35

city. Virtually every major family in central New Galicia sent at least one daughter to Santa María de Gracia, and these nuns all brought dowries of at least 3,000 pesos each, in addition to personal property which they often bequeathed to the convent. Any agricultural property, from the humblest rancho to the greatest latifundio, which borrowed money from the Church in any form was likely to have charged against it a *censo* from this convent. Unfortunately, it is not possible for us to estimate the total liquid capital at the disposal of the institution, or how much of it was lent out at any given time, but it must have amounted to at least several hundred thousand pesos.

The Church, then, apart from its limited role as a direct property-owner, performed a very important function in the agricultural economy as banker and redistributor of capital. Undoubtedly many landowners traded on the equity in their haciendas to secure ecclesiastical loans which they used in nonproductive expenditure. But there is also a great deal of evidence to suggest that personal loans from the various Church agencies were invested in the capital improvement of agricultural properties, and that this improvement was called forth by the broadened market demand in the latter part of the eighteenth century and the first decades of the nineteenth. The increasing property values in the eighteenth century bear witness to this investment in agriculture and to changes in the nature of large-scale agricultural production. It is to the nature of these changes that we now address ourselves.

CHAPTER 10

Hacienda Production—
The Changing Equilibrium

A consideration of the great rural estate from two perspectives—the urban market, and ownership and capital—has led us now to the same question: How did hacienda production change during the course of the eighteenth century? We have sketched the development of the urban market for foodstuffs, and especially the relatively greater increase in the demand for cereals than for meat. In the latter part of the eighteenth century, this enlarged demand steadily extended the effective pull of the Guadalajara market eastward to the Altos, so that the city drew its food supplies from an ever-larger area. Coupled with this, we have noted the increasing concentration of cereal production in large units, as well as a certain tendency for wheat to displace maize in the agricultural zones nearest the city. During the second half of the eighteenth century, hacienda ownership became notably more stable, the availability of investment capital increased, and the value of rural estates grew tremendously, through active investment by landowners.

The hacienda-dominated rural economy of central New Galicia was able to respond to the urban demand by a shift away from the traditional extensive livestock-raising toward a more intensive agriculture emphasizing both dry and irrigated cereal-production and the use of a larger labor force, and with it a more intensive husbandry. Under the old extensive economic regime, the major outlets for livestock lay outside the Guadalajara region itself, in the more prosperous and densely populated areas of central and southern New Spain. Our first step in tracing the important shift in the nature of hacienda production, therefore, is to examine the evolution of the long-distance livestock trade during the eighteenth century.[1]

The Livestock Trade

Before we embark on a detailed discussion of the livestock trade, the geo-historical basis for the concept of export employed here should be explained. In terms of the political entities involved, it is purely a historical accident that livestock shipped from New Galicia into New Spain crossed an administrative boundary and were therefore called "exported." To cite a more concrete example, livestock shipped to Mexico City or Puebla from León, in the Intendancy of Guanajuato, New Spain, were no different qualitatively or in economic importance from those shipped from nearby San Juan de los Lagos, in the Intendancy of Guadalajara, New Galicia. Yet the eighteenth-century documentation does make this distinction, so that "export" has an administrative meaning which may not correspond to any economic reality. The notion of exports does have meaning, however, for regional economic development, though a better set of terms might be "long- and short-distance livestock trade." If we substitute "western Mexico" for New Galicia, and divide it into subregions such as central New Galicia, the coast, and Los Altos, the notions of exports and long-distance livestock trade begin to converge in a more meaningful way. The shorter the distance between the origin and destination of the livestock, the less important becomes the distinction, of course; but in general, differentiation in terms of producing areas is useful.

The basic source for our study of livestock exports from New Galicia to New Spain is the yearly register of export licenses granted by the Audiencia of Guadalajara to stockmen within its jurisdiction—a system established by a *real cédula* of 1673 and later reinforced by additional cédulas of 1730 and 1735.[2] The main question about the reliability of these annual figures is whether there was consistent under-registration due to contraband movement of livestock during the period. Although there certainly was some, three facts point to the unlikelihood of a significant illegal live-

---

1. On the late-colonial sheep trade from northern Mexico to Mexico City, see Charles Harris, *A Mexican Family Empire*, passim.

2. Ramón María Serrera Contreras, "La contabilidad fiscal como fuente para la historia de la ganadería," *Historia Mexicana* 24 (1974), p. 180; Eucario López Jiménez, comp., *Cedulario de la Nueva Galicia* (1971), pp. 107-108.

stock trade between New Galicia and New Spain. First, no mention of it or of any legal measures designed to prevent it appears in colonial documentation. Second, the tax rate was so low (twenty reales on the first hundred head, and ten reales per hundred thereafter) that avoiding payment was hardly worth the risk of the heavy fines or confiscation which might have resulted from detection. Third, large numbers of cattle, horses, and mules could not move through the countryside without being noticed, and we are dealing here with possibly several thousand animals at a time.

The long-term decline of cattle exports over the course of the eighteenth century was quite marked. With the exception of the decade of the 1750s, the quantitative movement of this trade up to 1800 can be followed in Figures 13, 14, and 15. At the beginning of the seventeenth century, New Galicia as a whole was exporting to New Spain about 20,000 live cattle per

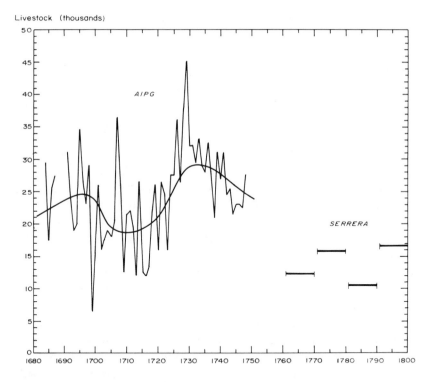

Figure 13.

Total livestock exports from New Galicia, 1684-1800

SOURCES:
AIPG-LG, various; Ramón María Serrera Contreras, "La contabilidad fiscal," *Historia Mexicana* 24 (1974).

Cattle (thousands)

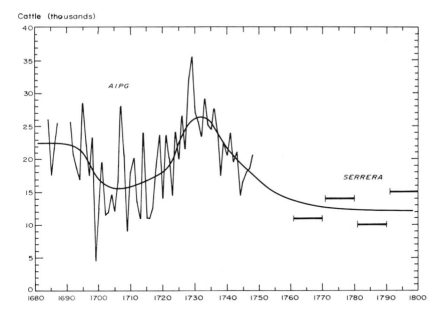

Figure 14.
Cattle exports from New Galicia, 1684-1800

SOURCES:
AIPG-LG, various; Serrera, "La contabilidad fiscal."

year, as well as large numbers of horses, mules, and sheep.[3] Whatever happened during the seventeenth century, by 1690 or so the level of cattle exports was virtually the same as it had been a century earlier, about 22,000 per year. Beginning with the disastrous year of 1699, in which cattle exports dropped to less than 5,000, there set in a period of recession which only began to be reversed after about 1715; recovery was particularly evident after 1725. Exports reached a peak in 1729, when more than 35,000 animals were sent into New Spain. From 1735 until the midcentury, when yearly figures stop, there was a fairly sharp fall in exports. Only the most general trend can be postulated for the latter half of the eighteenth century. Between 1760 and 1800, the number of live cattle shipped stabilized at levels considerably lower than the 20,000 per year of the late seventeenth century, and at about half the levels of the boom years of the late 1720s

3. Chevalier, *La formation*, p. 134. The following discussion deals only with live cattle, since horses and mules on the average accounted for less than 20 percent of annual exports, and since a change in the level of cattle exports would more directly reflect a change in the internal demand for foodstuffs. Unfortunately, there is only scattered circumstantial information regarding sheep exports to New Spain.

Cattle (thousands)

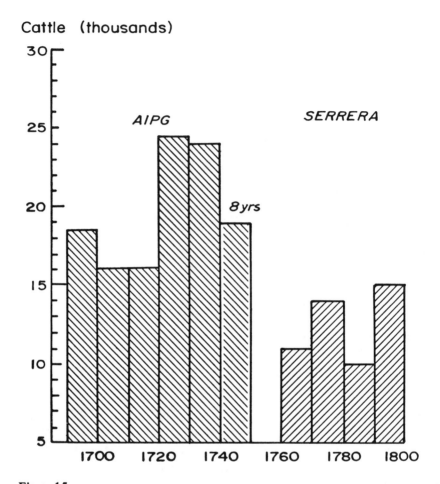

Figure 15.

Cattle exports from New Galicia, 1691-1800 (averages for ten-year periods)

SOURCES:
AIPG-LG, various; Serrera, "La contabilidad fiscal."

and early 1730s. The average annual shipment for the first five decades of the century was nearly 20,000, while for the last four decades it was barely 13,000 (see Figure 15).

The violent short-term fluctuations in cattle exports during the first half of the eighteenth century are largely ascribable to livestock epidemics and unfavorable weather conditions such as droughts.[4] The reason for the longer cycle of decline and recovery during the first third of the century is not clear, but livestock epidemics and droughts undoubtedly accounted

4. AIPG, prot. Mena mayor, 5:230-232v; 26:287v; prot. García, 19:120; AIPG, Tierras, leg. 58, exp. 18.

for much of the decline. One indication of this is the greater magnitude of yearly oscillations for both cattle and total livestock before 1725. We do not know the role of market conditions within New Spain, but there is no reason to assume that there was any slackening of demand during the first quarter of the century.

From the early 1730s, total livestock and cattle exports from New Galicia to New Spain showed a marked decline which bottomed out around 1770. Thereafter they remained virtually stable until 1800, with perhaps a slight rise just at the end of the century. This long-term decline in exports represented a progressive adjustment within the livestock-raising sector to the growing local demand for meat, work animals, and animal by-products, on the one hand, and an increasingly inelastic supply of land, on the other. As the populations of Guadalajara and the towns of its hinterland increased, ever greater numbers of cattle and other livestock remained within New Galicia to supply the expanding internal market. A breakdown of cattle exports from the various producing areas of New Galicia will give us a clearer picture of this process.

The absolute and relative contributions to the cattle export trade until 1750 by the three major producing regions within New Galicia—central New Galicia, the coast, and Los Altos—are represented in Figures 16, 17, and 18.[5] Exports from the central and Los Altos regions declined after the early 1690s, though the figures for central New Galicia hit bottom about 1712 or 1713, some seven or eight years earlier than those for Los Altos. Similarly, the recovery and peak of exports in central New Galicia antedated that in Los Altos by several years, and for both areas there was a falling-off thereafter until the midcentury.

The trends in the relative shares of these two areas resemble their absolute figures, except that recovery of the trade in central New Galicia only returned to the level—approximately 25 percent of total exports—of the beginning of the century. Rather than an increase and subsequent fall, as

5. Designation of these regions is admittedly somewhat arbitrary, but they correspond in general to geographical and ecological differences. Central New Galicia is the area we refer to here as "the Guadalajara region"; the coast means primarily Tepic, Compostela, and Purificación, though more northerly jurisdictions such as Rosario and Acaponeta also appear with some frequency; Los Altos means mainly Tepatitlán, Jalostotitlan, and Lagos, plus León—which was not a very important contributor. A fourth category—"other"—is not represented in the regional breakdowns, though it is included in the figures for total livestock and total cattle exports. This category includes Aguascalientes, northern and western Jalisco (Jala, Guachinango, Mascota, Juchipila, etc.), the northern mining areas (Sierra de Pinos, Zacatecas, Charcas, etc.), and shipments unidentifiable by region. Thus the regional breakdown graphs do not total 100 percent. For 1740, for example, when cattle exports from central New Galicia, the coast, and the Altos were 13, 52, and 14 percent, respectively, "other" areas exported 21 percent. The trends discussed in the text were established by adding up the yearly figures on livestock exports by district of origin, and then adding up the district figures within each region.

Percentage of Exports from New Galicia

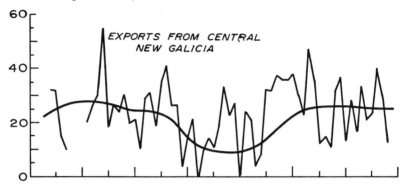

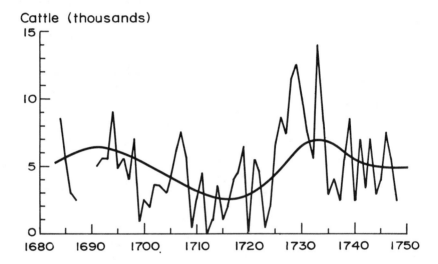

Figure 16.
Cattle exports from central New Galicia, 1684-1748 (in thousands, and as percentage of exports from all of New Galicia)

SOURCE:
AIPG-LG, various.

with its absolute shares, central New Galicia seems to have attained virtual stability in its percentage of the export trade after about 1735. If we assume that the central region's exports remained at about this same level until the end of the century, they would have amounted to something over 3,000 cattle in an average year toward 1800, compared to 5,000-6,000 dur-

Percentage of Exports from New Galicia

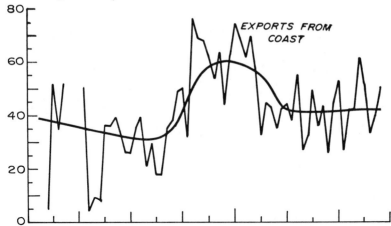

Cattle (thousands)

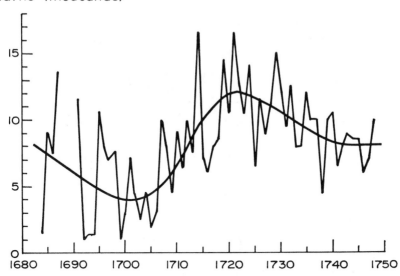

Figure 17.
Cattle exports from the coast, 1684-1748 (in thousands and as percentage of exports from all of New Galicia)

SOURCE:
AIPG-LG, various.

Percentage of Exports from New Galicia

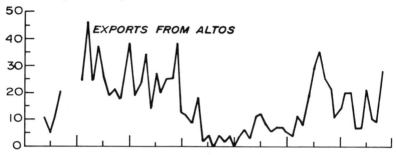

Cattle (thousands)

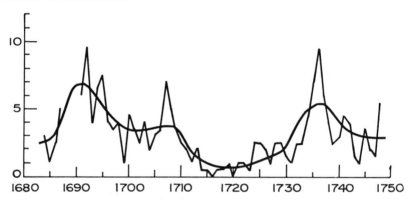

Figure 18.
Cattle exports from Los Altos, 1684-1748 (in thousands, and as percentage of exports from all of New Galicia)

SOURCE:
AIPG-LG, various.

ing the first half of the century. That central New Galicia did in fact continue to participate in the cattle trade is indicated by scattered export licenses from the early 1780s.[6] The Altos region, on the other hand, never returned to its percentage levels of the 1690s, even with its recovery in the second quarter of the century. The Altos had almost entirely ceased to export live cattle by the early 1780s, but maintained slightly under 10 percent of total livestock exports by concentration on horses and mules.[7]

The coastal area, though it experienced the same cycle of decline, recovery, and decline, had its peak for the half-century in about 1721, more

6. BPE-AJA, 135:7:1464; and Serrera Contreras, "La contabilidad fiscal," p. 182.
7. BPE-AJA, 135:7:1464.

than a decade before this occurred for the other two regions, and just about the time the trade was at its lowest ebb in the Altos. This contrast is even clearer if we look at the percentage of cattle exports contributed by the coastal region over the half-century 1700-1750. In 1712—the only year when central New Galicia failed to export any cattle at all—the coastal region contributed 76 percent of total cattle exports from New Galicia, a high for the period. Moreover, the period of recession in the Altos and the central region, from about 1705 until 1725, corresponded to a peak in the coastal area. Thus the relatively early and rapid recovery of the export trade in the coastal region mitigated the effects of its general decline in New Galicia during the first years of the eighteenth century.

It is impossible for us to say, on the basis of the available evidence, whether or not the number of live cattle exported from the coast and the Altos during the first half of the eighteenth century were by the end of the century being consumed locally or marketed in Guadalajara. It is clear that central New Galicia experienced not only an absolute drop in its cattle exports, but also an internal shift in export patterns outward from Guadalajara and its immediate grain-producing hinterland toward the drier, less intensively agricultural sections within the region. By 1750, the districts of Toluquilla, Tlajomulco, and Cajititlán, which appeared with some frequency as the origin of cattle shipments in the early part of the century, are already almost totally absent, and the districts of Tala, La Barca, and Cuquío—each with considerable uncultivated land—which were important contributors to the export trade early in the century, had come to dominate it. Tala and La Barca were important maize and wheat producers as well, but in relative terms they were certainly less intensively farmed than districts closer to Guadalajara.

That central New Galicia as a whole, and on occasion even the districts close to Guadalajara, could continue exporting cattle at all was due to two factors.[8] First, the supply of meat animals, as with any other commodity, was never so closely adjusted to local demand that there were not surpluses in some years which might be disposed of through other outlets. Second, with more land being put under the plow after 1750, the amount of irrigation and the available stubble-grazing land increased, especially near the city. This increase in the carrying capacity of the land enabled estate owners engaged in mixed farming to produce about as much livestock as previously, but on less land. This intensification of both farming and stock-raising would in a general way account for the ability of central New Galicia to satisfy the demand for foodstuffs by a growing urban center, and at the same time export some surplus livestock. Even so, there are occasional

8. *Ibid.*

indications that the city's meat supply was adversely affected by the increasing emphasis on cereal production.

Export licenses in a number of instances provide not only the district of origin of cattle being sent into New Spain, but also the name of the sender, so that it becomes possible to trace the activities of some individual stockmen over a period of years.[9] In general, this more detailed information points to the dominance in the trade of a relatively limited number of large landholders, particularly in the coastal area. For example, the second Conde de Miravalle and his successor, the Condesa, sent about 2,200 head per year to New Spain from their extensive properties in the Tepic-Compostela area for most of the period 1700-1750. Since the haciendas in central New Galicia were considerably smaller and more intensively cultivated than those of the coastal region, their cattle exports tended to be smaller, not only cumulatively but also in terms of individual shipments. Major estates in the neighborhood of the city—such as the haciendas of Mazatepec, Huejotitán, and El Cabezón—which raised cattle and might have been expected to participate in the export trade, did not do so. Others contributed animals for export only sporadically and in small numbers. A number of haciendas and ranchos in the area east of Guadalajara, on the fringes of the Altos, in the districts of Cuquío, Tacotlán, and Colimilla-Matatlán, sent cattle out of New Galicia, but generally in smaller quantities than the great livestock producers of the coastal region.

Throughout the eighteenth century, the most important external markets for the cattle and other livestock of New Galicia were Mexico City and the Puebla and Tlaxcala area. Bills of sale, instructions to herders, and other documents often state that livestock should be sold either in Mexico City or Puebla, depending upon the price or financial situation.[10] Among the most important purchasers of cattle from New Galicia were those merchants and city officials charged with running the municipal meat monopolies, particularly that of Mexico City. Sales to private individuals, most often merchants, were also common, however, and very often took place within existing commercial or credit arrangements. The practice of buying up livestock locally and reselling it in New Spain was widespread, even among hacendados, who purchased additional animals to round out what might otherwise have been herds of insufficient size.[11]

Throughout the century, there was in addition to the export trade a

9. The number of licenses which identify the exporter is much less than half the total, and some exporters specified by name in one year may not have been so specified in others.

10. E.g., AIPG, prot. García, 28:189v, 1729, and prot. Mena mayor, 6:392v-393v, 1716; *ibid.*, 18:178v-181.

11. AIPG, prot. Maraver, 4:412-415v; prot. Berroa, 14:334-335; *ibid.*, 8:372v-374; BPE-AJA, 102:2:1086.

substantial commerce in livestock within and among the various producing regions which made up New Galicia. Since these sales paid only the alcabala and did not require licenses, it is not possible for us to discuss them in quantitative terms. Notarial and hacienda records indicate, however, that most stock-raising estates disposed of large numbers of animals locally or at greater distances within New Galicia.[12] Most haciendas and ranchos raised their own work animals, but muleteers often depended upon purchases, and several major haciendas in central New Galicia consistently shipped mules and horses to outlying areas. A number of haciendas, large and small, apparently did not participate in the export trade to any great extent, but did sell cattle locally within New Galicia.[13] Aside from cattle sales to supply the city of Guadalajara with meat, the largest sales within central New Galicia seem to have been for the purpose of restocking rural estates.[14]

The economic and technical problems involved in moving large numbers of cattle or other livestock over long distances were great, making the export trade risky and cutting deeply into its profitability. Nonetheless, until Guadalajara developed as a significant market for cattle in the latter half of the eighteenth century, the differential between local prices and those in Mexico City was felt to justify the transport costs. There are no consistent data on prices in Mexico City or Puebla, but fragmentary evidence indicates that throughout the century they were about double those in the Guadalajara area.[15] In theory, this price differential should have made the cattle trade quite profitable; but in practice, the exporter was generally at the mercy of the buyer on the Mexico City or Puebla end. In 1740, an informal junta of hacendados, speaking in the name of all the stockmen in New Galicia, petitioned the viceroy regarding the cattle trade to New Spain. They complained that the meat-monopoly contractors of Mexico City were using viceregal regulations as an excuse for sharp dealing with exporters in New Galicia and elsewhere. The regulations stated that shipments of cattle coming into the Mexico City area had to remain at Guapango until the current needs of the meat monopoly had been met, and only then could they move on to seek purchasers in other places. The contractors thus offered exceedingly low prices for cattle, in the knowledge that the animals had literally been impounded at their pleasure. High labor

12. This discussion does not include sales of cattle in Guadalajara. Such livestock sales by haciendas were discussed more fully in Chapter 4.

13. AIPG, prot. Berroa, 19:118v-119v; AHMG, caja 20; AIPG, prot. Berroa, 10:326r-v, 12:383v-384, and 15:244.

14. AIPG, prot. Mena mayor, 8:84-86; prot. Echasco, 1:101v-103; prot. de Silva, 12:18-19; prot. Morelos, 8:20-29v.

15. BPE-BD, leg. 5, exp. 3; AJA, 202:24:2519.

costs and the rental of pasturage and water forced the exporters to make unprofitable sales in this situation.[16]

Various institutional infelicities and endless possibilities for extortion, many of them related to petty jurisdictional jealousies and differences in local customary usages, complicated the long-distance cattle trade and added tremendously to the expense and time involved. Local officials frequently extracted illegal registration and pasturage fees from the drivers of passing livestock herds. Although the mesta should have regulated herding and pasturage practices, conflicts often arose out of differences in local customs.[17] In the 1720s, for example, fees per head for pasturage were different in Tepic and Acaponeta, and difficulties were caused by varying local interpretations of grazing-rental agreements.[18] The movement of large droves of cattle over long distances entailed a high risk and considerable expense. Animals could only be shipped during the rainy season, from June to October, when there was sufficient pasturage along the route. But moving cattle during the rainy season meant that the sudden heavy downpours and swollen rivers caused heavy losses. Under normal conditions, losses of animals along the way due to all causes, including theft, ran as high as 40 percent.[19] And the expense involved in herding cattle and other livestock was considerable: when Ignacio de Estrada sent a herd of cattle from Mascota to Toluca, for which he expected to receive about 3,500 pesos, in 1794, the transport costs represented nearly 15 percent of the total value of the herd, not counting losses along the way.[20]

A revealing document from the latter part of the eighteenth century shows the cattle trade in microcosm. It is an account of a cattle drive in 1783 from the Hacienda del Palmito de Verde, belonging to the first Marqués de Pánuco, near Rosario. The hacienda was huge, and seems primarily to have functioned as a livestock supplier for the Marqués' extensive mining interests in the area. The estate did produce sufficient surpluses of cattle to export them from New Galicia to Mexico City, however—and even though it lay outside the area with which we are primarily concerned here, this unusual account touches upon most of the problems discussed above.

The herd of cattle of mixed description left the hacienda on July 30, 1783, in the care of mayordomo León Tejeda. It was to be received on the Mexico City end by José Joaquín de Ariscorreta, a wholesale merchant

16. AIPG, prot. Maraver, 4:412-415v.

17. AIPG, prot. Tapia Palacios, 2:149v-151v; prot. Maraver, 4:412-415v. On the history and powers of the mesta, see William H. Dusenberry, *The Mexican Mesta* (1963), passim.

18. BPE-BD, leg. 61, exp. 6.

19. AHMG, caja 27, 1814; caja 1, exp. 100, 1750; BPE-BD, leg. 61, exp. 6, 1725; AHMG, caja 23, 1803.

20. BPE-AJA, 102:2:1086; AIPG, prot. Morelos, 8:20-29v.

(*almacenero*) and the Marqués' factor there. Table 18 gives a condensed version of the financial account drawn up by the hacienda administrator. Tejeda left a detailed log of the journey in addition to the accounts. Shortly after the departure from Rosario at the end of July, the drive encountered two successive stormy nights which caused the loss of some cattle in rough country. Tejeda was continually riding ahead of the herd to reconnoiter the route and hire temporary help. Before crossing the Acaponeta River, he had to engage several men to clear the steep banks of the river for the cattle's descent, but despite his best efforts there was a stampede during the crossing and a number were lost. River crossings caused innumerable delays, since the fords themselves often needed work, and the frequent stampedes required regrouping the animals. On several days the Santiago River was too high to cross at all. The continued heavy storms and flooded *arroyos* added to the general chaos, and livestock were always straying into wooded areas and being lost. The herd was continuously losing animals which became lame and had to be left behind or sold along the way. The temporary herders tended to drift off, and new ones had to be hired. Every day or two the animals had to be counted.

After passing through Rosario, Tepic, Tequepespa, Magdalena, Tequila, Amatitlán, and the Hacienda de Guastla, the drive reached Guadalajara on October 21, crossed the bridge over the Santiago, and continued on by way of Zapotlanejo, the haciendas of Cerrogordo, Frías, and Salvatierra, and finally arrived at the Hacienda de San José de Hito near Mexico City on November 17. Shortly thereafter the cattle were sold by Ariscorreta to the meat monopoly of Mexico City, though the factor complained in a letter that because the animals had arrived so late and were in such bad condition, "me costó triunfo" to sell them at six pesos seven reales per head.[21]

It is hardly surprising, given these conditions, that stockmen within a reasonable distance of Guadalajara took the opportunity offered by the growing urban demand to market their cattle within New Galicia and thus increase their profits. By the early years of the nineteenth century, the high degree of risk involved in the cattle export trade was generally acknowledged, and risk was what stockmen and farmers alike sought to reduce above all. Thus the administrator of the great Hacienda de Cuisillos, writing to his *compañero* and agent in Tepic in 1803, advised him to stay out of the cattle trade:

Unless the cattle are three years or older, fat and healthy, and managed by a man who is honest and knows what he is doing, don't become involved in the cattle trade, because in one stampede you will lose everything.

21. BPE-AJA, 202:2:2519.

Table 18.

Accounts of an Eighteenth-Century Cattle Drive

	Number of animals
Shipments	
Left hacienda on July 30, 1783	1,360
Left subsequently and joined main herd on August 30, 1783	230
Total	1,590
Disposition	
Sold along the way because tired or lame	125
Left along the way because tired or lame	21
Died along the way	25
Killed for rations	1
Traded for two horses	2
Lost ("perdidos y extraviados")	401
Delivered in Mexico City on Nov. 17, 1783	1,015
Total	1,590

	Amount (in pesos and reales)
Proceeds	
Sold along the way: 125 cattle at various prices (average 2/1 per head)	265/3
"Fletes"[a] on cattle sent by private individuals	293/4
Sold in Mexico City: 1,015 cattle at 6/7 per head	6,978/1
Total	7,537/—
Costs	
Inventory value of 1,590 cattle (at hacienda), mostly at 2/2 per head	3,866/6
Rations and supplies	57/6
Wages:	
"Mozos conductores"	331/—
Temporary employees[b]	127/—
Mayordomo	100/—
Registration fees, export licenses, tolls, pasturage	107/—
Horses purchased along the way for drive and hacienda	117/—
Commission of factor: 2% of 6,978 pesos	139/4
Total	4,846/—

Table 18. (continued)

Accounts of an Eighteenth-Century Cattle Drive

	Amount (in pesos and reales)
Profit	
Proceeds (7,537/–) less costs (4,846/–)	2,691/–

SOURCE:

BPE-AJA, 202:2:2519.

NOTES:

[a]Transport costs paid by individuals for sending their cattle along with the hacienda's herd.

[b]Includes boatmen, swimmers (for leading the cattle across rivers), drovers, etc., hired along the way.

And again, speaking of the cattle export business, he advised his friend: "The cattle business involves high costs and losses, and in my opinion you should keep out of something you don't understand."[22]

The Shift Toward Cereal Production

The declining trend of livestock exports from central New Galicia, and capital investment in the grain-producing capacity of the great rural estates around Guadalajara, point to an intensification of agriculture in the late eighteenth century. This development is confirmed, particularly after the midcentury, by hacienda inventories and fragmentary accounts. In general, the numbers of livestock (both cattle and horses) raised for sale declined, as reflected by the shrinkage in the size of herds, while the numbers of draft animals, mainly oxen, increased dramatically. Irrigation works (dams, wells, ditches, and canals) and storage facilities increased in number and value. Yet another indication of the shift in production away from livestock and toward cultivation was the tremendous rise in the amount of fencing on late-colonial haciendas. Scattered data also show an increase in the area of tillage on a number of important properties, as well as a growing concern with the balance between tillage and stock-raising.[23]

Table 19 presents data drawn from a number of inventories of several important and widely scattered haciendas, indicating the kind and quantity

22. AHMG, caja 23, 1803.

23. For a discussion of a similar situation in the Bajío in the eighteenth century, see Brading, "La estructura de la producción agrícola," pp. 201-210.

Table 19.

Livestock Inventories of Selected Haciendas in the Guadalajara Region, 1704-1823

Hacienda and Location	Year	Cattle	Oxen	Horses	Mules and Burros	Goats and Sheep	Total
Huejotitán (Jocotepec)	1754	3,250	210	3,083	403	—	6,946
	1759	4,489	216	1,823	250	—	6,778
	1808	1,500	660	2,380	434	—	4,974
Potrerillos (Jocotepec)	1714	50	28	15	—	—	93
	1754	1,430	50?	680	136	38	2,334
	1823	923	203	863	107	—	2,096
Navajas (Tala)	1704	200	20	1,818	21	—	2,059
	1708	320	10	1,000	—	—	1,330
	1727	278	45	419	6	—	748
	1745	—	27	76	—	—	103
	1762	153	96	276	61	—	586
	1769	203	119	318	72	—	712

	1	2	3	4	5	Total
El Cabezón-La Vega (Ameca)						
1712	25,000[a]	—	10,000[a]	—	—	35,000[a]
1747	11,571	230	5,499	353	—	17,653
1763	—	70	50	—	—	120
1793	15,000	600	4,340	2,153	—	22,093
San Andrés del Monte (La Barca-Ocotlán)						
1722	838	—	261	8	—	1,107
1730	838	—	261	8	—	1,107
1737	830	—	261	8	—	1,099
1753	1,000	60	200	?	—	1,260+
1775	1,166	71	317	82	867	2,503
1778	1,129	63	270	83	830	2,375
1787	1,116	112	255	72	830	2,385
1819	178	140	48	24	—	390
La Concepción (Toluquilla Valley)						
1705	100	110	360	—	100	670
1710	200	80	500	—	—	780
1720	100	30	22	1	—	153
1739	—	60	100[a]	—	—	160[a]
1755[b]	400	80	535[c]	—	—	1,015
1791[b]	750	100	1,565	195	642	3,252

Table 19. (continued)

Livestock Inventories of Selected Haciendas in the Guadalajara Region, 1704-1823

Hacienda and location	Year	Cattle	Oxen	Horses	Mules and Burros	Goats and Sheep	Total
La Capacha (Toluquilla Valley)	1711	92	40	6	—	—	138
	1712	89	40	—	—	—	129
	1714	65[a]	40	26	—	—	131[a]
	1762	50	100	225	—	—	375
	1788	236	73	11	—	—	320
	1798	240	73	10	—	—	323
	1803	216	73	10	—	—	299

SOURCES:
AIPG, prots., various notaries; BPE-BD, -MC, and -AJA.

NOTES:
[a] Approximate.
[b] The data for this year are derived from estimates based upon joint inventories with the Hacienda de San Nicolás, with which La Concepción was consolidated about midcentury.
[c] Listed as "caballares."

of livestock they kept during the eighteenth and early nineteenth centuries. The most striking reduction in cattle and horses in favor of tillage occurred on the great Hacienda de Huejotitán, belonging to the Villaseñor family, on the western margins of Lake Chapala. During the last half of the eighteenth century, the number of cattle kept on the property declined by more than half, while the number of draft animals (oxen) more than tripled. This shift in favor of tillage is even more striking when we consider that a large part of the much-reduced stock of cattle was destined to replenish the huge number of oxen used in the production of maize and wheat. The Hacienda de Potrerillos, also owned from about the midcentury by the Villaseñor family, showed a similar increase in the number of draft animals between 1754 and 1823, although the number of horses and mules maintained on the estate also increased. The same trend is visible through the first two-thirds of the century for the Hacienda de Navajas, despite its highly unstable ownership history.[24]

Two slightly variant patterns were shown by the haciendas El Cabezón-La Vega, in the Ameca Valley, and San Andrés del Monte, in the Ocotlán area, which was long owned by the Augustinian monastery of Guadalajara. El Cabezón played a major role as a cattle producer into the first decades of the nineteenth century, at the same time that its owners, Manuel Calixto Cañedo and his successors, were greatly expanding tillage. Nonetheless, the contrast between the extensive economy of the early eighteenth century, when the hacienda supported some 25,000 cattle and 10,000 head of horses, and that of the last decade of the century, when the land resources of the estate were much more finely tuned to a balance between livestock and cereal production, is quite striking. On San Andrés, on the other hand, which was almost continually rented out, the number of cattle did not change appreciably during the century, while the number of draft animals more than doubled after 1750. The tremendous reduction in the total number of livestock on the property evident by 1819 is almost certainly due not to any conscious policy on the part of its monastic owners, but to the depredations caused by the revolt of 1810 and subsequent guerilla activity. It is interesting to note, however, that even while the herds of cattle, horses, and sheep were almost completely eliminated, the number of

---

24. A comparison of Guadalajara-region inventories with those of the Bajío and the Valley of Oaxaca at approximately the same time suggests that hacienda-based cereal production in central New Galicia was, if anything, more intensive, even at the end of the eighteenth century. None of these three regions demonstrates the high ratio of draft animals to land area characteristic of the relatively small production units of the Tlaxcala area in the early eighteenth century, however. See Brading, "La estructura de la producción agrícola en el Bajío," pp. 207-209; Taylor, *Landlord and Peasant in Colonial Oaxaca*, pp. 137-138; and González Sánchez, *Haciendas y ranchos de Tlaxcala en 1712*, passim.

plow animals was actually increased, suggesting the importance of tillage in the overall production pattern of the hacienda.

Two Toluquilla Valley haciendas, La Concepción and La Capacha, constitute something of an anomaly in this neat scheme. La Concepción quintupled its total number of livestock during the eighteenth century, with most of this increase in cattle and horses as opposed to draft animals.[25] Judging by the stability in the number of draft animals, tillage did not significantly expand during the late eighteenth century, and the same appears to have been the case on the nearby La Capacha. This is particularly notable in view of the considerable increase in the cultivated area of the neighboring Hacienda de Toluquilla, discussed below. Exactly what may account for this situation is not clear, but since both properties were relatively small (La Concepción was composed of one sitio de ganado mayor, one-half a sitio menor, and four caballerías), it is possible that they had reached some sort of natural limit on their cultivable area relatively early in the century and subsequently found themselves in a kind of technological and ecological cul-de-sac.

A more detailed examination of a few rural estates confirms the fact that cultivation was expanding at the expense of livestock production in the late eighteenth century, especially on the important haciendas, and that this shift in the traditional equilibrium of the great estate was a matter of concern to the important agriculturists of the day. Manuel Calixto Cañedo's testament of 1793, in which he left detailed instructions for the management of El Cabezón-La Vega, the superb estate he had developed in a quarter-century's effort, reveals much about the problem of balance between tillage and livestock and is worth quoting here at length. Since the portions (*tutelas*) of the non-inheriting Cañedo children were already provided for (El Cabezón-La Vega had been made an entail), Cañedo stated that the usual practice of selling off the livestock to settle among the coheirs was unnecessary. Cattle should thus be sold only in the customary way, and his son was every year to "take out the number by which the herds naturally increase, taking into account those which die, not less than 10 percent among the newborn animals." The mortality of livestock, particularly cattle, on the hacienda was to be avoided by not increasing the cultivated area (*labores*) to more than he had designated:

25. The situation of La Concepción is somewhat complicated by the fact that it was administered as a single unit with the neighboring Hacienda de San Nicolás after midcentury, so that it loses its identity in subsequent inventories. I have thus arbitrarily divided the number of livestock in half for the inventories of 1755 and 1791, attributing half to each estate, which may or may not represent the true picture on La Concepción.

. . . of fifteen or twenty fanegas of maize, and no more, because expanding the tillage restricts the livestock dangerously when they need more land during the rainy season, and destroys the useful scrubland which gives them pasturage and shade during the worst of the dry season; without these measures, the mortality among the livestock will be irreparable. Neither am I persuaded that it is better for the livestock, as some say, to open more plowed land, because when I was inexperienced at farming they advised me so, but experience and close observation have shown me that expanded tillage does great harm, as do renters on haciendas with great herds like mine.[26]

Whatever the objective merits of Cañedo's criticism of contemporary agricultural techniques, his remarks contain a number of interesting points which carry much credibility because of the obvious success of his enterprise. First, it is clear from his statement that there was considerable economic pressure at the end of the eighteenth century to expand tillage of both maize and wheat at the expense of livestock production, and that many large-scale producers were responding to the improved market conditions by doing just that. Second, the concrete way in which this production shift was accomplished was the clearing of new lands, as opposed to the introduction of more intensive technologies on old lands. Third, bringing into production formerly marginal lands exerted pressure on the traditionally extensive livestock-raising economy of haciendas by diverting land resources in favor of cereal production. Fourth, the intensification of agriculture was thought by contemporaries to be to the benefit of livestock, since it increased the carrying capacity of the land in use, primarily through better utilization of water (though Cañedo disagreed with this notion). Finally, Cañedo, at least, viewed renters as a threat to the equilibrium he had sought to establish between tillage and livestock, probably because they generally attempted to expand the cultivated area of their rented lands at the expense of pasturage. Fragmentary evidence from the years after 1793 indicates that Cañedo's son José Ignacio expanded the land devoted to maize cultivation, despite his father's advice, and oversold the cattle from the estate's large herds.[27] In the same period (1803), the Hacienda de Mazatepec was said to have overexpanded its tillage. Ignacio de Estrada, in connection with his financial difficulties at that time, claimed that it was ridiculous to extend the cultivated area on Mazatepec's sister establishment, Santa Ana Acatlán (known by then as El Plan), because grain supply and prices were already reasonable, while meat prices were climbing steadily.[28]

Even more detailed information on the transition from the extensive,

---

26. AIPG, prot. Ballesteros, 18:80-91v.
27. AIPG, prot. Sandi, 2: no page nos., 1797.   28. BPE-AJA, 235:2:3080.

livestock-based economy of the first half of the century to the later more intensive, cereal-producing economy exists for the Hacienda de Huejotitán, the entailed estate of the Villaseñor family. Huejotitán, consisting of some 37,000 acres of rich and varied lands on the western margins of Lake Chapala, was purchased by Lorenzo Javier de Villaseñor in 1733 and continued in the control of the Villaseñor family for the remainder of the colonial period. Almost entirely devoted to the production of livestock in the early decades of the eighteenth century, Huejotitán was more and more converted into a great grain-producing estate by Lorenzo and his successors as the century wore on. Although formal accounts were not found, two detailed inventories of the estate some fifty years apart (1759 and 1808) permit us to make a rough statistical analysis (Table 20) of the components of production.

During these fifty years of relatively continual capital investment and consistent management, the proportional values of cereal-related capital stock and livestock were almost exactly reversed. More specifically, the amount of fencing (*varas de cerca*) appears to have increased tremendously, though there is no figure on its amount in the 1808 inventory. The two dams of the 1759 inventory, valued at 350 pesos, were added to steadily, so that by 1808 the number of dams had grown considerably and the value of just the largest of them, which performed the dual function of irrigating wheat and watering livestock, was some 4,000 pesos. What is more, the area of tillage in both maize and wheat expanded dramatically over these fifty years. The 1759 inventory mentions a total area for the *labores de trigo* of 72 acres (24 *cargas de sembradura*), while the 1808 inventory includes some 540 acres of irrigated wheat land (180 cargas de sembradura).[29] There is no figure on maize for 1759, but by 1808 there were some 2,400 acres of *labores de maíz*, which probably represented at least a doubling of acreage over the period. The number of cattle kept on the hacienda had declined by about two-thirds between 1759 and 1808, as we have seen, while the number of draft animals had tripled. At these levels, it seems more than likely that the cattle herds served primarily to breed work animals rather than to bring in a large amount from sales, though cattle and oxen were sold to the city abasto in small numbers.[30] Many of the 2,380

29. The equivalence of one carga de sembradura of wheat to 3 acres is taken from Gibson, *The Aztecs*, pp. 323 and 559, n. 131. There may, however, have been some local variation, possibly quite substantial, in the size of this unit of measurement. The fanega de sembradura of maize equaled about 9 acres, according to Gibson, *ibid.*, p. 309; Bazant, "Peones, arrendatarios, y aparceros," p. 330; and Manuel Carrera Stampa, "The Evolution of Weights and Measures in New Spain," *Hispanic American Historical Review* 29 (1949), p. 19. But Brading found a local variation in the Bajío which put its size at 17½ acres, cited in his paper, "Hacienda Profits and Tenant Farming," p. 27.

30. E.g., AHMG, caja 25, 1789.

Table 20.
Value of Capital Stock, Hacienda de Huejotitán, 1759 and 1808

Capital Stock (not including land)	1759		1808	
Livestock	22,326 pesos	61%	26,830 pesos	22%
Irrigation, fencing, and sown lands	7,729	21	67,900	55
Buildings	2,900	8	27,200	22
Miscellaneous	3,749	10	1,000	1
Total value	36,704 pesos	100%	122,930 pesos	100%

SOURCE:
BPE-BD, leg. 106, exp. 3, 1759; leg. 180, no exp. no., 1808.

NOTE:
Percentages are rounded.

horses listed in the later inventory were used for threshing wheat, and also to breed mules for transport purposes.[31] The same tilt in the direction of cereal production characterized the two other haciendas owned by members of the Villaseñor family, Cedros and Potrerillos.[32]

We might think that the production emphasis of Huejotitán, Cedros, and Potrerillos, all located in the same district and owned by members of the same family, was not typical of late-colonial estates, but contemporary documentation on other properties reveals the same forces in operation. An unusually good opportunity to trace the relationship among urban demand, labor supply, and land use is offered by the important Hacienda de Toluquilla, in the Toluquilla Valley just southwest of Guadalajara. From 1587 until 1767, this fertile rural estate was owned by the Jesuit Colegio de Santo Tomás of Guadalajara, so that it had a continuous and notoriously efficient management.[33] After expulsion of the Jesuit Order from New Spain in 1767, Toluquilla was purchased by Francisco Javier de Vizcarra, the first Marqués de Pánuco. Under the ownership of Vizcarra's

31. BPE-BD, leg. 106, exp. 3, 1759; leg. 180, no exp. no., 1808. The same intimate relationship between working stock and breeding herds has been noted by Brading on Bajío haciendas in the eighteenth century, in "Hacienda Profits and Tenant Farming," pp. 25-26.

32. BPE-BD, leg. 106, exp. 3; AIPG, prot. Sandi, 11: no page nos., 1829.

33. On Jesuit landownership and estate management, see Chevalier, ed., *Instrucciones a los hermanos jesuítas*, and his *Land and Society*, pp. 239-250; James D. Riley's article, "Santa Lucía," and his doctoral dissertation, "The Management of the Estates of the Jesuit Colegio Máximo de San Pedro y San Pablo of Mexico City During the Eighteenth Century" (1972); and Germán Colmenares, *Las haciendas de los jesuítas en el Nuevo Reino de Granada* (1969).

heirs and then of Manuel García de Quevedo, the hacienda continued as one of the city's most important suppliers of wheat and cattle. Scattered but very revealing information from the seventeenth century relating to Jesuit management of the estate sheds light on the major problem which plagued local hacendados during that period, the shortage of agricultural labor, and discusses the solutions adopted by most landowners, lay and ecclesiastical.[34] A look at the economic structure of the Hacienda de Toluquilla before 1700 thus brings out strikingly the contrast with the later eighteenth century.

The Hacienda de Toluquilla had its origin in a donation of 10,000 pesos made in 1587 to the newly established Jesuit Colegio of Santo Tomás by the bishop and *cabildo eclesiástico* of Guadalajara. Eight thousand pesos of this donation was in the form of a rural property ("una heredad de labor") with land in irrigated wheat and maize which the donors had purchased from Francisco de Saldívar. This property, consisting of a sitio de ganado mayor, a sitio de ganado menor, and 6 caballerías, as well as livestock, equipment, and black slaves, was already called the Hacienda de Toluquilla in 1587, and was intended to support the Colegio with foodstuffs and a disposable income. Through subsequent purchases and royal grants, the hacienda had expanded in size to some 3 sitios de ganado mayor, 4 sitios de ganado menor, 36 caballerías, 24 suertes de huerta, and 2 millsites by the latter half of the seventeenth century, all in the heart of the fertile Toluquilla Valley. These 25,000 acres were still of quite modest value at the end of the sixteenth century, and indeed the Jesuits were able to enlarge the property because much of the Toluquilla Valley was not yet effectively occupied. A parcel of 600 acres acquired by a royal *merced* in 1603 was worth only about thirty pesos, and a witness said of it that it had been unoccupied and unworked for at least twenty-five years previously. In contrast, by 1700 most of the valley was at least claimed by titles, and by the midcentury there were thought to be no unclaimed lands at all, because the entire area was "poblada y cultivada."[35]

At the end of the sixteenth century, when the Jesuit Colegio acquired the hacienda, the main profit from the enterprise was based on a substan-

34. The discussion of Toluquilla in the seventeenth century is based upon documentary transcriptions made and graciously lent to me by Sr. Salvador Reynoso of the Universidad Autónoma de Guadalajara. The transcriptions, mostly from the Jesuítas section of the AGN, are unfortunately not as precisely cited as we might wish, and the dates of the documents have sometimes been arrived at by internal evidence or educated guess.

35. AGN, Temporalidades, vol. 87, exp. 7, ff. 1-55; Jesuítas, vol. 1, exp. 12; AIPG, Tierras, leg. 20, exp. 6, 1764. By the end of the nineteenth century, if not earlier, Toluquilla (by then known as El Cuatro) had shrunk back to nearly its original size of 1587, apparently as a result of land sales. The map of El Cuatro, dated 1887, is in roll 3 of the superb collection of hacienda maps in the Instituto de Geografía y Estadística de la Universidad de Guadalajara.

tial amount of land put down to wheat plus some 3,000 sheep, in addition to a few horses and cattle. Sufficient maize was grown on the estate to meet its own needs for rations, the wheat was sold in the nearby city and probably shipped to the coast as well, and the wool from the sheep was turned into cloth on the estate itself. The economy of the hacienda continued along these same lines into the early years of the following century, with a strong emphasis on wool production, but already by 1605 the decline in the local Indian population had caused a serious labor shortage. With no appreciable market and insufficient labor supply, the production of wheat was not very profitable, so the administrators of the hacienda constantly recommended the purchase of more land and expansion of the sheep-raising and textile-production activities. In a report of 1605, the hacienda's Jesuit administrator stated that he was renting a number of pieces of pasture land from neighboring Indian pueblos, but that this was still not meeting the needs of the hacienda (the property had yet to grow to its later 25,000-acre size). The obraje on the hacienda was having grave difficulty recruiting workers, which forced up wages and impelled the institution of a previously unknown weekly ration of maize and meat. The same labor situation obtained with the attempts to hire sufficient herdsmen. Not only were textile production costs increasing, however, but the local market for the cloth produced on the hacienda was weakening. The hacienda-produced cloth was actually being undersold in Guadalajara by textiles brought into Guadalajara from Mexico City, and attempts to sell in Zacatecas at a low price, even with transport costs discounted, had failed.[36]

Sometime about the middle of the seventeenth century, when the local Indian population had reached its nadir, the administrator of Toluquilla stated in a report that mules and cattle were "the products of greatest profit and least cost." By the mid-1660s, the number of cattle on the estate had increased to some 3,000, but there were only 200 sheep. Still, even though the major component of the hacienda's income was based upon the sale of cattle and mules, the Colegio continued its efforts to produce wheat on the estate, both for its own consumption and for sale in Guadalajara. But this effort was plagued by the twin problems of a weak market and the inadequacy of the local labor supply. The mid-seventeenth-century administrator's report is worth quoting at some length concerning the labor situation:

. . . If it were not for the mules, cattle, and horses sold, the Colegio could not sustain itself, because the wheat farm requires intolerable work and is so expensive that you cannot believe how little profit it yields. Since the president of the Audiencia has decreed that Indian laborers be paid at two reales and given a daily food

36. AGN, Jesuítas, vol. 1, exp. 12.

ration, without providing the number necessary, for the present harvest I have asked for help in securing labor from the alcalde mayor of the province and two friends from the parish of Lake Chapala. If it were not for this, we would have lost almost the entire wheat acreage, because the president only allotted forty Indians to us and we needed two hundred; but I found the necessary number and managed the harvest. . . .

An increase in the number of livestock, he continued, would allow the Colegio to save about 8,000 pesos within four years, "and then I would not bother with the farm, which causes us so much trouble, and only sow enough for our own needs."[37]

The situation regarding the availability of labor improved somewhat by the 1680s or so, and it is from this time that Toluquilla began the century-long process of developing into one of the growing city's major wheat suppliers. Early in 1681, for example, the rector of the Guadalajara Colegio, while on a *visita* of the corporation's properties, noted that there were some 400 cargas of wheat stored in the hacienda's granaries, a considerable amount for the place and time. It happened that most of this grain was too damaged by the weather to be sold, but his report, which also complained despairingly of the lack of credit available to the hacienda from city merchants ("I don't know who to turn to . . ."), indicates that wheat production was on the rise, even if substantial difficulties still existed.[38] By the end of the decade, the hacienda was being granted considerably larger contingents of *repartimiento* laborers for the wheat harvest, but labor costs were still high and manpower insufficient, given the scale of the enterprise. At about this time, the administrators of the hacienda were attempting to revive textile production and repopulate the sheep herds. In 1698 the Audiencia granted a license to the Colegio to establish an obraje on the hacienda, the older obraje apparently having fallen into disuse.[39]

By the end of the first third of the eighteenth century, the local economic situation had swung definitively in favor of cereal production. The Hacienda de Toluquilla was still receiving large numbers of repartimiento laborers, and was indeed consistently the largest and most frequent single recipient in the eighteenth century (see Chapter 11). Although figures on wheat production in the first half of the century are not available, the labor requirements of the hacienda indicate that cultivation was very important in the overall scheme of its management. By 1733, the number of cattle had

37. *Ibid.*

38. In fact, the financial position of the Colegio was very bad at this time, and at the conclusion of his report Padre Canto, the rector, asked the Provincial either that he be allowed to close the Colegio or that he be replaced by a more able man, so that he could use his linguistic abilities to better advantage in the northern missions (AGN, Jesuítas, vol. 1, exp. 12).

39. *Ibid.*; AIPG-LG, 14:130v-136.

dropped to 850, mostly for maintenance of the large numbers of draft animals needed on the estate.[40]

On the eve of the expulsion of the Jesuits in the mid-1760s, the primary income from the hacienda consisted of the 5,000-6,000 pesos it earned yearly from the sale of wheat and flour. The estate also produced maize and beans, mainly for consumption by the resident labor force. The wheat mill on the hacienda brought in about 400 pesos per year from grinding grain for neighboring haciendas as well as the estate's own wheat. A considerable number of horses were raised, mostly for the production of mules. The number of cattle had for some time been stabilized at around 1,000 head, from which the hacienda drew its draft animals and yearly sold a small number in addition (50 to 150 head).[41]

The new owner of the hacienda after 1767, the first Marqués de Pánuco, and his successors, continued this trend in production, though a considerable capital investment allowed them to somewhat increase the carrying capacity of the land and thus support more livestock. Around 1780, annual sales of cattle to the hacienda's major outlet, the Guadalajara abasto, were running at about 200 head—or, at prices then current, some 1,000 pesos. In 1786 the hacienda produced perhaps 1,000-1,200 cargas of wheat, which would have brought in around 10,000 pesos at normal (non-famine year) prices. Wheat harvests at this level represented a considerable extension of cultivation over that at the end of the Jesuit period. Even in the year 1796-97, a terrible year for wheat production, the sale of wheat from Toluquilla was equal in peso value to that of all livestock (each about 4,000 pesos). In fact, the high share of livestock-derived income for this year, in proportion to income from wheat sales, suggests strongly that the second Marqués was trying to recoup his temporary losses by slightly over-selling his cattle and horses. Maize was produced on the hacienda, but only in sufficient quantities to feed the labor force. The primacy of wheat production continued into the nineteenth century and may even have intensified, since there are signs of a land-enclosure movement in the Toluquilla Valley in the first decade of the century, with the Hacienda de Toluquilla (by then called El Cuatro) leading the way.[42]

The intensification of cereal production during the latter part of the eighteenth century was most obvious in the case of wheat, but was not restricted to it by any means. The exact nature of the changing relationship among livestock, wheat, and maize cultivation is extremely complex and varied. While, in general, tillage expanded at the expense of livestock on most great estates, and wheat showed a tendency to displace maize on

40. BPE-BD, leg. 76, exp. 6. 41. AGN, Jesuítas, vol. 1, exp. 12.
42. AHMG, caja 35, 1780; caja 11, exp. 2, 1786; BPE-AJA, 138:9:1489, 1796-1797; AIPG, Tierras, leg. 33, exp. 18, 1809.

these properties, maize cultivation grew tremendously in absolute terms during this period. Although most of this growth in maize production was probably within the subsistence sector of the rural economy, many haciendas increased their production as well, both for the city market and to feed their own resident populations. Such important wheat-producing estates as Huejotitán were also very important sources of maize for the Guadalajara market, either through direct demesne production or through renters. The emphasis we have placed upon the expansion of wheat production is justified not so much by any dominance it exercised in terms of absolute acreage, as by the fact that it seems to have been the most dynamic component in the agricultural production of the great estates near Guadalajara, both in terms of the demand it satisfied and the capital investment it attracted. The test of the importance of wheat production within the agricultural economy is the place it occupied in the overall composition of hacienda production and profit. What exactly did the great estates produce; and what role did cereals, particularly wheat, play in their economies? What part was played in hacienda economics by direct or, as we have called it, demesne farming, as opposed to renters, sharecroppers, or other types of tenantry?

Agricultural Technology

Before we attempt to answer these questions, we must devote some discussion to the state of agricultural technology at the end of the colonial period. The development of the agricultural economy around Guadalajara in the latter part of the eighteenth century was not mediated by any significant changes in technology such as those which occurred in northern Europe in the seventeenth and eighteenth centuries.[43] Instead, production was increased by a more intensive application of available technology and recombination of the major factors of production—land, labor, and capital.[44] There was little comment from contemporary observers concerning agricultural technology, and what there was indicates that New Spain in general was technologically backward.[45]

More specifically, there is no evidence that agricultural yields increased

43. See Slicher Van Bath, *The Agrarian History of Western Europe.*

44. A somewhat similar trend was responsible for the resurgence of Mexican silver production in the eighteenth century, though marginal improvements were made in the industry (Brading, *Miners and Merchants*, p. 139).

45. Florescano, in *Estructuras y Problemas Agrarios*, p. 128 ff., stresses the point that Mexican agriculture was of very low productivity, and that there was little reason for technological innovation. Humboldt, in *Ensayo político*, p. 256, noted the lack of expertise and technological knowledge among even the largest agriculturists.

very much during the course of the eighteenth century. The quantity of maize or wheat or beans harvested from a given unit of sown seed varied tremendously, of course, depending upon the quality of the soil, the care put into cultivation, the availability of water, and the vagaries of the weather. Generally speaking, maize yielded about 100 fanegas of grain for every fanega sown, with considerable variation.[46] The yield for beans, another important element in the late-colonial diet, varied between ten and fifteen to one.[47] The yield for wheat appears to have stood at about eight or ten to one throughout the century.[48]

Despite its demographic growth in the late colonial period, the rural population of the Guadalajara region, even concentrated as it was in certain small areas (e.g., Zacoalco, Cocula, etc.), never reached a high enough density to support the intensive agricultural techniques which so impressed contemporary observers in certain parts of Europe.[49] The New Husbandry —which integrated high labor inputs, complex crop rotations, the elimination of fallowing, and a more rationalized use of livestock—was simply not applicable to the human and geographic circumstances of late-colonial Mexico. There is little mention of agricultural techniques in eighteenth-century documentation, but the occasional references portray a simple and comparatively backward technology which relied generally on an elastic supply of land. Aside from the ancient symbiosis of maize, beans, and squash in small-scale *milpa* agriculture, crop rotation was virtually unknown. Given the indifferent-to-bad quality of the soils in the Guadalajara area, fallowing was a necessity. In the Cocula area at midcentury, for example, adjoining maize fields cultivated with plow and oxen were tilled on an alternating yearly basis.[50] On the coast, and in some spots around Lake Chapala, double-cropping was practiced, but this was manifestly impossible in most places because of the lack of water. Whatever may have been

46. 100:1, Cocula, 1739—BPE-BD, leg. 5, exp. 3. 80:1, Tala, 1762—BPE-BD, leg. 108, exp. 4. 100:1, Toluquilla Valley, 1782—BPE-AJA, 156:1:1736. 112:1, La Magdalena, ca. 1790—BPE-BD, leg. 134, no exp. no. The census and description of the *partido* of Guadalajara of 1813 gives the average maize yield as 50:1, which appears to be on the low side (AHMG, caja 41, 1813).

47. 15:1, San Cristóbal de la Barranca, 1722—BPE-BD, leg. 58, exp. 9. 8:1, Tala, 1762— BPE-BD, leg. 108, exp. 4. 20:1, Cajititlán, 1773—AIPG, Tierras, leg. 40, exp. 8. 10:1, Toluquilla Valley, 1791—AIPG, prot. Ballesteros, 14:93-109v.

48. BPE-BD, leg. 109, exp. 1, 1764; AHMG, caja 11, exp. 2, 1786. H. G. Ward visited the Hacienda de Atequiza in the 1820s and stated, in *Mexico in 1827* (1828), vol. 2, p. 364, that the yield for irrigated wheat was about 25:1, which seems greatly exaggerated compared to other more or less contemporaneous data. Generally the yields for irrigated wheat in the Guadalajara area were comparable to those for unirrigated wheat in northern Europe outside of the south Netherlands at about the same time. See Slicher Van Bath, *The Agrarian History of Western Europe*, table 3, p. 332.

49. Slicher Van Bath, *The Agrarian History of Western Europe*, pp. 239-243.

50. AIPG, Tierras, leg. 51, exp. 4, 1744.

the exact system of fallowing for maize and wheat when cultivated on a large scale, it must be remembered that the expansion of tillage required double or even triple the amount of acreage actually under cultivation in any given year. Seen in this light, the increasingly acrimonious conflicts over the possession of land which characterized the late eighteenth century are more readily understandable.

The use of fertilizers on a large scale was of course impossible, though stubble-grazing livestock on both maize and wheat lands was practiced on the great rural estates around the city. The most intensive agriculture was practiced in the immediate environs of Guadalajara on the multitude of small ranchos on the city *ejidos*, on the margins of Lake Chapala, and in the orchards and gardens which formed a part of many haciendas.[51] The grist mills in Guadalajara and its outskirts often had parcels of fairly intensively cultivated land attached to them, which were periodically treated with fertilizer collected in the city from excrement and various kinds of urban detritus. A rental agreement for the Molino de Sierra in 1741, for example, stipulated that the lessee throw over the wheat fields a thousand oxcart loads (*carretadas*) of fertilizer and topsoil within a five-year period.[52] Irrigated alfalfa was being produced on the small Hacienda de Santa Ynés very near the city at about the same time.[53] It was the proximity of these lands to the city which made such intensive cultivation possible, because of the night-soil available from Guadalajara itself and the nearness of the urban market.

Horticulture was possible not so much because of the use of fertilizer, however, as because of the accessibility and careful management of water. Indian horticulture was famous and widespread and was the major source of fresh fruits and vegetables for the growing city of Guadalajara. This form of agricultural production was particularly strong around Lake Chapala. The seasonal recession of Chapala and the nearby smaller lakes made for very fertile soils. The pueblo of San Martín Tesistlán (a *sujeto* of San Pedro Tesistlán), for example, had an *ancón* or *plan* covered for part of the year by the lake, but which in the summer months was very fertile and was planted with maize, wheat, squash, various types of melons, and vegetables. The pueblo of Jamay, also near the lakeshore, produced fruits and melons in great abundance, and the major Indian pueblo of Cajititlán, at the edge of a small lake of the same name, produced "los mejores melones que hay en la Galicia."[54] The list of Indian pueblos with horticultural specialties could be extended indefinitely. But there were also islands of inten-

51. AHMG, caja 19; caja 16, 1794 and 1796.
52. AIPG, prot. Vargas, 13:167v-169v.
53. AIPG, prot. Mena mayor, 32:126-129v.
54. AIPG, Tierras, leg. 33, exp. 13, 1803; BPE-MC, vol. 2, 1791.

sive cultivation on the haciendas of the Guadalajara region, both large and small, which depended for their success upon the availability of water and labor.[55]

The most important technological element in the mixed farming practiced in the Guadalajara region in the late-colonial period was the management of water. Thus, in this arid and semi-arid geography the expansion of agricultural production, particularly of wheat, was accomplished through the expansion of irrigation. The rather mediocre, sandy soils of the area immediately surrounding the city called for special management techniques which relied in the main on manipulation of the water supply. The land was very easily subject to damage because of sudden heavy rains, and topsoil was lost and ravines opened up through the least carelessness in tillage. The Indians of the pueblo of Analco, for example, invested much money and effort in the construction of various works (*galápagos* and *repechos*) which were intended to prevent the deepening of canyons and worsening of erosion.[56] These works, although of a fairly simple nature, were often built on a surprisingly large scale and required continual vigilance and repair. Neglect could lead to disaster during the rainy season. On the sugar-producing Hacienda de Guastla in 1766, the administrator's procrastination in repairing the feeder canals (*sacas de agua*) led to extensive damage of the irrigation network and cane fields. According to a peon resident on the hacienda who was an eyewitness, "a torrent of water came down the arroyo and carried off the dams and banks, wrecking the canals."[57] One technical problem which could not be solved in the late-colonial period was that of watercourses which were too deep to permit drawing off water for irrigation. Such lands, comprising a good deal of an area crisscrossed with barrancas, were simply not put under the plow.[58]

The main instrument for the management of water in cereal and livestock production was the earthen dam, often reinforced with masonry at considerable expense. We have already noted the marked trend toward greater capital investment in rural estates after the middle of the eighteenth century, and the large part played in this investment by irrigation works, fencing, and storage facilities. Dams themselves were often very large projects and were vital in the expansion of tillage. Just after the midcentury, the Hacienda de la Calera boasted at least one very large dam of earth and masonry measuring some 70 varas in length by 4.75 varas high and 2.25 varas wide (almost 750 cubic yards).[59] A common technique for collecting water was the construction of masonry-lined reservoirs which served both

55. BPE-AJA, 154:12:1736; AIPG, prot. Mena mayor, 24:350-352.
56. AHMG, caja 1, exp. 40, 1731.   57. BPE-BD, leg. 111, exp. 1, 1766.
58. E.g., the Hacienda de Cuspala, in Tala—AIPG, Tierras, leg. 14, exp. 5, 1727.
59. AIPG, prot. de Silva, 9:270v-276v, 1756.

for watering livestock and for irrigation.[60] Irrigation systems could be very elaborate and could bring water from considerable distances. In the 1760s, the small cane-growing Hacienda de Guadalupe, to the east of Cuquío, had some 3,000 varas of feeder canal to bring water from the Santiago River to its cane fields, as well as a number of lesser canals for the actual irrigation of various plots.[61] So important was the collection, retention, and distribution of water, in fact, that landowners occasionally overcame their perennially anomic impulses and managed to build and maintain dams in common and set up rotations for water use.[62]

Hacienda Profitability and Income Structure

Having looked briefly at the technological bases of agricultural production, we now return to the questions of the internal equilibrium within individual hacienda economies and the profitability of large-scale agriculture. What rate of profit could a late eighteenth-century hacendado expect to earn on his capital investment? More specifically, what were the respective roles of cereals and livestock within the overall production and profit structure of late eighteenth-century rural estates? What part of hacienda income was assignable to the direct participation of owner-entrepreneurs and what to the simple collection of rents in cash or in kind?

Despite the fragmentary nature of the data, we can assert that the average annual net return on agricultural capital was about 5 percent. This was subject, of course, to enormous variability, due chiefly to the vagaries of the weather—an inherent vulnerability accounting in large measure for the way in which late-colonial agriculture developed.[63] The 5-percent profitability figure was equal to the income from lending money at interest, and probably a good deal lower than the profits from large-scale commercial or mining enterprises. Brading and Bauer, for late eighteenth-century Mexico and early nineteenth-century Chile, respectively, both confirm the 5-percent figure suggested by records for late-colonial Guadalajara.[64]

Table 21 presents a summary of data drawn from accounts of four haciendas in the Guadalajara area, mostly from the late eighteenth and early nineteenth centuries, the single exception being the Hacienda de San Nicolás, near Tequila, for which earlier accounts were used. These four

60. E.g., Hacienda de Cedros, 1755—AIPG, prot. de Silva, 8:238-246v.
61. AIPG, prot. Berroa, 8:140-146v.
62. E.g., AIPG, prot. Mena mayor, 4:351v-355, 1714, regarding the Toluquilla Valley.
63. See in particular Florescano, *Estructuras y problemas agrarios*, pp. 102-124.
64. Brading, "Hacienda Profits and Tenant Farming," pp. 16 and 29; Bauer, *Chilean Rural Society*, p. 88.

Table 21.
Rates of Profit on Agriculture for Selected Haciendas in the Guadalajara Region, 1718-1812

Hacienda and Location	Years	Capital Value (pesos)	Annual Rate of Income (%)	Annual Rate of Profit (%)
San Nicolás (Tequila)	1718-1721 (4)	12,000	5.0	3.0
San Antonio de la Quemada (Magdalena)	1785-1788 (4)	19,000	9.0	5.0
Toluquilla (Toluquilla Valley)	1796-1797 (1)	97,000	11.0	7.0
La Sauceda (Cocula)	1807-1808 (1)	150,000	12.0	6.0
	1808-1809 (1)		15.0	8.0
	1811-1812 (1)		10.0	5.0
Average rate of profit				4.8

SOURCES:
Various.

rural estates were widely separated geographically and differed greatly in size, capital value, production emphasis, and history—yet their average profitability over the years represented in the table was about 5 percent. San Antonio derived most of its income from the sale of cattle, and San Nicolás from the sale of small surpluses of maize plus a few cattle and the collection of rents.[65] The important estates of Toluquilla and La Sauceda we shall deal with in more detail below.

The actual income composition of haciendas varied, of course, according to local soil conditions, the availability of water, access to labor and to a market, the financial capabilities of the owner, and a number of other factors. In general, the large, intensively farmed estates near the city, particularly those in the Toluquilla Valley and between Guadalajara and Lake Chapala, derived the major part of their income from the production of cereals and livestock for sale in the urban market. As distance from the

65. San Antonio—BPE-BD, leg. 134, no exp. no. San Nicolás—BPE-BD, leg. 54, exp. 4.

city increased, the degree of dependence upon livestock-related income tended to increase, along with the component of income from rents.[66] Table 22 presents a breakdown of the income of the great Hacienda de Toluquilla (later called El Cuatro) for a single year at the end of the eighteenth century. With total expenses for the year of 3,634 pesos, the rate of income for the hacienda on its capital value of 97,000 pesos was 11 percent, and the net profit 7 pecent.[67]

The most striking things about the composition of Toluquilla's income are the importance of wheat and the insignificance of income derived from renting out land. The sale of hacienda-produced wheat was the largest single component of estate income, accounting for 35 percent of the total, almost exactly equal to total livestock sales. Ground rents, on the other hand, provided only 3 percent of total income.[68] Since 1796-97 was a bad year for wheat production, the hacienda's income probably tilted even more in favor of cereal-related income in normal or good years. Another striking characteristic of the hacienda's income is the importance of rather odd categories which might not normally be expected to play much of a part: the rental of livestock, dairy production, and fees charged for use of the hacienda's grist mill, which together accounted for nearly 13 percent of the total. This indicates a surprising variety in the productive base of the estate, considering its optimal position vis-a-vis the urban market.

Other estates relatively close to the city, including the small sugar-growing haciendas to the north, also had a diversified production and a low ground-rent component in their incomes. Often haciendas further removed from the influence of the Guadalajara market demonstrated the same income structure, even where they were undercultivated. San Antonio de la Quemada, for example, located near the small town of Magdalena, had only three renters paying insignificant amounts on its 12,000 acres in the late 1780s, despite the fact that its gross income was only about 1,500 pesos per year.[69]

Nearer Guadalajara, there were some prime agricultural properties which did not follow the pattern of heavy grain production characteristic of the

66. For a good introductory discussion of location theory in agriculture, see Michael Chisholm, *Rural Settlement and Land Use* (1962).

67. The main elements in the hacienda's expenses were nearly 1,300 pesos in tools, equipment, and materials, and about 1,400 pesos in wages to temporary laborers and in rations (BPE-AJA, 138:9:1489).

68. There were 15 or 20 renters altogether (it is difficult to tell from the accounts); the largest rental was 50 pesos per year (*ibid.*). The importance of rental income to the mixed farming estates of the Bajío has been stressed by Brading, "Hacienda Profits and Tenant Farming," pp. 27, 29, and 38; and by Florescano, *Estructuras y problemas agrarios*, pp. 128-148, for Mexico as a whole.

69. BPE-BD, leg. 134, no exp. no., 1784-1798; leg. 54, exp. 4, 1715.

Table 22.

Income of the Hacienda de Toluquilla, 1796-97

Type of Income	Amount (pesos)	Percentage
Livestock-related		
Livestock sales:		
Cattle	2,610	
Horses	1,037	
Mules	340	
Subtotal	3,987	
Livestock rentals:		
Mules and horses for threshing; cattle (milking?)	376	
Bulls for fiestas (including payment for dead ones)	175	
Subtotal	551	
Dairy production	595	
Total livestock income	5,133	48
Cereal-related		
Sale of wheat	3,959	
Sale of maize (outside hacienda)	4	
Sale of barley	215	
Sale of wheat and barley straw	260	
Total cereal income	4,438	41
Rental income		
Rental land (ranchos)	319	
Rental magueyes	11	
Rental montes (6 months only)	15	
Total rental income	345	3
On account to employees		
Meat	213	
Maize	195	
Soap	119	
Total on account	527	5

Table 22. (continued)

Income of the Hacienda de Toluquilla, 1796-97

Type of Income	Amount (pesos)	Percentage
Miscellaneous income		
Milling fees (*maquilaje*)	264	
Chile production (sharecropped)	14	
Paving stones	13	
Total miscellaneous income	291	3
Grand total	10,734	100

SOURCE:
BPE-AJA, 138:9:1489.

Toluquilla Valley haciendas and the lakeside estates. One such was the Hacienda de la Sauceda, near Cocula, owned in the early nineteenth century by the Vizcarra family and valued at about 150,000 pesos in 1810. Table 23 summarizes the hacienda's income for the years 1807-08, 1808-09, and 1811-12.

The main elements in La Sauceda's income were the sale of livestock, the collection of ground rents, and the sale of "esquilmos." What exactly this last category was composed of is not clear, but traditionally it was taken to mean harvest grains, or livestock, or a combination of both. Inasmuch as the livestock component is specifically set apart in the accounts for all three years, it may be assumed that the "esquilmos" category for the years 1807-08 and 1808-09 corresponds to the sale of cereals raised on the hacienda, probably maize for the most part. It is interesting to conjecture on the basis of the above evidence as to the internal equilibrium among these three major income components. In the year 1808-09, a particularly good one for the hacienda, in which its profits reached about 8 percent of its capital value, livestock and grain sales were about equal and rental income was at its lowest level of any of the three years. Both livestock sales and ground rents increased greatly in 1811-12, a year of very mediocre harvests and high prices. This pattern suggests strongly that the hacienda's owners did rely on ground rents to make up for losses in demesne-farming operations, as Brading suggests, and also upon the sale of livestock. That rental proceeds alone could insure a steady flow of cash to cover wage costs and other operating expenditures, as Brading asserts, seems doubtful, however.[70] It must be kept in mind that a bad year for the hacienda as

70. Brading, "Hacienda Profits and Tenant Farming," pp. 29 and 38.

Table 23.

Income of the Hacienda de la Sauceda, 1807-08, 1808-09, 1811-12

Source of Income	1807-08		1808-09		1811-12	
	Pesos	%	Pesos	%	Pesos	%
Goods to workers on account	912	5	796	4	—	—
Sale of "esquilmos"	3,339	19	6,366	29	—	—
Sale of livestock	8,290	47	6,893	32	7,314	48
[Horses and mules]	[193]		[976]		[1,726]	
[Cattle]	[4,337]		[1,012]		[3,138]	
[Sheep and goats]	[3,760]		[4,905]		[2,450]	
Land rentals	3,473	20	2,749	13	5,148	34
Livestock rentals	391	2	279	1	96	—
Sale of sheepskins						
(*saleas*)	76	—	—	—	—	—
Sale of wool and tallow	220	1	1,776*	8	2,188*	14
Sale of soap	—	—	810	4	—	—
Sale of cheese	68	—	250	1	70	—
Sale of wood	33	—	100	—	57	—
Sale of sugar						
(*panocha*)	875	5	743	3	—	—
Sale of miscellaneous	76	—	272	1	263	2
Carried over from						
previous year	—	—	606	—	—	—
Total	17,753		21,640		15,136	

SOURCE:
BPE-AJA, 155:1:1736.

NOTES:
Numbers in brackets represent component parts of total livestock sales.

*Wool only.

a whole would have been a bad year for individual tenants as well, and that there was little cash to be looked for from small farmers struggling to survive a bad harvest or a drought themselves.

More detailed data which are available on La Sauceda's rental income in the late-colonial decades throw some light on the role of rents in the overall economy of the estate.[71] Table 24 presents these data for various years between 1790 and 1812.[72] Several rather interesting things can be

71. In addition to the work of Brading, cited above, see Jan Bazant's article, "Peones, arrendatarios y aparceros," and his *Cinco haciendas mexicanas* (1975).
72. The original data, which include information on the number of renters paying at a given rate per *fanega de sembradura*, have been much simplified for tabular presentation.

Table 24.

*Number of Renters and Rental Income of the
Hacienda de la Sauceda, Various Years, 1790-1812*

	1790	1791	1792	1808	1809	1811	1812
Number of fanegas de sembradura rented	243	——	140	——	——	282	369
Number of renters:							
Fanegas[a]	75	——	60[b]	——	——	129	146
Ranchos and pasture	30	——	30	——	——	31	73
Total	105	——	90[b]	——	——	160	219
Rental income (pesos):							
Fanegas[a]	2,012	——	987	——	——	2,572	3,465
Ranchos and pasture	428	——	388	——	——	556	1,683
Total	2,440	1,300	1,375	3,473	2,749	3,128	5,148

SOURCE:
BPE-AJA, 154:12:1736 and 155:1:1736.

NOTES:
[a]Renters of "huertas de riego" for the years 1811 and 1812 have been included under the category "fanegas de sembradura," since irrigated horticulture was more closely related to maize-farming than to stock-raising. In fact, the average yearly rental per huerta was close in value to that of a fanega de sembradura (6-8 pesos in 1811-1812).
[b]Approximate.

noted about La Sauceda's income from rentals. It must be pointed out that the apparently precipitous rise in rental-derived income in 1811 and 1812 was due in part, at least, to particular circumstances in the history of the hacienda's management. In the year 1811-12, following a period of thoughtless exploitation by the Vizcarra heirs, a new administrator took over. In the immediately preceding years, the livestock of the estate had been oversold ("se delapidaron y consumieron"), so that land formerly occupied by the hacienda's own stock was available for renting out. Also, rents which had been in arrears were collected, inflating the rental-income figures for 1812.

Despite these distortions, both the number of renters and the rents charged did rise after 1810. Rents for rancho and pasture (i.e., non-arable) lands increased almost 50 percent between 1811 and 1812. Moreover, the number of renters of non-arable land more than doubled in this period, while the number of renters on arable land increased only slightly. The rental charged on maize-farming land increased considerably between the early 1790s and the decade after 1810; most renters of fanegas de sembradura were now paying eight and ten pesos per fanega, compared to six or seven pesos in the earlier period. On the whole, the data show that the amount of arable land rented out by La Sauceda increased very little after the turn of the century, while its non-arable and marginal lands became increasingly desirable for small farmers.[73] In both cases, rents rose. Furthermore, the share of arable rentals in the total rental income of the hacienda declined from about 82 percent in 1790 to 67 percent in 1812, indicating a weakening in the relative position of farming as opposed to ranching lands. This suggests that even La Sauceda, which was not a major supplier of cereals for the urban market, felt an increased pressure on its arable lands in the last years of the colonial period.[74]

In terms of acreage occupied and rents paid, the distribution was very skewed: most renters occupied only one or two fanegas de sembradura, but a very few held much larger parcels. On La Sauceda's sister establishment of Estipac in 1790, for example, 5 renters, out of a total of 25 in one *potrero*, occupied well over half the land. Such men, who might almost be compared to the old-regime Russian *kulaks* in terms of the position they occupied in the rural economic scheme, were often styled "Don" and were themselves paid rentals amounting to several hundred pesos per year. Nor was the internal distribution of stock-raising lands any more democratic.[75]

The practice of renting out hacienda lands was virtually universal at the end of the colonial period. The major question about renting turns upon its importance in the overall economy of rural estates and why certain haciendas rented out more of their lands than others. Some hacendados lived as rentiers and drew a major part of their incomes from the rental of lands which they could not, or would not, cultivate directly themselves. This was largely the situation with the holders of the Porres Baranda mayorazgo.[76] Other large property-owners rented out explicitly only those

73. The number of *arrendatarios* did change from one year to the next, though apparently the maize-farming rentals were more variable in this respect. Rentals derived from ranchos were referred to by one expert around 1810 as "seguros," and those from fanegas de sembradura as "accidentales" (BPE-AJA, 155:1:1736).

74. BPE-AJA, 154:12:1736 and 155:1:1736.

75. BPE-AJA, 154:12:1736.

76. AIPG, prot. Mena mayor, 10:662v-667v, 1720; BPE-AJA, 235:2:3080, 1803. For a detailed discussion of the fortunes of the Porres Baranda family, see Chapter 8 above.

lands which were not essential to their own demesne-farming operations. Thus, for example, Miguel del Portillo y Zurita's power of attorney allocated to his wife in 1714 for the management of his Toluquilla Valley hacienda specified that she must give in rental "whichever lands and ranchos do not appear necessary to her for the main farming operations."[77]

Geography, however, did not necessarily dictate similar policies on renting. Almost all of the 100,000 acres of land in the La Barca area sold by the Marqués del Villar del Aguila in 1766 had been rented out.[78] The Hacienda de Frías, in the same general area, between Tepatitlán and León, was occupied solely by its owner, without a single renter on the property.[79] Several of the haciendas in the San Cristóbal de la Barranca area to the north of the city (San Martín, Guastla, San Isidro) each had many small renters at the end of the eighteenth century. The haciendas of El Carmen and Santa Lucía, however, owned respectively by the Guadalajara Carmelite monastery and the Sánchez Leñero family, had no renters at all.[80] Nor did rentals for hacienda lands often bring in the large sums typical of the Porres Baranda holdings, or even of La Sauceda. At the end of the century, Toluquilla, as we have seen, was taking in only about 3 percent of its yearly income from rentals.[81] Renters were frequently in arrears in their payments or simply did not pay their rents at all, for one reason or another. The extant accounts of La Sauceda and Estipac indicate a multitude of defaults. In 1790, Estipac was carrying on its books nearly 400 pesos in unpaid rents, and La Sauceda experienced similar arrears in most years. The reasons adduced in the accounts for these nonpayments constitute fascinating glimpses into the economic life of the rural lower class of the late colonial period. "Fled," "absent," and "died" appear most frequently, but other statements include "uncollectable," "insolvent," "denies debt," "no one knows anything about him," "unknown," and "has the money to pay."[82]

As the eighteenth century progressed, the structure of rural renting seems to have grown both more complex and more precarious. Up until the midcentury, it was not at all uncommon to find single arrendatarios who had occupied the same parcels or ranchos on haciendas for thirty or forty years in succession.[83] Toward 1800, the catgories of renters proliferated to include a bewildering array of arrendatarios, subarrendatarios, arrimados, and other small tenants who were explicitly not hacienda laborers with subsistence plots.[84] Temporary small-scale renting had also become com-

77. AIPG, prot. García, 8:66, 1714.   78. AIPG, prot. Berroa, 9:14-31v.
79. CG-ASC, leg. 3.   80. CG-ASC, leg. 12, 1789.
81. AIPG, prot. Berroa, 8:140-146v; BPE-AJA, 196:15:2378.
82. BPE-AJA, 154:12:1736.
83. E.g., AIPG, prot. Mena mayor, 9:661-663v, 1719; prot. Mena menor, 6:158-159v, 1747, and 20:404-405, 1758.
84. AIPG, Tierras, leg. 71, exp. 30, and leg. 14, exp. 8; BPE-MC, leg. 50, vol. 3, exp. 8, 1778.

mon, as in the Tlajomulco area, which had many "small ranchos of little value which at certain times of the year are established on lands rented by poor people from the town commons and haciendas of this parish. . . ."[85] In general, where leases were involved, tenures became shorter while rents increased, and the position of renters of all types became increasingly precarious.

Hacendados were putting other pressures on renters besides shorter leases and higher rents. In the area around Tlaltenango, Teul, and Jérez, to the north of Guadalajara, for example, the local subdelegado noted in 1813 that for the past twenty years or so the largest landowners had been systematically expelling their renters to convert their land to sheep-raising.[86] Just how far this process went in the immediate Guadalajara area itself is not clear. In addition, in the latter part of the century some of the more aggressive hacendados and their administrators were attempting to convert a rent-paying tenantry into a service tenantry, somewhat along the lines of Chilean *inquilinaje*.[87] In 1765, for example, a renter of long standing on the Hacienda de Cuisillos complained that the administrator of the property was pressuring him to supply labor to guard the roads and the hacienda's rough grazing land (*montes*), without wages, whereas he had previously paid only a money rent.[88] The creation of a service tenantry appears not to have progressed very far, despite the relatively weak economic position of both renters and laborers.

One form of tenantry whose role in the rural economy is not at all clear to us is sharecropping.[89] Evidence on the extent of sharecropping in the late-colonial period is both fragmentary and contradictory. Even had the practice been common, however, it would be difficult to determine, since sharecropping was generally an informal, subnotarial arrangement, and would therefore not often show up in contemporary documentation. In a

85. BPE-MC, leg. 50, vol. 3, exp. 8, 1778.

86. AHMG, caja 28. Expulsion, whether for nonpayment of rent or any other reason, was not always so easy, however. One tenant expelled from her small rancho on an hacienda in the Sayula area in 1789 tore down her house, cut down all the trees on her parcel, and tore up all her mescales after delaying her expulsion judicially for several months (BPE-AJA, 102:1:1094).

87. On Chile, see Arnold J. Bauer's *Chilean Rural Society* and his article, "Chilean Rural Labor in the Nineteenth Century," *American Historical Review* 76 (1971). For similar pressures on renters to convert them into a service tenantry, see Brading, "Hacienda Profits and Tenant Farming," pp. 17-18.

88. AIPG, Tierras, leg. 33, exp. 3.

89. Sharecropping was apparently a common practice in the eighteenth century among all types of landowners—Indian caciques, monastic orders, and Spanish laymen—in the Oaxaca area, according to William Taylor, *Landlord and Peasant*, passim, but esp. pp. 131 and 171. This form of tenantry was almost entirely absent in the contemporary Bajío; see Brading, "Hacienda Profits and Tenant Farming." For a comparison with France, see Marc Bloch on *metayage*, in *French Rural History* (1966), pp. 145-149.

period of rising agricultural prices and falling real wages such as the late eighteenth century, it would be in the interest of large landowners to retain as much direct control over production as possible, so that they would benefit from rising prices. On the other hand, where real wages and other production costs were rising, it would be in the interest of landlords to let tenants assume the burden of these costs. In any case, the use of share-cropping arrangements would also be influenced by the amount of capital available to a given hacendado, as well as the interest he showed in directly administering his property.

The available evidence strongly suggests that wheat production in the latter part of the eighteenth century was dominated by demesne farming, and that where sharecropping in wheat occurred at all, it was on a small scale. The tithe reports requested from the country districts by the cabildo of Guadalajara in 1786 indicate that most wheat production was in the hands of the great hacendados and their administrators. On the Hacienda de Atequiza, there were sharecroppers (*medieros*) producing wheat, but they accounted for only 130 cargas as against the hacienda's direct production of about 500 cargas. The haciendas of the Toluquilla Valley had no sharecroppers at all, and neither had Cedros or Santa Lucía, major suppliers of wheat for the urban market. The one major exception was the Hacienda de Mazatepec, whose "arrendatarios" (probably sharecroppers) produced in one year about 1,000 cargas of wheat, as against demesne production of some 600 cargas. But this distribution, it must be remembered, was fairly typical of Mazatepec and the other properties of the Porres Baranda entail, whose owners preferred to live more as rentiers than did other major landowning families.[90]

Sharecropping was more common in maize production. There were undoubtedly many small sharecroppers who worked land on certain haciendas; and rancheros who owned their own properties, or rented them from other landowners, were often given to sharecropping, or subrenting parcels for payments in kind.[91] As to the proportion supplied by sharecroppers in the huge amounts of maize sent to the city market by the haciendas of the area, no definitive answer can be given. There is a distinct possibility that when major properties contracted to supply large quantities of maize to the city's granary, as did the Hacienda de Huejotitán in 1802, 1808, 1815, and 1820, they expected to draw upon other crops than those produced directly by demesne farming.[92] Where did Tomás Ignacio Villaseñor, the owner of Huejotitán, expect to obtain the 10,000-15,000 fanegas of grain

90. AHMG, caja 11, exp. 2, 1786.
91. E.g., Hacienda San José de la Isla, La Barca—AIPG, prot. García, 5:452v-459v, 1711; BPE-BD, leg. 131, exp. 1, 1782.
92. AHMG, caja 11, 1786.

he committed to the city pósito in these years?[93] All that we can say at present is that the production and sale of wheat were almost completely dominated by demesne production, and that most of the maize marketed in Guadalajara by the great rural estates was probably produced directly by them, rather than bought up locally from other, smaller producers or taken as rents from sharecroppers.

The shift in the emphasis of farming in the late-colonial period was induced by the growth of a local urban market and facilitated by the availability of investment capital. The other important structural factor in the triumvirate was the rural labor force, which supplied the manpower necessary for a more intensive agricultural regime.

93. Richard Lindley, in his doctoral dissertation, "Kinship and Credit," claims that Huejotitán could not possibly have produced all this grain on its own lands, and must perforce have relied on buying up and marketing maize produced in the neighborhood. This is a possibility, but according to Lindley's own figures (pp. 168 and 173-174), the hacienda had enough maize lands to procuce most, if not all, of its maize, even at moderate yields.

CHAPTER 11

Hacienda Labor

As historians have struggled with defining the concept of the traditional hacienda, it has become increasingly obvious that one of the major variables is the use of labor.[1] In the last decade, particularly, a number of researchers have concentrated on the origins, functions, and implications of the various labor systems which evolved to fill the needs of rural estates in Latin America, and especially upon debt peonage.[2] In this chapter, we will turn our attention to the ways in which demographic growth in the countryside dovetailed with the availability of agricultural capital and increasing urban demand to produce a rural labor force based largely upon debt peonage, with an admixture of temporary wage-labor. We will examine the evolution of the labor system, the institutional arrangements through which rural labor was mobilized and remunerated, and the reasons for the rural impoverishment which underwrote much of Guadalajara's late-colonial prosperity.

The history of the rural labor system in central New Galicia before the end of the seventeenth century is at present *terra incognita*. The main elements in the situation, as they have been outlined for central Mexico by Woodrow Borah, Lesley Byrd Simpson, and Charles Gibson, among

1. See Chapter 6 above; and Wolf and Mintz, "Haciendas and Plantations," pp. 389-393.
2. The pioneering efforts on this question for Mexico were those of Silvio Zavala, "Orígenes coloniales del peonaje en México"; Woodrow Borah, *New Spain's Century of Depres-*

others,[3] were certainly present. A declining Indian population, a growing Spanish and mixed (*mestizo*) population, white seizure of Indian resources, and a significant if restricted demand for agricultural and livestock products (for both local use and export outside the region) all characterized the region in the late sixteenth and seventeenth centuries. And the institutional arrangements developed by the Spanish to utilize Indian labor in the countryside, by now so familiar from the study of central Mexico, were also present: the *encomienda*, the labor *repartimiento*, and free labor. The question turns upon the mix of these elements, and upon the timing with which the major institutional arrangements made their appearance.

Gibson's statement of the problem, that "the sequence of agricultural labor institutions—encomienda, repartimiento, private employment—may be understood as a progressive adjustment to a shrinking labor supply,"[4] is probably valid for the Guadalajara area. All three systems seem to have coexisted around 1600, much as they did in central Mexico at about the same time. A lengthy *visita* of the towns of New Galicia conducted by oidor Lic. Juan de Ábalos y Toledo in 1616 gives the names of holders of extant encomiendas as well as information on repartimiento working conditions.[5] A year later, the sales contract of the Hacienda de la Sauceda, in

---

sion; and François Chevalier, *La formation des grandes domaines au Mexique*; and, of course, the work of Zavala, Lesley Byrd Simpson, and others on the encomienda and repartimiento. Charles Gibson took up the debate on debt peonage in *The Aztecs Under Spanish Rule*, esp. chap. 9. More recently, Charles Harris, in *A Mexican Family Empire*, and William Taylor, in *Landlord and Peasant in Colonial Oaxaca*, have both dealt extensively with labor as a part of longer monographs on agrarian history. For the increasing importance of "free" wage-labor in the seventeenth century, see Charles Verlinden, "El régimen de trabajo en México," in García Martínez, ed., *Historia y sociedad* (1970). Specifically for eighteenth-century Mexico, Isabel González Sánchez has written on "La retención por deudas y los traslados de trabajadores tlaquehuales o alquilados en las haciendas, . . ." (the title is almost longer than the article itself), *Anales* 19 (1966). The nineteenth century has received considerable attention in the work of Jan Bazant, "Peones, arrendatarios y aparceros en México, 1851-1853," and *Cinco haciendas mexicanas*; Friedrich Katz, "Labor Conditions on Haciendas in Porfirian Mexico," *Hispanic American Historical Review* 54 (1974); and Harry E. Cross' doctoral dissertation, "The Mining Economy of Zacatecas in the Nineteenth Century" (1976). Rather further afield, Chile provides some interesting points of comparison with Mexico, as seen in the work of Mario Góngora, *Orígen de los inquilinos de Chile Central* (1960); and of Arnold Bauer, "Chilean Rural Labor in the Nineteenth Century" and *Chilean Rural Society from the Spanish Conquest to 1930*. A short but useful review of the literature is given by Magnus Mörner in "The Spanish American Hacienda: A Survey of Recent Research and Debate."

3. Borah, *New Spain's Century of Depression*; Simpson, *Exploitation of Land in Central Mexico in the Sixteenth Century*; and Gibson, *The Aztecs*.

4. Gibson, *The Aztecs*, p. 346.

5. AIPG, Tierras, leg. 1, exp. 3. This interesting document apparently remains unpublished. The greatest *encomendero* of the immediate Guadalajara area in the early sixteenth century was, of course, the egregious Nuño de Guzmán, who held, among others, the towns of Tonalá, Tlaquepaque, Tlajomulco, Cuyutlán, Atemajac, and Tetlán. Borah remarks, in "Los tributos y su recaudación," pp. 27-47, that although the privately held encomienda was

the Cocula area, included in the hacienda's inventory the "debitos de los indios, que le servían [the former owner] en dicha labor."[6] This is clear evidence that debt peonage existed at least by the turn of the century, though its exact role in the overall labor picture remains obscure. The most that can be said at present is that by 1600 or so the encomienda was probably on the decline as a supplier of labor and foodstuffs, that the repartimiento was assuming ever greater importance, and that free wage-labor was already established and waiting in the wings for the demise of the repartimiento.

The next few pages are devoted to a discussion of the role of the repartimiento in rural labor supply. This forced wage-labor draft was the first major institutional response to the growing importance of the Guadalajara market, and its decline will lead us directly into the eighteenth century, into the age of wandering labor gangs and debt peons.

The Repartimiento

The earliest evidence for the existence in New Galicia of the repartimiento system of forced Indian wage-labor appears very early—in 1550, just eight years after the permanent settlement of Guadalajara—in reference to the construction of monasteries.[7] The agricultural repartimiento, already in full swing in the Valley of Mexico by the early 1560s and in the Valley of Oaxaca by the 1570s, probably made its appearance in New Galicia in the last quarter of the century.[8] The apparent lag can be ascribed to the later foundation of Guadalajara (twenty years later than Mexico City, a decade later than Antequera) and its relatively slow development as a market for Spanish-produced agricultural commodities. Records are scanty for the repartimiento in New Galicia over the next century, full documentation beginning only around 1685, when the institution was already moribund. Nonetheless, an examination of the twilight period of the agricultural repartimiento, from 1685 to 1750, can tell us a good deal about the changing

---

relatively more important in New Galicia than in New Spain, the tribute system followed basically the lines laid down by the royal government of New Spain. For a discussion of the significance of the encomienda within the general context of Spanish economic life, see José Miranda, "La función económica del encomendero," *Anales del Instituto Nacional de Antropología e Historia* 2 (1946). There is no reason to suppose that encomenderos did not engage in similar kinds of activities in New Galicia.

6. AIPG, Tierras, leg. 39, exp. 2, 1761.

7. AIPG, Tierras, leg. 1, exp. 3; López Jiménez, comp., *Cedulario de la Nueva Galicia*, p. 3; Simpson, *The Repartimiento System*, p. 34.

8. Gibson, *The Aztecs*, p. 226; Taylor, *Landlord and Peasant*, p. 144; Simpson, *The Repartimiento System*, p. 88.

Number of Men in Contingent   Number of Repartimientos

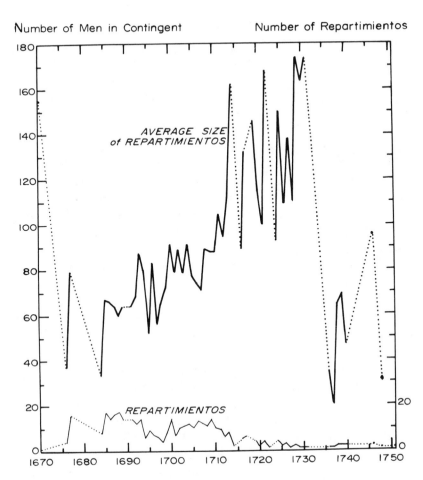

Figure 19.
Repartimientos de Indios in New Galicia, 1670-1751

SOURCE:
AIPG-LG, various.

structure of agricultural production and labor requirements in the area around Guadalajara in the early eighteenth century.

As shown in Figure 19, the number of agricultural repartimiento assignments made each year in New Galicia was declining in the last fifteen years of the seventeenth century, recovered somewhat in the first decade of the new century, and thereafter declined slowly to a level of only one or two per year from 1730 to 1750. The interesting thing to note, however, during this period of decline, is that while the yearly number of repartimiento assignments dropped from almost 20 in 1685 to one or two in 1730, the average size of contingents of Indian laborers doubled, going from around 70 to 140. In the late 1730s, with the number of repartimiento assignments at one or two per year, the average size of contingents dropped to about 50.[9] Although the repartimiento may have been used occasionally on an emergency basis to supply agricultural labor after the midcentury, it was effectively dead as a major means of labor recruitment in the Guadalajara area from at least 1730.

The repartimiento contingents were overwhelmingly drawn from Indian pueblos near the haciendas to which they were assigned. In the Guadalajara area, laborers were rarely if ever required to travel more than forty kilometers from their pueblos.[10] Since most grain-producing haciendas lay to the south and west of the city, it was from these areas that Indian workers were drawn. Altogether, repartimiento laborers were drawn from some 65 Indian pueblos in the greater Guadalajara area during the period 1670-1751, ranging in frequency from only once during that time span to more than once per year. These accounted for the vast majority of both village and individual assignments made in New Galicia during these years.

The available information on the destination of repartimiento contingents in this period indicates that areas and individual estates which were important suppliers of wheat to Guadalajara in the late eighteenth century were already so in the early part of the century. These estates were all located in areas of relatively dense Indian population, and there is every reason to suppose that they had equal or even greater access to local free labor than smaller producers. They apparently could not meet their requirements from these available resources of free labor, however, and turned to the repartimiento to make up the difference. Of the 371 assignments for which data are available, about 40 percent, or 114, were destined for the handful of small but intensively cultivated haciendas of the Zapotepec Valley—later in the century generally called the Toluquilla Valley—lying to the south of Guadalajara. The Jesuit Hacienda de Toluquilla, in this area, received 34 assignments, and in the last years of the repartimiento (1727, 1729, 1730, 1731) was occasionally the only hacienda receiving one. Production of wheat for the Guadalajara market was not limited to the immediate environs of the city itself, however. Farther afield, a handful of great haciendas also required repartimientos to meet their labor needs— among them Cuisillos, Mazatepec, Cedros, Atequiza, and Miraflores. The recipients of agricultural repartimientos in the years 1670-1751 were overwhelmingly private-property owners. Of the 385 such assignments made, 86 percent went to laymen and secular clergy, 11 percent to the Jesuits (all

9. AIPG-LG, 24:47; Gibson, *The Aztecs*, p. 226; Taylor, *Landlord and Peasant*, p. 144.
10. Moisés González Navarro, *Repartimiento de indios en Nueva Galicia* (1953), p. 14.

for their Hacienda de Toluquilla), and 3 percent to convents and monasteries of Guadalajara.[11]

The great majority of repartimiento allotments—84 percent—were intended for the harvesting of wheat. About 3 percent (10) were for sowing or harvesting maize, and about 1.5 percent (5) for sowing sugar cane, plus only one—an emergency drainage operation—for mining, and one—on the Hacienda de Toluquilla in 1708—for sheep-shearing. In about a half-dozen instances, assignments were made to cover both the maize harvest and the sowing of wheat, as at the Hacienda de Cuisillos in November 1693.[12] It is significant that the agricultural repartimiento was used almost exclusively for harvesting wheat, and that the hacienda receiving the largest allotments—Toluquilla—was located in the most important wheat-producing area, and was the last estate to drop off the repartimiento rolls. The harvest was the most intensive labor period of the agricultural year for wheat, and repartimientos assigned in New Galicia were probably at the 10-percent-of-tributaries level in use in New Spain for this peak season of agricultural labor (*dobla*).[13] Whatever the case, it is obvious that the normal resources of locally available free labor were sufficient at most times for all agricultural operations except the wheat harvest.

These ordinary needs were met by a combination of resident peones and temporarily employed wage-laborers. Producers of wheat for the urban market were obviously unable to mobilize sufficient numbers of workers for the peak season of the year through these methods, and relied upon the forced-labor draft to fill the gap. As recovery of the Indian population of central New Galicia accelerated during the first decades of the eighteenth century, however, local labor availability increased. Only the largest producers could not fill their needs at peak seasons through these mechanisms, and this disparity between the largest producers and their smaller competitors accounts for the increasing average size of repartimientos through the early 1730s. As the Indian population recovery continued through the midcentury, the average size of repartimientos dropped and eventually the system fell into disuse entirely, to be replaced by dependence on the free-labor market.

Wages paid to repartimiento laborers remained the same throughout the period from 1670 to 1750. With infrequent variations (all attributable to

11. González Navarro, *ibid.*, reports only 212 repartimientos. He differentiates secular clerical owners of property from nonclericals—which seems unnecessary, since secular priests typically inherited or purchased haciendas under the same conditions and obligations as laymen.

12. AIPG-LG, 25:126v-127, 241-242.

13. Gibson, *The Aztecs*, pp. 231-232; Zavala, "Orígenes del peonaje," p. 710; Isabel González Sánchez, "La retención por deudas," p. 242.

ambiguities in the documentation), the wage scale reached in the repartimiento in New Spain by 1630 was applied to New Galicia until the institution fell into disuse.[14] Indians working on wheat cultivation and the
planting and harvesting of maize typically received two reales per day
throughout the period, ideally in cash.[15] In addition to cash wages, Indian
laborers were to be provided with daily rations of food and with travel
expenses.[16] They were sometimes required to bring their own oxen and
tools to their work, in which case it was customary for them to be paid
rental on these items in addition to their wages and rations.[17]

Administration of the repartimiento—the actual mechanics of assigning
contingents of workmen to agricultural properties—seems to have followed
much the same pattern as that described for New Spain,[18] except that
petitions by agriculturists or their representatives were made directly to the
Audiencia in Guadalajara, which in turn considered the requests and assigned repartimientos. There was a definite tendency for certain Indian
pueblos to be traditionally associated with nearby estates for repartimiento
purposes, and proximity and custom are recurrent themes in repartimiento
orders.[19] This association of repartimiento assignments with given properties was so strong that even when lands were divided up, the separate
parcels could continue to receive proportionate shares of the original number of workers.[20]

Although repartimiento assignments tended to be the same size year
after year and to go to the same haciendas, occasionally the size of allotments was altered. Rarely, a smaller assignment was made than had been
requested, but special circumstances which could be adduced by the peti-
tioner usually led to increased size.[21] The normal functioning of the repartimiento was occasionally overriden entirely to provide labor in emergency
situations, always justified by public utility. Thus, for example, in 1688 the
renter of a *labor de trigo* in the jurisdiction of Santa Ana Acatlán received
a contingent of 40 laborers normally assigned to other producers in the
area because of the importance to the city of his harvest.[22] Similarly, repartimientos could be initiated to insure the availability of a normally voluntary labor force. Miraflores, one of the only important grain-producing
estates to the east of Guadalajara, traditionally drew the workers for its
harvest from several local pueblos "voluntariamente y sin apremio nin-

14. Gibson, *The Aztecs*, p. 250; Zavala, "Orígenes del peonaje," p. 719.
15. AIPG-LG, 38:302v.
16. AIPG-LG, 63:122 and 70:236v; Gibson, *The Aztecs*, p. 252.
17. AIPG-LG, 15:121r-v.
18. Gibson, *The Aztecs*, p. 227; Isabel González Sánchez, "La retención por deudas," p. 242.
19. E.g., La Barca, 1693—AIPG-LG, 9:78r-v.
20. AIPG-LG, 21:51 and 108v, 1705.
21. AIPG-LG, 24:167v.   22. AIPG-LG, 23:55.

guno." In 1709, however, its owner, Juan de la Mota Padilla, expressed the fear that these laborers would not arrive to work on time (the rains had been heavy, and he feared partial loss of the crop), and he asked for and received an allotment of 64 laborers from the same pueblos.[23]

Indian resistance to the repartimiento levies, while it did not paralyze the system, had a good deal of nuisance value and occasioned official reaction by the Audiencia. For two years running, 1688 and 1689, Indians from several different pueblos simply refused to appear for the wheat harvest on the Hacienda de Miraflores. In 1689, they complained that they were not paid the stipulated wages the previous year, so the recipient of the assignment was ordered to deposit the total amount of wages to be paid with the corregidor of Juanacatlán as bond, and the Indian alcaldes and *mandones* were commanded to send any Indian resisters to jail.[24] There are other similar instances of Indian resistance in the later seventeenth century, though mention of them is conspicuously absent after 1700, when the repartimiento itself was beginning to decline in importance.

If the justification for the repartimiento labor system was public utility, the necessity for it arose from the inadequacy of free labor to meet the needs of grain producers around Guadalajara. Repartimiento petitions and grants of the time are full of references to shortages of free wage-labor.[25] Before 1700, hacendados had sought to remedy this insufficiency by recruiting workers from other jurisdictions outside the Guadalajara area.[26] The labor shortage was primarily ascribed to the Indian population's decline, which only began to be reversed in central New Galicia by the 1680s.[27] In 1689, for example, Indians from the pueblos of Tala and Ahuisculco, normally assigned elsewhere, were drafted for labor on the great Hacienda de Mazatepec. The reason given for this innovation was that "the Indians of the towns assigned to this hacienda have fled, and there are not a sufficient number because most of them have died, and entire villages have been consumed."[28] To be sure, repartimientos based upon the same rationale were being made after 1725, but the nature of the shortage had changed. Only the very largest producers were now at any loss for labor, and the official policy of the Audiencia was now to discourage the use of forced Indian labor except in rare instances. If forced labor was to be used at all, it was to be drawn from among the free non-Indian population.[29] Certainly by the 1720s, much of the demand for agricultural labor was being met by the non-Indian population; but in the agricultural heartland around Gua-

23. AIPG-LG, 27:92r-v.   24. AIPG-LG, 23:195 and 70:130.
25. AIPG-LG, 23:72v.   26. AIPG-LG, 25:51v-52v.
27. Cook and Borah, *Essays in Population History*, vol. 1, p. 320.
28. AIPG-LG, 70:35.   29. AIPG-LG, 45:104v and 46:33.

dalajara, most rural laborers were Indians working for wages on a voluntary basis.

The repartimiento labor system was officially abolished in New Spain by Viceroy Cerralvo in 1633, after three decades of temporizing and palliative measures on the part of the viceregal government.[30] In various guises, it survived into the early eighteenth century in a de-facto form or as an emergency measure, but it was clearly no longer the mainstay of the agricultural labor supply. Its administrative history in New Galicia is not so clear, but the draft-labor system served as a vital source of workers for the grain-producing estates around Guadalajara through the first decade of the new century.[31]

The striking thing about the agricultural repartimiento in New Galicia is that it seems to have served a very different function within the developing Spanish economy than it did in the Valley of Mexico. Although the repartimiento in New Galicia was instituted in response to the declining Indian population of the sixteenth century, the system was not abandoned when the Indian population reached its nadir at about the midcentury. In the Valley of Mexico, it was just at this low point in the demographic curve (about 1630) that the repartimiento was abolished in favor of total reliance on private employment in the form of debt peonage.[32] In New Galicia, in contrast, the system was of importance through and long after the point at which Indian population bottomed out and began to recover. Yet we also know that the two labor systems of repartimiento and debt peonage co-existed in both regions, and that peonage grew immensely in importance during the eighteenth century. What accounts for the much longer survival of the labor draft in New Galicia and its continued importance into the early eighteenth century?

A possible explanation for this difference lies in the relationship between urban demand for cereals and recovery of the Indian population in the countryside. By 1650, Mexico City had a Spanish population alone of about 50,000, while the total population of Guadalajara at about the same time amounted to less than 5,000. Thus, at the nadir of Indian population decline, the demand for foodstuffs to supply Mexico City would have been substantially greater than Guadalajara's. This would have led to an earlier and more rationalized use of land by Spanish grain-producers in the Valley of Mexico, and a concomitant pressure upon the land resources of the even much-reduced village population. Under such circumstances, the rural Indian population would need to participate increasingly in the Spanish money economy to obtain with the proceeds of its labor those items which

---

30. Gibson, *The Aztecs*, p. 235; Isabel González Sánchez, "la retención por deudas," p. 245.
   31. López Jiménez, comp., *Cedulario*, p. 66.   32. Gibson, *The Aztecs*, p. 246.

could no longer be supplied directly from the land or from the sale of agricultural products in the city.

In the Guadalajara area, on the other hand, there is evidence to indicate that continued use of the repartimiento served to force the necessary labor into the Spanish money economy through the first years of the eighteenth century. The urban demand represented by Guadalajara itself was much smaller than that of Mexico City, perhaps a tenth to a twentieth in about 1700. This would have provided less incentive for fairly intensive, rationalized land use around Guadalajara than around contemporary Mexico City, and therefore less demand for Indian labor. At the same time, there appears to have been enough land available to Indian agriculturists in central New Galicia to enable them to produce marketable surpluses and thus to earn the money to pay their taxes and purchase necessary goods and services. Thus, although the growth of an urban market and demographic pressure in the countryside encouraged the spread of debt peonage in the Valley of Mexico during the eighteenth century, it antedated by several decades a similar occurrence in the Guadalajara region. The most important operative factor appears to have been the earlier and more intensive response of Spanish landowners to the greater demand of Mexico City for food, accompanied by the Spanish seizure of Indian resources.

The General Role of Labor and Production Costs

Our major concern with free rural labor in the Guadalajara countryside is not its existence, but the approximate date at which it became the dominant form of rural wage-labor and the extent to which it was based upon debt. Certainly it must have been common by the latter part of the seventeenth century. By the first decades of the eighteenth century, notarial and judicial documents and hacienda records are full of references to estate laborers (*gañanes, indios laboríos, peones*, etc.) who were at least nominally free, worked for wages, rations, and in some cases perquisites, and owed credit advances to hacienda stores or merchant aviadores.[33] From the middle of the century onward, most hacienda labor was performed by resident laborers, supplemented at peak labor-requirement seasons (primarily harvest times) with temporary wage-labor. We are dealing here with several interrelated questions. How were rural laborers attracted and settled upon colonial haciendas? What was the role of debt in this process, and did it change during the course of the eighteenth century? How wide-

33. Just a few of the many examples are from the haciendas of Epatán, 1699; San Antonio (Tequila), 1707; Navajas, 1711; Nuestra Señora de Guadalupe (Cuquío), 1712; San Nicolás (Tequila), 1717; Miraflores, 1722; Izcuintla and La Higuera (Cuquío), 1724; Cuspala, 1728; and Santa Cruz (Toluquilla Valley), 1728.

spread was debt peonage in the late-colonial countryside? Did debt in fact limit the physical mobility of laborers, tying them to one estate for years at a time? What was the trend of wages during the eighteenth century? What part did temporary wage-labor play in filling the manpower needs of late-colonial haciendas?

The entire economic structure, rural and urban, was shot through with complex credit arrangements, not only because of the chronic scarcity of cash, but also because of the cyclical nature of commerce (the *flotas* and great trade fairs) and agricultural income (seasonal fluctuations, the harvest cycle).[34] The rural labor system was no exception, and from this point of view the extension of credit to the hacienda labor force can be seen as having had a number of functions. First, within the particular context of the late seventeenth and early eighteenth centuries, when labor was relatively scarce, institution of the wage-credit system allowed the large rural estate to attract a permanent labor force. Second, the existence of debt was one factor which encouraged the stability of the rural labor force by tending to limit physical mobility, though admittedly it was not the only factor.[35] Third, the system of the *tienda de raya* provided a means to distribute manufactured and other goods in even the remotest areas of the countryside. Finally, the extension of credit to estate laborers and others functioned to adjust the wage system to the cycle of agricultural income in a cash-scarce economy. Even this brief enumeration of the functions of debt peonage points to the symbiotic nature of the institution. That is, debt served not only as a means of social and economic control exercised over the labor force by landowners, but also provided certain very real benefits to the laborers themselves. If in addition one accepts the view that the hacienda constituted a kind of surrogate nucleated social system in place of a weakened Indian pueblo community, then debt peonage becomes one of the central characteristics of late-colonial Mexican society.

The changes in the rural economy of the Guadalajara area during the eighteenth century put increasing emphasis on labor inputs and called forth concomitant changes in the way labor was recruited and remunerated. The shift away from livestock-raising and toward cereal-growing meant that labor became an increasingly important factor in production. It must be emphasized that this change in the rural production structure was not an abrupt one, nor can its exact chronology be pinned down. Certainly the process had begun by the second or third decade and was in full swing by the middle of the eighteenth century, to continue up to and beyond 1810.

34. On the pervasiveness of credit relationships vis-a-vis landownership and commerce, see Lindley, "Kinship and Credit," passim, but esp. chap. 4.

35. On this point, see Gibson, *The Aztecs*, p. 255; and Florescano, *Estructuras y problemas agrarios*, pp. 160-162.

In the simplest terms, it required more manpower to produce cereals, with the operations of sowing, weeding, irrigation, harvesting, and threshing, than it did to herd livestock.[36] Since almost all rural estates at the end of the eighteenth century were mixed farming operations producing both live-stock and cereals as well as garden crops, each hacienda's labor requirements were determined by its particular mix.

On the basis of the available evidence, we cannot make any statement concerning the productivity of labor or the unit labor costs for the production of a given amount of grain or meat during the eighteenth century, but it is possible to say something about the share of labor inputs in overall production costs. Table 25 summarizes data covering the five-year span 1725-1729 from the accounts of the Hacienda de Epatán, one of the major sugar-producing estates of the area to the north of Guadalajara. On the average, over these five years labor of all sorts accounted for 70 percent of yearly production costs, a very high proportion. Other sugar-producing haciendas, for which the most readily analyzable data exist, demonstrated a similarly high reliance on labor as their main economic input. The Hacienda de Santa Cruz, also in the jurisdiction of San Cristóbal de la Barranca, had 63 percent of its operating budget in 1748-49 absorbed by labor costs.[37] Since sugar production was probably more labor-intensive than grain production, even in the case of irrigated wheat, these figures are not strictly representative. Nonetheless, a labor cost component of 50 percent or more for mixed-farming properties is a reasonable supposition, even for the late eighteenth century when the relative cost of labor of all kinds had declined. A rough estimate for labor costs on the wheat-producing Hacienda de Toluquilla in the last years of the century would put the share of labor at about 50 percent of all production costs.[38]

Not only did labor absorb a significantly greater proportion of total costs in the expanded agriculture of the eighteenth century, but it was used in different ways than under the simpler regime of livestock-raising and limited maize cultivation. Whereas in the seventeenth century even the largest haciendas around Guadalajara seldom showed much functional differentiation within the labor force (a few *gañanes*, some *vaqueros*, and administrative personnel), by the early and middle eighteenth century labor

36. Maize, of course, was not generally irrigated, and required less intensive care during its growing cycle than wheat, but it did need to be threshed, or taken off the ears.

37. BPE-BD, leg. 94, exp. 7, 1749. The same picture is seen from records for the Hacienda de Guastla, in the same area—BPE-BD, leg. 111, exp. 1, 1766. The 70-percent figure for Epatán is remarkably close to the 67 percent cited for the sugar-producing Hacienda de Atlacomulco in the Cuernavaca area for the period 1768-1795 by Ward Barrett, who goes on to state, in *The Sugar Hacienda*, pp. 100-101, that labor in all forms accounted for more than half of all costs throughout the three centuries of the plantation's existence.

38. BPE-AJA, 138:9:1489, 1796-97.

Table 25.

Labor Costs, Hacienda de Epatán, 1725-1729

		Percentage of All Labor Costs				Per-centage of Total Costs
Year	Peones	Adminis-trative Per-sonnel	Slaves	Special and Seasonal	Rations (food)	
1725	45%	19%	7%	11%	18%	76%
1726	53	14	6	4	23	75
1727	53	16	4	5	22	63
1728	50	16	5	7	22	72
1729	44	18	4	12	22	66
Average	49%	17%	5%	8%	21%	70%

SOURCE:
BPE-BD, leg. 90, exp. 10.

was not only used on a more lavish scale, but it was also more specialized. In the eighteenth century, mixed-farming estates employed a bewildering array of specialists whose functions frequently overlapped, and who themselves often worked under several different titles during any given year. The administrative and executive personnel included *administradores, mayordomos, sobresalientes,* and *caporales*; livestock and transport specialists included *vaqueros, sabaneros, manaderos, rancheros, pastores, ahijadores, guardas, aviadores de requa, arrieros,* and *cargadores,* to name a few; and agricultural laborers included *gañanes, peones, laboríos, labradores, regadores, segadores,* and others.[39]

Wage Levels and Debt

Most researchers agree that the system of debt peonage in Mexico grew out of the need to control the scarce free-labor force available to Spanish agriculturists at the end of the sixteenth and the beginning of the seventeenth centuries.[40] In the labor-scarce situation which prevailed in the Gua-

---

39. E.g., Hacienda de Puerto de Cuarenta (Lagos), 1732—BPE-BD, leg. 73, exp. 9. San José (Toluquilla), 1764—BPE-BD, leg. 109, exp. 1. San Antonio de la Quemada (Magdalena), 1784—BPE-BD, leg. 134, no exp. no. Hacienda de Guajuquilla (Chihuahua), 1790—BPE-BD, leg. 150, exp. 5.

40. Woodrow Borah, *El siglo de la depresión* (1975), pp. 108-137; Gibson, *The Aztecs,* pp. 220-256; Florescano, *Estructuras y problemas,* pp. 148-162; Taylor, *Landlord and Peasant,*

dalajara region until well into the eighteenth century, the system of credit advances to workers was a manifestation not of the weakness of their position in the free-labor market, but of their strength. Rural laborers could and did demand substantial advances of cash and goods, as well as the payment on credit of tributes, ecclesiastical fees, legal fines, and other obligations. As late as the 1730s and 1740s, apparently, the advantage was still on the side of the sellers of labor rather than the buyers. In 1735, the *fiscal* of the Audiencia advised rejecting the request of a tributary Indian of the pueblo of Nestipac that he be allowed to pay a twenty-six-peso debt to a former employer by remaining in his village and liquidating the balance a little at a time. The *fiscal* argued that granting the waiting period (*espera*) would hurt the interests of hacendados and farmers "who with difficulty find people to work on haciendas and farms only by advancing something to the laborers."[41] Not only could workers in a scarce labor market demand credit advances, but in some cases Indian pueblos used the situation to insure their access to land in exchange for the availability of their labor. Such appears to have been the case, for example, with the conflict in the third quarter of the eighteenth century between the Hacienda de San Lucas and the pueblo of the same name, in the Cajititlán area. In the middle of the seventeenth century, the owner of the hacienda had tacitly allowed the village to occupy a portion of the estate's titled lands to insure the proximity and good-will of a labor force. By the 1750s and 1760s, good farming land was at a higher premium than agricultural labor and the hacendado came to loggerheads with the pueblo over legal ownership of the land so casually disposed of in the preceding century.[42]

By the late eighteenth century, however, the situation in the countryside had changed substantially in favor of the buyers of agricultural labor. An increasing rural population in Indian pueblos, as elsewhere, with its access to land absolutely reduced, was forced into a labor market in which manpower was no longer the scarce commodity it had been even up to the early decades of the century. Rural laborers were basically forced to compete among themselves. The results of this situation were declining real wages (virtually stable money wages, in the face of generally increasing prices); a decline in the per-capita indebtedness of resident peones, reflecting decreased bargaining power vis-a-vis employers; and also, probably, a general decline in rural living standards.[43] In tracing this complex process, let us

p. 5; Verlinden, "El régimen de trabajo," pp. 225-226; Isabel González Sánchez, "La retención por deudas"; Zavala, "Orígenes del peonaje"; Katz, "Labor Conditions," p. 40. For a general review of the question, see Mörner, "The Spanish American Hacienda," pp. 199-203.
41. BPE-AJA, 45:10:605.
42. AIPG, Tierras, leg. 12, exp. 2, 1750-1772.
43. Charles Gibson has suggested, in *The Aztecs*, p. 255, that a decline in indebtedness

first address ourselves to the trend of wages for rural labor during the eighteenth century.

Figure 20 sets forth data mostly derived from hacienda accounts on wage levels for resident hacienda laborers (*peones acomodados*) during the period 1730-1800.[44] Although the sample is limited, it covers a broad range of types of enterprise and is therefore fairly representative. It is readily apparent that money wages paid to resident peones, gañanes, laboríos, and vaqueros (the largest groups of employees generally mentioned in estate records) remained basically stable during most of the eighteenth century. Since prices for food, cloth, and other articles of primary necessity were increasing during the same period, the real wage of the resident hacienda worker—what he could actually buy with his labor—declined during the century.[45] The money wages of temporary hacienda laborers—those workers hired for the peak seasons of the agricultural year, the sowing and harvest, whether of maize or wheat—show an even more striking stability. If one includes the repartimiento laborers of the late seventeenth century, the daily wage of this type of labor stayed at two reales at least until the end of the eighteenth century.[46] We do not have data on the movement of rural money wages after 1800, though they probably remained stable until 1810. The effects of the intermittent political and military turmoil of the years after 1810 are not entirely clear, but if wages demonstrated any tendency to rise, there was also the countervailing tendency for agricultural production and markets to be disrupted and for the demand for labor to diminish accordingly.

---

represented a worsening in the position of rural laborers in the Valley of Mexico in the late-colonial period, as the result of a growing population. See also Brading, *Haciendas and Ranchos*, pp. 196-197.

44. The data for Figure 20 are drawn from the accounts of a number of different properties, but they do represent fairly large samplings of workers. For the Hacienda de Toluquilla in 1796-97, for example, they are based upon a total labor force of 281 men, 241 of them earning four pesos per month (BPE-AJA, 138:9:1489). Most of the wage figures represent averages of a number of employees earning at slightly different rates. It is not entirely clear in all cases if the monthly basis upon which laborers were reimbursed covered 24 or 30 days. Again in the case of Toluquilla, for example, 76 percent (184 out of 241) of those who earned four pesos per month worked a 24-day month, while the rest worked a 30-day month. On a strictly prorated basis, of course, this would raise the wage of the larger group above that of the smaller one.

45. In central Mexico, Gibson, *The Aztecs*, pp. 251-252, found that the basic money wage for agricultural laborers remained stable from 1650 to 1800. A similar situation seems to have prevailed in northern New Spain, though the overall scale in the north was somewhat higher; see Charles Harris, *A Mexican Family Empire*, pp. 67-68.

46. For the agricultural repartimiento, see above. For the later eighteenth century, examples, among many, are the Hacienda de Guastla (San Cristóbal de la Barranca), 1766—BPE-BD, leg. 111, exp. 1; and Toluquilla and Santa Cruz (Toluquilla Valley), 1790-1792—BPE-AJA, 155:1:1736. Again, wages farther north were higher: temporary laborers for the maize harvest were receiving three reales per day in 1790 on the Hacienda de Guajuquilla (Durango?)—BPE-BD, leg. 150, exp. 5.

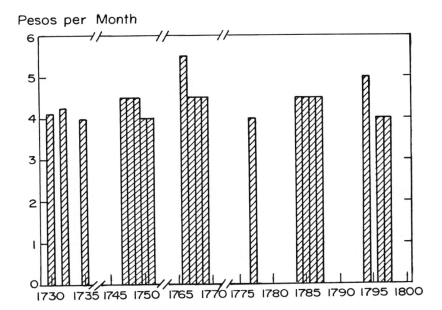

Pesos per Month

Figure 20.
Wages of resident peones in the Guadalajara region, 1730-1800

SOURCES:
1730 (Hacienda de San Martín, Tequila)–BPE-BD, leg. 69, exp. 5. 1732 (Hacienda de
Puerto de Cuarenta, Lagos)–BPE-BD, leg. 73, exp. 9. 1735 (Tala area, unspecified
property)–BPE-AJA, 45:10:605. 1747-1749 (Hacienda de Santa Cruz, San Cristóbal de
la Barranca)–BPE-BD, no leg. no., 1751. 1750-1751 (Santa Cruz, San
Cristóbal)–BPE-BD, leg. 94, exp. 7. 1766 (Hacienda de Guastla, San
Cristóbal)–BPE-BD, leg. 111, exp. 1. 1777 (Hacienda de San José, Toluquilla
Valley)–BPE-BD, leg. 124, exp. 7. 1784-1787 (Hacienda de San Antonio de la Quemada,
Magdalena)–BPE-BD, leg. 134, no exp. no. 1794 (Hacienda de Guadalupe,
Cuquío)–CG-ASC, leg. 12. 1796-1797 (Hacienda de Toluquilla)–BPE-AJA, 138:9 :1489.

By way of comparison with rural wages, Figure 21 shows the money
wages paid to laborers (peones) employed by the municipal government
working on construction and maintenance projects in Guadalajara for the
period 1774-1820. The slightly higher daily wage of construction workers
in the city may be explained by their not receiving rations. What is puz-
zling is that urban wages for unskilled workmen showed some tendency to
rise after 1810 despite the influx of people into the city, many of whom
were completely without a livelihood and whose presence should have
forced urban wages down, if anything. As to the comparative living standards of urban and rural laborers, it is impossible for us to say anything
definitive, since cash income does not necessarily reflect the total subsistence resources available in either case.

Money wages, whether actually paid in cash or in the form of goods,

Reales per Day

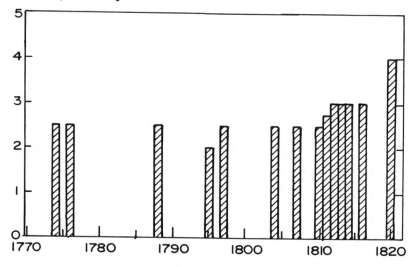

Figure 21.

Wages of urban construction workers in Guadalajara, 1774-1820

SOURCE:
AHMG, various cajas.

were not the only reimbursement received by resident rural laborers. A food ration, consisting primarily of maize but sometimes also of beans and meat, was virtually universal on rural estates. Many haciendas which did not produce sufficient maize to market commercially nonetheless raised enough to supply rations for their *gente operaria*.[47] The size and composition of the weekly ration depended both upon the family status of the laborer (married men received larger rations than unmarried men) and his functional importance in the hacienda labor force. *Mayordomos, administradores*, and foremen tended to receive larger rations than simple laborers, with skilled artisans and specialists somewhere in between.[48] The size of the weekly maize ration did fall into a rough range, but it was by no means as standardized as under the regime of repartimiento labor. In general, toward the end of the century married estate laborers received three or four *almudes* of maize per week, unmarried ones two or three.[49] Often laborers received rations of meat in addition to what they could buy on credit from the hacienda. During the year 1747, for example, 129 cattle

47. Gibson, *The Aztecs*, p. 252, discusses food rations on haciendas in the Valley of Mexico. For northern Mexico, see Harris, *A Mexican Family Empire*, p. 69.
48. E.g., BPE-BD, leg. 150, exp. 5, 1790.
49. BPE-AJA, 259:21:3522, 1811-1815; BPE-BD, leg. 150, exp. 5, 1790.

died on the Hacienda del Cabezón, and all the edible beef was given to the workers in the form of rations.[50] Whether the standard range of ration size changed at all over the course of the eighteenth century is not clear, but it is certain that at the end of the century the weekly ration was still considered a standard perquisite of estate laborers, so much so that during the famine of 1785-86 haciendas which had lost their maize crops used their wheat for rations, therefore being unable to market any grain at all in Guadalajara.[51]

As to the role of other perquisites in the wage structure of resident rural laborers, we simply do not have enough evidence to draw any conclusions. Probably most laborers had small garden or maize plots available to them on the hacienda, but how large these were, and whether they were rented or given gratis, are open questions. Some laborers also had grazing rights for a limited number of livestock on hacienda lands, as well as the right to collect firewood, dig clay, or pick fruit. The myriad informal, interstitial arrangements which undoubtedly existed in the countryside, and which must have palliated the deteriorating position of rural dwellers to some degree, simply do not show up in written records. Despite this fact, it seems reasonable to assume that money wages, rations, and credit constituted the major income components of those who relied for their living on the sale of their labor.

The conventional wisdom regarding debt peonage in Mexico is that per-capita debts were high and that they served effectively to bind the available labor force to the land in a serf-like condition. In fact, debt levels in the Guadalajara area in the latter part of the eighteenth century do not seem to have been particularly high in comparison to the earning capacity of estate laborers. Table 26 presents data on debt levels drawn from eight different rural estates widely separated in space and time. It will be readily apparent from these data that in the latter half of the eighteenth century, at least, per-capita debt levels generally did not represent more than one or two months' wages on haciendas around Guadalajara (the figures for the Chihuahua estate are included for comparative purposes). Such a level of debt conformed roughly to the viceregal limit of three months' indebtedness which prevailed throughout most of the century, and was not grossly in excess of the five-peso limit set for laborers by the Audiencia of New Spain in 1785.[52]

---

50. BPE-AJA, 54:11:682; also, on the Hacienda San Diego del Mesquite (Cuquío)—BPE-AJA, 259:21:3522.

51. E.g., various haciendas—AHMG, caja 11, especially Milpillas, Margaritas, and Cerro-gordo (La Barca), 1786— exp. 2.

52. Taylor, *Landlord and Peasant*, p. 149, traces viceregal regulations of debt levels in the seventeenth and eighteenth centuries. These regulations applied only to Indian laborers; but since a large proportion of estate workers in the Guadalajara area were in fact Indians, the viceregal limits are useful as a rule of thumb.

Table 26.

Debt Levels on Selected Haciendas in the Guadalajara Region in the Eighteenth Century
(in pesos and reales)

Years	Hacienda	Location	Number of Employees	Average Debt per Man per Year	Number of Months of Labor to Pay Off Debt	Number of Debtors	Average Debt per Debtor
1732 (1)	Puerto de Cuarenta	Lagos	28	55/2/–	11.0	—	—
1747-1751 (4)	Santa Cruz	San Cristóbal	275	6/7/–	1.5	—	—
1784-1787 (4)	San Antonio de la Quemada	Magdalena	25	3/5/–	1.0	—	—
1790 (1)	La Sauceda	Cocula	157	10/4/–	2.0	120	13/6/–
1790 (1)	Estipac	Cocula	63	9/2/–	2.0	46	12/4/–
1791 (1)	Nuestra Señora de los Dolores	Chihuahua	99	20/2/–	4.0	—	—
1796-1797(1)	Toluquilla	Toluquilla Valley	241	2/2/–	0.5	96	5/5/–
1800-1801 (1)	Labor de Rivera	Ahualulco	206	5/–/–	1.0	—	—

SOURCES:
Cuarenta—BPE-BD, leg. 73, exp. 9. Santa Cruz—BPE-BD, leg. 97, no exp. no. La Quemada—BPE-BD, leg. 134, no exp. no. La Sauceda—BPE-AJA, 154:12:1736. Estipac—BPE-AJA, 154:12:1736. Dolores—BPE-BD, leg. 150, exp. 2. Toluquilla—BPE-AJA, 138:9:1489. Rivera—BPE-AJA, 241:26:3215.

The figures given in Table 26 do not show the whole picture of debt, however, even though they are fairly representative of contemporary conditions. On the one hand, it is difficult to tell from contemporary estate accounts what is actual debt and what is an advance of credit. The extant records of laborers for the colonial period most often appear in the form of *ajustes de cuentas*—account adjustments, literally—which were done for the entire labor force of a given estate at the same point every year, usually depending upon the harvest cycle and not upon the calendar year. At this time, the number of days or months the individual had worked at a given wage-rate or at different rates was computed against the wages in goods or cash he had received during the previous year from the estate, and the difference constituted either his debt or what was owed to him. Wages received during the accounting period in the form of goods were generally known as *avíos*; and the workers who received them, *peones habiados* or *acomodados*. It is often not entirely clear, however, which avíos received during any given year were already worked off and which remained to be paid in the succeeding accounting period. In the latter case, a negative balance in the individual laborer's account would represent a real debt—a sum in excess of his earning capacity in that year; in the other case, it would represent an advance of credit which he might have every reasonable expectation of paying off. This is more than a technical caveat and should always be borne in mind when looking at putative levels of debt.[53]

On the other hand, very few laborers actually worked a full year during any given accounting period, so that their debts, even if low, represented a larger proportion of what they might really earn than would seem to be the case from a casual perusal of hacienda records. To take but one example: on the Hacienda de San Antonio de la Quemada, in the jurisdiction of La Magdalena, some 25 resident peones worked during the four-year period between January 1784 and December 1787. Their aggregate debt to the hacienda for avíos during this period came to 358 pesos. From the point of view of the hacienda accounts, their average yearly debt accrued was thus about 3 pesos 5 reales. They actually worked in these four years a total of only 25 man-years among them, however—so that computed from the point of view of what they earned, their average yearly debt came to nearly 14 pesos each.[54]

The available evidence indicates that somewhat fewer than half of resident hacienda laborers owed debts to the estate upon which they worked at

53. The figures in Table 26 have been adjusted, where possible, to take this problem into account, and the debt levels may therefore be construed as actual unpaid balances of credit advanced during the given accounting period.

54. BPE-BD, leg. 134, no exp. no.; also the Hacienda de Toluquilla—BPE-AJA, 138:9:1489.

any given time.[55] It would not be entirely correct to state, however, as does Gibson for the Valley of Mexico, that debt peonage in the Guadalajara region affected less than half the working force. Here we should add the caveat "at any given time," since laborers could owe several months' wages at the end of one accounting period and be owed back-wages in cash by the hacienda by the next *ajuste de cuentas*. This was tied in to the seasonal cash-flow problem of estate management, and fairly dramatic shifts—real shifts, not just accounting changes—could occur within a few years' time.[56] The cash-flow problem of rural estates in particular, and the acknowledged scarcity of specie in general, were important factors in initially encouraging and then sustaining the avío system for paying rural wages. Hacendados and their administrators were chronically short of cash throughout the eighteenth century, though the situation may have eased somewhat toward 1800. In 1765, the administrator of the Hacienda de Navajas complained that the payment of wages in coin was very difficult and that the principles of good estate management demanded payment instead in the form of food and goods ("and this is the general practice, followed by every good administrator").[57] This sentiment was echoed by the administrator of the Hacienda de Cuisillos at the beginning of the nineteenth century, who found himself scissored between the owners of the hacienda and its laborers: "the owners of this estate and the laborers always demand the payment of their income and their wages; they are always on me, and I have no other resources except what the soap and wheat bring in."[58] Testimony from contemporary observers bears ample witness to the fact that even far into the eighteenth century, laborers simply refused to work without advances. As one witness in a judicial action concerning the sugar hacienda of Santa Cruz stated at midcentury: "it is just as incredible that laborers work without advances as to catch a star in your hand."[59]

Advancing credit to estate laborers in the form of goods, then, had its advantages for estate management: it attracted a scarce labor force by insuring workers a much greater access to goods than their money wages would have allowed, and it reduced the need for cash outflow. As labor became more abundant during the eighteenth century, however, these advantages began to lose their importance. For one thing, the large stocks

---

55. Gibson, *The Aztecs*, pp. 254-255, found a similar situation in the Valley of Mexico in the late eighteenth century. Debt appears to have been more pervasive among the labor force, and debt levels higher, in both Oaxaca and northern Mexico at the same time, according to Taylor, *Landlord and Peasant*, pp. 147-150, and Harris, *A Mexican Family Empire*, pp. 70-71. In Oaxaca, Indians retained more extensive communal lands and were therefore reluctant to work on haciendas; in northern Mexico, the rural population was sparse; in both cases, debt peonage served to fix a relatively small labor force.

56. BPE-BD, leg. 69, exp. 5.   57. BPE-BD, leg. 110, exp. 2.

58. AHMG, caja 23, 1823.   59. BPE-BD, leg. 94, exp. 7.

which had to be maintained in the hacienda's tienda de raya represented substantial investments which generally made estates vulnerable to the demands of urban merchants and which might not be amortized (in the form of debt labor) for years at a time. In fact, tienda inventories for the first part of the eighteenth century seem to be rather larger than those later in the century.[60] For another thing, the aggregate debt of an hacienda's laborers represented a somewhat risky investment, much of which could be expected to be written off. The chance of recovering these debts depended, of course, on the control landowners and local authorities were able to exert over the mobility of the laboring population, and we will discuss this question in detail below. It should be noted, however, that it was precisely those individuals with the highest per-capita debts (on the average) who were the worst risks.[61] Like tienda de raya inventories, aggregate debts were large before the midcentury. After 1760 or so, one very rarely sees in the documents aggregate debts on the scale of the 2,732 pesos owed to the Hacienda del Cabezón by its resident laborers in 1747, or the 3,294 pesos owed to the Hacienda de Cedros in 1754.[62]

Of what did avíos consist? The major elements of wages and credit advances were cash in hand, paid in small amounts; tributes (for Indians and other tributaries) and ecclesiastical fees (marriages, baptisms, interments, indulgences) generally paid directly to the local corregidor-subdelegado or priest; foodstuffs; and manufactured items, primarily cloth and clothing. The exact proportions of these items in the total wage structure would of course vary with the size of the laborer's family, the amount of his salary, the credit available to the owner of the estate, the nature of production on a given hacienda, etc. In general, dry goods of various kinds seem to have been more important earlier, and cash later in the century, concomitant with the lessened ability of laborers to demand credit advances from haciendas.

A few examples drawn from laborers' accounts will illustrate the nature of the goods concerned and the trend toward cash remuneration as the eighteenth century advanced. Efigenio Antonio, a herdsman on the Hacienda del Puerto de Cuarenta, in the Lagos area, received an avío amounting to 106 pesos in September of 1732. Of this amount, which he was expected to work off at the rate of 6 pesos per month, 87.5 pesos were in the form of cloth and yardgoods and 18.5 pesos in foodstuffs and cash. The cloth goods included blankets, ponchos, a rebozo made in Puebla, and one pair of English women's stockings; lengths of serge, wool, cotton, linen, and silk originating in Mexico, China and a variety of other places;

60. AIPG, prot. García, 29:395-417v; BPE-BD, leg. 106, exp. 3.

61. BPE-AJA, 51:11:682; BPE-BD, leg. 106, exp. 3.

62. BPE-AJA, 154:12:1736.

various kinds of thread and ribbon; and two "sombreros finos." The food-stuffs and household goods consisted of two pounds of fine chocolate, salt, soap, and sugar. He received 9 pesos 3 reales in cash, and had his 20 reales of tribute paid for him by the hacienda administrator.[63] Other workers on the estate received advances of a similar nature.

About midcentury, Andrés Figueroa, a peon resident on the Hacienda de Santa Cruz near San Cristóbal de la Barranca, received in avíos for one year 101 pesos 3 reales. Of this amount, 28 pesos 6 reales were in cash, 62 pesos 3 reales in cloth and clothing, 5 pesos 2 reales in payments to a tailor for making clothing (*hechuras*), 2.5 pesos for his tributes, and 2.5 pesos in unspecified goods (tobacco, soap, sugar, etc.).[64] The larger cash compo-nent in his wage-credit payments is striking. Finally, an Indian vaquero named Nasario who lived and worked on the Hacienda de San Antonio de la Quemada, near La Magdalena, received during the year 1785-86 some 101 pesos 1 real in wages and credit. The largest component was in cash, 41 pesos; the rest consisted of 30.5 pesos in unspecified goods (probably most-ly cloth), 6 pesos in the value of an ox, 5 pesos for his tribute for the two years, and 13 pesos paid to the local priest for the burial of two of Na-sario's children.[65]

We do not have unequivocal evidence one way or the other as to whether hacienda stores gouged estate laborers by charging more than the going market prices for goods advanced on credit. In the first place, prices varied widely, and we cannot tell from contemporary records whether goods—yardgoods, for example—which were designated with similar names were in fact of equivalent quality. In the second place, many tiendas de raya did not exist in a commercial vacuum—there were wandering merchants (*mer-caderes viandantes*) and small merchants in provincial towns. Thus, while the hacienda store held a certain advantage by the very reason of its prox-imity and the fact that it offered extensive credit, it did not enjoy a perfect monopoly in provincial retail commerce. All kinds of country-dwellers, including Indian villagers and hacienda peones, dealt at small, indepen-dent country stores.[66] If prices for goods in hacienda stores were higher than the normal, it was not by much, and the price differential itself was not the main mechanism for encouraging indebtedness. Insofar as the sale of hacienda-produced foodstuffs is concerned, there is even some evidence

---

63. BPE-BD, leg. 73, exp. 9.   64. BPE-BD, leg. 89, no exp. no.

65. BPE-BD, leg. 134, no exp. no. The mechanics of tienda de raya operations and ac-counting are fascinating in themselves, but need not concern us here. Despite certain stan-dardized procedures and terminology, the whole process had a distinctly ad-hoc air about it and depended, as one midcentury observer put it, "on the good faith of the administrators" (BPE-BD, leg. 110, exp. 2, 1765).

66. E.g., accounts of the tienda of Santiago González (Atotonilco el Alto), 1806—BPE-BD, leg. 177, no exp. no.

to suggest that, especially in times of hardship, haciendas sold on account to their resident employees at below the going market price.[67]

We have suggested in the foregoing pages that the role of credit in recruiting a resident labor force for the hacienda, and the role of indebtedness in keeping it there, diminished during the eighteenth century. Proof is admittedly inferential, but circumstantially very strong. In the first place, the population, both Indian and non-Indian, was increasing in the Guadalajara countryside during the eighteenth century, and access to land resources was increasingly restricted because of this population pressure, on the one hand, and the expansion of hacienda production on the other. Second, in the face of an increasing availability of rural labor from this growing labor pool, rural money wages remained basically unchanged at least through 1800. Third, it seems fairly clear that both the aggregate debts of individual estate labor forces and the per-capita debts of individual laborers were greater at the beginning of the eighteenth century than at the end of it. Finally, evidence from other areas in Mexico at the same time tends to corroborate this conclusion. In sum, if debt peonage was still widespread around 1800, and if most resident estate laborers could expect to be in debt to the hacienda management at some times, the degree of indebtedness had declined substantially. The very function of debt—to insure a steady supply of rural labor—had largely been taken over by demographic pressure in the countryside.

Debt, Coercion, and Mobility

Ultimately, of course, whatever the trend in the amount of indebtedness during the eighteenth century, the efficacy of debt peonage as a system for the control of labor depended upon the degree to which the payment of debts was enforced, either within the law or extrajudicially. A determination on this point turns primarily upon two questions. First, was the physical mobility of debt laborers restricted—and if so, how? And second, were debts contracted on a given estate always recognized as payable only in labor on that same estate? And related to both of these questions is the role of the Spanish state in mediating between employer and employee, or in leaving them to their own devices to settle disputes.[68]

Most resident hacienda laborers who contracted debts from their employers stayed on the estate until they had liquidated the amount owing—this is clear from accounts spanning the eighteenth century. Probably in

67. E.g., Hacienda de Guadalupe (Tequila), 1810—AIPG, Tierras, leg. 41, exp. 1.
68. On all of these issues, see the interesting paper by James D. Riley, "Landlords, Laborers, and Royal Government: The Administration of Labor in Tlaxcala, 1680-1750" (1977).

most cases enforcement of debts never even became an issue—it was simply accepted by both parties that credit advances, even if constantly renewed, would be repaid with labor. Even when per-capita debts were relatively high, up to midcentury or so, the incidence of gañanes decamping after receiving their yearly avíos was low. In most cases, then, force or the threat of legal action was not necessary, and debt functioned reasonably well in recruiting labor for agricultural purposes. But conflicts did arise over the payment of debts. Most legal complaints of Indians against estate-owners and administrators arose over physical coercion or confinement related to debts. Viceregal efforts to establish norms for working conditions and debt ceilings continued throughout the seventeenth and eighteenth centuries, but their application in New Galicia was inconsistent.[69] In fact, although the famous *bando* of Viceroy Matías de Gálvez of 1785 set a debt ceiling of five pesos, required the ajuste de cuentas of gañanes to be made every five months, and established Indian laborers' freedom of movement, all of these regulations were ignored in greater or lesser degree in New Galicia as elsewhere in New Spain.[70]

The real question, all during the course of the eighteenth century, seems not to have been so much the sanctity of debt per se, but the kind of coercion which could be used in enforcing it. The principle was widely accepted by royal authorities, even in the early eighteenth century, that physical force was not admissible in insuring that workers paid off what they had borrowed. Physical punishment to discourage laziness or to enforce discipline in work situations, while not recommended by anyone, was apparently seen as inevitable and justified as long as it was not excessive.[71] But beating or incarcerating gañanes for debt was consistently disallowed by the Audiencia in the cases which it heard, most of which arose from attempts by Indian laborers with extant debts to leave estates. Nor was the retention of laborers for the putative debts of their fathers or other relations considered legitimate.[72] Even in cases where the royal authorities

69. For the history of viceregal legislation concerning rural labor conditions, see Zavala, "Orígenes del peonaje," pp. 732-744; Isabel González Sánchez, "La retención por deudas," pp. 245-248; Taylor, *Landlord and Peasant*, pp. 148-151; and Riley, "Landlords, Laborers, and Royal Government," passim.

70. For the Gálvez *bando*, see *Documentos para la historia económica de México*, vol. 3, pp. 64-72.

71. This attitude was certainly reinforced by the notion of the perpetual legal and moral minority of Indians and the paternalism of Spanish landowners. A witness in a 1726 case concerning debt and physical abuse on a Toluquilla Valley hacienda stated that the estate administrator had given an Indian laborer "dos o tres bofetadas en que siendo sirviente el referido indio no se cometió excesso alguno pues a los hijos se castigan por muchas menores cosas" (BPE-AJA, 36:3:456).

72. For three cases on the Hacienda de Epatán, in 1699, 1729, and 1730—BPE-AJA, 30:10:404; and BPE-BD, leg. 67, exp. 15, and leg. 70, exp. 34. For the Hacienda de San Nicolás in 1726—BPE-AJA, 36:3:456.

did uphold the physical freedom of debt laborers, however, they admitted the principle that other arrangements must be made to satisfy legitimate debts. The most common arrangement of this sort was the posting of a bond (*fianza*) by vecinos of the laborer's pueblo if he was an Indian.[73]

Lest it be thought that laborers with debts were completely free to move about at will, it should be emphasized that, barring physical abuse on the part of estate-owners or their representatives, workers were under an obligation to remain on the estate until their debts had been paid off. On occasion, hacendados sought and obtained orders from the Audiencia which legally forced workers who had fled without justification or without making alternative arrangements to return to haciendas and liquidate their debts.[74] The apparent willingness of the Audiencia to uphold the absolute principle of the physical freedom of Indian laborers and probably of laborers in general prompted landowners to complain even when the validity of the debt itself was never called into question.[75] Still, despite such laments and the implicit attitude of landowners that they should be absolute masters of their retainers, the insistence on the principle of physical liberty did not significantly interfere with the labor system in general. By the end of the eighteenth century, labor was so plentiful, relatively speaking, that neither debts themselves nor the loss of an individual worker's services represented much of a threat to the functioning of a given estate. This is why cases of incarceration or physical coercion on haciendas for unpaid debts so seldom occurred at the end of the colonial period. Certainly landowners were not casual about having employees with debts leave their service, but they were not as obsessively concerned with it as they had been in the early decades of the century. Many haciendas perennially carried on their books large numbers of gañanes and other workers who had fled or temporarily absented themselves.[76] While landowners were of course loath to write off such debts, no untoward efforts were made to recover them. The difference in attitude on the part of the landlords is quite simply explained by the change from a labor-scarce to a labor-abundant economy.

Temporary Wage-Labor

The more relaxed attitude of landowners toward debts in the last decades of the colonial period was largely due to the fact that less of the necessary labor was performed by resident debt-peones than in the early part of the

73. BPE-BD, leg. 70, exp. 34, 1730, and leg. 76, no exp. no., 1733; BPE-AJA, 36:3:456; AIPG, prot. Morelos, 8:15v-17, 1732.

74. E.g., the Hacienda de Santa Cruz (San Cristóbal de la Barranca), 1749, "para recogerlos [gañanes] y que desquiten el dinero con su trabajo"—BPE-BD, leg. 94, exp. 7.

75. BPE-AJA, 36:3:456.   76. E.g., BPE-AJA, 154:12:1736, 1790.

century. The gap was filled by temporary wage-laborers drawn from local villages or from the floating population of the country districts. It is impossible for us to arrive at a precise estimate of the percentage of yearly labor inputs accounted for on most haciendas by temporary wage-labor, but we can get a rough notion of its importance. On the sugar-producing hacienda of Epatán during the late 1720s, seasonal (that is, temporary) labor represented about 8 percent of total labor costs.[77] A more careful evaluation is possible at the end of the eighteenth century for the Hacienda de Toluquilla, one of the great wheat-producing estates of the Guadalajara region. In the mid-1790s, Toluquilla employed about 125 men per year for the wheat harvest, equal to about half its resident force of 241 gañanes. In terms of total labor input, this temporary labor represented about 2,500 man-days per year, or about 10 percent of that supplied by the resident labor force. But since these temporary wage-laborers worked only an average of twenty days apiece, their impact at the most critical time of the year was immense.[78]

The cost of this kind of seasonal labor was quite predictable and for many estates showed a remarkable consistency over several years, even more so than other production costs. While the costs themselves were in most cases not very great, it must be remembered that they represented large labor inputs concentrated into short periods of time (usually two to three weeks). Table 27 gives a notion of the cost of seasonal labor for several estates. For purposes of accounting and the payment of wages, a clear distinction was always made between temporary laborers, generally known as *mozos alquilados*, and the permanent or long-term residents, frequently called *sirvientes*.[79] These seasonal workers were almost always paid cash in hand at the end of their stints, and received rations apart from their wages.[80] The standard wage for seasonal labor of this sort all through the eighteenth century was two reales per day.

The methods for recruitment of labor, both resident and seasonal, are something of a mystery. In the case of seasonal labor, hacienda owners and their administrators often actively went out into the countryside, especially in the early decades of the eighteenth century, to solicit laborers themselves. This was the practice of the administrator of the Hacienda de Santa Cruz, near San Cristóbal de la Barranca, who in 1749 personally went to several pueblos "and other distant parts" in search of workers for the cane harvest (*zafra*) of that year.[81] Most temporary workers seem to

77. BPE-BD, leg. 79, no exp. no.   78. BPE-AJA, 138:9:1489 and 155:1:1736.

79. E.g., BPE-BD, leg. 71, exp. 1, 1731.

80. E.g., the Hacienda de Santa Cruz (San Cristóbal de la Barranca), 1749—BPE-BD, leg. 94, exp. 7.

81. BPE-BD, leg. 94, exp. 7.

Table 27.
Seasonal Labor Costs on Selected Haciendas in the
Guadalajara Region in the Eighteenth Century

Estate	Year	Amount
San Nicolás (Tequila)	1719	56 pesos
	1720	54
	1721	60
	1722	100
Epatán (San Cristóbal)	1725	120
	1726	80
	1727	100
	1728	120
	1729	130
Navajas (Tala)	1763	120
	1764	100
	1765	100
Toluquilla (Toluquilla Valley)	1792	700 (appr.)
	1797	736

SOURCES:
San Nicolás–BPE-BD, leg. 54, exp. 4. Epatán–BPE-BD, leg. 79.
Navajas–BPE-BD, leg. 108, exp. 4. Toluquilla–BPE-AJA, 155:1:1736 and
138:9:1489.

have come from villages close to the estates where they worked.[82] In the
latter part of the eighteenth century, seasonal workers often traveled in
labor gangs (*cuadrillas*), coming from the same pueblo or local area and
working in one harvest after another during the peak labor season. Even
though most rural dwellers stuck closely within the precincts of their own
town, the range of physical mobility was surprising, especially for those in
search of work. The Hacienda de Epatán, during the years 1725-1729,
counted among its laborers men from Jiquilpan, Zacatecas, and Santa
María de los Lagos.[83] There is even some evidence to indicate that the
more densely populated areas, such as the margins of Lake Chapala, were
net exporters of labor to those areas which were relatively underpopulated.
As to the origins of permanent or semi-permanent estate residents, they
also tended for the most part to come from local villages. Certainly by the
end of the century it was not uncommon to see people who had lived all or

82. BPE-BD, leg. 124, exp. 7.
83. BPE-BD, leg. 79, no exp. no.

almost all of their lives on the same estate, such as the Indian who in 1810 had lived fifty of his seventy-seven years as a laborío on the Hacienda de Copala.[84]

Hacienda Life and Social Control

By all indications, resident hacienda populations were quite large and showed a tendency to increase in the latter part of the eighteenth century. It was not at all unusual for even modest estates to support on a permanent basis upwards of 200 people, including laborers and their families. Thus the middling-sized Hacienda de la Labor de Rivera, in the Ahualulco area, showed about 200 permanent (as opposed to seasonal) personnel on its books in the year 1800-01, which would indicate a total population of perhaps 600 to 800 people.[85] The Hacienda de Toluquilla probably had upwards of a thousand people living on it in the late 1790s (the permanent laboring population was 281 men in 1796-97).[86] The range was considerable even among haciendas located in favored agricultural areas.[87]

With such large permanent and semi-permanent resident populations, haciendas inevitably assumed the character of surrogate pueblos. This in turn helped to weaken the traditional Indian social structure and encouraged what may be called the secularization of Indian society. Pueblos which saw their populations dispersed on rural estates and their native sons and daughters refusing to pay tributes or community contributions, or assume community offices, did not relinquish their control without protest.[88] Fairly typical was the complaint of the Indian alcalde of the pueblo of Buenavista, in the jurisdiction of Lagos, who in 1794 appealed to the Audiencia of Guadalajara. He said it was the custom of the Spanish vecinos of the area to have the Indians of the pueblo living and working on their haciendas, so that the Indians did not recognize the claims of the pueblo: they refused to honor the authority of the alcalde, to contribute toward fiesta

84. AIPG, Tierras, leg. 37, exp. 4.
85. BPE-AJA, 241:26:3215. The total population figure is based upon a multiplier of four for deriving the number of individuals from the number of families, which is on the conservative side; see Cook and Borah, *Essays in Population History*, vol. 2, pp. 119-200. As we have no way of knowing in the case of La Labor de Rivera or other properties what proportion of the resident laborers were married, the estimate has been adjusted downward to account for this.
86. BPE-AJA, 138:9:1489.
87. AHMG, caja 28, 1813. By way of contrast, the 53 haciendas in the partido of Aguascalientes had an average of 279 people living on them in 1813, ranging from a high of 1,400 to a low of 28 (AHMG, caja 28, 1813).
88. On pueblo-hacienda jurisdictional disputes, see Gibson, *The Aztecs*, pp. 55-57; and Riley, "Landlords, Laborers, and Royal Government," p. 4.

expenses, to work on the church or *casas de comunidad*, or to accept pueblo offices. Furthermore, the pueblo officials had great difficulty in collecting tributes from putative townsmen resident on local haciendas, because the hacendados paid them whenever they felt like it instead of on a fixed schedule, and the officials were "matando caballos" from the frequent trips necessary to collect them. The hacendados were very uncooperative, the alcalde claimed, maltreating the pueblo official who went to remonstrate with them and threatening any laborers who were tempted to leave with the loss of their employment and the small parcels of land they rented from the haciendas. In the end, the Audiencia recognized the claims of the pueblo and established a kind of withholding tax whereby the hacendados would pay not only tributes but community contributions for fiestas against the accounts of their laborers. But the justice of the claim stopped at this financial arrangement, and the Audiencia did not attempt to repatriate Indian workers living on rural estates.[89] Such instances point to a real deterioration in the traditional bonds of village life, and their replacement to some degree by hacienda communities.

The hacienda offered more as a place of residence than just steady work and access to credit. It had a social life of its own, often centering on the chapel with a resident priest. In fact, most major haciendas had at least a chapel where the people heard mass, were confessed, and could be baptized, married, and buried.[90] All kinds of social rituals helped to integrate the hacienda community, from the establishment of compadrazgo bonds between workers and the hacendado or his administrator to the customary issuing of wine rations on completion of the harvest.[91] There was often a real sense of community built up on the hacienda, an identification by the gañanes and other employees with the estate and its masters. Such allegiances emerge perhaps most clearly in the violent clashes which occasionally occurred between the retainers of one estate and those of another over land boundaries.[92] Nor was this loyalty one-sided: workers could often count upon hacendados or administrators to intercede for them with local authorities, both civil and ecclesiastical. In a vivid and rather amusing incident in 1764, for example, the administrator of the Hacienda de Cuisillos, Matías Gómez Marañón, went to great lengths to protect two of his gañanes. In connection with a protracted land suit between Cuisillos and the neighboring Hacienda de Buenavista, Gómez Marañón had had a contretemps with the corregidor of Tala during which he was alleged to have called the official a *cornudo*, among other things. The enraged cor-

89. BPE-AJA, 205:3:2570, 1794; and the interesting case of the pueblo of Cocula—BPE-AJA, 228:3:2695.

90. BPE-MC, leg. 50, vol. 3, exp. 8. 91. BPE-BD, leg. 71, exp. 1, 1731.

92. E.g., AIPG, Tierras, leg. 71, exp. 30, 1761.

regidor then arrested two of Cuisillos' sirvientes on the pretext that their tributes were unpaid. At this point, Gómez Marañón threatened to burn down the jail and release the men. After himself spending a few hours in jail, Gómez did, in fact, secure the release of the two hapless laborers.[93]

Despite the integrative mechanisms that made the hacienda in many instances a kind of surrogate village community, there nonetheless underlay the social relations between landowners and their laborers a certain tension and fear. On their side, Spanish landowners realized that they were in all times and places a small minority compared to the Indians and mixed castes living in the rural districts, and the skewed distribution of power and property must have been obvious to even the most complacent among them. Ultimately, of course, even if Spaniards believed in the legitimacy of their civilizing mission, their power rested upon the selective threat and use of force. Because of the great distances and the relative attenuation of Spanish civil authority in the countryside, landowners were frequently able to successfully solicit commissions as officers in the semi-official rural constabularies (the *acordada*, *hermandad*, and *mesta*) charged with keeping the peace and apprehending wrong-doers.[94] One of the most obvious examples of this sort of thing was Manuel del Río, who owned several haciendas in the Ahualulco area and was at one and the same time subdelegado of the district and alcalde of the Santa Hermandad.[95] Legitimating with a legal commission the de-facto authority which hacendados enjoyed over their laborers and other country-dwellers was rather like setting the cat to watch the canary. Just how much abuse actually occurred is difficult for us to determine, but the potential certainly existed.[96] Also, in the last years of the colonial period there seems to have been an increase in the incidence of rural violence and vagabondage and a concomitant effort on the part of officials and the propertied classes to reassert their authority in country districts.[97] The possibilities of all this ad-hoc law enforcement for social control of the rural population are striking.

On individual rural estates, as we have seen, physical coercion and restraint of debtors did occur. The lack of accountability by hacendados and their administrators to local civil authorities who might (or might not) attempt to defend the liberty of Indians and other laborers was notorious. While we cannot determine the extent of physical abuse which occurred, it is clear that it was not unusual. Nor were the laboring masses, on their

93. BPE-AJA, 121:5:314. For more on this famous suit, see Chapter 14 below; and Amaya, *Ameca*, pp. 100-113, who ascribes the bitterness of the conflict partially to the fact that Cuisillos lay within the jurisdiction of New Galicia and Buenavista within the Provincia de Ávalos, New Spain.

94. AIPG-LG, 42:64-65v; AIPG, Tierras, leg. 62, exp. 17; BPE-AJA, 219:11:2811.

95. AIPG, prot. de Silva, 30:30, 1789.   96. AIPG, Tierras, leg. 1, exp. 3, 1616.

97. BPE-AJA, 171:17: 1804.

side, always docile about such treatment. Aside from the kind of sub-rosa sabotage so familiar with slave populations (theft, foot-dragging, and outright incompetence), estate laborers occasionally showed signs of resistance ranging from sullenness to hatred and even violence. The statement of Francisco Juan, an Indian laborer from the pueblo of San Sebastián el Grande, in the jurisdiction of Tlajomulco, who was serving on an hacienda in the Toluquilla Valley in 1726, is worth quoting. He had received two or three blows from the estate administrator, ostensibly in an argument which arose over a debt he owed to the hacienda:

> . . . and the administrator even had the audacity to give me two or three slaps without good cause. I was so upset by the incident that, after being slapped, I have thought to myself that I am not a slave of the hacienda to be treated in such a manner; I do not want another, worse beating that, although I am a poor and humble man, might drive me to a revenge which would make things worse for me. And so I ask and entreat Your Lordship, be pleased to order that they let me go to my pueblo, first settling my account, and if I owe anything I will pay it off from my pueblo. . . .[98]

Francisco Juan's resentment of this mistreatment shines forth clearly from his statement, the implicit threat of violent retaliation against the estate administrator more menacing than an oath or a blow.

Occasionally, though not often, the resentment and violent impulses directed toward the owner-managerial group by the rural lower classes broke through the surface.[99] A particularly spectacular case was the murder of José Leandro de Siordia, a member of a prominent landowning family of Ahualulco, by one of his estate laborers in 1752. José Leandro, who was apparently managing the Hacienda de la Labor de Rivera for his elder brother, José Luis, had discharged (*despedida*) a resident laborer named José Tomás, originally from Irapuato, after settling accounts with him. Whatever the reasons for his discharge, José Tomás was not satisfied with them and sought redress and reinstatement from the elder Siordia brother. Early on the morning of August 21, as José Leandro made his rounds of the peones' huts to roust them out for work, he discovered the fired laborer sleeping in a corner of one family's home, by the hearth. A peremptory challenge by Siordia ("Díme, hombre, no te eché de aquí y te ajusté las cuentas? Para qué volvistes?") angered José Tomás, who stabbed Siordia to death on the spot. The ironic element in the story is that Siordia was described convincingly by several witnesses not as a cruel taskmaster,

98. BPE-AJA, 36:3:456.

99. It is interesting to note that among the several hundred persons executed by the insurgents under Hidalgo when they took Guadalajara at the end of 1810, landowners were conspicuous by their absence. See Hugh M. Hamill, *The Hidalgo Revolt* (1966); and Ramírez Flores, *El gobierno insurgente en Guadalajara, 1810-1811*, pp. 95-110.

a sadist, or an exploiter, but as a man who was "agreeable, courteous, and of good and kind words."[100] While this incident was certainly not typical of life in the Guadalajara countryside, it is nonetheless indicative of the kind of tension which lay just beneath the surface of the deferential words and polite formulas.[101]

Two statements of a general and somewhat speculative nature can be made in summarizing the situation of rural laborers at the end of the eighteenth century. First, it is apparent that in spite of the paternalism of the Spanish Crown and royal bureaucracy, tempered as it so often was by local allegiances and *realpolitik*, colonial elites pretty much disposed of labor resources as they liked. It would be a mistake to think of judicial intervention in favor of freedom of movement of laborers as a mere legal nicety, to be sure. But the institutional safeguards which were erected and often enforced to counteract the centrifugal tendencies of colonial life were undermined by the hard facts of rural demographic growth, and the all too nonfeudal tendency of colonial landowners to maximize their profits in the context of a growing urban market.

Second, it is possible to speak of an ever-increasing impoverishment among the mass of rural inhabitants during the last century of Spanish domination. As we have seen, money wages for those who sold their labor in the countryside remained stable during the eighteenth century. In the face of rising prices, this meant a decline in the purchasing power of the individual laborer. Apparently the prices of primary necessities such as maize, beans, lard, meat, sugar, salt, and cloth all rose during the course of the century, particularly after 1780 or so.[102] Furthermore, the access of most rural laborers to credit diminished as the labor force increased in size. The land available to the individual pueblo-dweller, whether Indian or *casta*, decreased during the eighteenth century because of population pressures in the countryside, as we shall see. One concrete sign of the lessened ability of rural laborers to buy what they needed with the proceeds of their labor is the stability in the volume of goods sold in market towns: the amount of taxable goods moving through rural markets, as reflected by the levels in alcabala (sales) taxes in the late eighteenth century, simply does not increase in proportion to rural population growth.[103]

All these factors—decreasing real wages, and a lessening access to land, credit, and goods—point to a declining living standard in the countryside

100. BPE-BD, leg. 98, exp. 3, 1752.

101. The above version of the Siordia murder case is much shortened for reasons of space. In its entirety, the testimony constitutes a vivid, highly circumstantial, and occasionally lurid portrayal of life on a mid-eighteenth-century hacienda.

102. This is based upon a random sampling of price data from very heterogeneous sources, such as notary records, municipal records, and judicial documents.

103. Various alcabala records in BPE-AFA.

around Guadalajara in the last decades of the colonial period. This situation is the exact opposite of that which prevailed in central Mexico in the sixteenth and seventeenth centuries. During that period, a drop in the Indian population led to concentration of the survivors upon better lands, an increase in the per-capita consumption of traditional foodstuffs, and an increase in real wages due to the growing shortage of labor.[104] In a certain sense, then, the demographic growth of the rural population around the city subsidized the growth of the city itself by insuring a supply of food. In conjunction with the investment in agriculture of capital generated in more dynamic sectors of the economy (commerce and mining), the low level of rural living standards underwrote a transfer of resources from the countryside to the city. We are confronted then, at least in the late-colonial period, not with an atrophied urban civilization dominated by a feudal countryside, but with a "great wen" which drew its sustenance from a hinterland characterized by growing impoverishment.

104. Cook and Borah, *Essays*, vol. 3, chap. 2, pp. 129-176.

PART IV. "DESDE TIEMPO INMEMORIAL": LATE-COLONIAL CONFLICTS OVER LAND

CHAPTER 12

Population Pressure in
the Countryside

Indian Population Growth and Land Scarcity

The effects of rural population growth, particularly in Indian villages, were important and complex. Indian participation in the economy shifted from land-intensive to labor-intensive activities. Indians withdrew from the market as sellers of certain commodities (notably maize) and re-entered the economy in a disadvantaged position, as sellers of labor. Interstitial, labor-intensive economic activities in the countryside and in the environs of the city increased in importance. The upsurge in the available labor force, combined with growing urban demand, allowed the system of hacienda agricultural production to expand, but at the same time induced a decline in real wages and living standards in the rural areas most dependent upon wage labor. In turn, mounting pressure in the countryside increased the vulnerability of the rural population to the effects of famine and disease, and may have brought about a reduction in the rate of population increase by the last years of the colonial period.

All these changes in rural economic life during the eighteenth century did not result solely from population growth, but were mediated by the man-land relationship. Under ideal conditions, the preferred occupation of the Indians, as of most other rural dwellers, was farming. To the degree that access to land was limited for these groups, they were forced first into increasingly labor-intensive agricultural activities and then into more marginal agriculture-related activities, crafts, and wage labor. The evidence is overwhelming that during the eighteenth century Indians, particularly, had their access to land resources progressively restricted due to the conjunction of population pressure with expansion of the hacienda system.

The decline and resurgence of Indian population had two dramatic and visible effects in the countryside: the occupation by Spanish landholders of the abandoned lands of extinct pueblos, and the resuscitation of old villages and formation of new nucleated settlements around older, surviving ones. This situation created as much conflict within Indian society as between Indians and hacendados. Indian villages became involved with each other in struggles not only over land, but also over political jurisdiction and fiscal status. In the long run, of course, the proliferation of Indian settlements and their claims for access to land and political autonomy also contributed to the economic competition between Indians and hacendados.

During the catastrophic decline in Indian population of the sixteenth century, entire Indian communities disappeared completely. A number of those which did remain, hanging on desperately to a vestige of civil autonomy, were consolidated with larger population nuclei under the royal measures for *congregación* promulgated at the close of the century.[1] The decline or outright disappearance of many landholding villages left a vacuum into which moved the Spanish hacienda, with its early emphasis on extensive livestock production.[2] Many land grants to Spaniards embraced unoccupied Indian lands, and by 1700 or so numerous haciendas included such lands in their titles. In 1696, for example, title was confirmed to Leonora Briçeño for the sitio de ganado mayor of Guastla, north of Guadalajara, where "antiguamente [was] fundado el pueblo de Huasta." The center of the grant was the site of the church of the former pueblo. Similarly, the "pueblo despoblado" of Epatán served as the basis for formation of the sugar hacienda of the same name, near Guastla, in the jurisdiction of San Cristóbal de la Barranca. In this same area, mercedes were also granted for the lands of the extinct pueblos of Cuyutlán, Quelitlán, and Acatlán de San Gaspar, all of which later came to be part of haciendas. Northeast of Guadalajara, the extinct Indian village of Izcuintla, in the jurisdiction of Tacotlán, was by the end of the seventeenth century the center of the Hacienda de Izcuintla, with nothing left of the pueblo but ruined buildings of great antiquity.[3]

1. Simpson, *Studies: II. The Civil Congregation*.
2. For the rest of Mexico, see François Chevalier, *Land and Society* (1966), pp. 216-218; Gibson, *The Aztecs*, pp. 407-408; Taylor, *Landlord and Peasant*, pp. 117 and 131.
3. Guastla—AIPG-LG, 12:145-148. Epatán—AIPG-LG, 4:264r-v. Cuyutlán et al.—AIPG, Tierras, leg. 3, exp. 89; LG, 3:17. Izcuintla—AIPG, Tierras, leg. 10, exp. 5.

It is no accident that several of the richest haciendas of central New Galicia included within their boundaries tracts of land formerly occupied by extinct pre-Hispanic pueblos, since the denser centers of Indian population had naturally developed where the possibilities for agriculture were greatest. At the beginning of the nineteenth century, for example, the Hacienda de Atequiza occupied, among other lands, the site of the long extinct pueblo of Cactlán, on the northern margins of Lake Chapala. Around 1810 the place still bore the name of the pueblo, though all that remained of the settlement itself were a few foundations of its church and the graveyard. There were also some trees not native to the area, such as lemons, guamuchiles, zapotes, and mesquites, "fruits generally cultivated by Indian villagers."[4]

Indians were often far from passive in defending their right to lands occupied by Spaniards with the pretended or real excuse of pueblo depopulation. The resurgence of Indian population in old *barrios* or *sujetos*, and formation of new settlements through the splitting off of excess inhabitants, were part of the same process. There are a great many such cases, all of them dating from the latter half of the century. Some of them involve only two Indian parties, generally the older, larger pueblo and its recalcitrant offspring; and some involve three groups, including a Spanish landowner. Despite the overtones of village politics and personal opportunism,[5] the immediate cause of conflict was generally a claim to independent pueblo status and the concomitant access to land.

A revived barrio asserting its claims to independent-pueblo status and communal land is well illustrated by the case of the pueblo of San Nicolás, near Jalostotitlán, in the Altos of Jalisco. In 1802 the Indians of the pueblo petitioned the Audiencia at Guadalajara to expel the inhabitants of the pueblo of San Gaspar from San Nicolás' land, and to grant San Nicolás a license to re-erect its church. San Nicolás, a league distant from San Gaspar, had been founded after the Conquest, ". . . and although because of adverse times it suffered great decline, it never was completely without inhabitants." San Nicolás was in due course reduced to a barrio of San Gaspar, but with subsequent population growth it sought to re-establish its separate identity. By 1802 all its lands had been taken over by San Gaspar for its church confraternity (*cofradía*), so that the inhabitants of San Nicolás were obliged to pay an annual rent to the parish priest of Jalostotitlán for arable lands.[6] We do not know the disposition of the San Nicolás case, but the basic issue of population growth is clear enough.

4. AIPG, Tierras, leg. 25, exps. 13-14. E.g., also: Asuchitlán and Çitala—AIPG, prot. Mena mayor, vol. 19, no page nos., 1757. Cacalutla—AIPG, Tierras, leg. 62, exp. 24. Santa Catalina —AIPG, Tierras, leg. 49, exp. 21, and leg. 62, exp. 17.

5. See Gibson, *The Aztecs*, pp. 50-57.   6. AIPG, Tierras, leg. 27, exp. 12.

A more complex case involving not the revival of an old pueblo, but the formation of a new one by the splitting-off process, is that of the pueblo of San Martín Tesistán, in the area of Jocotepec.[7] Around 1750, the inhabitants of what was later to become the pueblo of Tesistán were living in San Martín, one of the four barrios of the important village of Jocotepec. The expanding population was overcrowded, and the barrio had sought to establish itself as a separate pueblo at a nearby site where there had appeared a miraculous image of Santo Cristo de la Espiración "under the bark of a tree." The Indian officials of Jocotepec objected to the separation of San Martín, because they themselves would then have to bear the "cargos concejiles" formerly divided among all the vacinos, and there would also arise a problem in honoring Jocotepec's written contract with its resident priest. The fact that Jocotepec itself had earlier moved from another townsite in the area, and that there was a Spanish landowner whose interests were involed in the whole matter, led to considerable complications, but in the end sufficient land was found for the establishment of the pueblo of San Martín Tesistán. The *alcalde mayor* awarded possession of the religious image, reposing in the Jocotepec church, to the new pueblo, and de-facto occupation of the townsite began. By 1773, when the pueblo applied to Viceroy Bucareli for a formal license, it had a well-developed structure. There was a school with a *maestro* paid by the villagers, where they learned not only Christian doctrine but also reading, writing, and arithmetic. The inhabitants were electing their own officials, so that the administration of civil affairs and justice was easier and more effective than previously. Construction of the church had been planned but not yet executed. In 1748, the population of the new settlement consisted of 50 families, including *viudos*; twenty-five years later it had increased to 72 families, not including the widowed members of the community.[8]

Another permutation of what may be called the "new pueblo syndrome" involved only the new or revived settlement itself and a local non-Indian landowner. The conflict in the 1770s between Miguel de la Joya, owner of the small but fertile Hacienda de San Lucas just south of the Laguna de Cajititlán, and the Indians of the pueblo of San Lucas illustrates a number of issues discussed above and conveys something of the flavor of late-eighteenth-century rural life. The difficulties between the pueblo and the hacienda began in about 1750, when Pedro Gerónimo Rodríguez Vidal, the owner of the hacienda, petitioned the local corregidor to enforce attendance of the Indian officials of the pueblo at the placing of boundary markers for the hacienda. Rodríguez Vidal asked that the Indians attend

7. For this process among the modern Maya, see Robert Redfield, *Chan Kom* (1934).
8. AIPG, Tierras, leg. 78, exps. 3-12, and leg. 33, exp. 13. E.g., also, the case of Santa María, a barrio of Poncitlán—leg. 49, exp. 5.

"without everyone talking at once or arguing among themselves, but with only the head of the village speaking, and not the entire pueblo as they habitually do," and that they be enjoined not to provoke or to abuse him, which was apparently also their custom. This was the beginning of a long suit in which the Indians were to dispute with the hacienda the ownership of some of its best lands, and the hacienda's owners were continually to claim that the pueblo of San Lucas had no legal existence.

Miguel de la Joya purchased the hacienda sometime around 1770, after it had passed through the hands of two owners subsequent to Rodríguez Vidal. In 1773 Joya stated that the Indians, "under the furtive name of a pueblo, settled on the boundaries of the hacienda." It is from this point in the history of the suit that the terms of the argument shift from the right of Indians to occupy certain lands on the margins of the hacienda to their right to maintain a pueblo at all. Joya claimed that "the Indians extend their invasion from day to day with increasing damage . . . having arrived by now at the innermost part of the hacienda. . . ."

Joya's case was buttressed by the fact that the original merced for the Hacienda de San Lucas, dating from 1569, was for a tract of land lying between the pueblo of Cuyutlán northwest of the hacienda and the then estancia (but by 1773 pueblo) of San Juan, to the southeast. This 1569 grant made no mention of the existence of the pueblo of San Lucas, and it became clear from later testimony that the pueblo of San Lucas had formerly been a barrio of Cuyutlán which had split off from the older settlement sometime in the late seventeenth century. Joya claimed that the so-called pueblo of San Lucas had not proved itself either to be a pueblo or a *congregación*, but was only a "conjunto" of Indians. No one's land was safe, and royal grants were worthless, he said, if Indians could establish pueblos wherever and whenever they liked. He argued that the original merced would never have been made if an Indian settlement had already existed there, and that the hacienda had occupied the land in question for a century before anyone even knew that there were any Indians there. From this he went on to conclude that the Indians must have arrived from other pueblos after the establishment of the hacienda. Joya cited a number of recent examples of similar invasions in the jurisdiction of the Audiencia, including that of the nearby Hacienda de San Martín (near Jocotepec) and the pueblo of Aposol (northeast of Guadalajara, near Teocaltiche). One such pueblo "en la tierra dentro" was ordered extinguished by the Audiencia,

. . . and with justification, since such settlements are made up of fugitive Indians from other pueblos or reductions who gather to live at the expense of other people, lazy and licentious, which is not allowed to them, without a priest to indoctrinate them or to say mass except from year to year, and without any official to correct them except for one of themselves. . . .

The pueblo of San Lucas claimed on its side that in 1644 Juan Rodríguez Vidal had made de-facto recognition of the pueblo's existence by agreeing in the measurements of that year to accept less land than was actually specified in the original titles of the hacienda. The Indians also maintained that Joya and his administrator had harassed them and destroyed some of their cultivated fields.

Allowing for the vehemence of Joya's statements and for certain inconsistencies on the part of the Indian claimants, the truth probably lay somewhere in between the two positions, and certainly the royal authorities saw it that way. In 1775 an oidor with a special commission ordered the litigants to make a formal compromise settlement in which the disputed land was divided equally between them. The division deprived the Indians of access to a stone quarry and a water-hole, but in return for a specified annual amount of labor from the pueblo as a whole, Joya agreed to rent these to the pueblo on a limited basis. The Indians attempted to delay formalization of this agreement by appealing the entire matter to the Viceroy, but he returned it to the Guadalajara Audiencia and eventually both parties signed an official document.[9]

The impact of Indian population resurgence upon the landholding situation and the growth of new settlements emerges clearly from this case. The change in the land-labor equation from the mid-seventeenth to the late eighteenth century is striking. In 1644, Juan Rodríguez Vidal was apparently willing to sacrifice a part of his land in order to secure his access to labor in the form of the newly settled and very small pueblo of San Lucas, which for vague reasons had split off from the larger village of Cuyutlán. As Joya noted at one point, the Indians had made no claims against the hacienda until the middle of the eighteenth century. By the 1770s, however, Joya probably had sufficient access to labor but needed to defend his access to land. This change reflects the pressures created by rural population growth and the commercialization of agriculture in response to growing urban demand in the latter part of the eighteenth century. Certainly litigation over barrio-vs.-pueblo status was often used as a pretext, both by older villages and by non-Indian landowners, to prevent a more equitable distribution of land resources in the countryside. But the essential fact remains that the increase in the Indian population led to the revival of old settlements and the creation of new ones, particularly from the third quarter of the eighteenth century.[10]

9. AIPG, Tierras, leg. 12, exp. 3, and leg. 40, exp. 8; BPE-MC, vol. 3, exp. 8.
10. E.g., Analco—AIPG, Tierras, leg. 5, exp. 12, and leg. 46, exp. 13. Santa Cruz—leg. 21, exp. 10. Tonalá—leg. 5, exp. 9. Santa María—leg. 4, exp. 1. La Barca—leg. 20, exp. 10. Poncitlán—leg. 22, exp. 1.

The increasing frequency and acrimony of suits over land after the mid-century, not only between Indian pueblos and non-Indians but also among Indians themselves, is strong presumptive evidence that conflict was building in the countryside over the possession and use of land. The vast majority of suits initiated over the course of the century were concentrated in the years after 1750. There were earlier conflicts, to be sure, but these were generally less bitter, took less time to settle, and were often disposed of by extrajudicial agreements.[11] Even though the cost of litigation increased during the course of the century, Indian pueblos were more and more loath to compromise in disputes over land. Indian communities were by the end of the century spending substantial amounts drawn from their village treasuries (*arcas de comunidad*) in defense of their legal claims to land.[12] The notorious litigiousness of the Indians was noted by contemporaries and was reinforced both by their objective need to defend their access to the land and by the considerable degree of success their suits enjoyed before the Audiencia of New Galicia.[13]

More direct evidence on the question of decreasing access to land comes from the large number of credible statements that many Indian pueblos simply lacked sufficient lands to sustain their growing populations. In a number of instances, there is sufficient information, mostly in the form of land suits, to trace the growing scarcity of land in some detail. A particularly good example is the case of the pueblo of Tizapán el Bajo, more generally known as Tizapanito, in the area between Acatlán and Cocula, west of Lake Chapala. This fertile and densely populated area was long dominated by several important haciendas, the largest and richest of which was Santa Ana Acatlán, part of the Porres Baranda mayorazgo. In 1756 the pueblo, under considerable pressure because of its enlarged population, initiated a suit before the Audiencia with the haciendas of Santa Ana Acatlán and Estipac, owned respectively by Francisco Porres Baranda, then holder of the great Porres Baranda entail, and Francisco de Soto Posadas. At issue was legal ownership of several parcels of land in the neighborhood which the pueblo claimed by virtue of a viceregal merced of 1603 (the pueblo lay within the Provincia de Ávalos, in New Spain), and which amounted to about three sitios de ganado mayor. The titles to this land presented by the villagers were found upon examination to be false, and new measurements of the whole area were ordered made. The pueblo,

11. AIPG, Tierras, leg. 46, exp. 13.

12. E.g., both La Barca and Tlajomulco in 1803—AIPG, Tierras, leg. 20, exp. 10, and leg. 5, exp. 8, respectively.

13. AIPG, Tierras, leg. 27, exp. 5, and leg. 5, exp. 9; and Taylor, *Landlord and Peasant*, p. 53.

composed of four barrios, was found to be occupying only slightly less than the sitio mayor to which it was legally entitled.[14]

In 1756 the population of Tizapanito was over a thousand people, almost all of whom were dependent upon farming for their support. In addition to the need for farming land, the two *cofradías* and two *hermandades* required grazing for their 1,800 cattle and horses and 500 sheep. "Because they have scarcely enough land for their own needs," one witness said, "they have rented out none to other people." In fact, pueblo lands which had fifty years previously been rented out to non-Indians had been reoccupied by the villagers themselves, and by midcentury the pueblo was renting extensive lands from both Santa Ana Acatlán and Estipac. Eventually more than half of the land in question was found to be without legal title (*realengo*); of the rest, part was found to belong to Santa Ana Acatlán and part to Estipac. The pueblo was allowed to settle with the Crown for some 200 pesos and thus gain legal title to much of the land it had claimed.[15]

The substantially favorable decision of 1758 was hardly the end of the matter, however. Subsequent counterclaims by Soto Posadas led to a series of suits in which the pueblo was forced to defend its interests against those of the Hacienda de Estipac. The administrator of Estipac in the 1760s ordered his retainers to destroy the fences put up by the Indians on the adjudicated land. The villagers were told that if they persisted in trying to cultivate the disputed areas they would be kidnapped one by one, taken to the hacienda, and whipped to death. Further difficulties of this sort led to an injunction by the Audiencia in 1773 to the then-administrator of Estipac not to interfere in any way with the Indians' peaceable occupation. Despite this degree of judicial protection, problems continued, and Tizapanito never paid its fee (*composición*) to the Crown to legitimize its title. By 1805, fifty years after the initial suit, the pueblo still had not obtained unequivocal possession of the lands in question, but it was renewing its claim and promising to pay the original 200 pesos. Its petition of that year stated:

14. The question of the amount of land to which Indian pueblos were legally entitled simply by their status as pueblos is confused for the Ávalos towns by the inconsistent application of the 600-vara rule established for New Spain by a *real çédula* of 1697. This confusion is compounded by early jurisdictional conflict between New Spain and New Galicia over the area, and also by the fact that suits over land in the Provincia de Ávalos were generally heard before the Audiencia of New Galicia. In New Spain the rule was apparently interpreted to mean that where *no other* lands were held by legal title, a pueblo was allowed a *fundo legal* of 600 varas in all four directions from the site of the village church (e.g., AIPG, Tierras, leg. 33, exp. 38). In the present instance, the sitio de ganado mayor was admitted to be the minimum size of the fundo legal. (See Chevalier, *Land and Society*, passim.)

15. AIPG, Tierras, leg. 62, exp. 24.

Now we have not even a small piece (*palmo*) of unsown land to use, because of the large number of villagers and the great scarcity of land, since our powerful neighbors have callously destroyed us with repeated suits and have encroached on our lands as far as they want.[16]

In 1819 Tizapanito was said to be in an "estado miserable" due to a lack of land. The population had grown to about 1,700, but the pueblo still had the same land base. Individual Indians were paying some 400 pesos a year for rental of land from the surrounding haciendas. Despite the reopening of the case with a search for the pueblo's titles in 1819, by 1827 the Hacienda de Estipac was occupying the disputed parcels by virtue of the favoritism shown toward its owner, Juan Manuel Caballero, by the "despot" General José de la Cruz, Intendant of Guadalajara.[17]

The two main factors in the late-colonial struggle over land resources are clearly highlighted in the case of Tizapanito. The combined effect of village population growth and the cupidity of hacendados was to reduce the per-capita availability of farming land to Indians and to increase economic and social tensions in the countryside. Of course, not all Indian communities felt the same kind of pressure upon their resources, to the same degree, or beginning at the same time. Land was more at a premium in certain areas because of the possibilities for commercial agriculture, and similarly, the Indian population started on a denser base and increased faster in some areas than in others.

While generalization is difficult because of the chaotic nature of the evidence, some chronological and geographical patterns do emerge. The Indian villages on the northern margins of Lake Chapala and in the Jocotepec-Zacoalco area seem to have experienced the earliest and most serious pressure on their communal lands because of population growth. In 1703 the Indians of the pueblo of Santa Cruz, just west of Ocotlán in the jurisdiction of La Barca, complained that they had insufficient land for farming because of a growing population.[18] Cases of land scarcity in lakeside pueblos were complicated by the fact that Lake Chapala itself, and smaller bodies of water to the north and west (the lagunas of Cajititlán and Zacoalco), tended to shrink or increase in size with seasonal variations in rainfall. Thus what was *milpa* or garden land during the spring might become swamp during the rainy season, and the supply of land available for farming was therefore not constant. Still, the effects of population pressure are clear.

16. AIPG, Tierras, leg. 27, exp. 7.
17. AIPG, Tierras, leg. 62, exp. 25, and leg. 27, exp. 7.
18. Santa Cruz—AIPG, Tierras, leg. 60, exp. 21. E.g., also: San Miguel—AIPG, prot. Morelos, 2:51v-53. San Lucas—AIPG, Tierras, leg. 41, exp. 25.

Another striking case is that of the pueblo of Zacoalco itself. In 1726 the village was involved with Francisco Porres Baranda in a suit over possession of the sitio mayor of Santa Catalina, located between the lagunas of Zacoalco and Atotonilco. The Indians of Zacoalco claimed that Santa Catalina had existed as a subject pueblo until 1610, that it had been almost entirely depopulated, and that the survivors and therefore the right to the town lands had been absorbed by Zacoalco itself. This was also said to have been the case with another extinct *sujeto*, the pueblo of San Juan. By 1726 the population of Zacoalco had grown to more than 4,000, and there simply was not sufficient land to support them. Added to this basic insufficiency was the problem created by the seasonal advance of the nearby lake onto pueblo lands. The Indians went on to say that even if the land in question were found to be the property of a private individual (Porres Baranda), the clear necessity for enlarging the village's holdings should override this right and the sitio should be ceded to them.[19] We do not know the final outcome of this case.

As the century progressed, old conflicts over land continued in the lake area and more signs of population pressure appeared. The important pueblo of Jocotepec, for example, on the western extremity of Lake Chapala, was already cramped at midcentury owing to population increase (at least one new pueblo split off at about this time) and pressure from the great Hacienda de Huejotitán nearby. Fifty years later, the situation was grave. The pueblo was composed of four barrios "which are actually four pueblos reduced to one," with a total population of about 1,300. A number of vecinos had no farming land allotted to them, though this was partially due to illegal sales of communal lands to certain Indians by former alcaldes of the pueblo.[20] Another of the many cases which occurred after the midcentury was that of the pueblo of Santa Cruz de la Soledad, just northeast of the village of Chapala. By 1786, the pueblo had a population of upwards of 400 people without sufficient farming land. A spokesman for the neighboring hacienda of San Nicolás de la Labor maintained in a suit of that year that Santa Cruz had always been a barrio of Chapala and that it was therefore only entitled to a townsite (*fundo legal*) of 600 varas on a side, instead of a square league. It was later proved that Santa Cruz was in fact an independent pueblo which had existed since the end of the sixteenth century, and a quantity of land which the hacienda had occupied without title was returned to the pueblo in 1806. The growth of population is highlighted in the documents as the major cause of land pressure, whatever the legal merits of the individual case may have been.[21]

19. AIPG, Tierras, leg. 62, exp. 17.
20. AIPG, Tierras, leg. 71, exp. 32, and leg. 78, exps. 3-12.
21. AIPG, Tierras, leg. 28, exp. 1, and leg. 27, exp. 28.

Farther west, in the Cocula area, population pressure is noticeable from fairly early in the eighteenth century but seems to have become really important and widespread somewhat later than in the neighborhood of Lake Chapala. In 1744, the pueblo of Cocula itself was woefully short of land not only for cultivation but also for houselots for the Indian inhabitants.[22] Here, as in the neighboring pueblo of San Martín, there were numerous non-Indians; indeed, Cocula was specifically known for this peculiarity. Still, despite the dual pressure from surrounding haciendas and from non-Indians within the area itself, it is clear that population increase within the Indian sector caused substantial pressure upon available land. Another area characterized by both a strong Indian demographic recovery and intensification of hacienda agriculture in the eighteenth century was Tlajomulco, lying midway between the Valley of Toluquilla and the western end of Lake Chapala.[23]

The area which experienced the earliest and most intense development of commercialized agriculture was that immediately surrounding the city of Guadalajara, especially in the fertile Toluquilla Valley to the south and around Tlaquepaque and Tonalá to the east. Tonalá and the nearby towns were important suppliers of agricultural repartimiento labor from very early, and continued to furnish agricultural laborers for the local haciendas throughout the eighteenth century. Arable land in this neighborhood was at a premium from at least the beginning of the eighteenth century, and the boundaries among private and pueblo holdings were well established. Still, the growth of Guadalajara itself, the increase in village population, and the further intensification of agriculture produced strains on the local landholding structure and endemic conflict over land.

The case of the pueblo of San José de Analco, east of the city, indicates the early scarcity of arable land in the immediate environs of Guadalajara and casts an interesting sidelight on the problems of urban growth. In 1731, the Indians of San José, without any authorization from the Audiencia or cabildo, opened a long, deep trench (*vallado*)—either for purposes of irrigation or boundary division, or both—on the eastern side of the city. The area into which the villagers intruded to increase their arable land was called in the documents of the case the "ejido cordonal" of the city. The effect of their action was to cut the roads into Guadalajara from the east, interfering with the daily supply of foodstuffs to the city and preventing the pasturing of animals for the city's meat monopoly as well as privately owned dairy cattle. The soil in this area was very sandy and therefore easily subject to erosion. Many barrancas had been created by the normal action of the rains, and much money had already been spent by the city

22. AIPG, Tierras, leg. 1, exp. 1, and leg. 51, exp. 11.
23. AIPG, Tierras, leg. 8, exp. 6, and leg. 27, exps. 1 and 15.

and private individuals in constructing *galápagos* and *repechos* (types of earthworks) at the heads of these ravines to keep them from worsening. It was feared that the carelessly opened trench would aggravate this condition. Also, the cabildo's lawyer claimed that the growth of the city depended on having lands open toward the east, since it was blocked on the south by the pueblo of Mexicaltzingo and on the north by barrancas and the pueblo of Mezquitán. Since the main civic buildings should always remain in the center of the city, equal urban growth both east and west was essential to maintain balance. Eventually the Indians of Analco were required to withdraw and close up their trench.[24] Tonalá itself and nearby villages were continually involved in disputes over land among themselves and with the important haciendas close by.[25]

The conditions of land shortage among Indian pueblos which prevailed around 1800 in what may be called the "fertile crescent" to the south of Guadalajara were not nearly so marked in the more arid, less densely populated areas to the northwest, north, and east of the city. The area east of the city and north of Zapotlanejo, between the Río Santiago and the Altos of Jalisco, contained several important Indian pueblos (Matatlán, Tacotlán, Cuquío), but these had in large measure lost their Indian identity by the end of the eighteenth century and become communities of rancheros. What remained of the village population had sufficient land at its disposal, and mentions of land shortages are rare. Nor are land shortages due to population pressure prominently mentioned for the Indian pueblos surrounding San Cristóbal de la Barranca, due north of Guadalajara, though here a number of well-developed haciendas (Santa Lucía, Epatán, La Magdalena, etc.) did come into conflict with the Indian villagers over land resources. Around the town of Tequila, northwest of the city, the situation became rather more heated at the end of the eighteenth century, owing to the combination of both Indian and non-Indian rural population increase and a vigorous and expanding distilling industry dominated by the patriarchal figure of José Prudencio Cuervo.[26] Here the problem was not so much one of inadequate lands for cultivation as of use of the marginal and wooded lands which were becoming increasingly important both to the local Indians and to the distillers and producers of sugar.

Completing the circle, the district of Tala, to the west of Guadalajara, was dominated by the great Hacienda de Cuisillos. Legal actions and complaints by Indians about land shortages were much less bitter and frequent in this area than in Indian pueblos to the south and east. A detailed cir-

24. AHMG, caja 1, exp. 40.
25. Tonalá—AIPG, Tierras, leg. 33, exp. 24, and leg. 5, exp. 9. Tololotlán—AIPG, Tierras, leg. 27, exp. 18.
26. AIPG, Tierras, leg. 41, exp. 1, and leg. 40, exps. 30 and 31.

cumstantial account of the *bienes de comunidad* of Tala and its five sub-ject pueblos made in 1796 provides a partial picture of the local situation with regard to land. The main town of the district (*cabecera*), San Fran-cisco de Tala, had had its *fundo legal* measured in 1696 and a century later was still in possession of its full square league of lands. These lands were distributed in plots to the Indian vecinos of the pueblo, except for about 160 acres of arable land which were rented out to eight local Spaniards in parcels of nearly equal size. The proceeds of these rentals were deposited in the caja de comunidad and used primarily to defray the cost of religious festivals. Of the five sujetos, only two—Ahuisculco and San Juan de Ocotlán—had any lands in addition to their basic square league, and these were fully occupied by local Indians. Santiago de Nestipac, San Juan de Ocotlán, and Santa Ana Tepetitlán (Santa Ana de los Negros) all enjoyed rights to their full square leagues and rented none of their lands to non-Indians. Of all the six pueblos, only Ahuisculco found it necessary to rent land from outside sources to supplement its communal lands (*tierras de repartimiento*). None of the pueblos had any communally worked land (*siembras de comunidad*).[27] Thus in the Tala area, although there appears to have been no pressing need for additional arable pueblo lands, nearly all the land available was fully occupied by Indian farmers.

Social and Economic Differentiation Within Indian Communities

While we cannot assess the effect of rural population growth upon the distribution of land in precise quantitative terms, it was clearly the most important internal cause of land shortages among the Indian pueblos. A second important factor was the social and economic differentiation going on within Indian society: the solidarity of many Indian communities was undergoing tremendous strains in the latter part of the eighteenth century. This socio-economic differentiation aggravated the land shortages in the countryside, and the two situations reinforced each other. The myth of the ethnic solidarity of Indian society at any time during the colonial period has been exploded by the research of Charles Gibson, William Taylor, Eric Wolf, Marvin Harris, and Karen Spalding, among others.[28] Conditions in central New Galicia in the late eighteenth century, however, appear to

27. *Colección de acuerdos sobre tierras*, vol. 2, pp. 307-317.
28. Charles Gibson, *The Aztecs* and "The Aztec Aristocracy in Colonial Mexico," *Comparative Studies in Society and History* 2 (1960); William Taylor, *Landlord and Peasant*; Eric R. Wolf, *Sons of the Shaking Earth* (1959); Marvin Harris, *Patterns of Race in the Americas* (1964); Karen Spalding, *De indio a campesino* (1974).

have been particularly conducive to weakening the substantial bonds which remained within village communities.

Several variables besides population growth and socio-economic differentiation were at work in the countryside to produce this effect. For one thing, increasing *mestizacion* of the Guadalajara region's rural population in general, and especially in certain areas, makes it misleading to speak loosely of "village society," because of the ethnic and cultural blurring which occurred. The acculturation process in colonial society worked against the indigenous tradition and in favor of the homogenizing tendency of Spanish culture. Ethnically marginal elements within Indian society thus inevitably influenced the distribution of wealth and power and complicated the traditional structure considerably. Second, as the commercialization of agriculture advanced during the eighteenth century, there was a concomitant increase in the demand for rural wage labor. Haciendas linked to the urban market required ever larger numbers of permanent workers, who were in some measure drawn from the village population.[29] This produced an attentuation of village society which became increasingly obvious in the latter part of the century and reinforced the fragmenting effect of the other factors at work in the countryside.

As the economic value of land increased, the rural economy became more and more monetized. The amount of buying and selling of land increased, along with the amount of credit and debt at all levels of the economy. In some ways the opportunities for economic accumulation and for social mobility, both upward and downward, grew markedly. It is not surprising, then, that socio-economic differentiation within Indian society was linked strongly with access to land, and that the two were mutually reinforcing. In speaking of Indian wealth in land, there are two aspects to be considered. The first is property ownership in general and the accumulation of wealth. This was a kind of random process—not unlike Brownian movement in fluids—in which there might be change but not necessarily any long-term mobility. The second aspect is how power-holding groups (*caciques, principales,* and pueblo officials) used their positions of authority to acquire wealth and to manipulate the resources of the entire community for their own benefit.

That there were Indian commoners who amassed relatively substantial wealth is indicated by notarial records and contemporary testimony.[30]

29. The exact steps in this process of long-term labor recruitment in Mexico are at least as subject to debate as the effects of enclosure in England. For England, see R. H. Tawney, *The Agrarian Problem in the Sixteenth Century* (1967); Slicher Van Bath, *The Agrarian History of Western Europe*; Joan Thirsk, *The Agrarian History of England and Wales*, vol. 4 (1967); and J. D. Chambers, "Enclosure and Labour Supply in the Industrial Revolution," *Economic History Review*, 2nd series no. 5 (1953).

30. The sample of Indian testaments upon which this discussion is based is admittedly small

Most Indians, of course, like most other rural dwellers, did not make wills unless they had considerable property to dispose of to their heirs, but the testaments which do survive are often detailed and fascinating. Francisco Miguel, a tributary Indian born in the pueblo of Santa Cruz in the jurisdiction of Tlajomulco, left a testament upon his death in 1743. His parents were locally-born Indians still alive at the time of his death. He was married to María de los Reyes, a mestiza of the same pueblo, and they had eleven married children. He had had no capital at the time of their marriage, nor had she brought any dowry, so that virtually all of their property had been acquired by their own labor during the course of their marriage. Miguel's will enumerated eighteen separate parcels of arable land: a dozen devoted to maize, totaling some ninety acres, and six, of unspecified size, planted in wheat.[31] Of the parcels whose origins can be determined, eleven had been purchased from Indians of the neighborhood—four from the same man— and three were inherited; at least some of the rest were held by Miguel through his right as a vecino of the pueblo. He owned a large number of livestock, including over 100 horses, 10 cattle, 5 yoke of oxen, and a number of pigs. His other property included two small houses, a saddle and harness, agricultural implements and carpentry tools, clothing and furniture, and 8 cargas (almost 2,500 pounds) of unthreshed wheat. He was owed a number of small debts in cash and kind by local farmers, which may help to explain the manner in which he built up his small empire. One of the houses and at least one of the parcels of land were in payment of debts to him from local people. The total value of all this property was estimated to be about 700 pesos. After the costs for the funeral and liquidation of the estate were deducted, the widow received about 300 pesos and each of the eleven children about 30 pesos.[32] Thus, unless the heirs came to some arrangement to settle all the property on one of their number, Miguel's small fortune was probably dissipated within a short time after his death.

Other Indian testaments from the mid-eighteenth century confirm the pattern discernible in Francisco Miguel's will. Wealth was typically based upon ownership of several small parcels of land, one or two houses, and surprisingly large numbers of livestock.[33] The wealth of Indian families

---

(about a dozen wills); but it is drawn from one pueblo, Tlajomulco, during the latter part of the eighteenth century.

31. The size of maize plots was very often given in terms of *fanegas de sembradura* or *cuartillas*, areas of 8.8 and 4.4 acres, respectively. Conversions of weights and measures are based upon Manuel Carrera Stampa's "The Evolution of Weights and Measures in New Spain," except where otherwise noted. The cultivation of wheat by Indians was fairly common, especially in and around the pueblo of Santa Cruz.

32. AIPG, prot. Tlajomulco, 2: no page no., 1743.

33. E.g., Antonio Almao—AIPG, prot. Tlajomulco, 2: no page no., 1746.

(for the family was the primordial unit of production) was often based upon the fairly slim foundations of a small inheritance from parents or grandparents and a dowry brought by the wife, usually consisting of livestock.[34] Typically, the property was divided among several heirs at the death of the head of the household, so that the hard-won wealth of one generation was dispersed in the next, leaving the children to sink back into the morass of village poverty from which their parents had emerged. Nor did the basis of Indian wealth change much during the late colonial period. Testaments from around 1800 indicate the same reliance upon multiple small plots of land, house ownership, and livestock. Possibly there was a tendency for Indian agriculturists in densely populated areas to own less livestock than at midcentury, because of the increasing scarcity of land. The same patterns of inheritance, dowry, property accumulation, and dispersement prevailed at the end of the eighteenth century as at the middle.[35] There were few who attained this level of wealth; an estimate of 5 percent, even for the end of the eighteenth century, is probably very generous. An 1803 report by the *teniente* of San Martín de la Cal, in the jurisdiction of Cocula, discussed the relative nature of Indian wealth and the pattern of accumulation and dissipation outlined here:

In these pueblos they call "well-off" an Indian who has his own tanning stone for hides, which may pay him two or three pesos a year in rentals or, if he uses it himself, a half-real a day more than a common laborer; they call "comfortable" the man who has a yoke or two of oxen with which he sows a half-fanega or a fanega of maize which may yield, with hard labor, two or three cartloads, hardly enough to feed him and his family. Others are called comfortable because they have three or four cows, ten or twelve sheep; so that if the man dies and his family has to pay for a funeral, the property hardly covers it and the orphaned little ones are left without anything. . . .[36]

The general point to be made here is that many village Indians who achieved relative wealth, be they commoners or caciques, did so primarily on the basis of acquiring land, mostly by purchase. In fact, land was always changing hands in small pieces within village society.[37] Such minis-

34. E.g., the testament of Almao, cited above; and of María de la Trinidad, also of Tlajomulco—AIPG, prot. Tlajomulco, 2: no page no., 1746. In connection with livestock, the available evidence indicates that in areas less favored for agriculture, Indian wealth, much like non-Indian wealth, was based more upon the possession of cattle and horses than upon arable land. For example, the substantial estate of Josefa María, an Indian woman of Juchipila who died in 1721, was composed almost entirely of livestock (BPE-BD, leg. 57, exp. 7).

35. E.g., the wills of Mariano Cecilio Cuervo, 1793, and Ventura Canal, 1803, both Indian commoners of Tlajomulco—AIPG, prot. Tlajomulco, 2: no page no., 1793, and 1: no page no., 1803.

36. BPE-AJA, 228:3:2965.

37. The author observed this same process among the modern Otomí Indians of the Mezquital Valley in the state of Hidalgo, Mexico, on an anthropological field trip in the summer of 1970.

cule transactions rarely show up in contemporaneous notarial documents, for a number of reasons. It was often inconvenient for Indians or other rural dwellers to travel to the nearest notary for registration of their property transfers. Also, these countrymen were suspicious of outsiders, particularly where land was concerned. Even if there were a notary available locally, peasants living in small pueblos were unused to dealing in this way. Finally, the value of the land sold might not justify the expense of legally formalizing the transaction before a notary. Thus, the sales of land by Indians and other village dwellers which appear in local notarial registers are only the tip of the iceberg.[38] Most transactions involving Indian lands, even those that appear in local notarial records, were concerned with very small amounts of money, generally less than ten pesos.[39] Viceregal authorities were well aware of the frequency of these subnotarial transactions in land within the Indian community and between Indians and non-Indians, and tried to regulate the practice without much success.[40]

The personal wealth of power-holders within village society—the caciques, principales, and Indian alcaldes—was based upon much the same sort of goods as that of ordinary peasants: houses, livestock, and land. The only differences were that the fortunes of caciques and principales were perhaps larger than those of Indian commoners and that they embraced a broader range of types of wealth. Another distinction may have been that the wealth of Indian nobles was more stable than that of ordinary pueblo dwellers, with less tendency to dissipate after one or two generations.

For example, Juana Micaela, a cacique of Analco, and her non-Indian husband, José de la Cruz Osorio, made their wills in 1716.[41] Between them they owned their house of residence, which they had constructed themselves; an orchard with an irrigation system; a rancho with lands sown in maize and wheat; various livestock including cattle, oxen, horses, and a flock of sheep; and some 2,000 pesos on loan at interest to a *compadre* of Osorio's in Guadalajara. After Osorio's death, Juana Micaela remarried, this time to a native-born Spaniard from Navarra, Andrés de Villamayor. By the time of her own death, sometime in the 1740s, the rancho of the early years of the century had been dignified with the title Hacienda de Tetán—surely because of the intensity of its cultivation rather than for its size, since it only had about 100 head of livestock. By 1758 the property had fallen into the possession of the pueblo of Analco in the form of a religious bequest (*obra pía*) probably established in Juana Micaela's will, since she had no children by either of her husbands. At that time the rancho

38. E.g., various transactions in AIPG, prot. Zapotlanejo, vol. 1, 1788.
39. AIPG, prot. Tlajomulco, 1: no page no., 1809.
40. AIPG, Tierras, leg. 41, exp. 20; *Colección de acuerdos sobre tierras*, vol. 2, pp. 287-289.
41. Marriages between Indian noblewomen and non-Indian men seem to have been fairly common.

(as it was subsequently referred to) was being rented out by the pueblo to a vecino of Guadalajara for 100 pesos per year, which would make its capital value roughly about 2,000 pesos. In 1807 the property was still held by the pueblo of Analco.[42]

The wealth of Indian village elites was distinguished from that of ordinary pueblo-dwellers less by its nature than by the means of its acquisition. What ordinary Indians or non-Indians might achieve through their own industry or by granting credit to their less perspicacious neighbors, the cacique, principal, or Indian alcalde might also accomplish through the power of his office or the prestige of his social position. There are enough instances of outright expropriation of common lands, particularly by caciques, to make it clear that this was not an unusual practice. To cite but one example, in 1798 Don Francisco de la Asunción García, a cacique of the village of San Pedro Tlaquepaque in the jurisdiction of Tonalá, petitioned the Audiencia for permission to sell or rent out two "ranchitos" and a house in the pueblo which he claimed to have inherited from his father. Don Francisco was about to embark upon his studies for the priesthood and apparently required the income. The *fiscal* of the Audiencia, supported by a careful examination of the titles and testimony by the local subdelegado and others, determined that the documents presented by García did not constitute proof of his ownership and that the land in question was in fact part of the fundo legal and not García's private property. He was, however, allowed to rent the land out, since his father had occupied it by right of allotment as a vecino of the pueblo, and this principle of hereditary usufruct was admitted as generally applicable. Five years later García revived his claim and was asking for copies of his presumptive titles from the *juzgado*, though we do not know the outcome of this effort.[43] In all fairness to the village elite group, it must be said that Indian commoners on occasion claimed as pueblo lands property to which there was clear private title by caciques and principales.[44]

More important, perhaps, than the direct expropriation of communal lands by Indian power-holders was their manipulation of these resources for their own benefit. As the economic value of both arable and grazing land increased in the second part of the eighteenth century, those Indians

42. AIPG, prot. García, 11:187v-191; BPE-BD, leg. 94, no exp. no.; AIPG, prot. Berroa, 1:102v-103v; Tierras, leg. 5, exp. 12. E.g., also: Jose Pantaleón de Lara—AHMG, caja 25, 1789. Francisco Cortés de Velasco—AIPG, prot. Tlajomulco, 2: no page no., 1753. Juan Gaspar—*ibid.*, 1780. Antonio Lorenzo—*ibid.*, 1: no page no., 1789.

43. AIPG, Tierras, leg. 40, exp. 11. It is interesting to see that in the intervening five years, García's signature had been transformed, presumably under the influence of his seminary training, from a crabbed and childish scrawl into a beautiful, open, and flowing hand (AIPG, Tierras, leg. 14, exp. 7).

44. AIPG, Tierras, leg. 41, exp. 20, and leg. 22, exp. 8.

who controlled the distribution of these lands found themselves in an advantageous position. They could favor their kin and clients within the pueblo and utilize the money which the rental of pueblo lands brought in from non-Indians. Even putting aside a certain tendency for purely factional struggles within Indian communities to polarize around issues involving land,[45] it is clear that the distribution of land within pueblos was increasingly becoming a source of conflict after about 1760. Even where such practices had been in use for a long time, the population pressure in the latter part of the century sensitized the issue. In the pueblo of Jocotepec, for instance, certain vecinos had held a number of parcels of communal land since the early part of the century by means of illegal sales and rentals made to them by former Indian alcaldes, but the issue did not become really critical until the 1790s.[46]

The situation became yet more complex when powerful outsiders used their influence to insure that they themselves or their clients would have access to pueblo land resources. This often came about through the rental of village lands to non-Indians. The most common cases were those involving collusion between the local Spanish corregidor, subdelegado, teniente, or priest, and non-Indian farmers. In 1805, for example, a group of Indians from the pueblo of Tlajomulco brought a suit claiming that the teniente and priest of the pueblo had influenced the pueblo officials to rent out a large piece of land, the sitio de Cacalutla, to some nonresidents of the village. They maintained that the land had been occupied by them for some time, and pointed out that royal ordinances allowing the rental of excess pueblo lands specified that they be unoccupied. In the words of their petition:

. . . the priest and the teniente, in whom we should find our protection and help, according to their responsibilities, have shown themselves to be our greatest enemies, inclining to favor the powerful in the face of our poverty.[47]

One of the most blatant and notorious cases of this sort of manipulation occurred toward the end of the century in the pueblo of Ahualulco, where the Del Río family had established a virtual hegemony as the most important Spanish landowners of the district. In 1790 a group of caciques and elders (*viejos*) of the village complained of collusion by the subdelegado of Ahualulco, Don Manuel del Río, with the local priest and the current alcalde of the pueblo, in acquiring the use of pueblo lands to round out his haciendas. Del Río had arbitrarily razed some houses within the limits of

45. E.g., the formation of parties within the principal group regarding the petition for a merced of land by the pueblo of Tlajomulco—AIPG-LG, 29:3r-11v, 1711.

46. AIPG, Tierras, leg. 78, exps. 3-12; prot. Berroa, 22:95v; Tierras, leg. 27, exp. 4.

47. AIPG, Tierras, leg. 27, exp. 5.

the pueblo, torn up gardens, and made roads to insure access to his own holdings. The Indians claimed that the subdelegado had also imposed his own alcaldes on the village, and that these creatures of his had then sold, given, and rented communal lands to him. In return for this, Del Río had allowed his men to make use of community funds (some from the rental of pueblo lands) and tribute money. These claims were supported by the testimony of a number of witnesses.[48]

We do not know what proportion of such contracts for rental of communal lands to non-Indians was made under some kind of duress, or for the sole benefit of Indian power-holders, without the consent of the villagers themselves. The private utilization of communal funds by caciques, principales, and alcaldes, including the income from the rental of communal lands which such men were in a position to make, definitely occurred.[49] Certainly, among the scores of rental agreements made by Indian pueblos with outsiders, many were legitimate, made with the tacit or active consent of Indian vecinos, and the proceeds were used for the benefit of the entire community. Very often villages did hold unoccupied parcels or were able to arrive at more rational land-use by renting out some communal lands and using the income to lease holdings from non-Indians. The fact remains that some of the land hunger in pueblos which apparently held sufficient land to meet the needs of a growing population can be ascribed to the kind of manipulation described here. How else can one explain, for example, the rental of an entire sitio by the pueblo of Tlajomulco in 1805, when at this very time there is definitive evidence of a chronic lack of land for cultivation? Seen in this light, Hidalgo's famous decree of December 5, 1810, is quite understandable. The order stated that all renters of lands belonging to Indian pueblos within the "distrito de ésta capital" (Guadalajara) were to pay up their back rents and have them deposited in a "caja nacional," and the Indians were then to reassume possession of the lands in question and work them only themselves in the future.[50] Certainly this measure was intended to cement the loyalty of the Indian villages around Guadalajara.

The distribution of land within the Indian communities of central New Galicia, then, if not completely skewed, was at least unequal. The developing agricultural economy of the late eighteenth century favored the accumulation of wealth by some individuals within both the Indian and Spanish economies. Indeed, the increasing integration of these two traditionally separate sectors is one characteristic of the period. Compounding the general phenomenon of social and economic differentiation in rural commu-

48. AIPG, Tierras, leg. 60, exps. 1-5.
49. E.g., the cases of Tlajomulco, 1711—AIPG-LG, 29:3-11v; and Ahualulco, cited above.
50. *Colección de acuerdos sobre tierras*, vol. 2, p. 5.

nities was the increasingly anomic behavior of Indian elites, both traditional and of more recent origin.[51] The Indian population, scissored between its own growth and the increasing need of the hacienda economy for land, was thus subjected to pressure from within the Indian community as well as from without.

51. Both Taylor, in *Landlord and Peasant*, p. 52, and Pedro Carrasco ("The Civil-Religious Hierarchy in Mesoamerican Communities," *American Anthropologist* 63 (1961), have drawn attention to the dualization of the Indian elite into an older group based upon hereditary status and a newer one based upon elective office, rural commerce, and the acquisition of land.

CHAPTER 13

Formation and Stability of
the Hacienda

The General Trend Toward Consolidation

The great age of hacienda expansion in the Guadalajara region was not the eighteenth century, but the seventeenth.[1] Here a distinction must be made between productive expansion and physical expansion, as well as between the de-facto and de-jure acquisition of land. Changes in the nature of estate agricultural production brought more land under the hoof and plow during the eighteenth century, in response to the growing urban demand for foodstuffs. This process, combined with demographic growth in the countryside, resulted in an increase in the value and scarcity of land and in the frequency of judicial conflicts over its ownership, particularly between rural estates and indigenous communities. While it is true that haciendas occasionally nibbled away bits of land which were either unclaimed or belonged to indigenous communities or other landholders, it is wrong to

1. This has been the finding of several researchers, studying different parts of Mexico: Chevalier, *Land and Society in Colonial Mexico*, pp. 270, 314, whose data primarily, though not exclusively, pertain to northern Mexico; Gibson, *The Aztecs*, p. 289, on the Valley of Mexico; and Taylor, *Landlord and Peasant*, pp. 200-201, looking at the Oaxaca area. Florescano, on the other hand, in his synthetic *Estructuras y problemas agrarios*, pp. 44, 140-148, and 189-190, strongly implies that the expansion of hacienda landholdings continued full-tilt into the eighteenth century, mostly be extra-legal means as opposed to the formalistic grants and title settlements of the sixteenth and seventeenth centuries.

characterize the eighteenth century as a period of aggressive expansion, at least in terms of the actual seizure of land resources. Furthermore, Indian villages frequently managed to assert their legal claims, even to areas for which they could adduce no formal titles; in this, the protective legalism of the Spanish Crown was not merely a codified nicety. What was very often at issue in the voluminous late-colonial litigation over land was not so much the actual ownership of property as the prescriptive rights of peasants to the use of certain resources.

One of the most striking things about the great rural estates which ringed the city of Guadalajara and dominated its regional economy in the eighteenth century was their stability in terms of the land they occupied. Most haciendas, whether great or small, were essentially the same size in 1800 or 1820 that they were in 1700. The major change which occurred during the century concerned the uses to which already legally-titled lands were put. The major adjustments to the newly commercialized agricultural regimen were thus economic, and not primarily formal or legal in nature. The pushing and pulling over boundaries, the judicial arguments between and among haciendas and communal peasant villages, and the signs of an incipient enclosure movement toward the end of the century are thus not incompatible with the view that haciendas were basically stable in the amounts of land they held after 1700 or so, and were not aggressively expanding in the late-colonial period. On the whole, title adjustments and legal wrangles occurred as the commercial sector of the agricultural economy intensified its use of existing resources and filled in a legal tenure structure already in existence when the process began.

The stability in hacienda size is all the more striking in contrast to the frequency with which rural estates changed ownership, even in the late eighteenth century. In most cases, however, such changes in ownership did not affect the size of the estate: assets were generally not liquidated to pay off debts or to raise capital. There were some instances of important properties fragmenting into small holdings, and similarly, a few of what might be called compound haciendas—agglomerations of properties with distinct identities which were under the control of one individual or one family —broke up during the late seventeenth and early eighteenth centuries; but such occurrences were comparatively rare. Some of the compound haciendas came to be reconstituted during the eighteenth century. But the process of disaggregation and reaggregation so common to peasant landholdings, and of which vague hints emerge from contemporary documentation, was not characteristic of the great rural estates.

The formal legal means by which the hacienda consolidated its position was the title settlement with the Spanish Crown. The efforts of Philip II to raise money for his European projects had given rise to a series of cédulas in the 1590s, modified and amplified during the seventeenth century, which provided for the regularization and confirmation of lands held by questionable title. For the payment of a fee into the royal coffers, any landowner could have his property holdings covered by the issuance of a new title, as long as it did not injure the rights of any third party.[2] Enforcement of these decrees was inconsistent and did not take place all over Mexico at the same time, but by the beginning of the eighteenth century the *composición*, as such a settlement was called, had made its full weight felt in New Galicia. A wave of such settlements following a royal cédula of 1692— mostly in the form of individual contracts, as opposed to those made by towns—legally established the property bounds arrived at by purchase or appropriation during the seventeenth century.[3]

The post-hoc nature of these turn-of-the-century settlements is obvious. Even so, they were in many cases accepted in subsequent litigation. In fact, most of the usable land in New Galicia was already granted out to Spanish landholders by 1650 or so, even if it was not yet exploited.[4] Thus rural estates within central New Galicia did not gain nearly such huge amounts of land through the composiciones of the later seventeenth century as did estates in more peripheral areas. This is not to say that the Guadalajara region was in any sense congested already by 1700, but simply that the groundwork had been laid for the later agricultural expansion which characterized the area. The acreage to which formal title was acquired by composición in the 1690s and early 1700s rarely exceeded one or two sitios de ganado mayor. For example, a confirmation of 1653 obtained by Celedón González de Apodaca for the Hacienda de Cuisillos, which came to be the largest hacienda in the Guadalajara region, enumerated 20.5 sitios de ganado mayor, 5 menor, and some 59 caballerías. By 1730, when the hacienda reached its maximum size through various settlements with the Crown, it measured 22 sitios de ganado mayor, 6 menor, and 68 caballerías.[5] The relatively small extent of regularized-title lands in the Guadalajara region contrasts markedly with the huge expanses absorbed by haciendas, and subsequently accepted, in more marginal areas. Nothing in the region even began to compare with the dealings of the Rincón Gallardo family, for instance. In 1697, Capitán José Rincón Gallardo had his Hacienda de la Ciénega de Mata, in the Lagos area, measured. The property was found to encompass 181.75 sitios de ganado mayor, of which only 94 were properly

2. Chevalier, *Land and Society*, pp. 265-277, discusses this process in some detail.

3. Chevalier, *ibid.*, p. 270, states that the process was "completed" by 1696-97 for New Galicia, when actually it appears to have gone on into the early 1700s, and sporadically thereafter. E.g., in particular, the documents on title confirmations in AIPG-LG and Tierras.

4. Chevalier, *Land and Society*, p. 216.

5. AIPG, Tierras, leg. 25, exps. 16-18; prot. García, 29:395-417v, 1730.

titled. Eventually he paid a fee of 1,980 pesos to the Crown for the title-settlement of 65.5 sitios de ganado mayor, 18 menor, and 219 caballerías.[6]

The year 1700 rather coincidentally marks the beginning of the mature period of the hacienda system in the Guadalajara region. After that date, land boundaries were more or less stable and the important changes that took place were in the mode of agricultural production, not in the size of large landholdings. Table 28 presents data on the size of a select group of haciendas over the course of the eighteenth century. A few rural estates in the Guadalajara area grew substantially in size after the mid-seventeenth century through the absorption and later title-settlement of lands. The Hacienda de Estipac, for example, located in the Cocula area and owned in the last decades of the eighteenth century by the Marqués de Pánuco, measured 4 sitios de ganado mayor when its titles were confirmed to Cristóbal Camacho Bravo in 1644, but encompassed 7 sitios de ganado mayor by the end of the colonial period.[7] It must be emphasized, however, that such instances were relatively rare and that the quantities of land involved were much smaller than in districts outside the core area of fairly dense population and commercialized agriculture.

Hacienda Expansion

Starting with the end of the process, rather than the beginning, we have briefly outlined some aspects of the consolidation of large rural estates which developed in the Guadalajara region in the sixteenth and seventeenth centuries. As with the careers of individuals, the best way to illustrate that process is by looking in detail at a few cases. This section deals not so much with the issues of how lands were originally appropriated or how they were used, or even whether the means of their acquisition were legally or morally legitimate, but with the development of large, stable rural estates on the basis of putatively legitimate titles. Here we are concerned only with the question of how haciendas came to have individual identities, and in some instances how they came to lose them.

The modal case for the formation of a large rural estate was the agglomeration of a great many small individual land-grants, many of them dating from the sixteenth century. This process was largely completed by the middle of the seventeenth century, and acquired the imprimatur of the Spanish Crown with the composiciones of the late seventeenth and early eighteenth centuries.[8] Single mercedes, usually for sitios de ganado mayor

6. AIPG-LG, 13:202-204v, 1697.
7. AIPG, Tierras, leg. 51, exp. 4, 1750-1800, and leg. 14, exp. 1.
8. Jean Borde and Mario Góngora, in their remarkable study *La propiedad rural en el Valle*

or menor with attached caballerías, or groups of them, were made in great abundance by the Spanish authorities in the sixteenth century. Most of these primordial grants were authorized by the Audiencias of Compostela (until 1560) and Guadalajara (after 1560), but some of them date from the pre-Audiencia period and bear the signatures of royal governors such as Francisco Vázquez de Coronado (1538-1540 and 1543-1545).[9] Mercedes of lands within the jurisdiction of New Spain proper (including the areas of Jocotepec, Cocula, Zacoalco, and Ameca) were made by the viceroys in Mexico City.[10]

The recipients of the original grants were a mixed bag of individuals, few of whom retained the holdings. Among them were royal officials, conquistadores, and simple soldiers and settlers who have left little or no trace in the written records of the time. Prominent among them were such men as Nuño de Guzmán,[11] Alonso de Ávalos, and Juan de Urbina, to mention just a few of the more famous military figures of the conquest of western Mexico. But mercedes were also granted to humbler men such as Pedro Flores de Arellano, Gaspar de Tapia, Pedro de Plasencia, Andrés de Villanueva, and Hernando Martel, among a host of others.[12] Most of these early grantees did not hold onto their mercedes, for whatever reasons. Sometimes they died or moved elsewhere or were forced by indigence to sell their holdings. In some cases, it is obvious that the ostensible grantees merely acted as fronts for men with larger resources and ambitions who

---

del Puangue, vol. 1, passim, describe basically the same process within the same chronology for colonial Chile. See also Chevalier, *Land and Society*, pp. 134-143, which includes much specific data on New Galicia.

9. On the development of the political identity of New Galicia, see Parry, *The Audiencia of New Galicia*; for a chronology of political governments in New Galicia, see Instituto Nacional de Antropología e Historia, *Lecturas históricas sobre Jalisco*, pp. 94-95.

10. For a fastidious and extremely useful reconstruction of the districts within the jurisdiction of New Spain, see Peter Gerhard, *A Guide to the Historical Geography of New Spain*, esp. pp. 58-61 and 239-242 for Autlán and Sayula, respectively. The jurisdictional tangle caused by the administrative and political division between New Spain and New Galicia in these districts was formidable, and in many cases it is extremely difficult to trace the evolution of landholdings in this key agricultural zone.

11. E.g., AIPG, Tierras, leg. 77, exp. 14, referring to a merced made to Guzmán by Coronado in 1548.

12. E.g., AIPG-LG, 10: no page nos., 1694. These names are all drawn, for purposes of illustration, from the list of original grantees of the lands of the important Hacienda de Atequiza, on the northern shore of Lake Chapala. Tapia, Plasencia, and Villanueva were all Spaniards who came to the New World very young and served in the conquest and pacification of New Galicia (Icaza, *Diccionario autobiográfico de conquistadores y pobladores de Nueva España*, vol. 2, pp. 339, 267, and 265, respectively). Aside from Icaza and the standard biographical compilations and works on the Conquest, there is a wealth of biographical and genealogical information on the conquerors and early settlers of western Mexico, many of them landowners, in the works of Jesús Amaya; see particularly *Ameca, protofundación mexicana* and *Los conquistadores Fernàndez de Hijar y Bracamonte*.

Table 28.

Size of Titled Lands of Selected Haciendas in the Guadalajara Region,
1695-1804

Property	Location	Year	Size
Santa Lucía	San Cristóbal de la Barranca	1697	3.0 sitios mayor
			3.0 sitios menor
			15.0 caballerías
			11.0 suertes de huerta
			2.0 heridos de molino
		c.1785	4.0 sitios mayor[a]
			3.0 sitios menor[a]
			17.0 caballerías
			11.0 suertes de huerta
			2.0 heridos de molino
La Concepción	Toluquilla Valley	1720	1.0 sitio mayor
			0.5 sitio menor
			4.0 caballerías
		1739	same
		1755	same
		1791	same
Huejotitán	Jocotepec	1679	6.0 sitios mayor
			5.0 sitios menor
			13.0 caballerías
		1733[b]	same
Atequiza	Chapala	1703	4.0 sitios mayor
			0.5 sitio menor
			28.0 caballerías
			1.0 herido de molino
		1725	4.0 sitios mayor
			0.5 sitio menor
			20.0 caballerías
		1751	4.0 sitios mayor
			0.5 sitio menor
			22.0 caballerías
		1784	same
		1804	4.0 sitios mayor
			0.5 sitio menor
			26.0 caballerías
			1.0 herido de molino

Table 28. (continued)

Size of Titled Lands of Selected Haciendas in the Guadalajara Region, 1695-1804

Property	Location	Year	Size
Cuspala	Tala	1742	4.3 sitios mayor
			1.0 sitio menor
			7.0 caballerías
		1789	same
Navajas	Tala	1695	1.0 sitio mayor
			1.0 sitio menor
		1704	same
		1711	same
		1727	same
		1745	same
		1769	same

SOURCES:

Santa Lucía, 1697–AIPG, Tierras, leg. 58, exp. 16; 1785–*ibid.* La Concepción, 1720–AIPG, prot. Mena mayor, 10:984v-99lr; 1739–*ibid.*, 27:193-200; 1755–prot. Blas de Silva, 8:104v-110v; 1791–prot. Ballesteros, 14:93-109v. Huejotitán, 1679–AIPG, Tierras, leg. 78, exps. 3-12; 1733–prot. Morelos, 8:78-101. Atequiza, 1703–AIPG, prot. Morelos, 2:28r; 1725–prot. Mena mayor, 14:78v-82v; 1751–*ibid.*, 35:143-147v; 1784–prot. Ballesteros, 2:275-278v.; 1804–Tierras, leg. 20, exp. 7. Cuspala, 1742–AIPG, prot. Maraver, 7:142r; 1789–prot. Ballesteros, 10:287v-289v. Navajas, 1695–AIPG, Tierras, leg. 41, exp. 12; 1704–prot. Morelos, 2:no p. no.; 1711–*ibid.*, 3:40-47; 1727–BPE-BD, leg. 63, exp. 12; 1745–AIPG, prot. Mena mayor, 32:237v-240v; 1769–prot. Berroa, 12:290-293v.

NOTES:

[a]The extra sitio de ganado mayor on Santa Lucía was acquired by purchase from a Spaniard in 1750.

[b]Although no measurements of Huejotitán are available for the later eighteenth century, there is strong presumptive evidence that it remained basically the same size as in 1733.

thus gained control over huge tracts of land through the use of proxies. Still other smaller landholders were forced by general conditions to sell out, which appears to have been the case in the Ameca area, for example.[13]

A typical instance of the agglomeration of separate parcels into a single stable unit was the important Hacienda de Atequiza, composed of about 25,000 acres of fertile arable and prime grazing lands northeast of the town of Chapala.[14] Atequiza, one of the most valuable estates in the Guadala-

13. Chevalier, *Land and Society*, pp. 141-142; and Amaya, *Ameca*, passim.

14. There is perhaps nothing more tedious for the researcher in agrarian history than the perusal of documents on landholding, unless it is trying to understand them; and a like

jara region at the end of the colonial period (worth nearly 200,000 pesos by
1821), was originally composed of a great many individual mercedes which
had come to form a large estate with a definite identity already by 1650, if
not earlier. In fact, the size of the property changed very little during the
next 170 years. A composición of 1694, initiated to gain clear title to the
sitio de ganado mayor called Mira el Río, lists the documented parcels, all
of them contiguous, which then made up the property, as shown in Table
29. These lands had all been settled for in one lump—to clear any questions regarding their titles and to add any odd, untitled pieces (*huecos*)—
by the owner of the estate, Br. Domingo Casillas de Cabrera, before the
Audiencia of New Galicia in 1649. Cabrera's heirs eventually sold these
lands to Capitán Andrés Fernández Pacheco, who sought another composición in 1694, adding to the hacienda's legally titled lands the sitio de
ganado mayor Mira el Río, which he claimed had been occupied by the
estate de facto for more than a century. Thus, Atequiza had by 1650 actually, and by 1694 legally, come to occupy 4 sitios de ganado mayor, half
a sitio menor, 26 caballerías, and 1 *herido de molino* (mill site). In 1813 the
hacienda measured exactly the same size—though in the interim there had
been a few minor alterations, such as the purchase of some caballerías and
the selling of others in the early eighteenth century, in an apparent attempt
to rationalize the layout of the estate.[15]

In the cases of several important haciendas, one individual not only
consolidated a number of holdings initially granted to other people, but
also added mercedes made to himself in the same area. This procedure
suggests a quite conscious ambition to build up a large estate centered in
one zone, and in fact the few compound haciendas which emerged during
the seventeenth century (those associated with the names Porres Baranda,
Ahumada, and González de Apodaca) were constructed in this way. A
well-documented instance of the agglomeration of a great property through
a combination of purchases and land-grants is the magnificent Hacienda

---

boredom must envelop even the most committed reader if he is subjected to page after page on
the unraveling of land titles. Yet this type of documentation is among the most basic and
valuable for the theoretical reconstruction of a rural society. Interestingly enough, when one
tries to trace the evolution of a single landed estate, for example, through the legal documentation, it is rare to encounter complete records which can be read more or less unambiguously.
The few examples adduced in the following pages deal for the most part with the most
important haciendas of the region—Huejotitán, Atequiza, Mazatepec, Santa Lucía—and not
with smaller or less economically developed estates. But the process seems to have been
universal across the spectrum, from haciendas of a few thousand acres to the huge Hacienda de
Cuisillos and the compound haciendas which later broke apart into estates which were important in their own right. These are the cases for which the documentation is best, but they are
also a fairly representative sample.

15. AIPG, Tierras, leg. 25, exps. 13, 14, and 19, 1805-1816; prot. Morelos, 1:320-321v, 1699;
2:51v-53v, 1707; and 3: no page nos., 1710.

Table 29.
Land Titles of the Hacienda de Atequiza, 1694

Type of Parcel	Date of Merced	Granting Agency or Official	Original Grantee
sitio mayor	27 Aug. 1549	Audiencia N.G.	Pedro Gómez de Contreras
sitio mayor	20 Apr. 1556	Audiencia N.G.	Juan de Urbina
caballería	15 Sept. 1570	Audiencia N.G.	Pedro Flores de Arellano
caballería	7 Sept. 1570	Visitador Orozco[a]	Gaspar de Tapia
2 caballerías	27 May 1579	Presidente Orozco[b]	Lic. Sánchez
2 caballerías	26 Apr. 1554	Audiencia N.G.	Pedro de Plasencia
caballería	17 Sept. 1570	Visitador Orozco	Andrés de Villanueva
caballería	7 Sept. 1570	Visitador Orozco	Gaspar de Mota
caballería	7 Sept. 1570	Visitador Orozco	Hernando Martel
caballería	7 Sept. 1570	Visitador Orozco	Miguel de Orosco
caballería	7 Sept. 1570	Visitador Orozco	Antonio de Aguallo
2 caballerías	1 Dec. 1552	Audiencia N.G.	Juan de Urbina
4 caballerías	24 Mar. 1552	Audiencia N.G.	Juan Francisco de Ojeda
caballería	16 Sept. 1570	Visitador Orozco	Antonio del Rincón
2 caballerías	1 Sept. 1584	Audiencia N.G.	Francisco de Zepeda
caballería	(Sept. 1570?)	Visitador Orozco	Pedro de Plasencia
molino	25 Sept. 1597	Presidente Vera[c]	Juan López Romero
"una saca de agua"	18 Sept. 1584	Audiencia N.G.	Francisco de Zepeda
2 caballerías	24 July 1570	Visitador Orozco	Francisco de Plasa
sitio mayor, with 1 caballería	24 Aug. 1593	Audiencia N.G.	Andrés de Rivera
0.5 sitio menor with 2 caballerías	29 Nov. 1607	Audiencia N.G.	Bartolomé Alonso

SOURCE:
AIPG-LG, no. 10, 1694.

NOTES:
[a]Lic. Juan Bautista de Orozco, oidor-visitador of the Audiencia of New Galicia, 1565-1571.
[b]Dr. Jerónimo de Orozco, oidor and president of the Audiencia of New Galicia, 1572-1592.
[c]Dr. Santiago de Vera, oidor and president of the Audiencia of New Galicia, 1593-1606.

de Huejotitán, which eventually came into the hands of the Villaseñor family, was entailed, and became one of the most valuable estates of the late-colonial period.[16] This estate, encompassing something over 35,000 acres of prime agricultural and grazing lands in the neighborhood of Jocotepec, on the western end of Lake Chapala, was constructed by Juan González de Apodaca in the late sixteenth and early seventeenth centuries.[17] González de Apodaca, a Spaniard from the Basque province of Álava, apparently made his fortune from public office, including an *escribanía* in Guadalajara and a stint as alcalde mayor of Ameca and Sayula. In addition to his holdings in the Jocotepec area, González de Apodaca was the progenitor of what came to be the largest hacienda in the Guadalajara region, Cuisillos. His son, Juan González de Apodaca Rubín, continued to add luster to the family name and increase its fortunes through a good marriage and the acquisition of the offices of *alguacil mayor* of the Audiencia of New Galicia and *alcalde mayor de corte*.

The succession of legal titles to the lands which came to make up the Hacienda de Huejotitán clearly reveal Juan González de Apodaca and his son consolidating their hold on a prime agricultural area over a quarter of a century. The primordial grant from which the hacienda later took shape was that of two sitios de ganado mayor, called Jocotepec and Pixihuilitla, made by Viceroy Antonio de Mendoza to Alonso de Ávalos in 1546.[18] Ávalos took possession of the grants in 1547, acknowledging that he had held the land without formal title for at least twenty years previously. In 1571, Ávalos purchased a sitio menor from Francisco López Nieto and added it to his own contiguous holdings. López Nieto, who was the son-in-law of Juan de Urbina, one of the conquistadores of New Galicia, had received the grant from Viceroy Martín Enríquez only the year before (1570). Juan González de Apodaca enters the picture sometime during the 1570s, when he purchased one sitio mayor (from the 1546 merced—the other remained under the control of Ávalos' widow) and one sitio menor (from the 1570 merced to López Nieto) from Alonso de Ávalos' heirs.

González de Apodaca began to obtain mercedes for himself in 1558 around the nucleus of the former Ávalos holdings. This was a big year for

16. The handsome *casa grande*, dating from around 1800, is still to be seen there.

17. The biographical data on González de Apodaca are taken from Amaya, *Los conquistadores*, pp. 71-72. The González de Apodacas and Porreses were related through *compadrazgo* and acted in concert in dominating the food supply of the city in the early 1600s; see Chevalier, *Land and Society*, p. 163.

18. Alonso de Ávalos was one of the five Ávalos brothers, cousins of Hernando Cortés, who came to the New World and were active in the conquest of western Mexico. Alonso came to New Spain in 1523 and eventually held an encomienda in the province of Chapala; see Icaza, *Diccionario autobiográfico*, vol. 2, p. 4, for his statement made sometime in the decade of the 1540s. See also Amaya, *Los conquistadores*, pp. 75-78.

him. First he received the grant from the Marqués de Villamanrique of a sitio de ganado menor and two caballerías bordering on the parcels he had purchased from the Ávalos heirs. In the same year, Francisco de Zamudio, a vecino of Guadalajara, obtained a merced from Viceroy Villamanrique for a sitio mayor and two caballerías in the Jocotepec Valley. It was not by accident that this grant lay next to that of González de Apodaca, for Zamudio ceded the merced to him the same year. Also in 1588, González de Apodaca purchased a sitio mayor originally granted to Pedro de Ledesma (the date of this merced is not recorded), and yet another from the Ávalos heirs (probably the remaining parcel from the 1546 grant). In the following year, 1589, González de Apodaca bought another sitio menor from López Nieto. In 1592, Viceroy Velasco (the younger) awarded González de Apodaca a merced of one sitio mayor in the midst of his other holdings near Jocotepec. Finally, in 1615 the younger González de Apodaca was granted title to a parcel of two sitios mayor with six caballerías, also contiguous with the other holdings.[19]

The year 1615, then, marks the maturity of Huejotitán in terms of its size. The figures for that year—7 sitios de ganado mayor, 3 menor, and 10 caballerías, or altogether some 37,209 acres—accord quite closely with those for 1679 and 1733: 6 sitios mayor, 5 menor, and 13 caballerías, a total of 36,828 acres.[20] Exactly why the González de Apodacas did not hold onto the estate, which they had built with such perspicacity and energy, much past the middle of the seventeenth century (it apparently eventually passed to Celedón González de Apodaca, and thence out of the family) is not clear. But the formation of the great Hacienda de Huejotitán is yet another example of the early and rapid consolidation of the large rural estates in the environs of Guadalajara.[21]

Not all the important haciendas of the later colonial period had come into being with such speed as Huejotitán, or even at the only slightly more leisurely pace of Atequiza. It is tempting to speculate that the outward-spreading, concentric-ring pattern which was noticeable in agricultural development in the eighteenth century was characteristic of land acquisition

19. AIPG, Tierras, leg. 71, exp. 36, no date, but probably 1760s or 1770s.
20. There is admittedly an inconsistency in the count of sitios de ganado mayor and menor between the titles as they existed at the beginning of the seventeenth century and as they added up in 1679 and 1733. Just what adjustments took place after 1615 is not clear; but it was certainly not uncommon, as we shall see below, for merced measurements to be rectified many years after the fact, especially in the case of sixteenth-century grants. But the essential point to be grasped is that the estate remained almost exactly the same size for 200 years.
21. Amaya, *Ameca*, p. 111. For biographical data on Diego de Porres, see Amaya, *Los conquistadores*, pp. 115-116, and Chevalier, *Land and Society*, p. 162. For the fortunes of the Porres Baranda entail during the eighteenth century, see Chapter 8 above. The entail also embraced a very large amount of land to the east of Guadalajara, not included in the above figures (AIPG, Tierras, leg. 62, exp. 17).

in the sixteenth and seventeenth centuries, but the available evidence does not as yet bear this out. Still, there are indications that where the quality of the land was less attractive, where indigenous population was sparser at contact, and where natural barriers made access to the city difficult, there was a less frantic scramble to monopolize land and legitimize titles. This is certainly reflected in the lesser importance of middle- and late-seventeenth-century *composiciones* in the agricultural zones nearer to Guadalajara, and also in the tardiness in consolidation of some large rural estates. One such was the Hacienda de Santa Lucía, in the district of San Cristóbal de la Barranca, which developed relatively late in the eighteenth century, under the proprietorship of Juan Alfonso Sánchez Leñero, a wealthy city merchant. In contrast to Atequiza or Huejotitán, Santa Lucía was not really formed until the late seventeenth century and was still acquiring its lands as late as 1750.[22]

Eighteenth-century haciendas were not static, of course; their boundaries did change to some extent, and there was a great deal of pushing and pulling over land, judicial and otherwise. But the estates that did expand their landholdings in any important measure lay outside the major areas of commercialized agriculture, for the most part. They may have been linked to the urban market, but they were in more marginal areas, and the lands which they struggled over and sometimes absorbed were generally of marginal quality as well. In the zones of oldest and most intensive agricultural occupation, such as the Toluquilla Valley, the very idea of untitled, unoccupied lands available for estate expansion was absurd to eighteenth-century observers. On the occasion in 1764 of a denunciation of possible *realengos* in the Toluquilla Valley by the owner of the Hacienda de Santa Cruz, Miguel del Portillo, all the landowners in the area stated that there were no unoccupied lands because all of the valley was fully "poblada y cultivada."[23] A similar denunciation of nearly 10 caballerías in the Tlajomulco area by Portillo's son in 1801 threw the entire district into consternation, even though the land in question was acknowledged by all to be suitable only for pasture: it was rocky, uneven, and without water or wood.[24]

Even in areas farther removed from Guadalajara, or where grain production was less favored, such as Tequila, Ahualulco, and Tepatitlán, the agricultural expansion set off by the city's development in the late eighteenth century gave value to previously marginal lands. In these areas, the territorial expansion of haciendas was not so much directly for the purpose of putting newly acquired land under the plow as it was the result of the kind of outward displacement described in Chapter 10. The same kind

---

22. AIPG, Tierras, leg. 58, exp. 16. This summary of the estate's titles is undated, but probably was made up in the 1780s.

23. AIPG, Tierras, leg. 20, exp. 6, 1764.   24. AIPG, Tierras, leg. 47, exp. 3, 1801.

of absorption or redefinition of exploitation rights to marginal lands was characteristic of the better-situated properties in the Toluquilla and Ameca valleys and in the lake districts, but it was necessarily on a smaller scale. In Tepatitlán, for example,[25] in Tequila,[26] and in Ahualulco,[27] estate expansion in the late eighteenth century typically involved lands generally acknowledged to be useless for agricultural purposes. Furthermore, even in these areas the scale of late-eighteenth-century expansion was small, and in many cases the acquisition of title to lands in the 1780s, 1790s, and early 1800s was merely a matter of legitimizing claims made in earlier decades but never legally consummated.

Aside from the mechanisms of judicial denunciation and simple de-facto appropriation, haciendas expanded through the purchase of lands already titled. Such purchases were very common all during the colonial period, though somewhat less frequent in the late eighteenth century, judging from notarial records. This process may be viewed as a redistribution of already-titled lands as opposed to an aggressive expansion of the rural estate onto lands previously unclaimed. As with denunciations and composiciones, the scale of these transactions was directly related to the intensiveness of agricultural activity in a given area. Naturally, where agriculture was most developed on a commercial basis there would be less land available for sale, landowners would be more reluctant to part with valuable properties, and prices would be higher. Still, a more or less continual process of rationalization of landholdings went on, with parcels being bought and sold on the basis of their economic usefulness for a given estate. One prominent instance of such activity has already been mentioned above: the Hacienda de Atequiza in the early eighteenth century. Such examples could be multiplied indefinitely. Similar dealings rounded out the lands of the Hacienda de Toluquilla (later called El Cuatro), both under its Jesuit masters and during the ownership of the Marqués de Pánuco, and also expanded the holdings of José Prudencio de Cuervo's Hacienda de San Martín in Tequila,[28] among many others.

The essential stability of hacienda holdings after 1700 meant not only that existing haciendas maintained their boundaries, but also that very few new properties were created. To be sure, the devices of judicial denunciation and purchase could be used by ambitious and industrious interlopers to create new estates out of whole cloth, but this happened in very few instances—and the haciendas thus created were usually either small or short-

25. AIPG, Tierras, leg. 25, exp. 8, 1789.   26. AIPG, Tierras, leg. 49, exp. 6, 1803.
27. In the case of the aggressive Manuel del Río—AIPG, leg. 46, exp. 10, 1791, and leg. 49, exp. 36, 1792.
28. AIPG, prot. Castillo, 6:182-184, late 1690s; Tierras, leg. 18, exp. 3, 1808, and leg. 49, exp. 6, 1803.

lived or simply existed as fantasies on paper. Judicial denunciation was never effectively used to constitute an hacienda, though there were instances of such attempts. These generally assumed the form of legal fishing expeditions made by lesser landowners who might make a blanket denunciation of any potentially untitled land in a given area, thus forcing measurements and confirmation of titles in the hope that some parcels might break loose and fall to them. An example of this was the creation of the so-called Hacienda de San Cayetano in the 1770s, said to consist of "todo el hueco que hay" among the haciendas of Navajas, Cuisillos, La Calera, La Sauceda, Estipac, Mazatepec, the sitios of San Pablo and Los Sauces, and the pueblo of Ahuisculco, but which apparently never existed except on paper.[29]

The agglomeration of a number of smaller parcels of land into a larger property by purchase was effective in creating some new estates after 1700, but the frequency of this practice was much reduced in the eighteenth century, and so was the scale of acquisitions. This was the origin of the small but important grain-producing Hacienda de Rosario on the outskirts of Guadalajara, created by Capitán Francisco Fernández de Ubiarco in the early years of the eighteenth century. The small Labor de los Gachos (sometimes referred to as an hacienda) near Poncitlán, consisting of no more than 6.3 caballerías of arable land, was put together by Marcos Núñes Lambaren in the decade after 1710 from two small purchases and an even smaller merced. Similarly, the small estate of San Diego Guacome, referred to at the death of its owner in 1724 as an "hacienda de labor de maíz," had been made up of two purchases of land from the related Ahumada and Henríquez Topete families.[30] All of these properties, despite their late birth and relatively miniscule size, survived into the late-colonial period, but the number of instances of such creations probably did not exceed a half-dozen or so in the entire Guadalajara area.

Hacienda Fragmentation

As with social and economic mobility among individuals and families, the movement of land was not all in one direction, into the rural estate. Large haciendas sustained a certain amount of loss in their landholdings during

29. AIPG, prot. de Silva, 15:73-75v, 1771; Tierras, leg. 5, exp. 14.

30. AIPG, Tierras, leg. 46, exp. 13, 1713; prot. Mena mayor, 10:976-979v, 1720; prot. Morelos, 6:269-276v, 1724. E.g., also: AIPG-LG, 37:56-59v, 1719; prot. Maraver, 7:84-85, 1742, and 1: no page nos., 1754; prot. Berroa, 26:219v, 1782; prot. Mena menor, 17: no page nos., 1756; Tierras, leg. 41, exp. 10, 1802; and prot. Ballesteros, 5:210v-211v and 211v-212; 7: passim; 11:8v-11v and 60v-61v, 1789; 15:145v-146v, 1791; 16:316-317, 1792; and 22:382-385, 1794.

the late-colonial period, some through suits, some through sale for economic reasons (consolidation or debt), and some through inheritance. But in this regard, as with the expansion of already-existing estates and the creation of new ones, the prevailing trend was toward stability. In no known case during the eighteenth and early nineteenth centuries was an important rural estate divided to the point that it lost its identity as a production unit.[31] This appears not to have been due to any particular reverence for the traditional integrity of any given estate on the part of its owners, even though the seigneurial ideal did depend on continuing control of large, stable tracts of land, and entails were established partly to insure such control. Rather, the stability of rural estates was a question of economics, and the tendency was for owners to change rather than for haciendas to be dismembered. Where economic necessity such as debt might have been met through the sale of hacienda lands, either credit was available, enabling the hacendado to avoid sale of his most important asset, or the debts were already so large that the sale of some land would not have helped ease the situation in any case.

As to inheritance, the owners of large properties generally had sufficient resources that physical division of an estate among the heirs was unnecessary; other types of arrangements were made, often including the division of livestock, the settlement upon co-heirs of income from other properties, or liens upon the income of the estate. The one instance of a major hacienda which was actually parceled out among co-heirs (and possibly this occurred only on paper) was the Hacienda de Potrerillos, just east of the Hacienda de Huejotitán in the district of Jocotepec, which eventually passed to the heirs of Lorenzo Javier de Villaseñor. This property, measuring 2.5 sitios de ganado mayor (about 10,000 acres), was divided into five parts for his five children when their mother, María Manuela de la Cueva Villeseñor, entered a Mexico City convent. One of the heirs, José de la Cueva Villaseñor, eventually purchased his siblings' shares back from them and sold the entire estate in one piece to a priest.[32] Aside from this somewhat equivocal case, no important estates were broken up by inheritance.

31. This is admittedly a rather tricky criterion. The difficulty arises particularly in regard to groups of large properties gathered together by one owner, those estates we have called "compound haciendas," discussed below. Very often these were administered and managed as one property—as, for example, with the haciendas of La Concepción and San Nicolás in the Toluquilla Valley while they were owned by Antonio Colazo Feijoo in the late eighteenth century, or with the Toluquilla Valley properties of the first Marqués de Pánuco. In such instances, haciendas might lose their economic identity but retain their titular and traditional identity; but this happened relatively infrequently. For purposes of the present discussion, we may say that the identity of a production unit depended upon the retention of its name and the majority of its original lands, and its continued economic viability.

32. AIPG, prot. Mena mayor, 4:753v-756v, 1714.

Rancheros, however, generally lacked other resources to satisfy heirs and therefore subdivided their property among their children. This was done with such frequency that it would be pointless to cite examples; but suffice it to say that the multitudes of *parcioneros* who lived in country districts, and the large numbers of minifundia so characteristic of certain areas, had their origins in this process.

Those few rural estates which did diminish significantly in size during the late-colonial period most often did so through sale of parts of their titled lands. It is often difficult to tell the reasons for such sales, but they appear to have fallen basically into two categories: those for purposes of rationalizing estate management, and those for debt, which also included the raising of short-term capital. In the first category, it is interesting to note that most of the recorded instances of sales to rationalize estate management date from the period before 1750. This type of transaction involved lands which were either annexed to an estate in an odd manner, and therefore separate from it, or lands simply expendable in the land-plentiful conditions of the early eighteenth century. A very graphic example of this was the sale in 1758 of the sitio de ganado mayor Querémbaro by Gabriel Sánchez Leñero, owner of the Hacienda de Santa Lucía. He had purchased the land just eight years earlier, perhaps for speculative reasons, though its resale was certainly not because of financial difficulties. The 1758 sale for 300 pesos (indicating the scant agricultural potential of the parcel) had carried the proviso that the purchaser should give the owners of Santa Lucía first option to buy back the land if it should be sold in future. This, apparently, is what happened, since the titled lands of the property, when it was owned by Juan Alfonso Sánchez Leñero in the 1780s, included Querémbaro. By this time Santa Lucía had become an important grain-producing estate and was probably in need of additional lands for livestock.[33] Unfortunately for most hacendados, land alienated in an earlier period was very seldom available for repurchase later on.

The second category of sales encompasses those made for debts of various kinds, or to raise capital unavailable elsewhere on favorable terms. A clear example of land sales caused by debt is the Hacienda del Salitre in Cocula. Ana Fernández Partida, the widow of Tomás de Oviedo y Baeza, had inherited the hacienda from Brother Juan Pérez Maldonado in the early eighteenth century, but because of her husband's debts and other problems (*atrasos*), the property was by the early 1730s burdened with the yearly sum of 600 pesos in interest payments and she had personal debts of her own amounting to more than 2,000 pesos. To cut her way through a tangle

33. AIPG, prot. Leyva Carrillo, 1:437v-438v, 1758; Tierras, leg. 58, exp. 16. E.g., also: AIPG, prot. Mena mayor, 3: no page nos., 1713; and prot. Maraver, 7:565-567, 1742, and 11: no page nos., 1746.

of financial worries and insistent creditors, Ana agreed to sell the sitio mayor and attached lands known as the Labor de San Javier to Antonio de Medina for 5,000 pesos. With the 3,000 pesos cash she received in the transaction (2,000 pesos were assigned to redeem part of a censo on the property belonging to the convent of Santa María de Gracia), she hoped to be able to work profitably the remaining three sitios mayor of Salitre.[34] Similar circumstances seem to have been responsible for the sale of a large part (16,555 pesos' worth—the acreage is unknown) of the important Hacienda de Miraflores, located in the Colimilla-Matatlán area, by its owner, the widow of the famous Coronel Juan Flores de San Pedro, in 1750.[35]

The most important thing to note in all the cases we have examined is that even though the owners of rural estates may have parted with some of the lands of their haciendas, in no single instance did an estate lose its identity as a production unit. Even the limited dismemberments that we have looked at here—if such they may be called—were relatively rare, and they were all linked to specific circumstances in the histories of individuals or families, not to generalized trends in the late-colonial economy. If the divestiture of hacienda land did occasionally occur, it did not compromise the essential stability of the great rural estate as the chief landholding entity in the late-colonial countryside.

Compound Haciendas

Finally, there were several groups of properties formed and rounded out during the sixteenth and seventeenth centuries into huge compound estates, each one embracing a number of discrete, identifiable haciendas which were in many cases themselves small principalities. These holdings obeyed the same laws of formation as smaller ones: they were built up through the patient agglomeration of numerous single parcels, most of them early colonial mercedes. The difference was primarily in the scale of the agglomeration process, as well as the fact that while held by one owner or family these huge properties became differentiated into estates grouped together by geography and common ownership. Almost all of these huge holdings broke up before 1700, but two of them were reconstituted at least partially after that, even though they never reached the size of the original properties. Although subject to the same economic pressures as other holdings,

34. AIPG, prot. Maraver, 1: no page nos., 1734, and 11: no page nos., 1746. The very high price of the Labor de San Javier compared to land sold at about the same time in the San Cristóbal area, for example, indicates that land in the Ameca Valley was much more valuable because agriculture was more developed there.

35. AIPG, prot. Ballesteros, 5:187-188v, 1786; prot. Mena mayor, 15:701v-704, 1755.

these compound haciendas were so few in number (perhaps four, if one stretches the definition to its limits) that their histories are sui generis and each deserves at least a brief mention on its own.

The clearest and best-documented example of a compound hacienda is that of the Ameca Valley holdings of the Ahumada family, centering on the Hacienda del Cabezón.[36] The founder of the family and the builder of the estate was Luis de Ahumada, a man of somewhat obscure origins (probably born locally) who began buying up parcels of land in the Ameca Valley in about the 1570s. He received a half-dozen or so grants on his own and had still others obtained for him by intermediaries, but most of his eventually huge holdings came to him by purchases from landowners who had fallen upon hard times or left the area because of the decline of the local Indian population. Ahumada married the daughter of a royal official and died shortly before 1620 at a fairly advanced age. His daughter married Capitán Pedro Enríquez Topete, corregidor of Tlajomulco; and her two sons, Ahumada's grandsons, continued the labor of building up the family's holdings in the valley, obtaining various grants of land in the period 1650-1675. It is interesting to note that the grants made after 1600 or so were increasingly exact in their boundary delineations, because judicial conflicts had already arisen over the boundaries of older grants. The last mercedes, made in the 1670s, were probably brought about through the application both of money and of pressure upon the royal authorities by influential friends of the Ahumadas, with the object of keeping other landowners out of the valley.

In the meantime, the original Ahumada family had ramified through prolific alliances with outsiders, notably the Rico, Villaseñor, Arriola, and Fernández Partida families. This led to an increasing subdivision of the original unitary holdings built up by Luis de Ahumada and his grandsons, which already by the middle of the seventeenth century had been known as the various haciendas of El Cabezón, La Vega, Buenavista, La Calera, Jayamitla, etc. Finally, in 1697, after 125 years of almost uninterrupted territorial expansion, the Ameca Valley holdings were divided by the numerous heirs of Luis de Ahumada in an extremely complicated judicial settlement suggested by an influential family friend, Br. Juan Pérez Maldonado. At the time of the settlement, the holdings of all the Ahumada heirs together, which had been exploited "pro-indiviso" up to that time,

36. The following discussion of the Ameca Valley is based largely upon the magnificent and painstaking reconstruction of Jesús Amaya in *Ameca, protofundación mexicana*, which is essentially a work on local history but hints at a broader vision of colonial social and economic history as well; and also upon notarial records of the division of the Ahumada lands in 1697, found in AIPG, prot. Morelos, 1:12-28v, 1697, and other scattered documents. See also the useful short summary in Chevalier, *Land and Society*, pp. 141-142.

amounted to 27 sitios de ganado mayor, 10 sitios menor, and 43 caballerías (or nearly 141,000 acres), representing 36 of the 69 mercedes made for lands in the Ameca area.[37] These lands were divided by the compromise agreement into eight parcels of various sizes, each to a major heir or group of heirs, and in the ensuing further subdivisions the original latifundium was hopelessly fragmented, never again to belong to one individual or family.

There were two attempts, however, to reconstruct the Ahumada hegemony after the division of 1697. The first of these was almost immediate, by Juan Pérez Maldonado, the kindly priest who had engineered the compromise. Beginning as a renter of the Hacienda de la Vega (1694), Pérez Maldonado purchased in rapid succession some of the largest fragments of the Ahumada domains: El Cabezón in 1700, La Huerta (with annexed sitios) in 1702, La Vega in 1703. He also at one time owned the important haciendas of El Salitre and Las Navajas, which he eventually sold. The prices of the estates were all low (he paid 4,000 pesos to the great-grandson of Luis de Ahumada for the Hacienda del Cabezón), and Pérez Maldonado was able to pay off all the extant censos by 1710. But Pérez Maldonado died in 1712, and his empire—which had never embraced all the Ahumada lands, in any case—dissipated quickly.

A longer-lived and altogether more successful attempt at a reconstruction of the Ahumada compound hacienda was that of Manuel Calixto Cañedo in the latter part of the eighteenth century.[38] Cañedo, a wealthy miner who had made his fortune in the Real de Pánuco in Rosario in partnership with Francisco Javier de Vizcarra (the first Marqués de Pánuco), was able to buy up much of the Ameca Valley, centering on the great Hacienda del Cabezón. In 1790 he founded an entail which embraced El Cabezón, La Vega, Buenavista, La Calera, and other smaller parcels. But neither Pérez Maldonado nor Cañedo and his heirs approached the virtual hegemony which Luis de Ahumada and his grandsons had exercised over the lands of the Ameca Valley.

A far more shadowy case—but one which falls into the same category, albeit on a smaller scale than the Ameca Valley—was the Toluquilla Valley, south of Guadalajara. The major haciendas of this area, which served as one of the great breadbaskets of the city, were Toluquilla (belonging to the Jesuits for most of the colonial period), Santa Cruz, La Concepción,

---

37. Not all of the mercedes whose history is traced by Amaya pertained to the Ameca Valley proper. Some of them fell more into the Cocula area, and some as far east as Tala. Of the grants not accounted for in the Ahumada holdings, a few fell to the Porres holdings around Mazatepec and Santa Ana Acatlán, later to be entailed, and others were eventually taken up by the Hacienda de Cuisillos.

38. For a detailed discussion of Cañedo's career, see Chapter 8 above.

San Nicolás Zapotepec, and San José Zapotepec. Of these, all except for Toluquilla (and even possibly parts of it) had originally been included in one property belonging to one individual. According to testimony in a land suit from the mid-eighteenth century, the lands of these estates (amounting to perhaps 10 sitios de ganado mayor with attached caballerías) had all been granted in one merced or series of mercedes shortly after the Conquest. Circumstantial evidence suggests that the original grantee may have been Nuño de Guzmán. In any case, by the end of the seventeenth century the four distinct properties had long had separate identities. Several subsequent owners acquired more than one major estate in the valley (Antonio Colazo Feijoo; his heirs, the Echauris, by inheritance; and the first Marqués de Pánuco), but none ever succeeded in establishing a clear dominance over this rich agricultural area, perhaps because no single local fortune ever had the resources to make the necessary investment.[39]

Two other properties should be called compound haciendas, not so much because they embraced a group of estates under the aegis of one individual family, but because of the large scale upon which they were conceived and continued to exist: the two entails of Mazatepec and Cuisillos. In both cases, the estates were built up by one man (Diego de Porres and Juan González de Apodaca, respectively) and rounded out to some degree by his heirs. Both estates lasted undiminished in size throughout the colonial period. Neither estate ever suffered the dismemberment of the Ahumada or Toluquilla Valley properties, nor did they need to be reconstructed by late-eighteenth-century entrepreneurs. It is certainly not by coincidence that both of them were entailed (Mazatepec from 1619, Cuisillos from the early eighteenth century). Both estates seem to have been managed as single, unitary enterprises—though Santa Ana Acatlán, part of the Mazatepec entail, became increasingly differentiated as the eighteenth century progressed.

Despite the chronic instability in landownership, then, and the changes wrought in the agricultural economy by the development of the urban market during the eighteenth century, the greal rural estate *as a landholding entity* was basically stable after 1700. Yet there is undeniable evidence of the quickening tempo and increasing intensity of conflicts over land in the countryside, not only between Spaniards and indigenous communities, but also among and within all landholding groups. In the preceding chapters we have described the way in which Spanish landowners, in particular the important hacendados, gained control of and used the major agricultural production factors—capital, labor, and land—in response to a grow-

39. AIPG, Tierras, leg. 20, exp. 6, 1764, and leg. 77, exp. 14, 1764.

ing local market for foodstuffs and primary industrial products. We have also discussed (again, mainly in terms of the development of haciendas) the effects of these processes in the countryside and the countervailing pressures exerted by population growth and the needs of the traditional rural economy. What we have described, basically, are the two intersecting vectors of capitalist and peasant agriculture. In the following chapter we shall look more closely at the competition for land resources which grew out of these changes.

CHAPTER 14

The Clash

Land Suits as Historical Documentation

The major arena of conflict in the competition over land was the colonial court system, primarily the Audiencia of New Galicia. Here the contending parties in the struggle over an increasingly valuable and inelastic resource trotted out their claims to immemorial possession of land, their ancient grants and titles, their thousands upon thousands of pages of supporting documentation, and their witnesses. The judicial authorities, covered by the vast umbrella of Spanish legalism, on the whole did a fairly creditable job of administering justice. Even if no claim can be made for their impartiality, oidores and other royal officials were not merely the passive creatures of creole landlords. Given the constraints of class and culture and the pressures of local interest groups and royal policy, the striking thing about the performance of late-colonial judges is not of how much land they despoiled Indians and other peasants, but how often they confirmed the rights of the powerless, and particularly of communal landholding villages.

Certainly land did change hands during the eighteenth century, but the flow was not all in the direction of the great rural estate; and in any case, the quantity of land which changed ownership did not compromise the essential stability in landholding which obtained after 1700. More important than changes in the ownership of land were changes in the way land was used during the eighteenth century. These changes inevitably created conflicts over the control of land use, and such conflicts very often emerged as formal litigation.

The immense amount of documentation produced by colonial land suits is of uneven quality and importance for the historian investigating rural history.[1] Much of it consists of sterile legal formulas and endless wrangling over detail. Very often the extant documentation is only a fragment or a truncated record with little or no useful information. Nonetheless, colonial litigation over land is a vital source for study of the rural economic structure. The documents allow us to look at the specific pressures upon land resources created by the agricultural and demographic growth of the late-colonial period in the Guadalajara region. Amid the clouds of legal punctiliousness, we may occasionally glimpse very concrete data on local economic conditions, even down to ecological changes taking place (deforestation, for example), as well as the social cleavages and attitudes which were both cause and effect of specific conflicts over access to land.

It is important to note at the outset, however, some of the limitations of using land suits in trying to reconstruct late-colonial rural society and its economy; and we must be clear on what such documentation does not say, as well as upon what it does say. In the first place, much of the testimony in colonial records of land suits is boring, confusing, and trivial. Sometimes this is the result of the legal obfuscation and tendentiousness of the claimants and their lawyers, and sometimes of the inherently contradictory nature of the material, its fragmentariness, and the length of time it took to bring some suits to a conclusion. It is the province of the historian using these records, of course, to reconcile, simplify, and condense the endlessly contradictory evidence into a sensible fact which can be fitted into a historical trend of some sort. But very often it is the contradiction itself which is important, since it represents basically opposing views on the function of land in the rural economy, and on who had the prescriptive right to its use. Thus, eliminating the confusion and sheer triviality may divest the raw evidence of its significance. The reader may care very little whether a particular boundary marker should have been placed a few hundred paces in one direction or another, for example—but eighteenth-century Indians and

---

1. Most of the colonial documentation on land suits in New Galicia is located in the Archivo de Instrumentos Públicos de Guadalajara (AIPG) and is designated as the Ramo de Tierras y Aguas (Tierras; some 400 volumes); there are also scattered expedientes in other historical archives in Guadalajara. The Genealogical Project of the Church of Jesus Christ of the Latter-Day Saints (Mormons), headquartered in Salt Lake City, Utah, has filmed the Guadalajara Ramo de Tierras in its entirety, and I acknowledge with profound thanks the opportunity I had to use some hundreds of rolls of this microfilm during the course of my research.

hacendados cared very much, and pitched battles were sometimes fought over such apparently trivial questions.

Second, the reliability of the evidence contained in land suits is frequently suspect and on occasion nonexistent. These civil suits were most often conducted on an adversary basis, with all the possibilities for confrontation inherent in such a process. Individuals seldom made untrue statements in their testaments or contracts for the sale of land or goods (although they could), but they might very well do so when it came to defending their personal interests in litigation. Aside from a general and quite human tendency to bend the truth in such circumstances, there were particular social and historical conditions which impelled contending parties in land suits to fight stubbornly to uphold their rights, and occasionally to vilify their opponents.

Finally, colonial suits over land do not, in most cases, give certain kinds of information which we might think they would cover automatically. It is true that there is a great wealth of social and economic detail on how people in rural districts lived, where they lived, who held power locally, etc.—though we must often read between the lines to get at it. And of course there is a tremendous amount of material on physical geography— on the location and size of land parcels—including a great many maps of varying quality. The records of suits are replete with the minutiae of ownership histories—sales, donations, foreclosures, testaments, and every manner of property transfer. But lamentably, for our purposes, what most often goes unsaid is the use to which people put land, especially the land they sought to appropriate or confirm to themselves judicially. This was not, strictly speaking, relevant, since what was at issue in litigation was not the use to which land was put but its formal ownership.

Underneath the legal wrangling, however, the function of land was very much the issue. Except in the case of *monte*—forested or scrub-covered land, generally too wild or steep to be arable—which was specifically used for grazing animals or collecting wood, the agricultural use of land is not often described. Thus, for example, if we wish to discover a link between disputes over marginal (non-arable) lands and the agricultural and demographic expansion of the Guadalajara region in the late-colonial period, we must make a series of assumptions or inferences for which direct proof is not plentiful, but for which there is strong presumptive evidence. It is necessary to assume that land was to some degree an inelastic factor in production; that the competing needs of commercial and peasant agriculture pressed upon the existing supply; that less intensive activities, such as livestock-raising, were displaced outward, toward more marginal areas, by more intensive activities such as grain production; and that these previously marginal areas, which were the ones most often contended over in litigation, had for these reasons acquired a new value for all property-holders. It is only by making these inferences, in fact, that the general pattern of late-colonial land suits makes any sense at all.

Non-Economic Causes of Land Conflicts

The scheme outlined briefly above, and in considerably more detail in Chapters 10, 11, 12, and 13, deals with what may be called the economic forces behind eighteenth-century conflicts over land in the Guadalajara region. Before we look at land conflicts from the point of view of economic forces, however, we should say something about two other causes for conflicts over land, what we may call the social and the technical. In social terms, land conflicts, especially those between Indian communities and non-Indian landowners, may be seen to some degree as a sublimation of ethnic and class tensions.[2] From such a perspective, litigation appears to have served as a socially approved mode to express and channel hostility from both directions—though it did not, of course, preclude other, more antisocial forms of expression. The initiation of land suits by indigenous communities also functioned in some measure to preserve the identity of the pueblo, through its aggressive stance in defense of its right to land.

Evidence of the chronic social tensions in the countryside between Indians and non-Indians is not difficult to find. Spaniards, of course, expressed their opinions often and vehemently in written documents, commonly characterizing Indians as stupid, irresponsible, thieving, and lazy. This attitude was revealed not only among private citizens, but also at the highest levels of government. For example, in response to a viceregal project of the early 1790s to stimulate the textile industry by distributing seed and free instruction to Indians for the cultivation of hemp and flax, the *protector de indios* of the Audiencia of New Galicia expressed severe doubts about the efficacy of the plan because of the "natural rusticity" of the Indians. He added that their very nature "will always make very difficult the establishment among them of any activity requiring sweat and labor, of which they innately have such horror and resistance. . . ."[3] Recorded expressions of specifically anti-Spanish or anti-white sentiments on the part of Indians are rather less common because they had on the whole

2. The interrelationship between ethnicity and class status in Latin America as a whole, and in Indo-America in particular, is a vast and fascinating question which has been examined by both historians and anthropologists. See, among others, the work of Marvin Harris, *Patterns of Race in the Americas*; the interesting assortment of essays in Magnus Mörner, ed., *Race and Class in Latin America* (1970); and Moisés González Navarro, *Raza y tierra: la guerra de castas y el henequén* (1970).

3. AHMG, caja 13, 1791.

less access to written forms, but they do occur. Such expressions were often couched in terms of the powerlessness of Indians in the face of Spanish wealth and authority, but on occasion they took on a more virulent and explicit form. In 1742, for example, the Indians of the pueblo of Tizapán el Bajo were told by the local *teniente*, and apparently found no difficulty in accepting, that "one Indian was worth more than ten Spaniards"; buttressed by this reassurance, they invaded the lands of a local hacienda.[4]

One acceptable avenue for expressing this kind of hostility without rending the social fabric of which they had become a part was for Indians to engage in litigation. Not only the number of actual land suits, but also the number of powers of attorney issued by Indian communities to Spanish lawyers, mushroomed in the late-colonial period, particularly after 1760 or so.[5] One small rancher, a litigant against the Indians of Tlajomulco in 1805, complained:

That the spirit of the Indians of Tlajomulco is inclined and disposed to litigation requires no more proof than this: only to look at the voluminous actions over lands pending before the Audiencia, brought by them against the powerful inhabitants of the jurisdiction, including the Mayorazgo [Porres Baranda], the Echauris, and the Portillos; and if they can maintain litigation against them, with me, a poor man, they will consume my small property. . . .[6]

From the structural perspective of this man, the Indians were almost awesome in their persistence; but from above, they were more often viewed at best as a nuisance and at worst as pernicious and destructive. Thus, in a suit of 1807 involving the pueblo of Tonalá, the *asesor* in the case noted

. . . the ease with which the Indians in their simplicity are seduced or fooled by the rude and thoughtless traditions of their ancestors, mistaking the principles, confounding their own rights, and without understanding even each other; after the passage of time and with the excuse of their legal minority and exemptions, they become distracted and destroy themselves, causing equal or greater harm, according to the circumstances, to other propertyowners who have the misfortune to be their neighbors.[7]

We certainly need not take the asesor's opinion at face value, nor condemn Indian communities for asserting their rights, to see the confusion and expense that such endless litigation might cause.

The process of litigation itself, however, was not entirely capable of sublimating the inter-ethnic tensions and hostility which were a part of the relations between Indians and non-Indians. Physical violence was so frequent in disputes over land that it was regarded as a commonplace in the

---

4. AIPG, Tierras, leg. 58, exp. 18.   5. E.g., AIPG, prot. Berroa, various years.
6. AIPG, Tierras, leg. 27, exp. 15.   7. AIPG, Tierras, leg. 5, exp. 9.

late-colonial countryside.[8] It was characteristic not only of Indian-Spanish conflicts, but also of conflicts between Spanish landowners and between Indian communities. On the face of it, such physical aggression often looks like a simple extrajudicial defense of property interests where remonstrance and other means had failed. This violence most often took the form of forcible eviction of Indians and others from hacienda lands by estate retainers, or of forcible resistance or invasions by indigenous communities.[9] But in some cases the extreme violence and heated verbal abuse accompanying land conflicts suggest an almost ritualized expression of hostility, particularly between Indians and non-Indians.

To cite but one example, in 1818 the Indians of the Pueblo de San José de Tateposco in the jurisdiction of Tonalá brought a criminal action against the owner of the Hacienda del Cuatro, Manuel García Quevedo, for the "vexations, mistreatments, wounds, and fires" the hacendado and his retainers had committed against the village on the nights of November 30 and December 2, 1818. Apparently in a conflict over a piece of land, García had ordered his men to take a number of the villagers prisoner and lock them up in one of the hacienda's granaries (*trojes*). In the following two days, García himself and a "vast number of retainers called out and accompanying him for this purpose" burned the houses of the Indians and stole the *santos* out of their church.[10] This suggests that García meant to deny the very existence of the pueblo itself, to stamp it out by physically annihilating it and depriving it of the most important symbol of its communal identity, its holy images.

Such aggression did not run all one way, of course, though Indians were as a rule less aggressive and less organized than landowners. In 1750 the corregidor of Cajititlán, in providing for measurement of the Hacienda de San Lucas, specifically warned the Indians of the nearby pueblo of San Lucas not to provoke or abuse the owner during the surveying proceedings.[11] Much more violent than the villagers of San Lucas were those of Nestipac, in the jurisdiction of Zapópan. They were involved in a protracted suit in the early years of the nineteenth century with the Hacienda de Santa Lucía, belonging to the Sánchez Leñero family—not over the ownership of land, but simply the right to collect wood on the hacienda's non-arable lands. The suit led to such bitter feelings on the part of the Indians that on a number of occasions they attacked hacienda retainers on the roads in the vicinity, nearly killing them and shouting verbal abuses at them.[12]

8. E.g., the statement of the *comisario* in the Cuisillos-Buenavista suit—AIPG, Tierras, leg. 25, exps. 16-18, 1760.
9. E.g., Hacienda de San Nicolás (Sayula)—BPE-AJA, 102:7:1104, 1787.
10. BPE-AJA, 265:3:3615, 1818.   11. AIPG, Tierras, leg. 12, exp. 2, 1750-1772.
12. BPE-AJA, 256:7:3443, 1810.

Physical violence in conflicts over land was also frequent within ethnic groups. These intra-group hostilities often functioned to further concrete economic interests, of course, but their social implications are more interesting. Within the hacendado group, for example, one may speculate that violence in conflicts over land between the retainers of one estate and those of another were manifestations of intra-elite family rivalries. In the famous and protracted suit between the Hacienda de Cuisillos, in New Galicia, and the Hacienda de Buenavista, across a tiny river in New Spain, verbal hostility between the contending parties ran very high. An opponent of Don Domingo de Trespalacios y Escandón, an oidor of the Audiencia of Mexico and owner of Cuisillos, reported on one occasion: ". . . and he clearly said to me that while he lived he wouldn't even say good morning to me."[13] In the same conflict, the administrator of Cuisillos, clearly echoing his master's sentiments, said to one of his own retainers, in reference to the owners of Buenavista, ". . . that until he destroyed the Lomanas, and left them and their families perishing, he wouldn't rest content."[14] Manuel Capetillo, the owner of the Hacienda de Buenavista near Chapala, was accused by the Basauri family, in a suit with them over the boundaries of their Hacienda de Atequiza, of trying to bring the family low: "under cover of the interests of the royal treasury, some men try to ruin entire families."[15]

Nor was intra-group conflict limited by any means to elite landowning families. The *campanilismo* (localism) and lack of solidarity so characteristic among peasant villages was manifested in the multitude of suits and conflicts over land resources between Indian pueblos, often accompanied by the throwing of stones and epithets, by forcible evictions, and by physical beatings. In a land conflict of 1788, for example, the alcalde and some Indians of the pueblo of San José de Analco arrested some inhabitants of the neighboring pueblo of San Andrés at work in their fields, bound them, and conducted them to the jail in San José.[16] In such cases as this, the identity and immediate interests of the individual village community were clearly seen to be the paramount concern; and indeed, even where groups of villages contended with non-Indian landholders over lands or common rights, there were signs of intra-group tensions among the Indian villages.

In this connection, it is interesting to speculate on the internal structure of village politics vis-a-vis the initiation of land suits, either against other villages or against powerful non-Indian neighbors. If, as we have suggested above, land suits and other more aggressive forms of behavior served to preserve the identity of the Indian communal village by defining it in relation to hostile outsiders, it is equally true that villages were not monolithic

13. AIPG, Tierras, leg. 25, exps. 16-18, 1760.
14. AIPG, Tierras, leg. 33, exp. 3, 1765.
15. AIPG, Tierras, leg. 25, exp. 19, 1805-1816.   16. AIPG, Tierras, leg. 30, exp. 8.

internally. Social differentiation and opportunism within indigenous communities were facts of life, especially in the late-colonial period. Since land suits were generally brought by village officials in the name of the community as a whole and ostensibly using communal resources to defend communal interests, there exists the distinct possibility that some officials (alcaldes, caciques, and *principales*) brought such suits to consolidate their own hold on political power within the community. The village's hold over its sons and daughters, its claims upon their participation and allegiance, were increasingly at issue in the late-colonial period, and an aggressive assertion of communal identity would have served to reinforce the slackening bonds of communal life and thus bolster the position of village power-holders.

The second non-economic cause of conflict and litigation over land was technical—the difficulties of accurately surveying and subsequently identifying land boundaries. Contemporaries were well aware that methods of surveying were imperfect, and often admitted so.[17] This problem, certainly, was often used as a pretext for calling into question old mercedes and land titles in general, and arguments over the starting points of measurements raged on and on in litigation over land. In a suit between the pueblo of Tonalá and the Marqués de Pánuco in 1808, for example, one of the contending parties said of an earlier survey of the land in question:

The surveyor has done even better, for with taking the center-points for boundaries, overturning the legitimate locations, he has had in mind, as well as on paper, sufficient cloth from which to cut, and could have had more if he had established the boundary of the hacienda in its very house, or in the church of Santa Anita, or in Guadalajara.[18]

There is no doubt that much willful falsification took place in land surveying, or at least in the subsequent interpretation of it, but there were also real problems inherent in this highly imperfect art.

The three most common problems in land surveying and identification of boundary markers were inconsistencies in the standard form of land parcels, the roughness of the terrain, and changes in the geography which made subsequent identification difficult or impossible. In the first instance, it was not the size of standard land units (the sitios de ganado mayor and menor, the caballería, and the suerte were the major ones in use) which caused argument, but their shape and orientation.[19] For example, the practice in New Galicia very early on was to lay out sitios in a circular

17. E.g., AIPG, Tierras, leg. 20, exp. 6, 1764.

18. AIPG, Tierras, leg. 18, exp. 3, 1808.

19. For the size of these units and a number of lesser ones also in use, see Carrera Stampa, "The Evolution of Weights and Measures."

rather than a square shape, while the square was always preferred in New Spain. Even though the square form quickly came into use in New Galicia, subsequent attempts to reconcile titles based on the two divergent methods ran into grave problems.[20] Another source of difficulty was the fact that not all mercedes or composiciones were made at the same time, so that subsequent land grants had to be fitted in as best they could. This was possible, since it was the overall size of a parcel, and not its equilateral shape, which was important. Nonetheless, irregularly shaped parcels created surveying problems—the more irregular, the more difficult.[21] Again, although it was generally acknowledged that the boundary lines of land grants should be oriented with the cardinal directions, such was not always the case, and subsequent attempts to rectify the measurements, or to reconcile them with ones which had been made "por vientos rectos," as the contemporary phrase went, could throw a whole series of titles into question.[22] Finally, simple human error was a factor in the imperfection of surveying, and miscalculations must often have occurred.[23]

The more strictly geographical factors involved in surveying difficulties were the roughness of the terrain and the changes wrought in local geography by the passage of time. Very often, the land to be measured for an original grant or to be surveyed to settle a dispute was simply too rough to map accurately in the days before sophisticated instruments and aerial photography. It is certainly no accident that most late-colonial disputes and litigations over land had to do with steep, hilly, and broken terrain. The ease with which flat areas, which were the arable farming zones, were measured, as well as their comparatively early occupation, meant that it was mostly marginal areas which came into dispute during the eighteenth century. Since land surveying and measurement were done by parties of men on foot, the difficult topography introduced much error into the process. In measuring a piece of denuncia land in the jurisdiction of Tequila in 1787, the surveying party went with "great effort, going up and down stony brush-covered hillsides and crossing creek beds."[24] In another case, the pueblo of San Francisco Huejotitán in the jurisdiction of San Cristóbal de la Barranca had its town lands measured and confirmed in 1694 by the corregidor of the district delegated as the *juez de medidas* by an oidor of the Audiencia. Measurement proved physically impossible to the north of the village, because of the roughness of the terrain, and almost as bad in the other directions as well, so the juez simply arbitrarily assigned a sitio de ganado mayor to the pueblo as its legal ejido, and the pueblo stipulated

20. AIPG, Tierras, leg. 14, exp. 9, Cuisillos vs. Buenavista, 1760.
21. E.g., AIPG, Tierras, leg. 27, exp. 6, 1798.
22. E.g., AIPG, Tierras, leg. 60, exps. 1-5, Manuel del Río vs. Pueblo de Ahualulco, 1790.
23. AIPG, Tierras, leg. 14, exp. 9, 1760.   24. AIPG, Tierras, leg. 46, exp. 12, 1792.

that it was satisfied.[25] Very often, such measurements and the titles based upon them were subsequently called into question because of their inexactitude, especially when such marginal lands became more valuable, later in the century.

Finally, the face of the land changed under the impact of human habitation, and with such change the landmarks established as surveying points and land boundaries also changed, or vanished entirely. The masonry markers and piles of stones which men erected to delimit their possession of the land could be torn down, washed away, or simply disintegrate with the passage of time; but natural landmarks could be altered too, throwing into confusion the minute descriptions and painstaking measurements upon which land titles were based. An eloquent statement of this problem was made by one of the contending parties to a suit over the boundaries of the Hacienda de Navajas in 1796:

[In placing markers], men in past times did not proceed with the utmost efficacy since, perhaps, they put them at a tree that now no longer exists; or on a hill then bare, but with the passage of time and the manure of livestock afterwards overgrown; or, on the contrary, on a hill at one time forested but now bare because it was cleared. . . .[26]

Both endemic social tensions and technical difficulties in surveying thus played their parts in causing conflict and litigation over land. Social factors, particularly, were interwoven in complex ways with the motives and claims of parties to disputes, sometimes serving as pretexts, sometimes as the covert causes of conflicts. But from the point of view we have assumed in this study, the most important strands running through late-colonial disputes over land ownership and use were the increasing economic value of the land and the growing competition between small-scale peasant agriculture, on the one hand, and large-scale commercialized agriculture, on the other.

The Denunciation of Realengos

The same basic issue—access to land for economic purposes—was at stake in most late-colonial conflicts and litigation over land, but it took a number of different forms. The same general mechanisms came into play in almost all cases, but the occasions which gave rise to disputes, and the circumstances surrounding them, were almost infinitely varied. Broadly speaking, there were three major forms of dispute, with a number of minor variations. The first was the denunciation by an individual, a group of

25. AIPG, Tierras, leg. 49, exp. 5, 1694.   26. AIPG, Tierras, leg. 41, exp. 17, 1796.

individuals, or a community (usually Indian) of *tierra realenga* (more commonly *realengos*), land which belonged to the Spanish Crown and which might therefore be granted to a claimant, usually upon payment of a fee to the Crown.[27] Although realengos might be, and in the late-colonial period usually were, occupied at the time of denunciation, the fact that the occupier putatively lacked a legal title to the land made it fair game for the *denuncia*. Most of the land thus denounced was either in the form of *huecos*—literally holes or odd bits of land not accounted for in formal titles or subsequent measurements—or marginal lands of low quality.

The second major form of land dispute was an invasion or illegal or unauthorized occupation of one owner's titled lands by another (or by a non-owner). In theory, this was a very different legal case from the denunciation of realengos, since it involved lands for which there already existed a clear title, and therefore the operating principle was more analogous to trespass or theft. In fact, however, one party to a case might justify such an invasion on the grounds that the land in question either lacked a proper title or was tierra realengo. When legal elements were combined in this way, it is hardly surprising that suits might drag on for years or even generations. In the case of invasions, the parties to the suit were usually Indian villages and haciendas, though other permutations might also occur.

The third important form of conflict involved common rights of various kinds, and the practice most often at issue was the restriction of rights of access by one party to others. This might consist of the actual enclosure of, or encroachment upon, town common-lands (*ejidos*, *dehesas*, etc.); or closing off lands to which parties other than the actual owner had prescriptive rights of limited usage, most often grazing or wood-collecting. Again, as with invasions, elements of a denuncia of realengo might become entangled with common rights, since both frequently involved marginal areas, useful chiefly for grazing and wood-collection, which might not have been firmly claimed or occupied before the mid-eighteenth century. The rights to graze livestock on non-arable land and to collect wood may seem insignificant; but, as we shall see, they were of transcendent importance in an agricultural system which was beginning to press upon the limits of arable lands and which depended upon wood for a wide range of purposes, from fuel to handicrafts.

The main elements of land suits (and of course not every conflict over

27. There was a clear legal distinction between *realengos* and *terrenos baldíos*, which might have been titled to private individuals, but subsequently became vacant and uncultivated. In actual practice, the term "baldíos" was rarely if ever used in colonial land suits, so it is not discussed here. For the difference between the two, see Gibson, *The Aztecs*, pp. 599 and 604, and the classic legal work of Wistano Luis Orozco, *Legislación y jurisprudencia sobre terrenos baldíos* (1895).

land came into the courts) were: one party's bringing a claim; the presentation of evidence regarding title to the land in question by documentation, testimony, or both; usually a physical examination and measurement of the land, accompanied by a map; and adjudication of the land to one party or the other, sometimes with payment of a fee to the Spanish Crown. The basic issue in the claim was the proof of possession by the claimant, either by direct title or by strong indirect evidence. There was, of course, a presumption of ownership residing with the party which could prove long occupation of the land, even where direct legal title was missing. This emphasis on effective possession and occupation gave rise to the well-known expression "de tiempo inmemorial" in describing the length of occupation of a given piece of land by one party or another to litigation. Just what this expression meant exactly was never defined in law, but it was certainly relative and should be looked at with a certain amount of skepticism.[28] In a suit of 1757, for example, Francisco García de León, owner of the haciendas Santa Cruz and El Jacal in the district of Ahualulco, affirmed his right to parts of the Cerro de Ameca based upon "immemorial possession, or at least for more than forty years. . . ."[29]

The frequent denunciations of Crown lands (realengos) which occurred in the late eighteenth century were occasioned by the expansion of agriculture after the midcentury, with the concomitant pressures this exerted on the land base of the Guadalajara region. The absorption of realengos by denuncia had both a temporal and a geographical dimension. The same objective before 1750, or even before 1700, had been achieved through the mechanism of the composición, which was the legitimization of a *fait accompli* rather than a sign of active expansion. If the composición was a more passive mechanism for land absorption, it also brought much larger pieces of land under legal title, while late-eighteenth-century denuncias generally embraced much smaller parcels. Certainly there were denuncias of realengos before 1750—but after that date, the composición very obviously gave way to the denuncia as the dominant legal means for the acquisition of land.

The geographical dimension was that denunciations of realengos were

28. Credulity regarding claims of possession "de tiempo inmemorial" led Eric J. Hobsbawm, in "Peasant Land Occupations," *Past and Present* 62 (1974), to accept uncritically the assertions of Indian villagers about land conflicts in Peru.

29. AIPG, Tierras, leg. 25, exp. 21, 1757. It should be noted here that the three major forms of land conflict discussed above represent only one set of variables. Another, crosscutting set is the nature of the parties involved: i.e., hacienda vs. hacienda, pueblo vs. hacienda, or pueblo vs. pueblo. Since both these sets of variables are of equivalent importance in looking at late-colonial land conflicts, but are analytically subordinate to the basic, underlying reasons for conflict, the following discussion does not hew strictly to the line laid down above—realengos, invasions, commons rights—but rather weaves them into an overall analysis which stresses structural factors.

almost universally limited to marginal areas. Those lands which were most fertile and easily accessible were generally claimed very early on, in most cases well before the end of the seventeenth century. To take but the most obvious example, the Toluquilla Valley, the very idea of untitled lands in the area was absurd to late-colonial observers. When Miguel del Portillo made a blanket *denuncia* of any realengo in the district in 1798, the *fiscal* of the Audiencia almost laughed in his face and concluded: "The improbability of unclaimed Crown lands among such properties is easily seen."[30] Two years later, a local propertyowner, Nicolás Henríquez, denounced any possible realengos between his own property, the Rancho de San Nicolás, and the neighboring Hacienda del Rosario. This denunciation, like Portillo's of two years previously, expressly did not specify such-and-such a parcel as being realengo, as such claims usually did in less densely occupied areas, but denounced *any possible* realengos in very vague and indeterminate fashion: it was quite clearly a fishing trip. In fact, the two properties together measured only 17.75 caballerías, and their boundaries had been known as fixed for some time. Rosario, though very small, had an elaborate house on it (including a chapel) and was almost entirely devoted to the cultivation of irrigated wheat. Henríquez' claim was so patently ridiculous that he later withdrew it and became rather crusty over the whole abortive attempt. When Henríquez at one point refused to show his own titles to the local subdelegado, that official reprimanded him by saying that not to do so would make the entire proceeding a "burlesque and child's game," which was not far from the truth anyway. Eventually the surveyor (*agrimensor*) determined that the denounced realengo was purely imaginary.[31]

What we have in the late-colonial *denuncia de realengos*, therefore, is a much more finely honed, more limited, and at the same time more aggressive judicial mechanism than the composición for the appropriation of untitled lands. This becomes particularly clear when one looks at those areas, some of which were already intensively cultivated, where realengos did in fact exist, and in which claimants were able to make their claims stick. In 1779, for example, Manuel del Río, who as subdelegado and landowner was later to make a fair bid to dominate the entire Ahualulco area, denounced a piece of putative realengo between his Hacienda del Jacal and the neighboring Hacienda de Santa Cruz (which he subsequently came to own himself). This led to a long suit with Francisco García de León, the owner of Santa Cruz, but in 1782 Del Río carried the day and was awarded possession of a realengo consisting of three small parcels bordering his hacienda to the north, west, and south, measuring one-

30. AIPG, Tierras, leg. 27, exp. 6, 1798.   31. AIPG, Tierras, leg. 14, exp. 8, 1800.

quarter of a sitio de ganado mayor. This was certainly not a big piece of land as these things went (about 1,000 acres of rough terrain), nor was it valuable (Del Río paid 12 pesos to the Crown), but under the conditions of the time it was apparently worth litigating over.[32] Although Spanish hacendados initiated most denuncias, they were by no means alone in doing so. Smaller propertyowners also attempted to acquire title to Crown lands, and Indian communities in particular were not bashful about pressing their claims, nor about contradicting the claims of neighboring landlords.[33]

One interesting aspect of the increasing importance of realengos after about midcentury was the frequency with which old denuncias were revived in cases where the original claim had been allowed to lapse for some reason. Such, for example, was the issue in the long suit between Manuel Capetillo and José Ignacio Basauri, the hacendados of Buenavista and Atequiza in the Chapala area. The original denuncia, made in the late eighteenth century by a previous owner of Buenavista, was revived in 1801 and engendered a protracted suit still unresolved in 1819. The amount of realengo actually involved, after extravagant claims and counterclaims, turned out to be slightly more than one-third of a caballería (about 35 acres).[34] A similar instance was the denuncia of nine caballerías of land to the north of the small Rancho San José del Guaje, very near the pueblo of Tlajomulco, in 1772. Experts characterized the land as worthless for agricultural purposes and useful only for rough grazing—it was rocky, uneven, and totally without water or wood. By the early years of the nineteenth century, Miguel del Portillo had acquired the rancho and sought vigorously to expand its production. He therefore revived the old denuncia and eventually won ownership of the parcel over the counterclaims of neighboring Indian villages.[35] Probably in both cases the lands claimed, since they were unfit for arable use, were destined for the support of livestock which had been displaced by intensified cultivation.

The revival of old denuncias, however, did not always eventuate in gaining land for the current claimant. In the years intervening between the original denunciation and the revival of the petition, other people might have occupied the land in question and established a strong presumptive claim to title. A complex case of such a preemption graphically illustrates some of the important themes of late-eighteenth-century agricultural development. In 1794, Miguel del Portillo, owner of Navajas (as well as the Rancho San José del Guaje, discussed above, and the Hacienda de San José Zapotepec, in the Toluquilla Valley), sought to revive a denuncia of

32. AIPG, Tierras, leg. 27, exp. 11, 1782; also, leg. 25, exps. 16-18, 1760.
33. AIPG, Tierras, leg. 40, exp. 15, 1718-1807; leg. 49, exp. 50, 1793; leg. 41, exp. 45, 1772.
34. AIPG, Tierras, leg. 20, exp. 7, 1801-1803; leg. 25, exps. 13-14, 1805-1816.
35. AIPG, Tierras, leg. 47, exp. 3, 1801.

some realengo pieces lying northwest of the estate. The original claim had been made in 1764 by Martín Calderón, then owner of the hacienda, in contradiction to a claim by José Simón Coronado, a small rancher who occupied part of the land in question. Calderón in his 1764 denunciation had tried to prove his "inmemorial posesión" of part of the land through testimony that he had rented it out to various people and had had an acknowledged right to exploit the wood on the land. In the late 1760s, counterclaims had been made by the Pueblo de Tizapán and the owners of the haciendas La Sauceda, Mazatepec, and Cuspala. Coronado had died by 1768 and passed on his claim to the realengo to another local man, who maintained an interest in the denuncia and occupied the land. The arable part of the land originally denounced by Coronado consisted of three small mesas "on the top of the said hill [of Navajas]" potentially fertile for the growing of wheat, but lacking readily available water and inaccessible except by mule. The value of the land in the 1760s was placed by experts at about 90 pesos, despite the fact that it measured at least a sitio de ganado mayor in size.

By the mid-1760s, Coronado had apparently maintained a precarious independence on the untitled rancho for many years, playing off his two powerful neighbors, the haciendas of Navajas and Mazatepec, against each other. Since the owners of both these estates tried to assert their claims to the realengos by proving that they had rented the lands out at one time or another, or had reserved to themselves the rights to collect wood on them, Coronado adroitly avoided acknowledging the jurisdiction of either:

. . . and paying rent [to Mazatepec], when he was urged to pay at the proper time he excused himself saying he was on the lands of Navajas; from which it may be deduced that sometimes he was on the lands of the Mayorazgo [Mazatepec], and was therefore not a tenant of Navajas to be bothered by its owner for rent; and when he was asked for rent by the Mayorazgo, he passed over to Navajas and refused to pay on the grounds of not being a tenant of Mazatepec; he thus managed to be a tenant of both haciendas as far as occupying their lands, but of neither one when it came to satisfying rents. . . .[36]

The case was even further complicated by the fact that the boundaries of several local haciendas, Mazatepec and Estipac among them, were not "fixed and known," but only vaguely established. Before Coronado sought to establish his claim to the parcel, the land had not been used at all for agricultural purposes, and he had been the first to sow grain there in an era when Calderón, on the Hacienda de Navajas, was also putting new ground under the plow. One witness in about 1770 asserted that the cultivation of the small patches of arable land on the realengo dated only from about

36. AIPG, Tierras, leg. 41, exp. 17, 1796.

1730, "because until forty years ago nothing was sown on the old Navajas."
Changes in ownership of the various properties involved caused the entire suit to lapse into inactivity for twenty years, until Portillo revived the
claim at the end of the eighteenth century, obviously intent (as with his
Rancho San José del Guaje) upon expanding production on Navajas. Eventually, after a decision by the Audiencia and then a later reversal, part of
the land went to Navajas and part to the successors to Coronado's claim.

Several themes are worth underlining as they emerge from the Navajas-
Coronado litigation. The first is the attempt of the large rural estate to
extend its hegemony in the countryside—but also the ability of smaller
landowners, in this case a squatter, to assert their property rights effectively through legal mechanisms. The second theme is the expansion of
agriculture from about the midcentury, in response to a growing local
market. And the third theme is the increasing economic value of formerly
marginal lands, the concomitant of agricultural expansion.

The Extinction of Common Rights

The appropriation of realengos was only one of a number of different
institutional forms assumed by the aggressive agricultural expansion of the
later eighteenth century. Another was the restriction of commons rights of
various sorts, sometimes through fencing off previously open private lands
or the unilateral extinction of commons rights by private owners, sometimes through the outright expropriation of common lands by private individuals. These conflicts took place not only between Spanish landowners
and indigenous communities, but also among Spanish landowners themselves. Furthermore, although they generally involved access to lands of
marginal quality, this was not always the case. For example, the right of
livestock owners to graze their animals on the stubble (*rastrojos*) left after
the harvest on neighboring lands, so firmly established in Spanish law,
came under fire in the Guadalajara region during the eighteenth century.[37]
The promiscuous access of livestock, particularly cattle, to arable fields
after the harvest made the control of private lands difficult, of course, and
as agriculture expanded, estate owners became more and more jealous of
this very real pasturage resource. In the Toluquilla Valley, which because
of its fertility and proximity to the city was one of the first areas to undergo
transformation to a more intensive, grain-dominated agriculture, this strain
was already visible by the early eighteenth century. In 1722, for example,

37. On grazing rights, see Dusenberry, *The Mexican Mesta*, esp. chap. 7: and Chevalier,
Land and Society, passim.

two prominent Toluquilla Valley hacendados, Miguel del Portillo and Luis de Vargas Ruíz de Moncayo, agreed to abrogate the traditional commons arrangement for the sake of their individual operations and to avoid any legal difficulties over damages by straying animals.[38]

An even more graphic example of the extinction of age-old commons rights under the pressures of a more rationalized agriculture and stock-raising is the conflict between the haciendas Cuisillos and Buenavista in the mid-eighteenth century. Mixed in with the elements of claims and counterclaims over land titles, the interfamily rivalries, and the jurisdictional disputes between New Spain and New Galicia, are signs of a very real change in the way land was used after 1750. Already in the 1720s, Pedro Pérez de Tagle, owner of Cuisillos, had sought through a suit to cut off the access of Buenavista and other neighboring haciendas to stubble-grazing and rough pasturage on his lands, maintaining that he needed this resource exclusively for his own livestock. Initially, Pérez de Tagle had been successful in obtaining an injunction from the Guadalajara Audiencia suspending an *auto acordado* of 1719 which guaranteed that all local lands were to remain open to common grazing after the harvest. This injunction was later overturned (1720) and the common rights of all local landowners reconfirmed.

A running battle over the next forty years between Cuisillos and Buenavista culminated in a long and complicated suit in the 1760s, one element of which was a revival of the argument over commons rights. In the later suit, José Luis de Siordia, owner of the haciendas La Laja and Labor de Rivera, in conjunction with the owners of Buenavista complained that the administrator of Cuisillos, Gómez Marañón, was impounding their live-stock to restrict the use of pasturage on Cuisillos which should have re-mained open to all local landowners. Gómez Marañón had denied that local grazing lands were "reciprocally common," thus "violating the terms recognized previously by his neighbors." Siordia stated that before the advent of Gómez Marañón, local landowners had enjoyed the use of avail-able pastures "promiscuously, all of them, with their cattle and horses," as specified in the Laws of the Indies. The then-owner of Cuisillos, Trespa-lacios y Escandón, replied that such an arrangement was no longer appro-priate for the hacienda because of its large plantings of wheat and maize and its "casi permanente" cultivation of sugar cane. On this occasion the Audiencia found Trespalacios' arguments convincing and stated that the *real provisión* of 1720 had only been for a limited term and did not pres-ently apply. The rights of common pasturage which had prevailed in the

38. AIPG, prot. Mena mayor, 12:240v–242v.

area by long tradition were therefore extinguished in favor of an expanded agriculture.[39]

A more frequent, or at least more visible and controversial, occurrence than the extinction of common grazing rights between Spanish landowners was the restriction by estate owners of village community access to grazing and woodlands. The two practices were certainly related, and the entire movement in this direction in the late eighteenth century bears a marked similarity to the enclosure which had taken place in the English countryside since the sixteenth century.[40] It is often difficult to disentangle what we may call "enclosure" from conflicts over realengos, but the restriction of access to common lands, or the fencing-off of formerly open private lands, was an increasingly common cause for contention in the colonial courts after midcentury. Non-Indian landowners were not the only ones to engage in enclosure, certainly. Particularly in areas of dense Indian population which experienced early demographic pressure, Indian villages were known to enclose town lands to reserve for themselves and their cofradías the exclusive rights to pasturage and wood-collecting.[41] The most egregious examples of this practice, however, and the ones which provoked the longest and bitterest controversy, were those in which Spanish estate-owners closed off their own lands or encroached on town commons.

The basic issue in such enclosures was the prescriptive access-right of Indians to *montes* for the purposes of collecting wood and presumably—as with Spanish stock-owners—for pasturage of their animals. In fact, since Indians rarely possessed much livestock as individuals, the main point of contention was almost always over their right to collect wood. This right, rooted in the notion of the Indians' legal minority and their economic vulnerability and marginality, was reaffirmed a number of times in court cases and administrative edicts. In 1756, for example, the Audiencia of New Spain stated in an *auto acordado* that Indians had a prescriptive right to the use of pasture and woods on privately owned land, but that this right was subject to certain restrictions. The rights of the legal owners of privately held lands were not to be interfered with, particularly in the use of pasturage. Indians were to be allowed to enter onto such lands "for the cutting of all kinds of firewood and lumber" which they required for fuel and in the construction and repair of their houses and churches. But Indian villagers were explicitly forbidden to overcut trees, on pain of being denied further access to the land, nor could they cut wood for sale without license of the land's owner.[42] Royal legislation attempted in this case, as in

39. AIPG, Tierras, leg. 71, exp. 30, 1761; leg. 33, exp. 3, 1765; leg. 51, exp. 2, 1644-1805; leg. 25, exps. 13, 14, and 19, 1805-1816.

40. On English enclosure, see Thirsk, *Agrarian History of England and Wales*, vol. 4, chap. 4.

41. AIPG, Tierras, leg. 62, exp. 17.   42. AIPG, Tierras, leg. 46, exp. 10, 1791.

so many others, to strike a balance of some sort between the needs of the Spanish economy and those of indigenous communities. It is hardly surprising that as arable land, water, pasturage, and woodland became more valuable resources after midcentury, the balance was harder and harder to maintain.

The importance of such marginal lands, or *montes* as they were called, was often attested to in colonial litigation and other documentation. They were important to rural estates for rough grazing, and the balance between the amount of such lands and the amount of land put under the plow became of increasing concern to hacendados as agriculture expanded in the later eighteenth century.[43] Indian pueblos, which depended heavily upon montes for a variety of purposes, were increasingly hard-put to stretch their inelastic resources as their populations increased. One solution to this problem was to rent montes from Spanish landowners, something Indian communities did with great frequency after midcentury. These leases almost always included a stipulation on the part of the landowner that trees should not be cut at the roots, "but so that they may renew themselves," "without exterminating the small growth so as to avoid the general destruction of the entire monte."[44] The very fact that such leases were made at all suggests strongly that by the mid-eighteenth century the right of Indians to collect wood on privately owned lands was honored more in the breach than in the observance.

The vital importance of montes, and the competitive pressures upon them from the peasant and commercial sectors of the agricultural economy, are clearly illustrated by the interesting case of the Cerro de Tequila at the very end of the eighteenth century. In 1799, José Prudencio de Cuervo, one of the major Spanish landowners of the area, made an official denunciation of the forested peak (*cima*) of the huge Cerro de Tequila, to the south of the town, as realengo. The slopes of the mountain, almost all the way up to the top, had already been granted in mercedes of varying dates to a number of private owners, among them the Indian pueblo of Tequila, which held a sitio de ganado menor; Cuervo himself; and the Convento del Carmen of Guadalajara for its Hacienda de Miraflores. Cuervo declared the reason for his denunciation to be "without other interest than the common good." He stated that the local Indians, in order to save themselves the considerable trouble of ascending the steeper parts of the mountain ("ahorrar un poco de camino"), had cut even the second-growth wood on the slopes ("hasta los renuevos"), so that now there was

43. E.g., the remarks of Manuel Calixto Cañedo—AIPG, prot. Ballesteros, 18:80-91v, 1793; and in general, Chapter 9 above.

44. AIPG, prot. Mena mayor, 9:500-502v, 1766; prot. Berroa, 8:274-275, 1765. Both of these leases were made to Indian pueblos by the owners of the Porres Baranda mayorazgo.

no usable wood available for any purpose, but especially for the distilling industry, upon which much of the livelihood of the district depended. He emphasized the necessity of conserving the wood from haphazard exploitation, and suggested that a systematic program of replanting be undertaken under the aegis of the town (Indian and Spanish) as a whole. The fiscal of the Audiencia congratulated Cuervo for his altruism in making the claim in the name of the town as a whole.

By the following year (1800), Cuervo had desisted from his denuncia and withdrawn in favor of the Indian pueblo of Tequila. If his selflessness seems suspicious in a more cynical age, it was perfectly credible to his contemporaries, who characterized him as having "an honorable character" and as being "the most beneficent citizen toward the poor of all classes seen until now in the district of Tequila." In the meantime, the surveyors had attempted to measure the realengo at the top of the cerro, only to find it too rough for accurate measurement. They estimated it as about one sitio de ganado mayor, totally useless for agricultural purposes, but good for wood collection. There was no water at all (wood-collectors had to bring their own with them), so grazing was out of the question, and roads would have to be opened up for the transport of wood down into the town. The overall value of the land was placed by the experts at 100 pesos.

The Indians, who had taken up Cuervo's denunciation, proposed to pay for the merced from their caja de comunidad and to set up certain rules for more rational exploitation of the woodlands. They further proposed that Cuervo direct the opening of roads on the mountain, that all vecinos (Indian and non-Indian) of the town contribute their labor at his direction, and that in return for Cuervo's services he and his heirs be allowed to take all the wood they required for his house and hacienda, without restriction, forever. Although this privilege was already open to every vecino of the town by law and custom, they noted, Cuervo should be singled out because of his efforts to stop the "desolation that has already begun." The proposed regulations included a proviso that the Indians and non-Indians of the town split the cost of the project in half; that all wood cut in future be seasoned ("en sazón"); that anyone cutting second-growth trees lose the wood, his cart and animal, and his tools, and spend a week in the village jail; that no firewood be cut for export from the jurisdiction; and that timber be exported only under explicit license of local officials (the Indian alcaldes and the subdelegado). The Spanish vecinos of Tequila agreed to the proposals in principle and subscribed half the cost of the legal operations and projected road-building.

By the time of the 1799 denuncia in Tequila, a shortage of wood had already long since begun to make itself felt locally. With increasing population pressure, a number of the wooded cerros nearer Guadalajara had already become completely deforested. The immediate reason for local concern was the fear that the distilling industry might collapse if something were not done to regulate use of the wood upon which it depended. A number of witnesses testified to the almost total desolation of the lower reaches of the mountain, and that in recent years they had had to go ever farther up the slopes in search of wood. Although some local landowners (among them Cuervo) possessed enough of their own montes to supply their needs, a great part of the town, Indian and non-Indian alike, depended solely upon the cerro for wood for domestic purposes and for distillation and processing sugar cane, the two major local industries. A calculation of the annual wood consumption in the district for firewood (*leña*) alone produced the figure of some 35,000 cargas (mule-loads), including domestic uses, distilling, and sugar-processing. The total value of this consumption at current prices amounted to almost 5,000 pesos per year, at one real per carga; but since most of the cost consisted in labor and transport, the local subdelegado suggested that the value would rise when wood was brought down from the top of the mountain. Happily for all concerned, the Crown finally made the merced to the town as a whole, and the Spanish and Indian vecino groups each paid 125 pesos for the grant upon its consummation in 1804.[45]

The Tequila case is unusual not only for the wealth of circumstantial detail included in the records, but also for its outcome. If the vecinos of Tequila, both Indian and Spanish, reached an agreement about conserving one of their most important economic resources, the inhabitants of most other towns could not manage to do so. It is true that conflicts over access to montes did not often come up in just this form—the presumptive right of all vecinos to share in its exploitation. But enclosure by an individual was the preferred method of resolving such conflicts, and there were cases of individuals enclosing town commons. One instance which stands out by contrast with the amicable arrangements made in Tequila involved the town commons of Cocula in the latter part of the eighteenth century. The same pressures were certainly at work in Cocula, if one substitutes soap-making for the distilling industry—and it is of course the underlying similarity between the two cases which is of primary interest to us here. But it is also fascinating to see the civic disinterestedness of José Prudencio de Cuervo contrasted with the Scrooge-like character, or the public perception of it, of José Mederos, the man who tried to enclose the town common of Cocula.

Mederos had purchased the small Hacienda de San Diego, south of Cocula, in the mid-1780s. He was a merchant of Portuguese origin who

45. AIPG, Tierras, leg. 40, exp. 22, 1799.

had lived in Cocula for some sixty years and had eventually made a good deal of money from the soap trade and a store in the town, having begun his commercial career with only "una guitarra y un biolín." Almost immediately after he purchased the hacienda, Mederos began to fence off land which had customarily been regarded as realengo, open to all inhabitants of Cocula for pasture and wood-collecting. This action led to "some dissensions with various neighbors" and eventually to a formal denunciation of the land in question by Mederos in 1792. A number of local witnesses testified that Mederos was generally disliked and had begun the suit out of vindictiveness. He had gone out of his way to bring in employees for his hacienda from outside the town, as well. Upon his death in 1796, Mederos bequeathed his entire estate to a priest in a distant town, leaving nothing to any local person and establishing no obras pías, as was generally the custom among the propertied classes.

The denuncia made by Mederos in 1792, and to which the township of Cocula as a whole responded with a counterclaim the following year, involved two parcels of land called Mesa Grande and Los Morrillos, amounting to some two sitios de ganado mayor and 8.5 caballerías. A multitude of local witnesses all agreed that the land had for most of the eighteenth century been regarded by the inhabitants of Cocula as realengo and by tacit consent used as a town common. Some attempt had been made by the previous owner of San Diego to establish a tenuous hold over the land by collecting rents from squatters and regulating its use for pasture and wood-collecting, but this had never really been successful. The land had been used in common by all the vecinos of the town for several generations, without distinction of race. Although it was chiefly the poorer inhabitants of the town who used the common for collecting wood and grazing their few livestock, wealthier members of the community also exploited it; the neighboring Hacienda de Estipac, for example, had often been known to graze its stock on the land. Except for a small piece of land to the south, the town had no other available common lands, but was completely surrounded ("lo amurallan") by the neighboring haciendas of San Diego, Santa María, Santa Clara, Estipac, and La Sauceda. The township as a whole had taken up a subscription, prorated according to wealth, to support the legal costs of resisting Mederos' claims. The town, on its part, claimed "inmemorial posesión" of the land, and Mederos on his part was not only fencing off the land, but confiscating the tools and animals of local woodcutters who ventured onto it.

The primary economic importance of the land in question was not for farming but for pasture and wood-collecting. The experts in the case placed the total value of the two sitios de ganado mayor at 150 pesos, because the terrain was almost impassable and there was only one water source, a natural spring. The town as a whole had never supplied itself with wood from any other place, and the only alternative source was some ten or twelve miles (three to four leagues) distant. If the inhabitants of the town were forced to go further afield for wood, the high transport costs would raise the price of the soap whose manufacture was the mainstay of Cocula's economy. Therefore it was vital that access to the land by the vecinos of the district be assured.

By 1797, the case had progressed from the subdelegado of the district, through the Audiencia of New Galicia, to the Junta de Real Hacienda in Mexico City, where an earlier decision in favor of Mederos had been appealed by the vecinos of Cocula. The Junta de Real Hacienda eventually decided that the land did not, in fact, belong to the town by right of commons or long-time possession, but that it was realengo and might be sold to the highest bidder. The land was to be put up at auction, but the township of Cocula was to be given preferred status in the bidding. In 1810, the sitio Mesa Grande was sold to one of the middling landowners of the town, Rosa Serrano, for 1,100 pesos. The fate of the other sitio and the caballerías is unknown, but probably they too were acquired by private parties.[46] The significant points to notice, in the Cocula case as in that of Tequila, are the vital importance of agriculturally marginal lands in the local economy; the increasing pressure upon such resources exerted by population growth in the countryside; and the competition which arose between landowners and peasants over the use of these resources.

More typical than the enclosure by private individuals of putative town commons was the enclosure by estate-owners of lands which had long remained open for certain kinds of exploitation, a procedure protested in many cases of land conflict. A fairly representative series of cases involved the Hacienda del Cuatro, in the Toluquilla Valley, and the Indian pueblos of the neighborhood. Despite the fact that all the land in the valley had early been claimed, and that property boundaries were well established even by 1700, some tracts of private land remained open to common pasture and wood-collecting, especially for Indian villages, until very late in the colonial period. In 1809, however, the owners of the hacienda, the heirs of the Marqués de Pánuco, decided to build a fence to enclose their property on the north side of the pueblo of Toluquilla. The Indians complained that they had always pastured their livestock there, in the area at the base of the Cerro del Cuatro, and they asked an injunction to prevent construction of the fence. The ownership of the land was questioned, but eventually the title of the hacienda was indisputably confirmed and the enclosure proceeded. Ten years later, in 1818, the new owner of El Cuatro, Manuel Gar-

46. AIPG, Tierras, leg. 51, exp. 13, 1644-1818.

cía de Quevedo, was again enclosing formerly open hacienda lands which had traditionally been accessible to the Indians of the area for pasture and wood-collecting. A temporary injunction against construction of the fences was eventually lifted, and Indian claims that certain of García de Quevedo's lands were realengo and certain others actually Indian town-lands were disallowed.[47]

Land Invasions

Aside from the denunciation of untitled lands, and the extinction in one way or another of rights to commons, landowners both private and communal simply invaded and encroached upon each other's land with dizzying frequency. Various excuses might be adduced for such illegal occupations, from the existence of realengos to the invalidity of titles, but the *leitmotiv* was always the same: the economic necessity of enlarging one's landholdings. It is true that such incursions were not always the result of conscious policy on the part of either Indians or non-Indians, and that they often occurred as the result of slow accretion over long periods of time. But it is also true that in many instances trespassers knew full well what they were doing and the benefits to be gained from it, and that once such illegal acquisitions of land were called into question, no landholder withdrew gracefully from the occupied territory. Furthermore, the increasing incidence of such conflicts after about midcentury is yet another indication that both commercial and peasant agriculture were pressing as never before upon land resources.

Spanish landowners were plainly guilty on innumerable occasions of encroaching on Indian lands, as well as upon each other's. This does not contradict the basic stability of Spanish holdings after 1700, since large tracts of land were never acquired in this fashion at the expense of the peasant sector. Nonetheless, unlike conflicts over realengos and commons rights, invasions of Indian lands by non-Indians did occasionally involve tracts of arable land. This was in fact the whole *raison d'être* for invasions, in many instances; the expansion of arable land was often not possible in any other way.

A typical example was the suit between the pueblo of Santa Cruz de la Soledad and the neighboring Hacienda San Nicolás de la Labor, both of which lay on the shore of Lake Chapala northeast of the town of Chapala. Relations between the pueblo and the estate had been friendly until the

47. AIPG, Tierras, leg. 33, exp. 18, 1809; leg. 5, exp. 10, 1818. And on a similar problem with García de Quevedo's nearby Hacienda del Rosario—AIPG, Tierras, leg. 4, exp. 1, 1818.

mid-1780s, when a new owner took over the hacienda. From that point on, the aggressive agricultural expansion of San Nicolás had steadily infringed on the pueblo lands until it had come to occupy several hundred acres of cropland on which the owner of the hacienda cultivated wheat and garbanzos. The hacendado took the position that the pueblo had invaded his lands, and one witness even stated that he had begun to charge the Indians of Santa Cruz rent for the use of their own lands for pasture and wood-collecting. Around 1800, the hacienda closed off its own lands, which had traditionally been open to the villagers for pasture during the rainy season. The hacendado attempted to justify his usurpation by claiming that the pueblo was not properly a village in its own right, but only a barrio of Chapala. In fact, the pueblo dated from at least 1591, and the location of the hacienda's casco *between* the pueblo and Chapala tended to confirm its independent status. The Indians' suit eventuated in a survey of the area, and in 1806 the Audiencia ordered restitution of the lands which had been occupied by the hacienda.[48] Nor was the owner of San Nicolás de la Labor the only hacendado to justify de-facto seizure of village lands on the grounds that the village lacked a legitimate identity.[49]

The notion of an illegal occupation of titled lands largely depended, of course, upon the construction the contending parties and the courts put on the facts of evidence; to resort to a homely image, the cut of the cloth depended upon who held the scissors. Thus one man's (or one village's) invasion was simply another's assertion of his rights. This element of relativity often makes it difficult to determine the justice of any claim over land, particularly where unauthorized occupations were involved. Nonetheless, it is clear that Indian communities were not just passive victims of hacendado rapacity in the late-colonial period; they too invaded lands and turned them to their own uses. This occurred with remarkable frequency, though probably Spanish estate-owners were on the whole more aggressive in this respect.

In the 1780s, for example, the Indians of the pueblo of Huentitán, north of Guadalajara, began to make incursions on the legally titled lands of the small neighboring Hacienda de Guadalupe. By 1790, most of the estate's one sitio de ganado mayor was occupied by the villagers, and to add insult to injury they had established their own canoe crossing on the Río Santiago, thus ruining the business of the crossing controlled by the hacienda.[50] In another case, the Indians of the pueblo of Tlajomulco systemati-

---

48. AIPG, Tierras, leg. 28, exp. 1, 1806.
49. AIPG, Tierras, leg. 22, exp. 1, 1803. Just a few of the many examples are: San Martin de la Cal, 1709—AIPG, Tierras, leg. 1, exp. 1. San Sebastian el Chico (Tonalá), 1761—leg. 85, exp. 4. Ahualulco, 1790—leg. 60, exps. 1-5. Tlajomulco, 1803—leg. 5, exp. 8.
50. CG-ASC, leg. 12, 1794.

cally invaded the lands of Miguel del Portillo's Rancho San José del Guaje in the early years of the nineteenth century, demolishing the accepted boundary markers and advancing almost to the patio of the house before he managed to contain them with an injunction from the local authorities.[51]

If one expects to see hacendados and Indian villagers invading each other's lands, it is more surprising, at least in the conventional wisdom, to see Indian pueblos engaging in conflict over lands. But of course the same forces—an increasing rural population, an expanding commercial agriculture, and concomitant pressure on land resources—were at work within the indigenous community as between it and non-Indians. Pueblo-dwellers did not hesitate to accumulate individual wealth within the village, and villages zealously defended their interests against their neighbors, with never a thought of ethnic solidarity in the face of Spanish power-holders. Often this was a matter of pride and local tradition and pueblo identity, but it could also be a matter of survival.

Indian pueblos disputed the ownership of both arable and wooded-pasture lands, but the latter seem to have been at issue more often as the eighteenth century drew to a close. Fairly typical is the case of the pueblo of Ajijic and its neighboring villages on the shore of Lake Chapala. In 1797 Ajijic was involved in a suit with the pueblos of San Juan Cosalá and San Antonio Tlayacapán—to the west and east of it, respectively—as well as with Patricio de Soto, a local Spanish landowner and Guadalajara merchant. As far as the Indian pueblos were concerned, Ajijic maintained that its two neighbors had occupied parts of its town lands (*fundo legal*) to the point that it now was missing nearly half its titled lands, and its "número... crecido de habitantes" found it impossible to live, resulting in a good deal of migration out of the village. On its side, Cosalá claimed that its population had also grown tremendously and was short of farming land. Eventually Ajijic had its missing lands restored and entered into a compromise agreement with Cosalá and Tlayacapán.[52]

Not all land conflicts between Indian pueblos were resolved with the apparent ease and amity of the Ajijic suit. Not infrequently, violence against persons and property broke out.[53] Sometimes the issue of independent-pueblo vs. barrio status was tied into conflicts over land, either as a pretext or an underlying factor, and this could complicate matters con-

51. AIPG, Tierras, leg. 60, exps. 13-14, 1802; leg. 18, exp. 3, 1808. Among the many other instances of this kind: Tesistlán, 1738—AIPG, prot. Mena mayor, 26:344-347. Istlahuacán, 1759—BPE-AJA, 63:3:793. San Pedro Tesistán, 1765—AIPG, prot. Berroa, 8:89v-92v. And the protracted suit between the hacienda and pueblo of San Lucas—AIPG, Tierras, leg. 12, exp. 2, 1750-1772, and leg. 40, exp. 8, 1773.
52. AIPG, Tierras, leg. 27, exp. 33, 1797.
53. E.g., Jocotepec vs. San Cristóbal Zapotitlán—AIPG, Tierras, leg. 78, exps. 3-12, 1767.

siderably.[54] And sometimes conflicts simply dragged on and on over decades because of obstinacy or incredible tangles of interests. In general, this kind of infighting among Indian villages was almost as common, and every bit as bitter, as conflicts between Indian communities and non-Indians.[55]

A good many conflicts over land in the late-colonial countryside probably never came to litigation at any level, but remained informal in nature. Such cases are not part of the public record and it is impossible for us to trace their existence. What form of resolution these cases took is not known, but many of them must have lapsed into a sort of chronic low-level state of irritation. Of those conflicts which did emerge into the public domain, most seem to have found some form of resolution in the process of litigation and adjudication itself, at least temporarily. Very often suits were simply dropped, for various reasons: lack of money to pay for legal costs; insufficient or faulty documentation; an extrajudicial agreement of some kind; or a change in the particular circumstances which had induced the suit in the first place. Just as often, the initial judicial resolution proved inefficacious and the case would come to law again if the pressures which had given rise to it continued to exist. In general, the solutions to conflicts over land appear to be palliative measures which could deal with problems temporarily, but not with the underlying causes. Conflict over the ownership and use of land had its origins in structural factors which may have been recognized by colonial lawyers and royal officials, but with which they could not, or would not, cope.

What, then, are we to make of this Hobbesian world in which neither the claims of race nor social class prevented landholders of all stripes from warring incessantly on all others? The fact is that, given the structural factors and the secular trends at work beneath the surface of day-to-day life, late-colonial Spanish officialdom and courts did a fairly decent job in reconciling the clashing interests of peasants and landlords. Of course it was infinitely nicer and more comfortable to be a wealthy urban merchant or an hacendado than an Indian peasant or a laborer on a rural estate. Of course the legality, not to mention the morality, of the Spanish seizure of Indian economic resources from the time of the Conquest onward is highly arguable. Of course the ruling structure of the Spanish state and society was sustained from the top down, in part, by the exercise of force. And of

54. E.g., Barrio de Santa María vs. Poncitlán—AIPG, Tierras, leg. 49, exp. 15, 1777; leg. 20, exp. 18, 1790; leg. 21, exps. 3-4, 1745 and 1748; leg. 46, exp. 9, 1790; and BPE-AJA, 173:1:1931, 1776.

55. Other examples are: Coyula vs. Tonalá, 1702—AIPG, prot. Ayala, 1:156v. San Lucas vs. Cuyutlán, 1717—AIPG, Tierras, leg. 41, exp. 25. Cuyutlán vs. Tlajomulco, 1736—AIPG, prot. Maraver, 1: no page nos. Tonalá vs. Salatitán, 1737—AIPG, Tierras, leg. 5, exp. 7. Chapala vs. Tlayacapán, 1756—leg. 20, exp. 15. Santa Cruz de las Huertas vs. Tlaquepaque, 1780—leg. 21, exp. 10.

course Indians were not only the objects of exploitation, but exploited other Indians as well. Nonetheless, given the time and the environment, the colonial judicial system extended a good deal of protection to the powerless, while facilitating the expansion of a capitalist agriculture centered on the Guadalajara market. The instances in which the Audiencia of New Galicia confirmed the rights of Indian communities to landownership are too many to count; the clear evidence of it is there in the colonial documentation.

It is true, of course, that there was a strong structural bias in the system in favor of those with power and wealth. But it is equally true that peasants and Indians were not always justified in their claims of "inmemorial posesión" of land, just as landlords and Spaniards were not always justified in theirs. If an increasing misery and exploitation of the rural masses underlay the cultural efflorescence and apparent prosperity of the late-colonial period, it was not because efforts to impose a reasonable balance in the access to landed resources in the countryside were lacking. Rather, at the root of the problem were long-term factors—demographic, social, economic, and technical—dictating a certain pattern of development which contemporaries might well recognize, but which they could not control.

CONCLUSION

The Guadalajara of 1800 was a good deal different from the fairly modest provincial town of 1700, though a centenarian would certainly have recognized it. The major change was one of scale. The city of 1800 was almost six times as large as it had been a century earlier. Its economic and social life was grander and more complex, its government larger, its influence more extensive. But with growth and development had also come a greater vulnerability. The city's food supply, sufficient in normal times, in fact hung by a slender thread, as was demonstrated by the disastrous years of 1785 and 1786. Prices were higher at the end of the eighteenth century, even if there was a larger variety of material things to be found in the marketplaces of the city. The greatly increased population of Guadalajara probably had a greater proportion of poor and underemployed people than at any point in its previous history, and vagrancy and crime had come with them. In short, the Guadalajara of 1800 shared the benefits, the glories, the disadvantages, and the malaise of growing cities the world over.

In the rural districts around the city, changes were also in evidence. There were more people traveling the country roads, collecting wood, working for other people, and tilling the soil in 1800 than in 1700. The houses of the rich were grander and those of the poor more squalid. Land which a century earlier had been unused, covered with thickets of scrub oak and other vegetation, was being grazed by herds of cattle; land which had been grazed was very often planted in maize; and land which had been planted in maize was devoted to irrigated fields of wheat. Individuals who were obviously Indians, though still numerous, were less visible than they had been in 1700. Rural villages and provincial towns were large and growing, but more people lived in the open countryside, on haciendas and ranchos, than ever before. Though most inhabitants of the countryside raised the food they ate themselves, they were more dependent than ever before on earning cash for the products available in the stores of town merchants and haciendas.

The development of commercialized agriculture in the Guadalajara region linked the growth of the city to the changes in the countryside. Increasing urban demand for the products of agriculture was met through the investment of capital drawn largely from other sectors of the economy: commerce and mining. Yet the changes in agriculture were essentially quantitative, not qualitative. The technology employed in farming remained backward and productivity low. Despite this backwardness, large-scale agriculture proved an attractive investment for those with sufficient resources to take the initial plunge and to make the periodic injections of capital necessary to keep a rural estate afloat economically. Levels of profit were low compared to more dynamic activities, but the risks were also lower, and occasional windfall profits were to be had. Moreover, the ownership of landed wealth conferred a high degree of social legitimacy and provided a way of consolidating family status. If much wealth went down the drain this way, at least the observed success of those family fortunes consolidated in the ownership of great rural estates provided a model for aspiration. The other major input in large-scale agriculture—labor—was kept relatively inexpensive through the growth of a rural population which had outstripped its land resources by the latter part of the eighteenth century. In general terms, then, the growth of Guadalajara was underwritten by the transfer of economic resources from the countryside to the city, and was subsidized through the investment of capital from more profitable economic sectors. The organizers of this system, the large propertyowners and landlords, extracted a brokerage commission for the transaction in the form of profits from commercial agriculture.

From the economic point of view, the major problem facing the Spanish sector in the Guadalajara region in the late-colonial period was the "depeasantization" or "proletarianization" of the Indian village-dwelling population, and of rural lower-class groups as a whole. This was necessary both because commercial agriculture required an ever-larger force of laborers, and also because foodstuffs and raw materials produced in the commercial sector of the rural economy required a market for their sale, and the cities and towns growing from rural emigration represented such a potential market. Drawing the peasant population into the money economy through taxation and the creation of needs for goods and services had proved to be the most effective means for accomplishing at least a partial de-peasantization before the eighteenth century. Debt peonage, tribute payments, the notorious *repartimiento de mercancías*, ecclesiastical fees, and the fiesta system were all means to this end, since the specie required for all these economic exchanges could be obtained only within the bounds of the Spanish money economy, and only at the cost of labor.

Under conditions of population decline, stability, or slow growth, with high wages and relatively great availability of land, the mechanisms instituted to draw peasants into the money economy were bound to be imperfect. Since there were economic alternatives to substantial reliance on the sale of their labor, and since a maximum degree of autonomy was the most prized condition, peasants, particularly Indians, were loath to enter the wage-labor economy. Inducements, either in the positive form of high wages and/or levels of debt, or in the negative form of reducing their resource base (expropriation of land) or legally compelling them (the labor repartimiento), had to be very strong. Even within this situation, recalcitrant peasants might escape the net and enter the money economy only on their own terms as sellers of agricultural products rather than labor: this appears to be the significance of the strong share of Indians, particularly, in the maize supply of Guadalajara up until the last decades of the eighteenth century. On the other hand, high levels of debt on rural estates before the late eighteenth century represented the mirror-image of the famous backward-bending supply curve in the labor market: they indicate a situation in which the position of laborers relative to employers was strong, since they could demand large advances as a quid pro quo for their labor, and one in which the de-peasantization process was necessarily incomplete.

During the last century of colonial rule, the push of demographic increase in the countryside replaced to a degree the pull of high wage and debt levels and legal compulsion in integrating large numbers of peasants into the commercial agricultural sector. This development parallels in some respects that in certain areas of Europe at about the same time, in which the combination of a population growth more rapid than ever before and new possibilities for capitalist agriculture led to changes in both agricultural methods and land-tenure arrangements.[1] The major difference in the Guadalajara region was that agricultural technology per se seems not to have improved. In fact, the agricultural expansion of the eighteenth century in this area of Mexico resembles even more closely the changes in Europe at an earlier period, the later medieval centuries before 1300 or so, during which—in the words of B. H. Slicher Van Bath—"the keynote was expansion" rather than technological innovation or intensification.[2] Irrigation and the methods of integrated cereal and livestock production had been known throughout the colonial period, but remained on a simple level even during the period of changing land use which began during the early eighteenth century. In place of technological innovation, a process of

1. For detailed treatments of this generally acknowledged trend, see, among others, Slicher Van Bath, *The Agrarian History of Western Europe*; Jerome Blum, *The End of the Old Order in Rural Europe* (1978); Marc Bloch, *French Rural History*; and Colin Clark, *Population Growth and Land Use* (1968), p. 135.

2. Slicher Van Bath, *Agrarian History*, p. 132; see also Murdo J. MacLeod, *Spanish Central America, 1520-1720* (1973), p. 3.

internal colonization occurred within already claimed lands which were previously unexploited because of a scarcity of labor and the lack of a strong local demand.[3] This may be thought of as a "semi-open" frontier situation, in which land was available for farming and stock-raising but had already been largely pre-empted by legal claims and titles. One aspect of this effective occupation of marginal lands was the extinction of putative rights of common usage, a practice which gave rise to sharp legal and social conflict in the countryside, especially between peasants and estate-owners. In fact, such conflicts over resources seem generally to occur with changes in agrarian structures associated with population pressure.[4]

In such a semi-open frontier situation, most of the peasant sector was effectively prohibited from taking advantage of the increasing market demand by a combination of constraining factors. The first constraint was demographic: the increase in rural population itself, with concomitant building of pressure on an essentially inelastic resource base. The second constraint, accounting for the resource inelasticity itself, was institutional: the existing land-tenure system, in which the putative legal title to most unoccupied land within the region had already been vested in non-peasant, or at least non-Indian, owners. The third constraint was economic: the inability of most peasants to meet the relatively high capital and labor requirements of cereal production for the urban market. Peasant agriculture did apparently intensify in some places, again on the basis of existing technology, to take advantage of increased market demand and probably to meet the subsistence needs of the rural population itself as well. But such intensification, along with craft production in rural areas, was not enough to absorb the energies of the growing population, given the demographic, institutional, and economic constraints. Under such conditions, excess rural manpower could only be absorbed by an economic sector or sectors with the potential for growth, and the commercialized agriculture centering on the local urban market supplied such an outlet.

The circumstances accompanying these changes during the late-colonial era in the Guadalajara region recall those of large parts of late-medieval Europe, say from 1150 to 1300, as described by B. H. Slicher Van Bath and Michael Postan. Both areas expanded their agricultural production, primarily of cereals, on the basis of an already-existing farming technology.

3. Juan Martínez Alier, "Relations of Production in Andean Haciendas," in Kenneth Duncan and Ian Rutledge, eds., *Land and Labour in Latin America* (1977), pp. 141-145, discusses this process of internal colonization, as opposed to land-grabbing or illegal encroachment on peasant lands, for Peruvian estates in the early decades of this century.

4. Ester Boserup, *The Conditions of Agricultural Growth*, pp. 84-86, and Clark, *Population Growth and Land Use*, p. 137, treat this tendency in a general fashion. For a specific historical case, very similar in its outlines to late-colonial Mexico, see Bloch, *French Rural History*, p. 198 ff.

In both areas, marginal lands acquired a new importance in the total farming picture, though they appear to have been used in somewhat different ways. In both late-medieval Europe and eighteenth-century New Galicia, the total amount of land devoted to livestock production declined under the pressure of expanding cultivation. In both areas, also, the distribution of landholdings among peasant cultivators showed a tendency to become quite uneven. A growing segment of tiny, highly fragmented holdings barely supplying the necessities for subsistence to peasant families faced a small but important segment of larger peasant holdings across a widening social gap. Furthermore, a growing landless rural population was available for labor in farming operations in both areas.[5] Here an important difference between Europe in the period 1150-1300 and the Guadalajara region in the eighteenth century does emerge, however, and that is in the realm of real wages of rural laborers. In Europe, real wages—that is, what a laborer could actually hope to buy with his labor—were on the rise during the thirteenth century, while in the Guadalajara region they appear to have fallen during the eighteenth century. The reasons behind this difference in the trend of real wages between late-medieval Europe and eighteenth-century Mexico are not clear, but a faster rate of population growth in Mexico may be one possible explanation.[6]

The internal structure of commercial agriculture and the equilibrium between city and country were both seriously affected by rural population growth. Arthur Lewis' suggestion that in certain circumstances high rates of population increase result in low wages, and therefore a decreasing pressure on profits, seems to fit the case of commercialized agriculture in the Guadalajara region.[7] The Guadalajara case indicates that profits subsidized by such low wage levels will encourage a tendency toward capital accumulation and investment at the expense of a per-capita rise in income.

5. Slicher Van Bath, *Agrarian History*, pp. 132-136. Michael M. Postan, *Essays on Medieval Agriculture* (1973), p. 16, suggests the primacy of population movement behind increases and declines in agricultural production in late-medieval England, but points to the difficulty of establishing a causal sequence. My doctoral dissertation, "Rural Life in Eighteenth-Century Mexico: The Guadalajara Region, 1675-1820" (1978), chap. 11, deals at length with economic differentiation within the peasant sector in the Guadalajara region at the end of the colonial period.

6. The agricultural boom in much of Europe in the period 1550-1650 was similar in some respects to the situation in the Guadalajara region in the eighteenth century. In Europe, population had increased, arable farming expanded at the expense of pasture, overall meat consumption apparently dropped, and real wages fell. The European situation had been complicated, however, by the effects of the influx of American silver and by signs of real innovations in agricultural technology in some regions, in contrast to the non-innovative expansion in eighteenth-century western Mexico. On Europe, see Slicher Van Bath, *Agrarian History*, pp. 195-206.

7. H. J. Habakkuk, *Population Growth and Economic Development Since 1750* (1971), p. 47; and W. Arthur Lewis, *The Theory of Economic Growth* (1955).

On the investment side of the equation, we have seen that the profitability of large-scale agriculture was sufficient to attract substantial capital from a number of sources, including mining, commerce, and the Church.

On the per-capita-income side of the equation, the data on income and living standards in the late-colonial countryside available to us are too limited to allow quantification of the trend, but this type of redistribution effect does seem to have been taking place in the Guadalajara region and perhaps elsewhere in Mexico as well. We have referred to this in Chapter 11 as a transfer of resources from the countryside to the city; but within the agricultural economy itself, it meant a shift in favor of the commercial sector at the expense of the peasant sector. The city of Guadalajara was not only provided with agricultural products from its hinterland, but also with people who swelled the ranks of urban consumers. To produce the doubling of the city's population which occurred during the decade 1760-1770, for example, the 1760 population would have had to sustain a net rate of natural increase amounting to 10 percent per year, a patent impossibility.[8] It has been suggested that under such conditions a labor scarcity may occur in the countryside because of migration to the city, bringing with it a rise in food prices.[9] That there was a rise in food prices during the late eighteenth century is undeniable, but wage levels in commercial agriculture indicate that the rate of rural population increase was apparently sufficient to keep wages low and to send a constant stream of migrants to Guadalajara at the same time.

In recent years, a number of economists and other social scientists have argued from their observations of primitive and peasant economic systems that population increase is the independent variable, and agricultural productivity the dependent variable, in changes in a rural economy. This view reverses the traditional Malthusian scheme, in which the movement of population is dependent upon the available food supply, in its turn dependent upon agricultural productivity.[10] Those theorists who assign primacy

8. Van Young, "Rural Life," p. 52.

9. Clark, *Population Growth and Land Use*, p. 136; Ester Boserup, *Conditions*, p. 118.

10. See especially Ester Boserup, *Conditions*; Clark, *Population Growth and Land Use*, pp. 60 ff. and 134 ff.; and Colin Clark and Margaret Haswell, *The Economics of Subsistence Agriculture*, 3rd ed. (1967), p. 51, for the clearest statements of this position. A number of historians looking at the relationship between population and agrarian change have confirmed such a causal sequence; see, for example, Habakkuk, *Population Growth and Economic Development*, p. 33. For a summary treatment of the general connection between population increase and economic development, see J. D. Chambers, *Population, Economy, and Society in Pre-Industrial England* (1972), esp. chap. 6. The population-primacy theory is by no means accepted by all social scientists, however. E. A. Wrigley, *Population and History*, p. 49, says the model specifically proposed by Ester Boserup is "difficult to support in its starkest form," but he acknowledges it as a "useful corrective" to the orthodox Malthusian view. Those who have closely studied economic growth in the North Atlantic economies, as well as in the underdeveloped areas of the world, have come to differing views on the subject.

in agrarian changes to population increase see demographic pressure as the force behind innovations in agricultural technology and productive arrangements. More specifically, Ester Boserup has ascribed the intensification of agriculture, through the shortening of fallowing periods, to the need to feed increasing human populations in historic tribal and peasant economies. This theory of agricultural growth explains, in a general way, the changes in the economic structure of the Guadalajara region in the late-colonial period. Certainly the importance of population growth as an initiating condition can be established in the Guadalajara case. All the production factors, techniques, and institutional arrangements involved in the commercial agricultural sector were present before 1700 or 1750, but it was only with the growth of population, especially after midcentury, that it experienced a quantum jump in its importance within the regional economy. The process of change in the countryside, and the drags upon it and resistances to it, have been detailed in the preceding chapters.

The usefulness of the population-growth theory has its limits, however, in explaining agrarian change in the Guadalajara region, and certain important modifications must be added. In the first place, in terms of market-oriented agriculture, the crop which received the largest relative injection of capital and labor resources during the late-colonial period was wheat. Under local conditions and with the available technology of the late eighteenth century, wheat was certainly lower than maize in its yield per land-unit and in its productivity per unit of labor input.[11] Nonetheless, the development of commercial agriculture was in large part encouraged by the returns to be had from the cultivation of wheat for consumption in the urban market. We are then faced with the apparent anomaly of economic development based upon a technological involution—that is, the partial transfer of resources from a more productive to a less productive form of agriculture. This directly contradicts the theory of increasing productivity under conditions of population pressure, and suggests that economic and social factors may be of equal or greater importance than ecological or technical ones in determining resource allocation.

For example, W.W. Rostow, in *The Stages of Economic Growth* (1965), p. 5, strongly suggests that the more traditional model is the correct one; while Albert O. Hirschman, in *The Strategy of Economic Development* (1958), pp. 176-182, treats the theory of population pressure as an inducement to economic development in a very cautious manner, acknowledging its validity in a general way. In fairness to Rev. Malthus, it should be noted that he himself showed some inclination to modify his ideas in later editions of the famous 1798 *Principles of Population*, particularly that of 1817, in which he obliquely suggested that population growth could be a stimulant to economic development under certain circumstances; see Clark, *Population Growth and Economic Development*, p. 60.

11. On the comparative yields of wheat and maize, see, for example, Colin Clark, *Starvation or Plenty?* (1970), p. 87 ff.; wheat is considerably higher in its protein content than maize, however.

In the case of wheat, specifically, which despite its lower yields absorbed a large share of capital investment and labor resources, we should look to the decisions of producers and consumers for an explanation of the growing importance of this food crop. On the consumption side, the surprisingly widespread desirability of wheat bread in the city (and probably larger provincial towns as well) may be laid to the processes of acculturation and socio-economic mobility in the urban environment. On the production side, the relatively high price of wheat compared to other cereals, and the constraints on its cultivation imposed by high capital requirements, made it an obvious choice for larger producers seeking to earn profits in commercialized agriculture. Such a situation does not contradict the primacy of population growth in initiating the process of change, but it does point to the need to look at more complex mediating factors in the relationship between demographic increase and changes in agrarian structure.

In the second place, the relationship between population growth and agrarian change in the Guadalajara region was predominantly distributional rather than technical. That is to say, the growth in aggregate production in agriculture, and the increase in complexity of the rural economy, depended upon alterations in the arrangement of production factors and the creation of an effective urban demand, rather than upon innovations in agricultural technology.[12] The major questions regarding the Guadalajara region, then, concern the process of resource allocation and the equilibrium between two distinct sectors of the agricultural economy, peasant farming and commercialized production. Any model of agrarian change based only on the response of tribal or peasant cultivators to demographic pressure, such as Ester Boserup's, and which does not take into account the competing economic claims of non-peasant agriculture, cannot adequately explain the economic history of the Guadalajara region, nor of large parts of Latin America as a whole. The major economic problem to be solved by the non-peasant sector was generation of a potential—a gap between resources and the subsistence needs of a large segment of the regional population. Increasingly during the course of the late-colonial period, the constraints on peasant agriculture and landholding, and the population growth itself, served to convert thousands of country-dwellers into rural proletarians and semi-proletarians whose only recourse was to sell their labor in the commercialized sector. This provided the manpower upon which commercial agricultural expansion was based. The creation of a market for the products of commercial agriculture was the contribution of urban growth, itself partially fueled by immigration from the countryside.

12. Eric R. Wolf has pointed out, in "Aspects of Group Relations in a Complex Society," *American Anthropologist* 58 (1956), p. 57, that the major innovation represented by expanding hacienda agriculture in the colonial period was in labor organization, not technology.

It is at this point that the economic function of the city of Guadalajara shows up most clearly. In fact, the role of the city in the development of commercial agriculture is often neglected in studies of rural transformations, even though it is a pivotal one.[13] In the case of the Guadalajara region, the growth of the city provided the effective demand which made large-scale agriculture profitable. Such a demand for agricultural products need not, of course, be local in origin: producing regions may be linked to national or even world markets through export agriculture. The resulting agrarian systems and the social relations which characterize them may be very different in the two cases.[14] In any event, the distinction between an externally-oriented system, such as a plantation area producing for export, and a more autocthonous system, such as the Guadalajara region, is not a rigid one. In the Guadalajara region, external demand for agricultural products and a variety of non-agricultural goods and services was effectively translated into a local demand through the ascendancy of the city as an economic, politcal, and social clearinghouse for western Mexico. Here the importance of regional commerce, mining activity, industrial and artisanal production, and government must all be acknowledged. The city, then, served as a point of economic crystallization in the transformation of the countryside around it, with its own growth due in some measure to exogenous factors. But if the economic development of Guadalajara was encouraged by external factors, the ability of the city to respond to those demands was underwritten by regional population growth. Thus ultimately we are led back to the primacy of population growth, both inside and outside the region, in initiating changes in the agrarian structure.

The de-peasantization process which fed the growth of the city and eventually provided a pool of inexpensive rural labor was considerably different in its historical outlines from that which occurred in Europe from the late-medieval period on. In Europe, the historical problem was for landlords to convert manorial peasants into tenants-at-will or proletarians. England is often cited as the classic example of this development, with landlords converting their feudal rights to private rights of landownership. In France after the sixteenth century, landlords reconstituted the demesne in order to engage in capitalist agriculture at the expense of customary rights of tenure, and of commons rights as well. The pervasiveness of landlord tenure in Europe, and the survival of the feudal principle of "nulle terre sans seigneur" well into the eighteenth century, was accom-

13. Ester Boserup, *Conditions*, p. 38, does mention a causal sequence in which increasing urban population may induce changes in agricultural technology through a growing demand for foodstuffs, but she takes the theme no further.

14. For a somewhat more detailed treatment of this idea, see my paper on "Regional Agrarian Structures."

panied by a general trend toward private rights in land and the elimination of labor relations not based on some form of free contract.[15] In Mexico, on the other hand, the problem was not for landlords to convert manorial peasants into proletarians, but to convert an independent peasantry which was only imperfectly integrated into the Spanish money economy.[16] In fact, this conversion process has been going on in large parts of Mexico ever since the eighteenth century at least, and has continued into the present century, though certainly not without much resistance and many setbacks.

The ongoing conversion of an independent peasantry into a rural proletariat has had two interesting implications for the social structure and social history of Mexico. First, the apparent resilience of the rural Indian community in the face of population pressure and the economic onslaught of non-Indians may have been due precisely to the partial entry of many village-dwellers into the commercial wage-labor economy. We are looking here at a kind of symbiotic relationship between hacienda and village. On one side, the symbiosis allowed the commercial agricultural sector to recruit necessary labor, whether through direct wage payments or some kind of service tenantry, or a combination of both. On the other side, the relationship allowed Indian peasants to earn cash and at the same time maintain their communal, village-dwelling lifestyle against the forces of demographic pressure and land scarcity. The symbiosis on the Indian side may thus have helped to underwrite the survival of a traditional way of life and a mutilated peasant economy which itself produced only exiguous surpluses.[17]

Second, the conversion of the independent peasantry, its integration into the larger economy, and the breaking open of the corporate Indian community to homogenize colonial, and later national, society, inevitably assumed the form of an ethnic conflict. In fact, the process—slowed down during the eighteenth century by the patriarchal hand of the Spanish royal government—was at bottom one of replacing social relations based upon ethnicity with those based upon class. The locus of the Indian peasant's economic identity, his village, also happened to be the locus of his ethnic

15. Ester Boserup, *Conditions*, pp. 86-87; Bloch, *French Rural History*, p. 135 ff.; Blum, *The End of the Old Order*, pp. 17-35; Mogens Boserup, "Agrarian Structure and Take-Off," in W.W. Rostow, ed., *Economics of Take-Off Into Sustained Growth* (1965), pp. 206-208.

16. Wolf, "Aspects of Group Relations," p. 56, pointed to this as the principal function of the hacienda, historically.

17. Van Young, "Regional Agrarian Structures"; Wolf, "Aspects of Group Relations," p. 57. For similar findings on the peasant-hacienda symbiosis in the Andean region, see Henri Favre, "The Dynamics of Indian Peasant Society . . . in Central Peru," in Duncan and Rutledge, eds., *Land and Labour in Latin America* (1977); and Karen Spalding, "Estructura de clases en la sierra peruana, 1750-1920," *Análisis, Cuadernos de Investigación* (Lima) 1 (1977).

and cultural identity. And even though the major force of the attack on traditional village society came not from Spanish officials or landowners, but from the increase in Indian numbers itself, the perceived cause of the increasing strain was the active encroachment on peasant resources of a growingly rapacious capitalist agriculture which happened to be in the hands of the whites. Thus the overlay of racial conflict upon the growth of an incipient class structure may be understood as the response of a hard-pressed peasantry to changes in its relationship to the means of production.

The basic changes in the regional rural economy which so altered relations of production in the countryside occurred in ways of which most contemporaries were probably not aware. Yet there were signs of increasing strains in the countryside, signs of resistance and resentment, and we have described some of these, including an obviously growing rural impoverishment and competition within and among contending groups for access to land. Both resort to the law to relieve these strains in the form of litigation, and the frequency of extralegal actions such as land invasions, increased. It also appears that the incidence of vagrancy, alcoholism, and crime rose significantly in the late-colonial period.[18]

Within this context of intensifying social and economic strain, the violent upheaval of the Hidalgo revolt, the first military phase of the Independence movement, leaps to our attention at the close of the period. Surely it was not merely by chance that, after the battle of Las Cruces, Hidalgo established his short-lived insurgent government in Guadalajara, that he received immense reinforcements of manpower from within the region, or that the huge but disorganized rebel force met defeat at the hands of the royalist army at the Puente de Calderón near Guadalajara. Hidalgo seems to have oriented some pieces of his revolutionary legislation specifically to local conditions—particularly the famous decree of December 5, 1810, regarding the rental of village communal lands—with an eye both to needed reform and a fertile ground for propaganda. Just as surely, it is not unreasonable to assume that conditions of social and economic strain in the countryside contributed as much or more than Miguel Hidalgo's propagandistic efforts to the swelling of the rebel ranks in late 1810.

18. For the Guadalajara region, this statement is admittedly impressionistic, based on contemporary comment rather than quantitative documentary evidence, but the trend seems to hold true for all of Mexico. Colin M. MacLachlan implies strongly in his essay on the Acordada, *Criminal Justice in Eighteenth-Century Mexico* (1974), esp. pp. 30-32, that vagrancy and associated forms of deviant behavior increased significantly in the late-colonial period in Mexico as a whole, though he nowhere gives specific figures. William B. Taylor, in his recent comparative study of central Mexico and Oaxaca, *Drinking, Homicide, and Rebellion in Colonial Mexican Villages* (1979), passim, states that the incidence of alcoholism, homicide, and local rebellion rose in the eighteenth century, but he points to regional differences related primarily to village community structure.

Yet such a knee-jerk explanation for the Guadalajara phase of the rebellion is not ultimately very convincing, or at best provides only a partial answer. There are several reasons why such an appealingly simple connection between conditions of rural impoverishment and rural rebellion is not acceptable. In the first place, we simply don't know very much about the social composition of the Hidalgo movement, either at its inception in the Bajío or during its later phase in Guadalajara, and this despite a torrent of historical scholarship and polemic by Mexicans and others.[19] For example, where did the 40,000 or more insurgent troops who flocked to Hidalgo's banner in the first weeks of 1811 come from?[20] Were they local people from near Guadalajara, or from farther away? Were they village Indians, hacienda laborers, mestizo smallholders, provincial townsmen? Thus, while we know a good deal about the directive superstructure of the early insurgency—about the creole-peninsular rift, lines of intragroup stress within the creole elite, and early liberal and reformist ideology—we know virtually nothing about the social relationships involved. Any attempt to tie the support of such a movement to social and economic conditions in the countryside must await the answers to these and other questions.

In the second place, a growing body of historical and theoretical literature has seriously called into question the simple cause-effect relationship between absolute deprivation and rebellion, and has pointed to the important intervening variables of relative deprivation, socio-economic disjunction, popular perception, and social structure as basic determining factors in the rise of popular movements against established authority. The present lack of data on the movement itself thus prevents any thorough application of theoretical concepts to it.

Finally, much of what we do know either contradicts the knee-jerk theory or complicates the picture greatly. For example, not only during the pre-Guadalajara phase of the revolt but in the protracted guerrilla phase after it, when the locus of military activity had shifted to southern Mexico but roaming insurgent bands (*gavillas*) still occasionally terrorized the coun-

19. Recent and sophisticated works by Mexican and non-Mexican scholars alike show a virtually complete lack of information on the social composition and dynamics of the Hidalgo movement below the level of the creole directorate; the Bajío phase of the rebellion receives some attention, but Guadalajara remains in a vacuum. See Ramírez Flores, *El gobierno insurgente*; Hamill, *The Hidalgo Revolt*; and Brading, *Los orígenes del nacionalismo mexicano*, except for the comments in the last few pages of the book. Significantly, Brading in his treatment of eighteenth-century agrarian structure in the Bajío, *Haciendas and Ranchos*, avoids speculating at all on the relationship between the leadership structure and the social origins of the Hidalgo rebellion. John M. Tutino, "Life and Labor on North Mexican Haciendas," in Frost, Meyer, and Vázquez, comps., *El trabajo y los trabajadores en la historia de México* (1979), makes some valuable and provocative comments on adherence to the Hidalgo movement in the near north of central Mexico.

20. Hamill, *The Hidalgo Revolt*, pp. 197-198.

tryside of western central Mexico, local landowners were able to field their own defense forces, drawn largely from the same groups of estate laborers and other retainers who are often presumed to have been part of Hidalgo's forces. Again, most of the victims of the insurgent government during the bloody purge in Guadalajara were European Spaniards, but very few of them were landowners, and we have as yet no particular evidence that large landowners or their properties were victimized in the countryside except for strictly military needs. It is clear, in fact, that the Hidalgo revolt was a complex, layered movement in which the selective use of violence, the choice of victims, and the social and political objectives were determined by contending groups for different reasons. It was no less a monolithic force rising from below in the form of a peasant *jacquerie* than it was a rational political revolution with fixed goals directed from above. The truth lay somewhere in between and is still buried in the contemporary documents. Notwithstanding these important reservations, it would indeed be surprising if regional development and agrarian conditions had not contributed to the history of the movement, especially in its Guadalajara phase. For the present that is the most we can say.

The economic development of the Guadalajara region stands in marked contrast to that of other areas of colonial Mexico which have been studied in detail, though substantially the same variables were at play. Taylor in his work on Oaxaca, for example, points to the viability of the Indian landholding community and the Indian landowning nobility at the close of the colonial period, in contrast to the relatively weak and unstable hacienda system and the minor role of large non-Indian landowners in valley life. In Oaxaca, the Indian economy was neither particularly hard-pressed nor marginal, and was certainly not on the defensive. A credible explanation for Indian economic dominance in the Oaxaca countryside may be found in the combination of a dense Indian population with a local urban market (Antequera) of relatively small size.[21]

In the Bajío, studied by Brading, the exiguous Indian population had largely lost its ethnic identity by the end of the colonial period. The rural economy, oriented toward supplying the local towns and mining centers, was dominated by a combination of large estates and small-to-middling farms and ranchos operated by non-Indians with a paid labor force. Here sharecropping and renting assured hacienda income, and demesne farming played a relatively minor role. The flow of capital and personnel between the mining and agricultural sectors underwrote the social and economic

21. The population of Antequera remained basically stable throughout the last half-century of colonial rule, while that of Guadalajara doubled. By the mid-1770s, Guadalajara's total population was very likely to be already bigger than that of greater Antequera, including the neighboring Villa de Oaxaca (Taylor, *Landlord and Peasant*, pp. 18-19).

dominance of large landowners in the countryside, even while a small but important group of provincial ranchers, merchants, and professional men formed a buffer between the white elite group and the mass of rural proletarians and peasants.[22]

In the Guadalajara region, the growing urban market of the late eighteenth century acted like a dynamo in the rural economy. Compared to the Oaxaca area, Indian landholding villages did not thrive, except in numbers, and if they managed to retain control of much land, they were definitely on the defensive economically in the face of a growing commercialized agriculture dominated by large production units. Compared to the Bajío, on the other hand, the Indian village population was relatively dense and provided a large, cheap labor pool. Demesne farming by large hacendados seems to have been relatively more important in the Guadalajara region than in the Bajío, with a concomitantly lessened role for renting and share-cropping in the hacienda economy and in the social structure of the countryside. The evolution of the rural economy in the Guadalajara region, then, constitutes yet another permutation in the regional development of Mexico; and if the elements of the picture are much the same in these three regions—city, population, rural village, labor institutions, availability of land—the final products are strikingly different.

The scheme elaborated in the preceding chapters helps to fill out our notions of colonial economic development, urban history, and the nature of the hacienda as an economic type. In particular, it points to the importance of an urban market in integrating a large region economically, and to the considerable degree of flexibility on the part of the hacienda in participating in that market. While hacendados generally strove to reduce their costs as much as possible, the rural estates of the Guadalajara region were never the vast, self-contained enterprises that haciendas have often been pictured. Thus there appears another crack in the monolithic model of the traditional hacienda as a rural economic type.

The wealthy hacendado families which took a commission for organizing the rural economy in the form of profits, prestige, and political power were only the proximate cause of change in the countryside. Basically, they were the intermediaries in a very long process which has occurred in the last few centuries not only in colonial New Galicia, or in Mexico, or even in Latin America, but all over the world: the death of the historical peasantry and the growth of modern urban-industrial society. This process has moved at different rates and has created different effects everywhere in the world. It has been set back temporarily by violent political upheavals, of which the Mexican Revolution itself is but one example. In much of the underde-

22. Brading, *Haciendas and Ranchos*, passim.

veloped world, the process has only recently begun and has not made much headway as yet. Yet the strains wracking the modern world are in large measure assignable to this complex happening.

More particularly, the history of Mexico may be seen in these terms, even if such a view provides only partial explanations for its evolution. The conversion of the Indian peasantry into rural proletarians and urban dwellers was well advanced already by the end of the colonial period, and its origins went at least as far back as the middle of the eighteenth century. The tremendous growth of Guadalajara and other Mexican cities has not been without its costs, therefore. In return for its subsistence, the city has offered a refuge to countless immigrants from the countryside—but at the price of a way of life which has forever vanished.

GLOSSARY OF SPANISH TERMS

abastecedor: meat monopoly holder

abasto de carnes: meat supply monopoly in a city or town, usually rented out by municipal government

alcabala: sales tax

alcalde mayor: district magistrate

alcalde ordinario: municipal magistrate

alhóndiga: central granary in a city or town

almacenero: wholesale merchant

ancón: floodplain

arrendatario: renter

Audiencia: royal high court of justice

aviador: supplier of working capital or goods to an agricultural enterprise; usually a merchant

avíos: working capital or goods

ayuntamiento: city council

barranca: ravine

barrio: a district of a city

bodega: storehouse

Br.: abbreviated form of Bachiller, the honorific title of a secular priest

caballería: unit of agricultural land measurement equivalent to 105.8 acres

cabildo: city council

cacique: Indian noble

caja: royal treasury; also, a box

calicata: sliding price scale for bread relating it to price of wheat

capellanía: ecclesiastical benefice or chaplaincy

carga: a load, generally of two fanegas, or about 200 pounds

casta: a person of mixed blood

çédula: an order

cofradía: a lay ecclesiastical brotherhood attached to a parish church; a sodality

compadrazgo: fictive or ritual kinship

composición: regularization of defective land titles; the fee paid to the Crown in such a transaction consulado: merchants' guild

corregidor: district magistrate

denuncia: a judicial claim to land

dobla: peak seasonal demand period in agricultural repartimiento

ejido: lands held communally by a township, generally used for grazing and wood collecting

encomendero: holder of an Indian encomienda; also, a commission merchant or factor

encomienda: a grant by the Spanish Crown of the right to collect tribute and labor from Indians within a specified area; also, the practice of commission sales in the grain market

escribanía: notarial office

escribano: public notary

estancia: livestock estate

fábrica: factory

fanega: unit of dry measure; about 1.5 bushels

fanega de sembradura: area sown with one fanega of maize; about nine acres

fiscal: Crown or city attorney

fundo legal: standard township site

gañán: peón; an estate laborer

hacendado: owner of a rural estate, or hacienda

hacienda: a large rural estate, typically based on a mixture of grain farming and livestock production

heredad: rural property

herido de molino: mill site

hospicio: poorhouse, orphanage

indio laborío: resident Indian estate laborer

jornalero: laborer

junta: a commission

juzgado de capellanías: ecclesiastical court having jurisdiction over chaplaincies and their distribution

labor: grain farm

labrador: farmer

maíz: corn

mayorazgo: entailed estate; holder of an entailed estate

mayordomo: foreman or supervisor

merced: land grant by the Spanish Crown

mesta: stockmen's association

mestizo: person of mixed European and Indian blood

monte: uncleared scrub land used for livestock grazing, usually on a hillside

obraje: workshop or factory, generally for textiles

oidor: judge sitting on an Audiencia

peón: laborer

plan: clearing

pósito: stock of grain (generally maize) maintained by municipal government for purpose of manipulating grain market

principal: an important Indian commoner

pulpería: a small store

ranchero: small agriculturist; owner or renter of a rancho

rancho: small agricultural property, generally combining farming and livestock production

real: unit of money equal to one-eighth of a peso; also, a mining camp

real çédula: a royal order

realengo: unoccupied land belonging to the Crown

regatón: small-scale speculator in foodstuffs; regrater

regidor: city councilman

regidor alférez real: senior member of city council

repartimiento: forced wage-labor draft applied to Indians, usually in agriculture

repartimiento de mercancías: forced sale of merchandise at inflated prices, generally by a district magistrate (corregidor) to local Indians

saladero: simple processing plant for salting down beef, developed in Argentine pampas region during nineteenth century

sembradura: farmed land

señoríos: small city-states

sitio de ganado mayor: land grant for grazing cattle and horses, measuring 4,388.9 acres

sitio de ganado menor: land grant for grazing sheep and goats, measuring 1,928.4 acres

subdelegado: district magistrate, similar to earlier corregidor and alcalde mayor

suertes de huerta: fruit and vegetable plots

sujeto: Indian town subject to political jurisdiction of a larger town

tabla: butcher shop

tapatío: a native of Guadalajara

temporal: farming without irrigation or unirrigated farm land

tendejón: a small retail store

teniente: a deput district magistrate

tesorero juez official: treasury official

tienda de raya: store on a hacienda selling goods on credit to resident laborers

tlatoanazgo: an Indian chieftainship

trigo: wheat

vaquero: herdsman

vara: unit of measure, about thirty-three inches

vecino: a householder; citizen of a city or town

visitador: investigator

BIBLIOGRAPHY

Archives

Archivo General de la Nación, Mexico City (AGN)

Documents from the AGN used in this study were exclusively those from the Ramo de Jesuítas, graciously lent to me in transcription by Sr. Salvador Reynoso of the Universidad Autónoma de Guadalajara. They concern chiefly the Jesuit (until 1767) Hacienda de Toluquilla and are few in number but important in content.

Archivo Histórico Municipal de Guadalajara (AHMG)

This rich repository of materials on the city's history contains some 250 boxes of documents covering the period from the seventeenth century until 1913; only about the first 50 pertain to the colonial period. This is the main source for studying the evolution of the urban market and the efforts of the city government to regulate the food supply of Guadalajara. Of particular value are the records of the city's granaries and meat monopoly.

Archivo de Instrumentos Públicos de Guadalajara (AIPG)

Libros de Gobierno de la Audiencia de Nueva Galicia (LG)

The 80 volumes in this series cover the period 1675-1750, approximately. They include land and repartimiento grants, licenses of all kinds issued by the Audiencia (for the use of livestock brands, for livestock exports, for the erection of mills, etc.), and confirmations of various kinds of minor officials.

Protocolos de notarios públicos (prot.)

An indispensable source for colonial (and modern) social and economic history, the protocolos are the records of the public notaries of Guadalajara. They contain legal instruments of all kinds, including testaments, dowry agreements, contracts, property sales, and rentals. There are many hundreds of volumes in the collection, running up to the modern period. For this study, most of the major eighteenth-century notarial series were consulted exhaustively. In alphabetical order, they are as follows:

Guadalupe Altamirano, 6 vols., 1822-1834
Miguel Tomás de Ascoide, 3 vols., 1674-1693
Antonio de Ayala Natera, 8 vols., 1699-1715
Urbano A. Ballesteros, 25 vols., 1783-1796

Antonio de Berroa, 26 vols., 1757-1782
Nicolás del Castillo, 14 vols., 1693-1706
José María Cruz Ahedo, 2 vols., 1797-1805
Antonio Fernández Echasco, 5 vols., 1720-1737
Juan García de Argomaniz, 36 vols., 1708-1737
Thadeo Leyva Carrillo, 3 vols., 1756-1781
José Antonio Mallen, 2 vols., 1790-1794
Alejo de Santa María Maraver, 16 vols., 1730-1752
Manuel de Mena[1] (the elder), 35 vols., 1711-1752
Manuel de Mena[2] (the younger), 23 vols., 1724-1762
Antonio Morelos, 9 vols., 1697-1734
José Antonio Sánchez de Lara, 2 vols., 1757-1760
José Tomás de Sandi, 16 vols., 1796-1822
Ignacio de la Sierra, 7 vols., 1766-1785
Blas de Silva, 36 vols., 1748-1795
José de Tapia Palacios, 2 vols., 1678-1735
Pueblo de Tlajomulco (no notary given), 2 vols., 1733-1820
Miguel de Vargas, 17 vols., 1722-1745
Pueblo de Zapotlanejo (no notary given), 3 vols., 1705-1833

Ramo de Tierras y Aguas (Tierras)

The more than 300 folio volumes of this collection provide a wealth of information on colonial land-holding patterns through the litigation records they contain. Also included are hundreds of maps detailing land boundaries.

Biblioteca Pública del Estado (de Jalisco), Guadalajara (BPE)

Archivo Fiscal de la Audiencia de Nueva Galicia (AFA)

The 1,500 volumes of this rich but uneven collection are largely unindexed. They contain records of royal tax collections of all kinds, including mintage records and sales tax (alcabala) receipts.

Archivo Judicial de la Audiencia de Nueva Galicia (AJA)

There are several hundred boxes of documents in this collection, consisting of records of civil and criminal proceedings at law. Aside from the legal records themselves, there are a large number of wills, inventories and evaluations of property, and accounts of various kinds.

Archivo del Juzgado General de Bienes de Difuntos (BD)

In this collection are some 200 legajos of documents relating to those peninsular Spaniards who died intestate in New Galicia. Since a great many of these men were landowners and merchants, the inventories and other records of the collection are an important source for the study of rural economy. Mixed in with this collection are also a large number of records which more properly belong in the AJA.

Manuscritos Catalogados (MC)

This is an uneven miscellany of several hundred manuscripts, including local description and history, documents relating to the city's religious establishments, and other items.

Catedral de Guadalajara (CG)
    Archivo del Arzobispado de Guadalajara (AAG)
        This collection was not extensively used in the preparation of the study. The documents consulted were a handful of pastoral inspections made by late colonial bishops of parishes in the Guadalajara region.
    Archivo de la Secretaría del Cabildo (Eclesiástico) (ACE)
        The documents consulted in this collection for the present study chiefly relate to the collection of ecclesiastical tithes on agricultural production; they are not so much actual records of production as administrative documents.

Books, Articles, and Manuscripts

Abler, Ronald, John S. Adams, and Peter Gould. *Spatial Organization: The Geographer's View of the World.* Englewood Cliffs, N.J.: Prentice-Hall, 1971.

Altman, Ida, and James Lockhart, eds. *Provinces of Early Mexico: Variants of Spanish American Regional Evolution.* Los Angeles: Latin American Center, University of California, 1976.

Amaya, Jesús. *Ameca, protofundación mexicana.* Mexico City: Editorial Lumen, 1951.

––––––. *Los conquistadores Fernández de Hijar y Bracamonte.* Guadalajara: Edición del Gobierno del Estado, 1952.

Anes, Gonzalo. *Las crisis agrarias en la España moderna.* Madrid: Taurus Ediciones, 1970.

Arregui, Domingo Lázaro de. *Descripción de la Nueva Galicia.* Edited by François Chevalier. Seville: Consejo Superior de Investigaciones Científicas, Escuela de Estudios Hispano-Americanos, 1946.

Bakewell, Peter J. *Silver Mining and Society in Colonial Mexico.* Cambridge Latin American Studies no. 15. Cambridge, Engl.: Cambridge University Press, 1971.

Banda, Lónginos. *Estadística de Jalisco.* Guadalajara: Tipografía de I. Banda, 1873.

Baraona, Rafael, Jimena Aranda, and Roberto Santana. *Valle de Putaendo: estudio de estructura agraria.* Santiago: Universidad de Chile, Instituto de Geografía, 1961.

Bárcena, Mariano. *Ensayo estadístico del estado de Jalisco.* Mexico City: Oficina tipográfica de la Secretaría de Fomento, 1888.

Barrett, Ward. "The Meat Supply of Colonial Cuernavaca." *Annals of the Association of American Geographers* 64 (1974): 525-540.

––––––. *The Sugar Hacienda of the Marqueses del Valle.* Minneapolis: University of Minnesota Press, 1970.

Bassols Batalla, Angel. *La división económica regional de México.* Mexico City: Universidad Nacional Autónoma de México, 1967.

––––––. *Recursos naturales (climas, aguas, suelos),* 2nd ed. Mexico City: Editorial Nuestro Tiempo, 1969.

Bauer, Arnold J. "Chilean Rural Labor in the Nineteenth Century." *American Historical Review* 76 (1971): 1059-1083.

―――. *Chilean Rural Society from the Spanish Conquest to 1930.* Cambridge Latin American Studies no. 21. Cambridge, Engl.: Cambridge University Press, 1975.

―――. "The Church and Spanish American Agrarian Structure: 1765-1865." *The Americas* 28 (1971): 78-98.

Bazant, Jan. *Cinco haciendas mexicanas: tres siglos de vida rural en San Luis Potosí (1600-1910).* Centro de Estudios Históricos, new series no. 20. Mexico City: El Colegio de México, 1975.

―――. "Peones, arrendatarios y aparceros en México, 1851-1853." *Historia Mexicana* 90 (1973): 330-357.

―――. "Una tarea primordial de la historia económica latinoamericana: el estudio de la economía de las haciendas en el siglo XIX, el caso de México." In *La Historia económica en América Latina,* vol. 2, pp. 111-116. Sep-Setentas no. 47. Mexico City: Secretaría de Educación Pública, 1972.

Benítez, José R. *Conquistadores de Nueva Galicia, fundadores de Guadalajara.* Guadalajara: Imprenta Universitaria, 1942.

Bentura Beleña, Eusebio. *Recopilación sumaria de todos los autos acordados de la Real Audiencia y Sala del Crímen de esta Nueva España.* 2 vols. Mexico City, 1787.

Berry, Brian J.L. *Geography of Market Centers and Retail Distribution.* Englewood Cliffs, N.J.: Prentice-Hall, 1967.

Berthe, Jean-Pierre. "Introduction à l'histoire de Guadalajara et de sa région." In Centre National de la Recherche Scientifique, *Villes et régions en Amérique Latine,* pp. 69-76.

Bloch, Marc. *French Rural History.* Translated by Janet Sondheimer. Berkeley and Los Angeles: University of California Press, 1966.

Blum, Jerome. *The End of the Old Order in Rural Europe.* Princeton, N.J.: Princeton University Press, 1978.

Borah, Woodrow. "Discontinuity and Continuity in Mexican History." *Pacific Historical Review* 48 (1979): 1-25.

―――. *New Spain's Century of Depression.* Ibero-Americana no. 35. Berkeley and Los Angeles: University of California Press, 1951. Spanish version: *El siglo de la depresión en Nueva España.* Sep-Setentas no. 221. Mexico City: Secretaría de Educación Pública, 1975.

―――. *Silk Raising in Colonial Mexico.* Ibero-Americana no. 20. Berkeley and Los Angeles: University of California Press, 1943.

―――. "Los tributos y su recaudación en la Audiencia de la Nueva Galicia en el siglo XVI." In García Martínez, ed., *Historia y sociedad,* pp. 27-48.

―――, and Sherburne F. Cook. *The Aboriginal Population of Central Mexico on the Eve of the Spanish Conquest.* Ibero-Americana no. 45. Berkeley and Los Angeles: University of California Press, 1963.

―――. *The Population of Central Mexico in 1548: An Analysis of the Suma de visitas de pueblos.* Ibero-Americana no. 43. Berkeley and Los Angeles: University of California Press, 1960.

Borde, Jean, and Mario Góngora. *La propiedad rural en el Valle del Puangue.* 2 vols. Santiago: Universidad de Chile, Instituto de Geografía, 1956.

Boserup, Ester. *The Conditions of Agricultural Growth.* Chicago: Aldine, 1965.

Boserup, Mogens. "Agrarian Structure and Take-Off." In W. W. Rostow, ed., *Economics of Take-Off Into Sustained Growth*, pp. 201-224. London: Macmillan, 1965.

Brading, David A. "La estructura de la producción agrícola en el Bajío de 1700 a 1850." *Historia Mexicana* 23 (1972): 197-237.

————. "Grupos étnicos, clases y estructura occupacional en Guanajuato, 1792." *Historia Mexicana* 21 (1972): 460-480.

————. "Hacienda Profits and Tenant Farming in the Mexican Bajio." Unpublished manuscript, 1972.

————. *Haciendas and Ranchos in the Mexican Bajío: León, 1700-1860.* Cambridge Latin American Studies no. 32. Cambridge, Engl.: Cambridge University Press, 1978.

————. "La minería de la plata en el siglo XVIII: el caso Bolaños." *Historia Mexicana* 18 (1969): 317-333.

————. *Miners and Merchants in Bourbon Mexico, 1763-1810.* Cambridge Latin American Studies no. 10. Cambridge, Engl.: Cambridge University Press, 1971.

————. *Los orígenes del nacionalismo mexicano.* Sep-Setentas no. 82. Mexico City: Secretaría de Educación Pública, 1973.

————, and Celia Wu. "Population Growth and Crisis: León, 1720-1816." *Journal of Latin American Studies* 5 (1973): 1-36.

Calderón de la Barca, Fanny. *Life in Mexico.* Edited by Howard T. Fisher and Marion Hall Fisher. New York: Doubleday, 1966.

Carmagnani, Marcelo. "Demografía y sociedad: La estructura social de los centros mineros del norte de México, 1600-1720." *Historia Mexicana* 21 (1972): 419-459.

Carrasco, Pedro. "The Civil-Religious Hierarchy in Mesoamerican Communities: Pre-Spanish Background and Colonial Development." *American Anthropologist* 63 (1961): 483-497.

Carrera Stampa, Manuel. "The Evolution of Weights and Measures in New Spain." *Hispanic American Historical Review* 29 (1949): 2-24.

Castañeda, Carmen, with the collaboration of Richard Lindley, Helen Ladrón de Guevara, and Eric Van Young. "Los archivos de Guadalajara." *Historia Mexicana* 25 (1975): 143-162.

Centre National de la Recherche Scientifique, Institut des Hautes Études de l'Amérique Latine. Recherche Coopérative no. 147. *Villes et régions en Amérique Latine*, vol. 1. Paris: CNRS, 1970.

Chambers, J. D. "Enclosure and Labour Supply in the Industrial Revolution." *Economic History Review*, 2nd series no. 5 (1953): 319-343.

———. *Population, Economy, and Society in Pre-Industrial England*. London: Oxford University Press, 1972.

Chávez Hayhoe, Arturo. "El establecimiento de Guadalajara." In Instituto Nacional de Antropología e Historia, *Lecturas históricas sobre Jalisco*, pp. 102-107.

———. *Guadalajara de antaño*. Guadalajara: Editorial Industrial de Jalisco, 1960.

Chayanov, A. V. *The Theory of Peasant Economy*. Edited by D. Thorner, R. E. F. Smith, and B. Kerblay. Homewood, Ill.: R. D. Irwin, for the American Economic Association, 1966.

Chevalier, François. *La formation des grandes domaines au Mexique, terre et société aux XVIe-XVIIe siècles*. Paris: Université de Paris, Institut d'Ethnologie, 1952. English version: *Land and Society in Colonial Mexico: The Great Hacienda*. Edited by Lesley Byrd Simpson; translated by Alvin Eustis. Berkeley and Los Angeles: University of California Press, 1966.

———. "The North Mexican Hacienda: Eighteenth and Nineteenth Centuries." In Archibald R. Lewis and Thomas F. McGann, eds., *The New World Looks at Its History*, pp. 95-107. Austin: University of Texas Press, 1963.

———. ed. *Instrucciones a los hermanos jesuítas administradores de haciendas*. Universidad Nacional Autónoma de México, Instituto de Historia, 1st series no. 18. Mexico City: Editorial Jus, 1950.

Chisholm, Michael. *Rural Settlement and Land Use*. Chicago: Aldine, 1962.

Clark, Colin. *Population Growth and Land Use*. London: Macmillan, 1968.

———. *Starvation or Plenty?* New York: Taplinger, 1970.

———, and Margaret Haswell. *The Economics of Subsistence Agriculture*, 3rd ed. London: Macmillan, 1967.

Coatsworth, John H. "Obstacles to Economic Growth in Nineteenth-Century Mexico." *American Historical Review* 83 (1978): 80-100.

Colección de acuerdos, órdenes y decretos sobre tierras, casas y solares de los indígenas. Bienes de sus comunidades, y fundos legales de los pueblos del estado de Jalisco. 6 vols. Guadalajara: Imprenta del gobierno del estado, 1849-1882.

Colmenares, Germán. *Las haciendas de los jesuítas en el Nuevo Reino de Granada*. Bogotá: Universidad Nacional de Colombia, Dirección de Divulgación Cultural, 1969.

Cook, Sherburne F. "The Hunger Hospital in Guadalajara, an Experiment in Medical Relief." *Bulletin of the History of Medicine* 8 (1940): 533-545.

———. "Las migraciones en la historia de la población mexicana: Datos modelo del occidente del centro de México." In García Martinez, ed., *Historia y sociedad*, pp. 355-378.

———, and Woodrow Borah. *Essays in Population History: Mexico and the Caribbean*. 3 vols. Berkeley and Los Angeles: University of California Press, 1974-1980.

———. *The Indian Population of Central Mexico, 1531-1610*. Ibero-Americana no. 44. Berkeley and Los Angeles: University of California Press, 1960.

————. *The Population of the Mixteca Alta, 1520-1960.* Ibero-Americana no. 50. Berkeley and Los Angeles: University of California Press, 1968.

Cooper, Donald B. "Epidemic Disease in Mexico City, 1761-1813." Ph.D. dissertation, University of Texas at Austin, 1963. Ann Arbor, Mich.: University Microfilms.

Cornejo Franco, José. *La Calle de San Francisco.* Guadalajara: n.p., 1945.

————. "El paseo del pendón." In Instituto Nacional de Antropología e Historia, *Lecturas históricas sobre Jalisco,* pp. 141-142.

————, ed. *Testimonios de Guadalajara.* Mexico City: Universidad Nacional Autónoma de México, 1942.

Costeloe, Michael P. *Church Wealth in Mexico: A Study of the "Juzgado de Capellanías" in the Archibishopric of Mexico, 1800-1856.* Cambridge Latin American Studies no. 2. Cambridge, Engl.: Cambridge University Press, 1967.

Couturier, Edith Boorstein. "Hacienda of Hueyapan: The History of a Mexican Social and Economic Institution, 1550-1940." Ph.D. dissertation, Columbia University, 1965. Ann Arbor, Mich.: University Microfilms.

Cross, Harry E. "The Mining Economy of Zacatecas, Mexico, in the Nineteenth Century." Ph.D. dissertation, University of California, Berkeley, 1976. Ann Arbor, Mich.: University Microfilms.

Dávila Garibi, José Ignacio. *El pequeño cacicazgo de Cocollán.* Guadalajara: Publicaciones de la Junta Auxiliar de la Sociedad Mexicana de Geografía y Estadística en el Estado de Jalisco, 1918.

Díaz, Sévero. *Geografía general y física del estado de Jalisco.* Guadalajara: Universidad de Guadalajara, 1946.

————. *El suelo de Jalisco.* Guadalajara: Editorial Jaime, 1933.

Documentos para la historia económica de México. Edited by Luis Chávez Orozco. 12 vols. Mexico City: Secretaría de la Economía Nacional, 1933-1938.

Duncan, Kenneth, and Ian Rutledge, eds., with the collaboration of Colin Harding. *Land and Labour in Latin America: Essays on the Development of Agrarian Capitalism in the Nineteenth and Twentieth Centuries.* Cambridge Latin American Studies no. 26. Cambridge, Engl.: Cambridge University Press, 1977.

Dusenberry, William H. *The Mexican Mesta: The Administration of Ranching in Colonial Mexico.* Urbana: University of Illinois Press, 1963.

Favre, Henri. "The Dynamics of Indian Peasant Society and Migration to Coastal Plantations in Central Peru." In Duncan and Rutledge, eds., *Land and Labour in Latin America,* pp. 253-268.

Flores Caballero, Romeo. "La consolidación de vales reales en la economía, la sociedad y la política novohispanas." *Historia Mexicana* 18 (1969): 334-378.

Florescano, Enrique. "Colonización, ocupación del suelo y 'frontera' en el norte de Nueva España, 1521-1750." In Alvaro Jara, ed., *Tierras nuevas; expansión territorial y ocupación del suelo en América (siglos XVI-XIX),* pp. 43-76. Centro de Estudios Históricos, new series no. 7. Mexico City: El Colegio de México, 1969.

———. *Estructuras y problemas agrarios de México (1500-1821)*. Sep-Setentas no. 2. Mexico City: Secretaría de Educación Pública, 1971.

———. *Precios del maíz y crisis agrícolas en México (1708-1810)*. Centro de Estudios Históricos, new series no. 4. Mexico City: El Colegio de México, 1969.

———. "El problema agrario en los últimos años del virreinato, 1800-1821." *Historia Mexicana* 20 (1971), 477-510.

———, and Isabel Gil, comps. *Descripciones económicas generales de Nueva España, 1784-1817*. Fuentes para la historia económica de México, vol. 1. Mexico City: Instituto Nacional de Antropología e Historia, 1973.

Fonseca, Fabián de, and Carlos de Urrutia. *Historia general de Real Hacienda escrita por órden del virrey, conde de Revillagigedo*. 6 vols. Mexico City, 1845-1853.

García Martínez, Bernardo, ed. *Historia y sociedad en el mundo de habla española; homenaje a José Miranda*. Centro de Estudios Históricos, new series no. 11. Mexico City: El Colegio de México, 1970.

Gerhard, Peter. *A Guide to the Historical Geography of New Spain*. Cambridge Latin American Studies no. 14. Cambridge, Engl.: Cambridge University Press, 1972.

Gibson, Charles. "The Aztec Aristocracy in Colonial Mexico." *Comparative Studies in Society and History* 2 (1959-1960): 169-196.

———. *The Aztecs Under Spanish Rule: A History of the Indians of the Valley of Mexico, 1519-1810*. Stanford, Calif.: Stanford University Press, 1964.

Góngora, Mario. *Orígen de los inquilinos de Chile central*. Santiago: Universidad de Chile, 1960.

González, Luis. *Pueblo en vilo: microhistoria de San José de Gracia*. Centro de Estudios Históricos, new series no. 1. Mexico City: El Colegio de México, 1968.

González Navarro, Moisés. *Raza y tierra; La guerra de castas y el henequén*. Centro de Estudios Históricos, new series no. 10. Mexico City: El Colegio de México, 1970.

———. *Repartimiento de indios en Nueva Galicia*. Museo Nacional de la Historia, scientific series no 1. Mexico City: Instituto Nacional de Antropología e Historia, 1953.

González Sánchez, Isabel. *Haciendas y ranchos de Tlaxcala en 1712*. Mexico City: Instituto Nacional de Antropología e Historia, 1969.

———. "La retención por deudas y los traslados de trabajadores tlaquehuales o alquilados en las haciendas, como sustitución de los repartimientos de indios durante el siglo XVIII." Instituto Nacional de Antropología e Historia, *Anales* 19 (1966): 241-250.

Goubert, Pierre. *Beauvais et le Beauvaisis de 1600 à 1730, contribution à l'histoire sociale de la France du XVIIᵉ siècle*. Paris: S.E.V.P.E.N., 1960.

———. *Louis XIV and Twenty Million Frenchmen*. Translated by Anne Carter. New York: Random House, Vintage Books, 1972.

Greenleaf, Richard. "The Little War of Guadalajara." *New Mexico Historical Review* 43 (1968): 119-135.

Greenow, Linda L. "Spatial Dimensions of the Credit Market in Eighteenth-Century Nueva Galicia." In Robinson, ed., *Social Fabric and Spatial Structure in Colonial Latin America*, pp. 227-279.

Guadalajara, Ayuntamiento de. *Estudios del régimen anual de lluvias en Guadalajara, período 1874-1964*. Boletín no. 1. Guadalajara: Ayuntamiento, 1966.

Guthrie, Chester L. "A Seventeenth-Century Ever-Normal Granary: The Alhóndiga of Colonial Mexico City." *Agricultural History* 15 (1941): 37-43.

Gutiérrez y Ulloa, Antonio [Intendant of Guadalajara]. "Ensayo histórico-político del Reino de la Nueva Galicia, con notas políticas, y estadísticas de la Provincia de Guadalajara." Manuscript, 1816. In the Bancroft Library, University of California, Berkeley.

Habakkuk, H.J. *Population Growth and Economic Development Since 1750*. Leicester, Engl.: Leicester University Press, 1971.

Hamill, Hugh M. *The Hidalgo Revolt: Prelude to Mexican Independence*. Gainesville: University of Florida Press, 1966.

Hamnett, Brian R. *Politics and Trade in Southern Mexico, 1750-1821*. Cambridge Latin American Studies no. 12. Cambridge, Engl.: Cambridge University Press, 1971.

Hardoy, Jorge E., ed. *Urbanization in Latin America: Approaches and Issues*. New York: Doubleday, Anchor Books, 1975.

————, and Richard P. Schaedel, comps. *Las ciudades de América Latina y sus áreas de influencia a través de la historia*. Buenos Aires: Ediciones SIAP, 1975.

Haring, C.H. *The Spanish Empire in America*. New York: Harcourt, Brace, 1947.

Harris, Charles H., III. *A Mexican Family Empire: The Latifundio of the Sánchez Navarros, 1765-1867*. Austin: University of Texas Press, 1975.

Harris, Marvin. *Patterns of Race in the Americas*. New York: Walker, 1964.

Hexter, J.H. *Reappraisals in History*. New York: Harper and Row, 1961.

Hirschman, Albert O. *The Strategy of Economic Development*. New Haven, Conn.: Yale University Press, 1958.

Hobsbawm, Eric J. "Peasant Land Occupations." *Past and Present* 62 (1974): 120-152.

Hoel, Paul G. *Elementary Statistics*, 2nd ed. New York: Wiley, 1966.

Hollingsworth, T.H. *Historical Demography*. Ithaca, N.Y.: Cornell University Press, 1969.

Humboldt, Alexander von. *Ensayo político sobre el Reino de la Nueva España*. Edited by Juan A. Ortega y Medina. Mexico City: Editorial Porrúa, 1966.

Icaza, Francisco A. de. *Diccionario autobiográfico de conquistadores y pobladores de Nueva España*. 2 vols. 1923. Reprinted, Guadalajara: Biblioteca de Facsimilares Mexicanos, edited by Edmundo Aviña Levy, 1969.

Instituto Nacional de Antropología e Historia, Centro Regional de Occidente, Departamento de Historia. *Lecturas históricas sobre Jalisco antes de la Independencia*. Guadalajara: Departamento de Bellas Artes del Gobierno de Jalisco, 1976.

Israel, Jonathan I. *Race, Class and Politics in Colonial Mexico, 1610-1670*. London: Oxford University Press, 1975.

Katz, Friedrich. "Labor Conditions on Haciendas in Porfirian Mexico: Some Trends and Tendencies." *Hispanic American Historical Review* 54 (1974): 1-47.

Keith, Robert G. *Conquest and Agrarian Change: The Emergence of the Hacienda System on the Peruvian Coast*. Cambridge, Mass.: Harvard University Press, 1976.

Kerblay, Basile. "Chayanov and the Theory of Peasantry as a Specific Type of Economy." In Teodor Shanin, ed., *Peasants and Peasant Societies*, pp. 150-160. Harmondsworth, Engl.: Penguin Books, 1971.

Ladd, Doris. "The Mexican Nobility at Independence, 1780-1826." Ph.D. dissertation, Stanford University, 1972. Ann Arbor, Mich.: University Microfilms.

Laslett, Peter. *The World We Have Lost: England Before the Industrial Age*. New York: Scribner's, 1965.

Lerdo de Tejada, Miguel. *Comercio exterior de México desde la Conquista hasta hoy*. 1853. Reprinted, Mexico City: Banco Nacional de Comercio Exterior, 1967.

LeRoy Ladurie, Emmanuel. *Les paysans de Languedoc*. 2 vols. Paris: S.E.V.P.E.N., 1966.

Lewis, W. Arthur. *The Theory of Economic Growth*. London: George Allen and Unwin, 1955.

Lindley, Richard. "Kinship and Credit in the Structure of Guadalajara's Oligarchy, 1800-1830." Ph.D. dissertation, University of Texas at Austin, 1976. Ann Arbor, Mich.: University Microfilms.

Lockhart, James. "Encomienda and Hacienda: The Evolution of the Great Estate in the Spanish Indies." *Hispanic American Historical Review* 49 (1969): 411-429.

———. "The Social History of Colonial Spanish America: Evolution and Potential." *Latin American Research Review* 7 (1972): 6-46.

———. *Spanish Peru, 1532-1560*. Madison: University of Wisconsin Press, 1968.

López Jiménez, Eucario, comp. *Cedulario de la Nueva Galicia*. Guadalajara: Editorial Lex, 1971.

López Portillo y Weber, José. *La conquista de la Nueva Galicia*. Mexico City: Secretaría de Educación Pública, Departamento de Monumentos, 1935.

López de Velasco, Juan. *Geografía y descripción universal de las Indias*. Edited by Justo Zaragoza. Madrid: Est. Tip. de Fortanet, 1894.

MacLachlan, Colin M. *Criminal Justice in Eighteenth-Century Mexico: A Study of the Tribunal of the Acordada*. Berkeley and Los Angeles: University of California Press, 1974.

MacLeod, Murdo J. *Spanish Central America: A Socioeconomic History, 1520-1720*. Berkeley and Los Angeles: University of California Press, 1973.

Martínez Alier, Juan. "Relations of Production in Andean Haciendas: Peru." In Duncan and Rutledge, eds., *Land and Labour in Latin America*, pp. 141-164.

McBride, George McCutcheon. *The Land Systems of Mexico*. New York: American Geographical Society, 1923.

McNeill, William H. *Plagues and Peoples*. New York: Doubleday, Anchor Press, 1976.

Mellafe, Rolando. *The Latifundio and the City in Latin American History*. Latin American in Residence Lectures no. 2. Toronto: University of Toronto, 1970-1971.

Mendizábal, Miguel Othón de. *La evolución del noroeste de México*. Mexico City: Publicaciones del Departamento de la Estadística Nacional, 1930.

Meyer, Jean. "Perspectives de l'analyse socio-historique de l'influence de Guadalajara sur sa région." In Centre National de Recherche Scientifique, *Villes et régions en Amérique Latine*, pp. 77-84.

Miranda, José. "La función económica del encomendero en los orígines del régimen colonial, Nueva España, 1525-1531." *Anales del Instituto Nacional de Antropoligía e Historia* 2 (1941-1946): 421-462.

Molina Enríquez, Andrés. *Los grandes problemas nacionales*. Mexico City: A. Carranza é Hijos, 1909.

Moorhead, Max L. *The Apache Frontier: Jacobo Ugarte and Spanish-Indian Relations in Northern New Spain, 1769-1791*. Norman: University of Oklahoma Press, 1968.

Moreno Toscano, Alejandra. "México." In Richard M. Morse, ed., *Las ciudades latinoamericanas*, vol. 2, *Desarrollo histórico* (1973), pp. 172-196.

Morin, Claude. "Los libros parroquiales como fuente para la historia demográfica y social novohispana." *Historia Mexicana* 21 (1972): 389-418.

―――. *Santa Inés Zacatelco (1646-1812): contribución a la historia demográfica del México colonial*. Mexico City: Instituto Nacional de Antropología e Historia, Departamento de Investigaciones Históricas, 1973.

Mörner, Magnus. "The Spanish American Hacienda: A Survey of Recent Research and Debate." *Hispanic American Historical Review* 53 (1973): 183-216.

―――, ed. *Race and Class in Latin America*. New York: Columbia University Press, 1970.

Morse, Richard M., ed. *Las ciudades latinoamericanas*. 2 vols. Sep-Setentas nos. 96 and 97. Mexico City: Secretaría de Educación Pública, 1973.

Mota Padilla, Matías de la. *Historia del Reino de Nueva Galicia en la América septentrional*. Colección Histórica de Obras Facsimilares no. 3. Guadalajara: Instituto Jalisciense de Antropología e Historia, 1973.

Mota y Escobar, Alonso de la. *Descripción geográfica de los Reynos de Nueva Galicia, Nueva Vizcaya, y Nuevo León*. Colección Histórica de Obras Facsimilares no. 1. Guadalajara: Instituto Jalisciense de Antropología e Historia, 1966.

Nava Otero, Guadalupe. *Cabildos y ayuntamientos de la Nueva España en 1808*. Sep-Setentas no. 78. Mexico City: Secretaría de Educación Pública, 1973.

Navarro y Noriega, Fernando. *Memoria sobre la población del Reino de Nueva España escrita en el año 1814*. Llanes, Spain: J. Porrúa Turanzas, 1954.

Negrete, José Vicente. *Geografía del estado de Jalisco.* Mexico City: Sociedad de Edición y Librería Franco-Americana, 1926.

Noticias geográficas y estadísticas del Departamento de Jalisco. Guadalajara: Imprenta del gobierno, 1843.

Noticias varias de Nueva Galicia, Intendencia de Guadalajara. Guadalajara: Edición de "El Estado de Jalisco," 1878.

O'Gorman, Edmundo. *Historia de las divisiones territoriales de México,* 4th ed., rev. Mexico City: Editorial Porrúa, 1968.

Orendáin, Leopoldo I. *Cosas de viejos papeles.* 2 vols. Guadalajara: n.p., 1968.

––––––, and Salvador Reynoso, eds. *Cartografía de la Nueva Galicia.* Guadalajara: Banco Industrial de Jalisco, 1961.

Orozco, Wistano Luis. *Legislación y jurisprudencia sobre terrenos baldíos.* 2 vols. Mexico City: Imprenta de el Tiempo, 1895.

Ortega y Pérez Gallardo, Ricardo. *Estudios geneológicos.* Mexico City: Imprenta de E. Dublán, 1902.

Osborn, Wayne S. "Indian Land Retention in Colonial Metztitlán." *Hispanic American Historical Review* 53 (1973): 217-238.

Páez Brotchie, Luis. *Guadalajara, Jalisco, México; su crecimiento, división y nomenclatura durante la época colonial, 1542-1821.* Guadalajara: n.p., 1951.

Palerm, Angel. "Distribución geográfica de los regadíos prehispánicos en el área central de Mesoamérica." In Angel Palerm and Eric R. Wolf, *Agricultura y civilización en Mesoamérica,* pp. 30-64. Sep-Setentas no. 32. Mexico City: Secretaría de Educación Pública, 1972.

Palomino y Cañedo, Jorge. *La casa y mayorazgo de Cañedo de Nueva Galicia.* 2 vols. Mexico City: Editorial Atenea, 1947.

Pares, Richard. *A West-India Fortune.* London: Longmans, Green, 1950.

Parry, J. H. *The Audiencia of New Galicia in the Sixteenth Century.* Cambridge, Engl.: Cambridge University Press, 1948.

––––––. *The Spanish Seaborne Empire.* New York: Knopf, 1967.

Payno, Manuel. *Los bandidos de Río Frío.* Mexico City: Editorial Porrúa, 1959.

Pérez Verdía, Luis. *Historia particular del estado de Jalisco,* 2nd ed. 3 vols. Guadalajara: Editorial Gráfica, 1951.

Phipps, Helen. *Some Aspects of the Agrarian Question in Mexico.* New York: Columbia University Press, 1925.

Postan, Michael M. *Essays on Medieval Agriculture and General Problems of the Medieval Economy.* Cambridge, Engl.: Cambridge University Press, 1973.

Potash, Robert A. *El Banco de Avío de México.* Mexico City: Fondo de Cultura Económica, 1959.

Powell, Phillip Wayne. *Soldiers, Indians, and Silver: North America's First Frontier War.* Berkeley and Los Angeles: University of California Press, 1969.

Ramírez Flores, José. *El gobierno insurgente en Guadalajara, 1810-1811.* Guadalajara: Publicaciones del Ayuntamiento de Guadalajara, 1969.

––––––. *El Real Consulado de Guadalajara, notas históricas.* Guadalajara: Banco Refaccionario de Jalisco, 1952.

Redfield, Robert, with Alfonso Villa R. *Chan Kom, a Maya Village.*
Washington, D.C.: Carnegie Institution, 1934.

Riley, James D. "Landlords, Laborers, and Royal Government: The
Administration of Labor in Tlaxcala, 1680-1750." Paper delivered at Fifth
Meeting of Mexican and American Historians, Pátzcuaro, Mexico, October
12-15, 1977.

_____. "The Management of the Estates of the Jesuit Colegio Máximo de San
Pedro y San Pablo of Mexico City During the Eighteenth Century." Ph.D.
dissertation, Tulane University, 1972. Ann Arbor, Mich.: University
Microfilms.

_____. "Santa Lucía: desarrollo y administración de una hacienda jesuíta en el
siglo XVIII." *Historia Mexicana* 23 (1973): 238-283.

Rivière D'Arc, Helène. *Guadalajara y su región: influencias y dificultades de
una metrópoli mexicana.* Sep-Setentas no. 106. Mexico City: Secretaría de
Educación Pública, 1973.

Robinson, David J. "Introduction to Themes and Scales." In *Social Fabric and
Spatial Structure in Colonial Latin America,* pp. 1-24.

_____, ed. *Social Fabric and Spatial Structure in Colonial Latin America.*
Dellplain Latin American Studies no. 1, 1979. Ann Arbor, Mich.: University
Microfilms.

Romano, Ruggiero. "Mouvement de prix et développement économique:
l'Amérique du sud au XVIIIe siècle." *Annales, Économies, Sociétés,
Civilisations* 18 (1963): 63-74.

Romero de Terreros, Manuel. *Antiguas haciendas de México.* Mexico City:
Editorial Patria, 1956.

_____. *El Conde de Regla, creso de la Nueva España.* Mexico City: Ediciones
Xochitl, 1943.

Rostow, W.W. *The Stages of Economic Growth: A Non-Communist
Manifesto.* Cambridge, Engl.: Cambridge University Press, 1965.

Rudé, George. *The Crowd in History; A Study of Popular Disturbances in
France and England, 1730-1848.* New York: Wiley, 1964.

Sánchez-Albornoz, Nicolás. *The Population of Latin America: A History.*
Translated by W.A.R. Richardson. Berkeley and Los Angeles: University of
California Press, 1974.

Schondube B., Otto. "La evolución cultural en el occidente de México: Jalisco,
Colima y Nayarit" and "El territorio cultural de occidente." In Instituto
Nacional de Antropología e Historia, *Lecturas históricas sobre Jalisco,* pp.
25-31 and 19-24.

Serrera Contreras, Ramón María. "La contabilidad fiscal como fuente para la
historia de la ganadería: el caso de Nueva Galicia." *Historia Mexicana* 24
(1974): 177-205.

_____. "Estado económico de la Intendencia de Guadalajara a principios del
siglo XIX." In Instituto Nacional de Antropología e Historia, *Lecturas
históricas sobre Jalisco,* pp. 201-205.

_____. *Guadalajara ganadera: Estudio regional novohispano, 1760-1805.*
Seville: Consejo Superior de Investigaciones Científicas, 1977.

Silva Herzog, Jesús María, comp. *Relaciones estadísticas de Nueva España de principios del siglo XIX.* Archivo Histórico de Hacienda, vol. 3. Mexico City: Secretaría de Hacienda y Crédito Público, 1944.

Simpson, Lesley Byrd. *The Encomienda in New Spain,* rev. ed. Berkeley and Los Angeles: University of California Press, 1966.

————. *Exploitation of Land in Central Mexico in the Sixteenth Century.* Ibero-Americana no. 36. Berkeley and Los Angeles: University of California Press, 1952.

————. *Many Mexicos,* 4th ed., rev. Berkeley and Los Angeles: University of California Press, 1967.

————. *Studies in the Administration of the Indians in New Spain: II. The Civil Congregation.* Ibero-Americana no. 7. *III. The Repartimiento System of Native Labor in New Spain and Guatemala.* Ibero-Americana no. 13. Berkeley and Los Angeles: University of California Press, 1934 and 1938.

Sjoberg, Gideon. *The Preindustrial City, Past and Present.* New York: Free Press, 1960.

Slicher Van Bath, B.H. *The Agrarian History of Western Europe, A.D. 500-1850.* Translated by Olive Ordish. London: Edward Arnold, 1963.

Spalding, Karen. *De indio a campesino; cambios en la estructura social del Perú colonial.* Historia andina no. 2. Lima: Instituto de Estudios Peruanos, 1974.

————. "Estructura de clases en la sierra peruana, 1750-1920." *Análisis, Cuadernos de Investigación* (Lima) 1 (1977): 25-36.

————. "Tratos mercantiles del Corregidor de Indios y la formación de la hacienda serrana en el Perú." *América Indígena* 30 (1970): 595-608.

Stein, Stanley J. *Vassouras, a Brazilian Coffee County, 1850-1900.* Harvard Historical Studies no. 69. Cambridge, Mass.: Harvard University Press, 1957.

Tannenbaum, Frank. *The Mexican Agrarian Revolution.* Washington, D.C.: The Brookings Institution, 1930.

Tawney, R.H. *The Agrarian Problem in the Sixteenth Century.* 1912. Reprinted, with introduction by Lawrence Stone, New York: Harper and Row, 1967.

————. "The Rise of the Gentry, 1558-1640." *Economic History Review* 11 (1941): 1-38.

Taylor, Paul S. *A Spanish-Mexican Peasant Community: Arandas in Jalisco, Mexico.* Ibero-Americana no. 4. Berkeley and Los Angeles: University of California Press, 1933.

Taylor, William B. *Drinking, Homicide, and Rebellion in Colonial Mexican Villages.* Stanford, Calif.: Stanford University Press, 1979.

————. *Landlord and Peasant in Colonial Oaxaca.* Stanford, Calif.: Stanford University Press, 1972.

Thirsk, Joan. *The Agrarian History of England and Wales,* vol. 4, *1500-1640.* General editor, H.P.R. Finberg. Cambridge, Engl.: Cambridge University Press, 1967.

Thurman, Michael E. *The Naval Department of San Blas: New Spain's Bastion for Alta California and Nootka, 1767 to 1798.* Glendale, Calif.: Arthur H. Clarke Co., 1967.

Topete Bordes, Luis. *Jalisco precortesiano: Estudio histórico y etnogénico.* Mexico City: "El Sobre Azul," 1944.

Tovar Pinzón, Hermés. "Las haciendas jesuítas de México, índice de documentos existentes en el Archivo Nacional de Chile." *Historia Mexicana* 20 (1971): 563-617, and 21 (1971): 135-189.

Trevor-Roper, H. R. "The Elizabethan Aristocracy: An Anatomy Anatomized." *Economic History Review,* 2nd series no. 3 (1951): 279-298.

Tutino, John M. "Hacienda Social Relations in Mexico: The Chalco Region in the Era of Independence." *Hispanic American Historical Review* 55 (1975): 496-528.

————. "Life and Labor on North Mexican Haciendas: The Querétaro-San Luis Potosí Region, 1775-1810." In Elsa Cecilia Frost, Michael C. Meyer, and Josefina Zoraida Vázquez, comps., *El trabajo y los trabajadores en la historia de México,* pp. 339-378. Mexico City: El Colegio de México and University of Arizona Press, 1979.

Van Young, Eric. "Regional Agrarian Structures and Foreign Commerce in Nineteenth-Century Latin America: A Comment." Paper delivered at the Annual Meeting of the American Historical Association, New York, 1979.

————. "Review of Ramón María Serrera Contreras, *Guadalajara ganadera: Estudio regional novohispano, 1760-1805.*" *Agricultural History* 53 (1979): 838-839.

————. "Rural Life in Eighteenth-Century Mexico: The Guadalajara Region, 1675-1820." Ph.D. dissertation, University of California at Berkeley, 1978. Ann Arbor, Mich.: University Microfilms.

————. "Urban Market and Hinterland: Guadalajara and Its Region in the Eighteenth Century." *Hispanic American Historical Review* 59 (1979): 593-635.

Vázquez de Espinosa, Antonio. *Compendium and Description of the West Indies.* Translated by Charles Upson Clark. Smithsonian Miscellaneous Collections no. 108. Washington, D.C.: Smithsonian Institution, 1948.

Verlinden, Charles. "El régimen de trabajo en México: Aumento y alcance de la gañanía. Siglo XVII." In García Martínez, ed., *Historia y sociedad,* pp. 225-246.

Villaseñor Bordes, Rubén. *El mercantil consulado de Guadalajara.* Guadalajara: n.p., 1970.

Villaseñor y Sánchez, José Antonio. *Theatro americano.* 2 vols. 1748. Reprinted, Mexico City: Editora Nacional, 1952.

Ward, H. G. *Mexico in 1827.* 2 vols. London: H. Colburn, 1828.

West, Robert C. *The Mining Community of Northern New Spain: The Parral Mining District.* Ibero-Americana no. 30. Berkeley and Los Angeles: University of California Press, 1949.

————, ed. *Natural Environment and Early Cultures.* Vol. 1 of *Handbook of*

Middle American Indians. 16 vols.; Robert Wauchope, general editor. Austin: University of Texas Press, 1964.

Whetten, Nathan M. *Rural Mexico.* Chicago: University of Chicago Press, 1948.

Wolf, Eric R. "Aspects of Group Relations in a Complex Society: Mexico." *American Anthropologist* 58 (1956): 1065-1078. Reprinted in Teodor Shanin, ed., *Peasants and Peasant Societies: Selected Readings*, pp. 50-68. Harmondsworth, Engl.: Penguin Books, 1971.

————. "El Bajío en el siglo XVIII, un análisis de integración cultural." In David Barkin, ed., *Los beneficios del desarrollo regional*, pp. 63-95. Sep-Setentas no. 52. Mexico City: Secretaría de Educación Pública, 1972.

————. *Peasants.* Englewood Cliffs, N.J.: Prentice-Hall, 1966.

————. *Sons of the Shaking Earth.* Chicago: University of Chicago Press, 1959.

————, and Sidney W. Mintz. "Haciendas and Plantations in Middle America and the Antilles." *Social and Economic Studies* 6 (1957): 380-412.

Wrigley, E. A. *Population and History.* New York: McGraw-Hill, 1969.

Zavala, Silvio. "Orígenes coloniales del peonaje en México." *Trimestre Económico* 10 (1944): 711-748.

INDEX

Designer:	Rich Hendel
Compositor:	In-House Composition
Printer:	Thomson-Shore, Inc.
Binder:	John Dekker & Sons
Text:	10/12 Times Roman (Compset 500)
Display:	Times Roman Bold